Encyclopedia
of
Canaries, Parrakeets,
and
Other Cage Birds

Canaries, Parrakeets, Love Birds, Finches, Parrots, Mules and Hybrids

BY NOLA MILLER FOGG

PREFACE

Mrs. Nola Miller Fogg

The canary hobby in the United States has increased yearly. With the coming of early springtime thousands of owners of a canary feel the urge to buy a mate for their pet and grant him the pleasures nature has deeply planted in all bird life.

With the selection of one or two hens to be mated with a male one can for two or three months enjoy a very pleasant and interesting pastime that will incidentally pay for all the costs of their hobby and grant a thrill obtained in no other way. One can usually sell in their neighborhood or through classified ads in the papers all of the birds they raise, which usually amounts to from 10 to 15 birds for a good working pair in the two or three nests that should be taken from one hen during a season, but over breeding begets weaklings, undernourished birds and always decreases the efficiency of the mother bird for any future breeding.

The canary fancy attracts so many new bird-lovers to its fold that a reliable, constructive book of authentic information from truly experienced breeders who have had years of experience has been necessary in order that the thousands of beginners may have before them at all times a comprehensive treatise of the canary keeping, rearing, feeding, training and treating. The Encyclopedia of Canaries and other cage birds of which this is the tenth revised edition has met with such great favor, that the author hereby announces that the meaning of the word ENCYCLOPEDIA has and shall continue to be used in this book (that is, not the sole opinion or the writing of some gifted writer with products to sell, or some narrator from hearsay, but articles from noted authorities in the art of rearing, training and ministering to canaries.)

The owners and lovers of man's great companion, THE DOG, have the trained Veterinarian; hence need have no grave fears as to the health of their pet, but we bird lovers must rely on experienced breeders and students of science for information, hence the justification of this Encyclopedia. The pictures of our associate authors are herewith presented and we wish to take this opportunity to extend our gratitude and very respectful thanks to each of those listed, and to others who have co-operated with us to obtain the desired information and if we are able to assist some despairing bird lover to save the life, or contribute to the health and comforts of the birds our greatest desire will have been gratified.

3

The great difference which exists between present day varieties in canaries, all of which have been evolved by breeding from the one source—THE ORIGINAL WILD CANARY—is well indicated in the above picture. This picture shows on one hand birds of graceful beauty and the master musicians of the feathered world, and to the extreme in type and color birds. That you may get acquainted with them we give the names to correspond with numbers given: 1, Roller; 2, Wild Canary; 3, Border; 4 Norwich; 5, Yorkshire; 6, Hartz Mountain; 7, Dutch Frill; 8, Scotch Fancy; 9, Crest; 10, Belgian.

ASSOCIATE AUTHORS

Mr. C. C. Mulligan

Arthur G. Griffiths

DR. HERBERT SANBORN

Mrs. W. A. Finney

Mrs. Amelia Jane Mayberry

L. Armitage

We are proud to present the photos of our co-authors in the compiling of this book—rcognized by many as renowned authorities in the different fields of bird lore in the United States, England, Canada and Australia. We have used some of the writings of these eminent authorities, and also articles of Budgerigars (Parrakeets) from the publication, American Cage-Bird Magazine, with the view of compiling a complete and comprehensive treatise dealing with all members of our feathered friends and wonders ever kept for companions or known as cage birds. With grateful thanks and the highest respect for our associates we herewith present The Encyclopedia of Canaries, Parrakeets and Other Cage Birds for your approval and benefit.

5

The Home Singer

The Purchase of the Right Bird

Never in the history of our country has there been such opportunity, or such assurance of a profitable business in raising birds, because never before have caged birds been as popular with the general public as they are today.

Individual fancy and taste will decide the question of what kind of birds you will have as your specialty.

If we were all of the same mind, then possibly we would not have the many different varieties to select from as we find at the present time.

Some like a Warbler, some a Roller, some a Type bird or Color bird. Some prefer a large bird, while others are not particular in this respect. With many the song is the prime consideration, while others like a bird which can be heard in other rooms than the one in which it is kept. This being the case it is a rather difficult matter to even advise until the individual fancy is known. In regard to color the Solid Green bird I believe should be given first place. They are admitted to be strong and healthy, and they do not show dust and dirt in soiled plumage as is the case with a Clear Yellow or Buff colored bird. In every home no matter how well kept there is always a certain amount of dust and as a cold water bath does not really clean the plumage, owing to the film of oil covering each feather, a clear colored bird will in time show the effect, which will not be noted in the case of the Green bird.

Unless the owner has previous experience it is not advised that a Roller of the Tutor class should be purchased for a home singer. The reason being that it is proposed to keep the bird under conditions which would in the end spoil the song of the Tutor. To keep a bird in an open wire cage, to include in the diet, food of a stimulating nature, and to allow the bird to sing at will and without restriction are the three principal points which tend to spoil the song of a Tutor. What is required in a home bird, is a singer with a good variety and a well connected song. One with a short, catchy delivery or with harsh, clattering faults becomes rather trying to listen to. If my advice should be asked for, I would without hesitation recommend a Roller, but not necessarily a Tutor. A medium priced bird will give equally as satisfactory results for the purpose required.

Usually the first singer is treated to a real fancy cage, and often the owner will put the question of looks before usefulness. Seeing that

The Best Type of Cage

cages vary in price from $2.50 to $25.00 or more, a wide range can be found to select from. Seeing that fancy work and ornamentations on the cage prevent proper cleaning, and form a harbor for red-mite and insect life, it is much preferable that the cage should be plain. The first consideration should be size. Exercise is essential to the health of the bird and a cage smaller than 14 inches long, 12 inches wide and 12 inches high is not suitable.

Wooden, cane or bamboo cages should not be purchased for they are hard to clean, and unless carefully watched will in time become the home for a large number of little pests which make the life of the bird a constant worry. A large plain white enameled cage is preferable to brass, and a square or oblong cage is better than a round one. It will be noted that there is a tendency to get away from the use of brass cages, and the reason is as follows: When a bird is given a bath in a brass cage, the water splashed upon the wires is allowed to dry. This in time destroys lacquer on the wires, and where the lacquer is removed rust will commence to form. This rust will be noticed in the form of a blue green powder which is known as "Verdigris." It is a strong poison, and should a bird pick at the powder mentioned, then a loss is almost sure to be the result.

If a brass cage is used, the bird should be trained to pass into another cage to take its bath, and while doing so the brass cage can be cleaned and well dried before the bird is returned to the same. There should be three perches in the cage, one at either side and close to the bottom, and from which the bird can easily get to seed and water in the cups provided for the purpose. The third perch should be in the center of the cage, and just low enough from the top, so that the bird cannot reach up to pick the wires at the point from which the cage will hang. The perches should not be small and round as often found in most store cages. The perches should be oval and varying in thickness, thus giving the bird a firm grip when passing from one to the other. The center perch being the one upon which the bird will roost, it should be the thickest of the three. Not less than five-eighths of an inch thick. The small swing which will be found in most store cages should be removed and not used. I have known of endless accidents resulting from them, and another disadvantage lies in the fact that as the bird is constantly passing under the swing, it will in time adopt a crouching position, which would not be the case if the swing was not left in the cage.

Where The Cage Should Hang

I cannot explain the reason, but in every home I have ever visited where one or more singers are kept, I have noticed without exceptions that the cages hang in the worst possible position. Directly in front of the center window is always a position. More birds are unintentionally killed in this way than would be imagined. It can be understood that as soon as the window and door is opened, the bird is then in the direct line of draught be it from the window to the door or vice-versa. In summer time windows are often left open, and as temperatures fall at night time, the bird will quickly take cold, and its owner will wonder why. I think that the cage stands now in use in many homes have been made to avoid this common mistake.

If a brass bracket is secured to a side wall, and the cage suspended from the end of the bracket by means of a small brass spring an ideal arrangement is provided. The bird should have plenty of light, but still be so situated in the room that draughts on the cage would not be possible. It is advisable to cover the cage at night time, so that the bird will get plenty of sleep and in comfort. Another mistake frequently made is to keep a bird in a kitchen were cooking is done, and very often by the use of a gas range. Gas fumes are extremely dangerous and birds should never be kept in a room where gas is used. Canaries do not require heat, and will be in better health if kept in a cold room. Fluctuating temperatures should be avoided, for a bird can quickly be put into a partial moult, if taken from a cold room into a warm one frequently. The dining or living room is therefore the best room to keep the singer in.

How The Singer Should Be Fed

The question is often asked. How long will a Canary live and be in song. The correct answer to this question depends upon three points. A bird will live and be in good condition in direct proportion to the way in which it has been fed, and its general care as regards cage, cleanliness and where it has been kept. In the feeding of the singer we find that the two extremes are followed. Some fanciers get a packet of store seed, and when the packet is used another one is purchased. The bird is never given food of any other kind but dry seed. Then they have the reverse. It is positively painful to go into some homes and to see the varied bill of fare in the cage of the singer. Red-Peppers. Bacon rind. Soda Biscuits. A cube of sugar. A small sack of sulphur suspended from the top of the cage. A piece of apple and a large leaf of lettuce. A piece of cuttlefish bone and other items too numerous to mention. The thought occurred to me, when I was reading an article in which boiled potatoes were advised, that a side order of Corned Beef and Cabbage would have been quite in order. In order to keep a Canary in perfect health all we have to do is use just a little common sense. First of all a Canary is what is known as a "Hard Bill" and therefore its natural food is dry seed, and Canaries can be kept in good condition by the use of Canary and Rape Seed only.

Canary Seed to a canary is exactly what bread is to ourselves, and Rape Seed can be considered as the butter to go with the bread.

Certain additions to the diet are advisable, but none should be given excepting those from which you wish to obtain certain results. During a year a bird passes through the seasons, and each brings changes which require certain additions to their diet. The best illustration of just what I mean will be found in the moulting period. At this time a double strain is forced upon the bird. The food given has not only to provide nutriment for the bird itself, but also for the production of the new growth of feathers. This being the case the diet must be liberal and stimulating, and in order to obtain these results we add items to the diet which are not required or advisable at other times. For birds which are not intended for breeding, a plain, wholesome diet is the best plan. While I have no desire to force my views upon my readers, I will be glad to give an outline of just how a singer in the home should be cared for.

The Staple Food

The staple food consists of Best Spanish Canary Seed and Best Roller Rape Seed. Only the best quality should be used. When a good sample has been located, purchase about two pounds of each kind. Mix these together and keep in a glass or tin container, which should have one small hole in the top for ventilation. Good Canary Seed can be recognized by the size, the color of the outside shell or husk, and the sample being entirely free from dust or foreign matter. A light creamy colored husk denotes seed which has been sun-dried, while a dark colored husk denotes seed which has been "kilndried." Of the two, always choose the former.

Rape Seed requires a little skill to decide the best quality. Some samples will be found to be treated with a certain oil, which gives the impression of sweetness, when a few seeds are placed in your mouth. If you will allow the seeds to remain for a few minutes before chewing you will find that the sweetness soon disappears, and when the seeds are broken, there is a hot biting or peppery taste. Such a sample is not genuine Roller Rape Seed, and it should not be purchased. With genuine Roller Rape you will not find the sweetness previously referred to before the seeds are broken. In good Roller Rape when the seeds are broken, there is a mild pleasant nutty flavor, closely resembling the taste of a "Walnut." When you find such a sample, you can purchase with confidence. If properly stored a good supply will keep indefinitely.

Condition Mixture

In the list of seeds which can be used as suitable food for Canaries, there are at least twelve which can be used to advantage. Each of these have a different chemical analysis, and it is for that reason that they are advised. A first class condition mixture can be made of the following seeds. One part by measure of each of the following seeds: Hulled Oats, Hemp Seed, Flax Seed, Inga Seed, White Italian Millet Seed, Red Indian Millet Seed, and Teazle Seed. Now add half of one part of the following seeds: Sesame Seed, Gold-of-Pleasure Seed and Best Blue Dutch Maw Seed. These should be well mixed together, and stored in the same way as the staple food. In feeding the condition mixture, the container should be well shaken before taking out the supply, for the small seeds get down to the bottom, and unless the bulk is well mixed, the birds will not get the benefit of the small seeds such as Maw and Sesame. Only a small amount should be given at one time for the mixture is stimulating, and will be found excellent for a conditioner before the breeding season.

Patent foods are not required or advisable, Song Restorer, Health Food, Bird Manna, (whatever that is) are placed on the market more with a view of sales rather than real worth. I think my own studs are as healthy as the average birds, but I have yet to purchase the first packet of any of these patent foods. I have never found them to be necessary. In cases of sickness medicines are sometimes necessary, but the less they are used the better.

Bird Grit and Cuttlefish Bone Necessary

Clean dry grit must always be before the bird. This is necessary for by its use the food is ground into digestible form in the crop of the bird. A Canary having no teeth, the grit is supplied as a natural substitute for the same. Cuttlefish Bone should be between the wires of the cage at all times. It aids the bird in keeping the mandible or beak trimmed, and as it is composed of a large percentage of lime, it is a bone forming food, and good for all birds to use, more especially those which are young and growing.

Care of The Beak and Claws

With some birds the growth of the mandible or beak, and also the claws seems to be much more rapid than others. You will find that the overgrowth is always on the upper half of the beak. This must be watched, for it is possible for a bird to go short of seed and almost starve, due to the overgrowth, it is not able to pick up and shell all the seed that is required. When the claws become overgrown, the free movement of the bird is prevented. Often the claws will meet around the perch. When this is the case they should be trimmed, and to do so is a very simple operation. Use a small sharp pair of bent nail scissors. Take the bird in the left hand, with both legs drawn between the second and third fingers. Close the fingers so that the bird can not withdraw the claws. Trim each nail about half its length. Care must be taken not to cut too close or bleeding will result. A small blood vessel runs half way down into the claw. In clear colored birds the blood vessel can be quite easily seen, but with green birds it is not so easily noticed.

To trim the beak, take the head of the bird between the thumb and the first finger of the left hand, while the body of the bird is held in the palm of the same. A little pressure upon the lower and upper halves of the beak will close them tight. Now with the scissors clip off the overgrowth from the upper half, at the same time being careful not to cut more than will make both top and bottom parts of the beak equal in length. A strip of fine sandpaper glued to the underneath of the upper perch will prevent overgrown claws. This must be narrow, so that there will be no chance of the fleshy part of the toes of the bird coming in contact with the same.

Training The Singer

Start early with a young bird, and you can get it to do most anything you require. A cage cannot be properly cleaned while the bird is in the same. It is a capital plan to give the bird its bath in a cheaper cage kept for the purpose. Start by opening the doors of each cage and placing them close together. Try to coax the bird to pass from one cage to the other. At first it will take a little time, but if you will place, say, a little green-food in the second cage, turn it toward the light, and cover the other cage with a cloth, the bird will soon go through to the other cage. You can then give the bath, and while this is being used you can give the good cage a real cleaning. Dipping the cage and perches in boiling soap water will sterilize the same. No insect germ, or bacteria can withstand boiling water.

ORIGIN OF OUR CANARY

THE WILD CANARY

A small group of islands lying off the northwest coast of Africa are called the Canary Islands and the Islands of Madeira, from whence came our beloved present-day canary, a creation entirely of man; during the centuries these charming companions have been bred as household companions.

These islands are not real tropical islands and the birds in their native habitat endure severe cold weather at times. Our present-day canary can stand well very cold zero weather if the change is not too sudden, but they cannot survive drafts; guard your bird from drafts, do not permit late baths, see that the bird never goes to bed wet or damp.

The canary is a native of the Canary Islands, whence comes its name. It is technically known as *Serinus Canarius*.

Several thousand canaries in the wild state were taken as part of a merchant ship cargo in the early part of the sixteenth century. On the homeward trip the ship was wrecked and the birds were set free by one of the sailors. They flew to Elba, a small island off the western coast of Italy; the climate here being so favorable that the birds increased quite rapidly in number and their power of voice attracted the Italians, who were the first to capture and breed these birds, and were by them shipped to Belgium, Russia, Germany and England.

The rage for breeding the canary with other birds, including the citril and serin in Italy and the linnet, greenfinch and siskin in Germany, became popular and the result was a curious intermixture of colors and sizes; the Norwich, Yorkshire Don, Scotch Fancy, Gold and Silver Spangled, Manchester Coppy and Belgian all being bred for color and size, making them more valuable as ornaments than as musicians, and being bred especially for appearance some of them being almost monstrosities. Hartz Mountain Canaries are usually of a very brilliant and beautiful color and are somewhat larger in size than the Roller Canary. The Hartz Mountain Canary's voice is rather loud, but sometimes clear and full of variety, some of the voices being softer than others. As these breeds do not receive the care and attention paid to the Roller Canaries relative to musical training, naturally they would be inferior as songsters compared to the Full Note Roller that has been bred through many years exclusively for melody of voice.

Every mother should provide some sort of pet for her child because all normal children are born with a natural love for the wild. This instinct if carefully encouraged is certainly not lost in the development of his own character. The growing generation is in urgent need of the right employment—why not begin early to cultivate the natural element by supplying that which will develop in each the lovable traits of responsibility and humanity? The author can well imagine that the inspiration of some of our skilled physicians and patient, competent nurses perhaps came from observation of helpless, ill or injured little creatures of Nature, and was recognized and thoroughly established in the early part of life.

So many people think it cruel to cage the birdies, but domesticated birds or animals, if properly fed and cared for, are indeed better off than those in the wild state. In the case of canaries, which have been kept in captivity so long, it would be very cruel to turn them into the open, with no experience or knowledge with which to care for themselves.

Personally, the author thinks every person aside from regular duties, ought to have a "Hobby,"—Birds or what-not,—and persistently give it as much of her individual intelligent thought and study as is possible. What could be more companionable that the melodious, silver-throated Canary, that is trained to sing, by people who are thoroughly acquainted with the art, to say nothing of the interesting care necessary to its welfare, and perhaps the rearing of nestlings?

The popularity of the Canary is daily increasing and he is rapidly becoming a universal household companion on account of his wonderful song ability, for which he is truly unexcelled.

Probably every layman knows that the cage-canary originated in the Canary Islands which

9

are located off the west coast of Africa; in fact the average person doubtless believes that the Islands get their name from the bird, instead of from *canis* the Latin word for dog. Possibly many of our breeders are under the impression that birds are still exported from the islands in considerable quantities to Europe and America, although this is, or up to 1919 was so far from being the fact that it is almost if not, indeed, quite impossible to secure a native canary even in Germany where the interest in experimental breeding with the canary is perhaps greater than in any other country. There have, however, even been doubting Thomases, who have gone so far as to raise the question whether the present cage-birds, or at least some of their varieties, are identical with the species found on the islands, although this is probably settled beyond any doubt. Whatever uncertainty exists is due to the meagre details handed down to us concerning the early importation of the bird to Europe.

The first account we have of the canary is given us by Conrad Gessner, who published in the second half of the sixteenth century a book entitled, De Avium Natura, in which he describes the bird called Canarian Aviculem, from an account given him by a friend; he had not seen the bird himself. This account of Gessner was repeated by Aldrovandi in his Ornithologiae Libri XII (Belogna 1599-1609), with the addition of some further details, such as the fact that the male differs from the female by having more yellow in its plumage; he also shows a picture of the bird and of the canary-grass upon which it delights to feed. In 1622, Olina published at Rome his "Uccellieria", in which he gives the best account of the bird of that time, which was frequently copied by later writers. All of these writers are acquainted only with the green bird, which had been brought immediately from the Canary Islands to Europe.

From 1478, when Spain took possession of the islands, the Spaniards kept a rigid control over the trade in these birds, which were sold at very high prices to only the richest families in Europe. The Canary became the inseparable ornament of the ladies, who received visitors with the bird sitting on the forefinger of the right hand. Portraits from this period show that it was quite the custom for the ladies to have themselves painted with the bird sitting on the finger. According to current reports the Spaniards kept the trade in their own hands, never allowing a female bird to be sent to the continent; and, according to the account of Olina, the breeding of the bird in Italy, and later in Germany, began through securing females from a vessel, having a large cargo of the birds, which was shipwrecked on the Italian coast.

These birds are said to have flown to the island of Elba, where they found favorable conditions for their development; here they increased in such numbers that the Italians began to pay attention to them, breeding them later with success and shipping them to Tyro and to the countries to the north. It is certain that in the last quarter of the eighteenth century canaries were being bred extensively in Switzerland and Southern Germany, and were thence exported to England, Russia, Constantinople, and Egypt. Sixteen hundred birds a year were exported to England alone at a price of about four dollars per bird, which was enormous for that time.

The traditional shipwreck story is largely discounted by modern writers, who point out that it is incredible the Spaniards should have been able to maintain a monopoly in this line of trade for a whole century. They insist that the desire of bird breeders in other countries to get hold of females could not have remained so long unsatisfied. Moreover, they call attention to the great possibility that either unwittingly, because of the size of the importations or purposely because of the desire for gain on the part of individual breeders, females would be sent along with the males. Furthermore, if the birds had become wild on the island of Elba, specimens would doubtless have been found there, when the story of the shipwreck first began to spread. There is no record except this tradition of the bird ever being found there.

The wild bird has never been found anywhere except on the Canary Islands and on the island of Madeira. Linnaeus thought that the canary is also native to the Azores, but this was due to confusing our songster with a finch found there which is closely related to our songster. It is indeed a remarkable fact that the bird has never migrated to the continent of Africa; but this is usually accounted for by the fact that it finds on the islands in question the food which it likes best, as well as by the further fact that the moist climate of the island, which is favorable to the development of its song, is for some reason preferred by the bird. It is a fact that it is found in the Canaries in greatest numbers on the moistest island of Teneriffe, which lies farthest to the West. From this, breeders may get a hint with respect to keeping the air in our breeding and training quarters sufficiently moist to secure proper condition for the best development of song. A too dry atmosphere is doubtless injurious for the bird's voice, as in the case of human singers.

The color of the wild bird, in contrast with that of our cage-bird, is uniform as with other wild birds. There is a greenish-yellow strip on his forehead, with the regions above and under the eye, on the sides of the head and on the neck also a lively greenish yellow. The top of the head is a grayish yellow-green. The feathers on the very top and the back of his head are pure gray with blackish streaks, and above the yellowish-green regions of the neck are areas of bluish or ash-gray, extending on toward the body. The shoulders and upper part of the back are olive-green, with touches of brownish color, and each feather has a broad middle stripe of black. The lower part of the back is of a grayer greenish color, shading into pure yellowish green on the rump. The primaries are blackish-gray, bordered on the outer edges with greenish-gray, with broad fawn-colored tips, and with secondaries fawn-colored to gray. The wings underneath are light ash-gray.

Becker, from whom this description is taken, says he noticed that the yellow color of the birds has grown more pronounced as they become older, and that it then stands in quite lively contrast with the brownish color on the shoulders and upper back. The chief difference between the male and female, according to this observer, is that, on the breast and abdomen of the female, grayish-white color takes the place of the greenish yellow of the male. The wild bird is, according to this authority, just a little smaller than the cage canary and appears to be more slender. Becker considers the wild bird to be more beautiful than any cage birds he had seen, and says also that its movements are much more graceful, as would, indeed, be expected.

The birds are found to-day principally on the islands of Teneriffe, Palma, Gomera, and Ferro, in districts where the open forest land is broken up by bushy plains, and from the level of the sea up to the height of over a mile on the mountain slopes. He frequents the gardens in the cities quite as regularly as the secluded points on the islands, but according to Becker, has disappeared from many regions where the timber has been entirely cut down. In 1886, Hartwig reports that there were more wild canaries on the island of Madeira than on Teneriffe itself. He says that in the fall and winter months one sees flocks of sixty or more of these birds, the cypress trees in which they roost at night being fairly alive with them.

In the first days of February the flocks break up into pairs and the breeding period begins. At this time the cocks fight frequently with each other; and their song becomes much more energetic, as is also the case with our cage-bird.

The wild canary makes its nest in gardens and vineyards as well as in cypress trees, avoiding the dark, damp laurel woods, and the mating and building of the nests usually takes place in the latter part of March. The nest is built at a height of from seven to twelve feet from the ground, usually by preference in an evergreen tree, although Becker reports nests in ornamental trees, palms, orange and other fruit trees. Bolle says that the material of the nest examined by him was a sort of soft white vegetable fibre like cotton, but Becker maintains that he never saw a nest composed entirely of this material, there being always grass, straw and roots mixed with this cotton.

As soon as laying begins, one egg is deposited each day, as in the case of most wild birds, with an average of five eggs per nest. These eggs are pale sea-green in color, covered over with reddish-brown to blackish spots, which sometimes are united at the large end of the egg in the form of a wreath; but frequently the eggs are solid in color. In size and form they resemble those of the cage-bird, but the outline of the shell in the direction of its length is said to be somewhat more than in the case of the cage-bird. In thirteen days the eggs are hatched, and in the same length of time the young are fledged. They are, however, fed for some time longer, chiefly by the male. According to Becker, they are fed not only by regurgitation but also given various seeds and greenfoods, as well as the seeds and juice of ripe figs. According to this authority there are three clutches raised each year, but Bolle says there are four. Probably the large number may be due to the fact that Becker missed one of the broods, or it may be that he examined the birds in some season that was less favorable for breeding than usual. Possibly, however, Bolle made his observations in an unusually favorable year. Hartwig reports for Madeira, which lies farther north than the Canaries, two and sometimes three broods per year; and his description of the other habits of the bird is in general identical with that given for Teneriffe and the other islands of the Canary group. The moult begins in the Canary group toward the end of July.

The Yorkshire
Canary.

The Yorkshire

THE YORKSHIRE CANARY is the most noteworthy member of its family. A long, slim bird with an erect carriage, it is a very handsome creature, even if not as imposing in appearance as the variety just passed under review, and, like it, is met with in all colors, as well as with and without a crest.

Self-colored and evenly-ticked specimens are those that are most in request, and fetch the best price, while such as are irregularly marked and blotched are justly held to be inferior.

A fair-sized Yorkshire will measure from 6 inches to 6½ inches in length, and be scarcely half the girth of the coppy. Its position when in repose is very upright, and when in motion much more so, so that a line drawn from the back of the head to the end of the tail will be almost perpendicular.

The Yorkshire cock is usually a good singer, but his voice is sometimes shrill and loud, which is rather the fault of his education than attribut-

able to his idiosyncrasy. Very frequently he repeats the notes of the Skylark, which are too loud for the house, and in point of resonance and force lose nothing by his rendering of them. When the Woodlark has been his tutor, the Yorkshire Canary is a much more pleasing inmate of the drawingroom, where his shriller-voiced brother is altogether out of place.

In selecting birds of this variety for breeding, attention should be paid to the following points: length, slimness of figure, good upright carriage, and a pleasing disposition of color if the bird is ticked or mottled, or perfect uniformity of tinting if self-colored, whether yellow, buff or green. The last-named color is more often met with in the Yorkshire than in the coppy class, and when the shading is clear and bright is by no means unhandsome, though perhaps not as pleasing, at least to some fanciers, as the lighter-colored birds.

An extremely pretty sub-variety has the wing-feathers, with the exception of the flights, of a very dark, almost black shade, a spot or tick of a corresponding tint proceeding backwards from the eye, the flights as nearly white as possible, and the rest of the plumage buff or primrose. When the bird is yellow, even one dark feather on any other part of the body or among the tail-feathers disqualifies for first place in an average competition.

The green Yorkshire must have the outer edges of the tail and wing-feathers black, and be lightly ticked with the same color on the back and shoulders; the lores and moustache must also be dark, and the nape of the neck should be a trifle darker than the surrounding parts. The breast and under-parts must be of a distinctly green, as opposed to a yellow, shade, and should be absolutely free from dark markings.

The Yorkshire Canary is a bird that is well known, and considerably fancied in the United States. The breed originated in the county of Yorkshire England. In the towns of Halifax, Sheffield and Rotherham, the fancy is still part and parcel of each working man's existence. There are very few of the miners in these industrial centers, who are not in possession of a few of the Yorkshire Variety, and of course like all other fanciers think that the bird of their choice is the only bird worth raising.

I am quite sure that in all other breeds there is no bird which can show its points to more perfection, and which is more elegant than a first class Yorkshire. With the exception of the Lancashire Coppy, the Yorkshire is the largest bird on the show bench in point of length. The standard length of this bird is not less than 6¾ inches, measured in the usual way, from the tip of the tail, to the point of the beak.

The show points in a first class Yorkshire are as follows: Beak, small and neat, neither large or small when considered in proportion to the head. Head round and neat, with no showing of flatness on the top, which is a bad fault. Neck neat and in proportion to shoulders, which must be well rounded. Too massive shoulders give the bird a top heavy appearance, while small shoulders do the reverse and make the bird look stalky. Wings are carried close to the body, and well braced. They should lie close and with the feathers of each wing meeting in the center, but not overlapping from the shoulders down to the tail at which point the wings should lay with the tips of the first primary feather just touching each other, but not overlapping. There must be no signs of roughness of frills in the feathers on the shoulders or the breast, which should be nicely rounded, but not full, as with the Norwich. The tail feathers should be well packed, and rounded like the stem of a pipe. A fan tail in Yorkshires is a fault that puts the bird beyond consideration on the show bench.

From the back of the head down to the tip of the tail, there should be the slightest inward curve, but this must be so slight, that only a critical examination will show this point. As with the breast the lower part or abdomen, must be close and smooth feathered, gradually tapering off towards the tail. The legs should be of neat length and very little thigh should be shown. The lower leg must be neat, well formed and in proportion to the general make-up of the bird. Eye, bright and dark, and well placed, giving the bird a bold appearance.

Valuable Yorkshires are often passed by, due to the fact that their training has been neglected, and owing to this omission, the bird will not show its good points to advantage. When I speak of training, I do not refer to the song, which I will deal with later. What I refer to at this time is the training necessary to have the bird come into position, and to stand while being judged, in the way that will bring out the good points of the bird to be judged. A special type of cage is used for the Yorkshire, and this cage has been designed to allow these points to be shown to advantage. The Yorkshire show cage is all wire, with the exception of a wooden base which is nine inches long and six inches wide. There are 19 wires in the side of the cage, and 11 in the width. The height of the cage is 14 inches, measured from the bottom of the tray to the top of the wires. These wires are bent so that when they are soldered into place, they form a dome to the top of the cage. There are three perches in the cage. Two are placed four wires from each end at the bottom, and the third perch is placed in the center, and is raised above the other two five inches. It is upon this center perch that the Yorkshire bird is judged. The position in which a good Yorkshire should stand, depends much as to the color of the card that we will be given. The best illustration that I can give of this position, and one which will impress itself upon the minds of those interested is as follows: Consider the hands of the clock. First let the hour hand point almost to the hour of one o'clock, and let this represent the head of the bird. Now consider the minute hand of the clock as pointing to the 25th minute to the hour, and let it represent the tail of the bird. When the

position of a Yorkshire standing right to be judged, can be resembled to the hands of the clock, when it is 25 minutes to one o'clock, you will then have the correct position of a show bird.

In the breeding of the Yorkshire as with other fancy breeds, strong points in the male bird are mated to weak points in the hen. To illustrate, if you have a large rangy male bird, then his mate must be a neat, trim hen, which is not up to standard length. A clear yellow male is mated to a clear, or ticked buff hen. A variegated male should, if possible, be mated to a clear hen or vice-versa. A loosely or rough feathered bird, should have a smoothly and tight feathered mate to give the best results. All birds are not perfect, and the idea of mating strong points to weak points, is to try and produce in the progeny the ideal, which, of course, is the object that all fanciers wish to attain.

There are many matters in connection with this breed, which would be of interest to the fanciers, but which would require considerable space to enter upon. For instance, careful consideration must be given before a cross is made, or an introduction of Cinnamon blood infused into the stud. This new blood should only be infused for good reason, such as the enriching of color, but it must be considered that while it only takes one year to make the introduction, it will take several seasons to breed out the cross. Two yellow birds should not be mated together. Yellow blood brings color and type, while buff blood produces quality, length, and silky texture of feather. It can, therefore, be readily seen that in mating yellow to buff, the fancier is more likely to obtain birds with a good showing of both of these desired points. In the large show the classifications for this breed are many. They are as follows: Clear Yellow, Clear Buff, Ticked Yellow and Ticked Buff, Lightly Variegated, Even Marked, Heavily Variegated, Self, or Solid Greens. Of course these classifications are given in all cases for male and female, which, while the two sexes are judged separately, cases will often present themselves, where male birds and females compete against one another. This, of course, would be in the cases of a championship. Referring briefly to the song, the Yorkshire while being a beautiful bird, is not by any means a Caruso. They are not valued as singers, but as show birds. The song is of course choppy, and is entirely without any resemblance of rolls or tours, as we find in our favorite the Roller. A Yorkshire does not have to sing to be shown, and it is most likely that owing to this fact, the song of this bird has never received any close attention from fanciers generally. Many attempts have been made to cross this bird with the Roller, with a view to improving its song, and while a certain degree of improvement has been noted, still this has been at the sacrifice of the type, the Yorkshire type being submerged into the reverse type of the Roller, producing a bird which would not be considered as anything more than a cross bred bird, and of course useless for showing in either Yorkshire or Roller classes.

Crested Yorkshire

Crested Yorkshires are not so much in evidence as some other varieties, but are occasionally met with, and show a decided cross with the Coppy. Some others are "crest-bred," that is, one of the parents or grandparents has worn a crown, but its descendant shows no sign of that particular distinction, which, however, in virtue of the law of heredity, may make its appearance in a subsequent generation, and spoil it. If, however, a Yorkshire is crested, the crest is judged as in the case of the Coppy and the Norwich, to which we shall come directly, and any tendency to baldness in the center of the crown, or to undue length or shortness in the side or front feathers composing it, is of course fatal to the bird's chance of getting a place where there is anything approaching to close competition.

The cage for breeding the Yorkshire Canary must be roomy, especially as regards its height, so that the bird shall not have to stoop, and run the risk of losing the upright carriage that is its chief characteristic. Space for exercise is also requisite, as this bird is an active creature, and more disposed to hop and jump about than some of its heavier and more phlegmatic cousins. It is a good plan to provide the bird with perches of different thickness, so as to prevent any risk of its contracting cramps or deformed feet. This is especially requisite when the birds are young.

Now as to type. The head must be small and nicely rounded in every way, moulded into a long straight neck. The shoulders are narrow with no trace of hollowness or prominence. The back must be long and straight. The tail also is long, close and compact, and should look as if it were only one feather. An open or fish tail is a great drawback to an exhibition bird. The breast must be narrow and well rounded, tapering away in a straight line to the tail. The legs must be long, straight and set not too far apart. This being a bird of position, it must stand as erect as possible, and must not on any account stand over the perch in a crouch.

Feather is of great importance in a Yorkshire, for a bird to win in competition must have quality, that is a fine soft silky feather, and there must not be a feather out of place. They must be close and tight to the body. Now, in the breeding of these birds there is no more trouble attached to it than the breeding of any other canary. The only thing to avoid is not to pair up two birds that have the same fault. For instance, two birds with a flat skull or with a frill breast or crossed wings, etc. The idea is if one bird has a flat skull, mate it to one that is perfect and so on. I would recommend a beginner to go to a reliable breeder. Tell him what you want and how much you are willing to pay, and leave it to him to select a well matched pair. It is useless to try and pick up a bird here and there unless you have a fairly good line on their pedigree. I have known prize winners bought right off the show bench and from different parties to produce nothing but moderate birds, so remember that pedigree has a lot to do with the mating of your stock. As I mentioned heretofore, the correct method is to pair yellow to buff, except on some special occasion we may double yellow or double buff. It is also advisable to have one of the birds clear and the other marked, the yellow marked for preference.

The show cage or exhibition cage is practically all wire except the bottom which is like a shallow box, 3 inches deep. The size of the cage is 9 inches long, 6 inches wide and 15 inches high. The wires are bent in a circle over the top and from side to side, which forms a very neat compact cage for this particular type of bird.

The standard of excellence and scale of points of the Yorkshire Canary:

Head small and round. Skull narrow .. 5 pts.
Neck moderately long and straight ...... 5 pts.
Shoulders narrow, rounded and well filled
in .... 5 pts.
Back—Long, straight and well filled, wings
long and evenly carried .... 5 pts.
Breast—Round and Smooth. The body
long and gradually tapering to a neat
waist .... 5 pts.
Legs—Long without being stilty. Thighs
well clothed .... 5 pts.
Tail—Long, straight and closely folded .. 5 pts.
Size—Length, 6¾ inches with corresponding symmetrical proportions ....10 pts
Position—Attitude erect with fearless carriage. Head, Neck, Back and Tail on a
straight line ....20 pts.
Feather—Close, short and tight for compactness of body feather, and close carriage of wing and tail ....20 pts.
Color—Pure body color, beak, legs and
feet clear .... 5 pts.
Condition, health, cleanliness and sound
feather ....10 pts.

The Standard of Perfection ....100 pts.

The Border

Border Fancy Canary

The Border Fancy is the smallest of the type breeds of canaries. They originated in Cumberland and Westmoreland on the "Borders" of England and Scotland. In the early days the breed was known as the "Common Canary" but it became so popular in England and Scotland that a more appropriate name was desired and it was called the Cumberland Fancy. Here the Scots kicked as it was not very popular in that country, and along the borders of England and they desired a more suitable name, so eventually it was settled upon the Border Fancy Canary.

This bird for large number of years was bred in the North of England and the South of Scotland, but now I am pleased to say that it is one of the most fancied breeds in the British Isles and in many other countries. The reason for this I put down several causes. First: All birds must be exhibited in their natural color. No color feeding is allowed. This being the only breed for which color feeding is barred, and this fact makes it a very popular breed with the novice, for no novice desires to color feed his or her birds until they have become thoroughly acquainted with the correct method. I am sorry to state however that there are a few exhibitors to-day that do not exactly color-feed their birds, but they assist color by giving "Nasturtium"

flowers and Marigold Blooms. These enrich the color so that it is very hard in some cases to detect, but if the same should be detected then the birds are disqualified.

The standard of perfection is as follows. The grand essentials then of a Border Fancy are type, and quality. Without these the birds are worthless. The general appearance is that of a clean cut, lightly made, compact proportionable, sprightly, close feathered smallish canary, showing no tendency towards heaviness, roughness or dullness, but giving the impression of fine quality and symmetry throughout. Standard and scale of points. Head and neck: small, round and neat looking. Bill fine, eyes dark and bright, neck rather fine and proportionate to head and body, 10 points. Body: back well filled in and nicely rounded, running in almost a straight line from the gentle rise over the shoulders to the point of the tail, chest also nicely rounded but neither heavy or prominent, the line gradually tapering away at the vent, 10 points. Wings: compact and carried close to the body. Just meeting at the tip, 10 points. Legs: of medium length showing little or no thigh, fine and in harmony with other points, feet corresponding, 5 points. Tail: close packed narrow, being nicely rounded and filled in at the root, 10 points. Color: rich soft and pure, and as even in tint as possible throughout, but extreme depth and hardness such as color feeding gives are objectionable in this breed and are debarred, 10 points. Plumage: close firm and fine quality, presenting a smooth glossy appearance and free from frill or roughness, 15 points. Position: semi-erect and standing at an angle of 45 degrees, 10 points. Carriage: gay and jaunty with a fine free poise of the head, 10 points. Health: condition and cleanliness shall have due weight, 10 points. Size: not to exceed one and one-half inches in length, measured in the usual way. Total 100 points.

Selection for Breeding

In selecting our birds for breeding we must select quality of feather first, for without it we have no chance whatever on the show bench. The feathers must be soft and silky in appearance and must lie close to the body. The next detail to consider is type, although on 5½ inches long this bird is not like the Yorkshire, which is long and slender, or the Norwich which is short and cobby, but comes in between the two, carrying the style, gracefulness and quality of the two varieties. The Border should travel from perch to perch with a free graceful movement and while doing so there should not be a feather out of place. Next comes color which is essential to a good bird, but we find that color and quality goes together, so if we look after the first point quality, then we will get color also. At the same time we must be always trying to improve. Never be content with what we have, but always forging ahead. If we should lose color we must go back to the Green variety, and which is known as the fountain of color. To do so we get the deepest Yellow Green Canary Male we can find, and mate it to a clear Buff hen. The offspring from this mating would contain heavily variegated birds, both yellows and buffs. Again we take the richest colored yellow variegated male, and mate it to the best clear buff hen we have, and the offspring this time would be clear and lightly variegated. The clear bird is preferred on the show bench, and the premier prizes always go to the clear or ticked birds, although there are classes for every variety of birds, and including Greens, Cinnamons, Clears, Ticked, Lightly Variegated and Heavily Variegated. Then there is at most shows a class for even marked birds. That is for birds which are marked on both eyes or both wings, they are known as two pointed, but if marked on both eyes and both wings they are known as four pointed, being the perfect markings that every breeder strives for. There are a few breeders that have created a strain that produce even marked birds quite freely. In the breeding for marked birds it is necessary to know your birds for if you take a pair of birds that have not been bred for that purpose, we find that the markings fall. That is for instance if we pair a bird with a nice cap to a clear one, the markings on the offspring would be over the eyes or on the neck. The next generation it would be on the back. I have watched the markings fall each year until they reach the tail. We find the Cinnamon marked birds breed the truest to markings, and the markings do not drop as in the green marked birds, so here we use the Cinnamon marked bird to cross into the green marked birds to fix the markings but do not forget that cinnamon marked birds can be exhibited as well as the green marked. In mating for marks do not mate two birds that have the same marks, or you will get the marking too heavy, but mate one that is marked on both eyes and wings to one that is clear, but bred from even marked birds. If you have one marked on the right eye and wing mate it to one marked on the left eye and wing and so on. This method will balance up the markings and avoid getting them too heavy.

On General Management

The Border Fancy is probably the most easily managed of all the Canary tribe. It is small, active, and very hardy, and is a most prolific breeder. Taken generally, it is the best feeder we have. It does not need any special getting into condition for either breeding or show. The hens could have a little inga seed, say half a teaspoonful twice or three times a week, from the beginning of March until after they have laid the first two eggs of the first clutch. This prevents egg binding, and excites the organs of production. It will not be necessary to use this seed afterwards; in fact, it is best kept out of the diet altogether until the breeding season is over. Soft food I do not recommend at all until the day the eggs are due to hatch. I have always found it best to keep the birds in good hard condition, and this can only be done by feeding on hard seeds.

I like to give plain seed alternately with a good mixed seed practically all the year round; soft food, crushed hemp and groats, and watercress whilst feeding young. A little extra linseed should be given during moult as a "glossy" feather producer, and a teaspoonful of mawseed will be found beneficial during the time the feathers are growing, as it keeps them warm and corrects looseness of the bowels—a thing they are very susceptible to during the changeable autumn weather. Plenty of good, coarse flint grit and a piece of cuttlefish bone in the cages all the year round, and baths must not be neglected. The only time that baths are out of place is during the first ten days after young are hatched, and in dull or foggy weather.

Cages 18 ins. by 16 ins. by 9 ins. are of a handy size for breeding purposes, and for keeping the young in afterwards. Flight cages are not desirable, the fine texture of the feathers suffering by too much knocking about, which is inseparable where too much room is given. Two, three, or even four can be moulted in the breeding cages together without any ill effects, so long as they are kept scrupulously clean. The clear and marked varieties will of course want washing for show; being so small and dainty they easily soil, but as they are free bathers as a rule, very slight tubbing keeps them in condition for the bench. Greens and Cinnamons very rarely want washing except, perhaps, the feet and tip of tail, that is, of course, if they are kept in clean surroundings.

A good plan during the show season is to throw a handful of crushed oats on the top of sand in cage bottoms. This keeps the feet clean, and does not hurt the birds if they pick amongst it.

The standard show case is "oval topped and all black."

The Crowned Head of Canaries

THE CRESTED CANARY

Crests and Crest Bred

Crests and Crest-breds are among the oldest varieties, but the present-day specimens bear very little relation to the birds shown 35 years ago, when they were looked upon as the most valuable breed of any.

The Crest is not, like some other breeds, located in a certain area, but its adherents are found North, South, East and West, in every country; but, unfortunately, many of the old breeders have either joined the great majority or have fallen out and the younger generation have gone in for Norwich, Yorkshires, or Borders as being easier to breed and keep in condition.

In taking up Crest-breeding as a hobby it must be remembered that good specimens are not so easily obtained as Plainheads; the supply is much more limited, prices rule very high, and they are a variety requiring a considerable amount of time and care expended on them. It is generally advisable also to keep a stock of foster parents. Some Crests make good parents, so far as breeding goes, but I frequently found that owing to the heavy feathering of the hen there was a tendency to lose young through sweating in the nest, especially during the June and July rounds.

When pairing, it is usual to trim the crest, feathers over the eyes and also to cut the tail feathers to about half the length and to trim away the feathers from the vent of the hens.

If no foster-mothers are provided, a sharp look-out must be kept after the youngsters are hatched to see that hens are not sitting too close. If such is the case it is often best to remove the cock from the cage and let the hen do all the feeding; this keeps her away from the young for longer periods and reduces the risk of loss. Another device is to put in a dummy egg: this acts as a cushion for the young and prevents the hen from sitting too heavily on them; but there is nothing to beat one or two spare Hartz Mountain hens and transferring the eggs to them; this takes less wear and tear from the breeder stock and enables an extra round to be obtained.

It is well to use birds of two and three years of age in preference to younger birds, as Crests do not mature quite so quickly as lighter-feathered varieties.

The Crested Canary takes its name, from the topping or crest, which covers its head. Years ago, when this breed was in its infancy, it was known as the "Topping" or "Turn-Crown." The aim of all breeders, is to get as chubby a bird as possible, with massiveness of head, and density and length of head feathers.

The Perfect Crest

A good crest should extend in front to the tip or over the tip of the beak, and should reach evenly round, to the beak of the head. Level with the eyes, which should be almost entirely hidden. A most important feature is size, shape, and density of feather, which should be broad and of a leafy texture. A small crest, with make the bird's head look mean and spare.

Some birds have small heads but carry a large crest, and show it off to perfection. So it will be seen, that it does not require, an extra area of skull, to hold the foundation, of a well feathered crest. The shape of the crest, is developed upon two things: a small center, and the position of that center. It should be sufficiently remote from the base of the beak, to ensure a good frontage. (Nothing will compensate for a bad frontal, and any defect there is fatal.

The center which gives the crested effect, is one placed behind the eyes, in the center of the top of the head. If it is too far forward, it takes greatly from the frontal crest. So it will be seen, then that it is of great importance to study the position of the center of the crest. This is the most important fact, as it assists, to give or mar a good finish.

Another point to consider of great importance, is the back of the crest. If you examine a young crest canary, in the nest before there is any sign of feathers appearing, there will be seen at the back of the skull, a scar like mark. The rest of the skull will be the color of the feathers that will cover the skull. For example in a dark crest, the skin will be black, on the scar-like mark, feathers never grow. If the head is examined, as the quills show themselves, it will be noticed that they grow from every portion of the surface, except the scar-like mark. This remains bare, and so the experienced fanciers look for this scar-like mark, for if it is large the probability is that the crest will have an inferior back. If the scar is small the crest will be well filled in behind, and will give the bird a neat appearance.

A good crest should not stand up in front, and a dark one should show no light feathers over the beak or in any other part. It should not be narrow or pointed in front, neither should it be tucked at the sides. It should not have any splits, or openings in the front. It should not be wider at the back than it is in the front. Nor should it be ruffled or resemble a mop at the back. The crest should not have a split or opening in the front, as this will give the appearance of being made up of two parts. This is what is termed a running center. The crest should not merely be a tuft of feathers, with no given center, as this is neither one thing or the other, and has the appearance of a mop. It must not be thin or spare, but should be dense and full of feathers. Radiating evenly all round, from a well filled neat center. Now we come to the birds themselves, and we must remember that a crest must have size, type, and quality and color. In selecting your birds, remember that size is the foremost important point. Do not start with undersized birds, or you will be simply living in a "Fool's Paradise." The clear body, dark crested is the ideal of all breeders, and if we take into consideration the difficulty of production, this is rightly so. The even marked dark crest, is also very difficult to obtain, and I think it should really stand before the clear body, dark crest. Try to breed a Clear Yellow with a dark crest. Now we come to the Grey crest, a most important bird in the breeding. A good grey crest is a very pretty bird on the show

bench. This is usually bred from the mating of two Buffs, and is a chance breed. Another peculiar thing about the grey crest, they are usually buffs, with a clear body. Now we come to the clear crest, really a most handsome bird. Besides these we have the Green Crests, and then the heavily variegated, which is the first removed from the green. The novice is inclined to give very little thought to color, or markings. His whole craze being to breed a winner, and as quickly as possible, not troubling a bit about color. Stop. This is a blind policy on the breeders part, as this is bound eventually to kill classification for the breed, and as the various marked and colored birds become scarce, they will all drift into the one channel of variegation.

What we want is classification, if we are going to breed the ideal. Therefore it is the duty of the breeder to fix the various markings and color, which he has once produced. Of course perfect birds will not necessarily breed perfect specimens. Nevertheless good typical points, when the birds possessing them, are at one's command, are to be by no means depreciated.

Now in the breeding of the crest, we have to deal with another distinct breed, and that is called the Crest-Bred. This bird is just as important as an exhibition bird, as the crest itself. The Crest-Bred like the Crest should be of massive build, with a thick set body. It should resemble in form the English Bullfinch, as near as possible, the Crest-Bred should have an abundance of feathers lying close to the body. Now we come to the most important point in Crest breeding, and that is the head of the crest-bred.

A crest-bred without a really good head, and head feathers, can hardly be called a crest-bred at all. No matter how many feathers it has on its body, it is the head of the crest-bred, which is the real factor, towards the making of the perfect crest, of typical perfection.

A good crest-bred's head should be large and broad. The entrance should be wide the feathers should rise suddenly from the very start of its growth, owing to its denseness, at the base of the beak. These feathers should expand in as they gracefully fall over the skull, to the back of the neck. Their density causing them to fall over the eyes at the sides, giving the bird a frowning appearance, which is called "Lashing." These feathers give a peculiar wide appearance to the skull, finishing off with a good expanse at the back of the skull. The bird should have a very short beak, as this adds to the beauty, of the massively shaped skull. In a good bird the feathers on the crown, when turned over, should reach to the end of the beak, or even further. The "Brows" or Lashings should give the bird a silky appearance, without brushing or artificial aid whatever.

The first rule to be observed in pairing birds for crest breeding, is to mate a Crest with a Crest-Bred. Before going further, perhaps I ought to explain, that the Crest-Bred is bred from pairing a Crest to a Plain-Head.

I cannot too strongly impress upon the fan-

CRESTED CANARY

The Crest-bred Canary

ciers who are about to take up crest breeding, and I feel sure and heartily hope there will be many, to get his start from some Crest Breeder of fame, or a straight forward Dealer, then he knows exactly how his birds are bred, which will be a very great help to him. I have noticed many people on going to a bird show, for the first time, observing the section devoted to the Crests, remark on their extreme beauty, but at the same time saying, "How expensive they must be." This is really a great mistake, as the majority of fanciers are only too pleased to meet the Novice on a fair basis, and to give him all the help that he requires. Now we will suppose that we are about to pair up the birds. Pick the best Crest Hen that you have, and pair your Crest-Bred male with her. By so doing you should get good results. The reason that we pair a Crest-Bred and Crest together, is somewhat obvious. If we bear in mind that a canary's crest is not a high spherical tuft, but a flat arrangement of feathers on the top of the skull, which radiating from a center, would have their character, from the radiated crest. They are more like rough mate than anything else. That is why we do not pair two crests together for it would lead eventually to this kind of crest. Of course sometimes we have to breed two crests in order to get the radiation, which is so dear to the fanciers eye, we have to use the crest-bred.

I want to impress upon the novice, that we do not as general rule, mate two crests together. It is very possible that you might procure a good bird with a good crest, of approved type but at the same time, there will be some very objectionable forms, which are not at all desirable of perpetuation. For instance ugly partings, splits, or gutters, may occur and these all spoil radiation.

This is by no means an uncommon defect. A split in front is the worst kind of a fault, as this class of split is very difficult to breed out. The centers of some birds have an inclination this way, only in a more modified form, which does not interfere, with the proper arrangement of the frontal crest, nevertheless it shows a tendency that way. They are what is called running centers, and I want to make it plain to the fanciers, when pairing such birds, to be very careful. Then we have the crest which is broken or licked inside. The birds with this fault are described as having weak or short sides. Now we come to the crest with the rough back, which we very often see, and

to pair such a bird to a crest-bred, which has not good lashings, or is in any way "Horned" at the sides, will only further intensify the fault, while if it is paired with a Crest-Bred that is smooth and has good lashings it will reduce the fault. So it only goes to prove to the fanciers, the great importance due to the crest-bred.

I want to draw the fanciers attention to the fact that because you breed two crests together, you do not always get crests. I have bred birds apparently Crest-Breds from two crests, a thing easily accounted for, as the crest has much of the crest-bred in it. I do not advise the novice to start pairing crest to crest, because he will only be courting failure, but to the more exerienced breeder, I do say this, that to pair two crests is a certain way to obtain density of feather, which can afterwards be regulated and brought into shape by pairing back to crest-breds, with nice smooth feathers over the head, but take care Mr. Fancier, for if you double crest repeatedly you will find your birds, born with running ulcers at the back of the head, or over the nostrils. What is wanted in crest breeding is markings, and we must furnish these at all hazards. Once obtained it will rest with the breeders to restore and maintain a balance of the other properties by the exercise of skill in his art. Do not be contented to breed a big bird and let it go at that, because that will never get you anywhere at the show bench. Perhaps one of the commonest mistakes the novice makes is the pairing of his stock wrong. Remember you are not breeding crest for song, you are breeding for the show bench. Here are some hints to the novice. By pairing a Yellow Crested Male to a Buff Crest-Bred Hen, you will get better quality of feather, and as a rule a larger percentage of Yellow young, then by pairing the young from one pair back to the other, I think that you will find that you keep up your size as well as quality of feather.

Do not pair two small birds together, or you will soon lose your size. Remember in crest breeding size counts the most. It does not follow that you are bound to have show birds to breed show birds. If you should breed a bird which looks a likely winner, only is a little on the small side, be sure to pair it to a bird with plenty of size. Do not put up two birds with the same faults. Whatever failing you see in one bird, try to counterbalance it on the other. Now I want to give the novice and those interested in this breed of Canary, one last bit of advice. Remember Rome was not built in one day, and the ideal Crest is not procured in one year or two. You want to start slow, and go slow all the time, then you will be sure to finish well. Do not when you come face to face with a disappointment, give up, what you do not know ask for, then plod, plod and plod again, with the sole determination to overcome all obstacles for this surely is the spirit of the real fancier.

Take a live interest in your hobby. Join a club or society. Exhibit for it is only by getting and keeping well in touch, that success will be yours.

Should circumstances compel you to utilize young stock, then pair a young cock to a two or three-year-old hen and young hen to an adult cock. This will give you more substance and stamina in the produce.

Not more than two nests of young stock should be taken, however they may be paired. If you are breeding exhibition stock do not discard youngsters which hardly come up to the standard the first season. Keep them over, and you will find that the adult moult will make a very great difference in their show points.

Extra care and attention during the moult must be given to this variety; a slow, dragging moult is very detrimental to the bird's chances. They must be kept free from draught and the bath must be freely given.

First Appearances Deceptive

In this variety of Canary a nestful of apparent wasters of moderate-looking youngsters, so long as they are bred from the best, may contain eventual winners. Even if they should not themselves develop into winners they may in the next generation produce young with all the desired points. They may even develop them themselves after the adult moult, for some of the most successful winners have not shown their qualities until three or four years old.

The Crest, being essentially an exhibition bird, requires considerable care and attention in preparation, and it will often be found that a local exhibitor's birds have a big pull over those which have to be sent a long railway journey, as the local team can be prepared later and staged in better condition and with more evenness of the head points. This means a great advantage when being judged.

There is a greater tendency toward blindness in Crests than in any other variety. Show writers say this is owing to the heavy feathering on the head, and others think it is hereditary. A blind, or partially blind bird, is not fit for showing, but such birds do sometimes put in an appearance, especially in the selling classes. Birds with defective sight should never be used for breeding

purpose, for many breeders are satisfied that blindness is hereditary and is often caused through injudicious in-breeding.

THE AGE AT WHICH YOUNG BIRDS SHOULD COMMENCE MOULTING

Young birds from the first nests will moult when two months old. The moult at this time is only partial, and it is referred to as the "Baby Moult." All secondary feathers are moulted, but the primary feathers (large feathers in the wings and tail) are not moulted until the season to follow. A young bird in its first season is therefore called an UNFLIGHTED bird, and when this bird has passed through the second moult (at which time all feathers, both Primary and Secondary are moulted) the bird is then referred to as a FLIGHTED bird, and which means that the bird in question has passed through its second moult, and the large feathers in the wings or FLIGHTS have been moulted.

AGE EGG-FOOD SHOULD BE STOPPED FROM THE DIET OF YOUNG BIRDS

It seems that quite a large number of losses are taking place, owing to the belief that young birds should be placed upon dry seed as soon as possible. Nothing of the kind. A young bird cannot be expected to husk and use the amount of dry seed that is required, and even if it could it is not able when so young to properly assimilate the food, from the time of taking the young birds from the parents, they should have a little egg-food twice each day, and given fresh each time. After they have been feeding themselves for one week, then you can stop egg-food afternoon feeding, and in its place give bread and milk. You will not find it necessary to use any form of green-food if you follow this plan. Keep this up right up to the time that the young birds have passed into the moult, and you can of course decrease the strength of the egg-food towards this period, by mixing in a larger proportion of biscuit. When the young birds are showing the small new feathers breaking through upon the neck and head, that is the time to consider reducing the quantity of soft food, getting them into the training racks. You can then start to reduce the quantity of Canary Seed given, but make quite sure of the quality of the Rape Seed, which will now become their principal diet. By following this plan, and giving the birds plenty of room for flying during their early life, you will not have any losses to record in your stud books.

THE NORWICH CANARY

THE NORWICH CANARY

The Norwich is altogether a shorter and stouter bird than the Yorkshire, for its girth is half as much again as that of the latter, and its length runs from 6 inches to 6½ inches.

If the two varieties already dealt with offer several well-established variations, the Norwich is more erratic in that respect than either of them. It is also more prone to put on color than they are. As a rule, Norwich Canaries are good parents, and rarely require assistance to rear their young.

As in the case of the other varieties, we have yellow Norwich Canaries, buffs, regularly marked or ticked, and others that are blotched and self-colored. The yellow birds assume a deep orange-red color when moulted on cayenne, and are less powerfully influenced by saffron and marigolds, as well as in a yet less marked degree by chlorophyl, turmeric, and chochineal.

The Norwich is the "crested Canary" properly so called, as the centrifugal arrangement of feathers on the crown is commoner in this breed than in any of the others, and assumes a number of different shapes difficult to describe, but readily understood when pictorially represented. No bald spot, however, should appear in the middle of the crest; and if such there be, it is a fatal defect, and relegates its possessor at once to a back seat.

It has frequently been asserted that the pairing together of two crested birds is apt to result in bald or imperfectly-crested progeny; but carefully conducted experiments have conclusively proved that this is a mistake and all analogy would lead one to believe that it would have the exact opposite tendency, namely to improve and enlarge the crest and make it permanent (fix it, so to speak), as happens in the case of every other variation. No one, therefore, need be afraid to mate a crested cock and hen Canary together, but should rather be encouraged to do so in the well-grounded expectation of their producing an offspring at least as well endowed with the capital adornment as themselves, and most probably with something better.

In-breeding is permissible in such a case, but must not be pushed too far, or the progeny will deteriorate in stamina, as well as in less material respects. For one or two generations it is permissible to mate a male bird with one of his daughters, or a hen with one of her sons, for the purpose of giving fixity to some desirable attribute: but it is unwise to pursue this in-breeding further.

As a rule, the Norwich Canaries are good parents and attentive to their offspring, but of course they must not be handicapped by the presence of parasites in the cage or nest, or have their energy and vitality depressed by unsuitable and irregular breeding.

This variety is a bird that responds to the fanciers demand for color, certainly and looks better through its increase in size when color fed.

They come, as all Canaries do, both in the yellow and buff kinds, even the greens are either yellow green or buff green. In this respect, in the Lizards, they are called gold and silver, in the London fancy it is called Jongree and Meaties.

Perhaps a word or two here, on the difference between a yellow and a buff in all breeds of Canaries, will be in order so that even the novice will be able to detect the difference between them, although to his untrained eye they look alike, though he can see that some are of deeper shades than others. The yellow may be of various shades, but the color extends

21

right through and over the ends of the webs of all the feathers, giving to the bird a rich and more even tone of color throughout, but a buff although of a rich color, it will be found on close examination that each feather on the edge is pure white. These white margins all over the body, give the appearance of frost, in fact we call it frosty. The peculiarity of this white edging is that it cannot be colored by anything, so that a bird well color fed, with his white frosting all over him is a picture so exquisite that no tongue can describe. I myself love to see a good buff although they are not the deep red hot iron color of the yellows.

In pairing a yellow and buff together, in the general way. Double yellowing is resorted to for increase of color. Double buffing for increase of size, and a dash of Cinnamon blood will increase the silkness and quality of the feathers, but the latter should be used only by experienced fanciers because of the peculiarities of the Cinnamon.

Norwich are six and one-half inches long, head full and round, neck short and thick, in fact no neck at all, chest full and broad, back wide and well filled in, not reached; wings short fitting tight to the body, and meeting feather to feather down the back, tail short and kind of penciled shape, a fish tail is an abomination. Feet and claws clear, no black stockings, except in the greens; back clear and short, feathers short and silky, always strive to get as much of the body in front of the perch as possible, body short and thick set, chubby and wedge shape from shoulders to tail, free from coarseness throughout, color even, not patchy.

As to markings, these birds come from the clear to the green in all the various markings from the ticked to the heavily variegated. The best marks, called technical marks, are the eyes, wings, and a few feathers each side of the tail. Such a bird is an even marked bird and called a six pointer, if evenly marked with four marks he is called a four pointer. Try and breed all marks above the breast as lots of good birds are spoiled for show purposes by having green splashes on the throat or breast.

Classes

1. Clear Yellow
2. Clear Buff.
3. Evenly marked Yellow or Buff.
4. Light Marked Yellow.
5. Heavily Marked Yellow.
6. Lightly Marked Buff.
7. Heavily Marked Buff.
8. Green Yellow.
9. Green Buff.

I have placed the even mark, both yellow and buff, in one class on account of their rarity.

Standard of Perfection Adopted By The Norwich Plainhead Club

	Points
Head—Round and neat, short, stout and clear beak	15
Neck—Short and thick	10
Chest—Deep, broad and full	15
Back—Broad and well filled in	10
Wings, Tail—Short, compact and carried well	10-5
Feathers—Soft, silky, with brilliancy and compactness	15
Legs and Feet—Legs well set back and clear	5
Color—Deep, bright, rich, pure and level throughout	15
Total	100

Condition—Health, cleanliness and sound feather essential.

Lengths—Not to exceed 6½ inches.

Streaked beak and marked legs not to be a disqualification but to count against the bird according to their extent.

A Tip

Be sure and clip the claws of your birds if they seem to be too long, also the tips of their beaks, it is not a delicate operation, but is easily done with a pair of manicure scissors. Excelsior in the flight cages keeps the bird's feet clean and can be turned over like a carpet after a few weeks use. Paper is not dangerous, but by far less valuable than sawdust, sand or excelsior which is much the best of all. It is not necessary that you clean your breeding cage more than once a week or ten days, paint the cage and nest with kerosene with some pine tar in it, this will prevent mites.

Eggs Dangerous Food For Canaries

Likely the above title will startle many, we do not mean in a sense that egg food is dangerous for birds, but wish to call to your mind and attention that only fresh eggs should be used, last year we had a number of letters from old experienced persons who had bought eggs for real fresh eggs. Mr. Westphall of Buffalo for instance, he found that the eggs were not fresh but were cold storage eggs and he lost quite a number of his fine birds. Bear in mind the eggs you use must be fresh, bad eggs are dangerous, in fact fatal to the birds, especially the young ones, therefore be careful of the quality of your eggs. Many birds die each year on account of the eggs not being absolutely fresh.

There being no established standard for the popular bird now termed Warbler, we henceforth want it generally known that the following standard has been established, which was shown to Judge Brooking after the judging and he and the other judges concurred.

Standard For Judging Warblers, And Open Beaked Mixed Songs

	Points		Points
Feather	15	Song Variety	15
Shape	15	Free Singer	5
Condition	10	Special Tours	5
Song	15	General Effect	10
Quality	10		
		Total	100

The Golden Capped Lizard

THE LIZARD CANARY

This is the most distinct variety that has yet been produced in the Canary world. The name of "Lizard" has been bestowed upon this Canary owing to the fancied resemblance of the scalloped markings on its back and side to the scales of its reptilian namesake. It can scarcely be termed a happy or an appropriate one: however, it is consecrated by long usage, and is likely to remain. Its origin is quite unknown, though a number of conjectures have been hazarded as to its parentage, one of the most unlikely being that it is a cross between the ordinary Canary and the Saffron Sparrow (misnamed Finch). The latter is a Brazilian species, with which the Canary has nothing in common beyond the fact that they are both small birds, for one builds an open nest, and the other rears its brood in a hole in a tree, rock, or building. The cock Canary feeds its mate and young with food disgorged from its crop, and the male Saffron Sparrow carries food to its offspring in its bill, as the Sparrows and Buntings do, and does not feed its mate. The eggs of the two species are also quite unlike: those of the Canary, as everybody knows, are blue, pale blue, or bluish-green spotted and speckled with reddish-brown; while those of the Saffron Sparrow very much resemble those of the common House Sparrow.

There are two principal types of the Lizard Fancy, namely, the golden-spangled and the silver-spangled, the former being perhaps the more beautiful of the two. In a well-bred bird of either sub-division the top of the head is covered with a cap, which should be of prim-

rose (or, rather, crocus yellow), unmixed with a single feather of any other shade—the cap is said to be "broken" if any such intrude upon it. Deep colored in the golden-spangled, the cap is much paler in the silver-spangled Lizard, and the light markings on the back and sides correspond in color with that of the cap and the under-parts of the body.

It is a pity to mar the extreme delicacy of the natural color of these birds by giving them color-food, particularly cayenne, which has the effect of confusing the two races, for by its action a pale cap becomes golden, and a bright yellow is turned into red.

The Lizard Canary is one of the smaller varieties rarely exceeding 6 inches in length. So much care has been expended on the development of the "spangle," golden or silver, that the cap has been neglected, and is rather rarely met with in a perfect state. So well, indeed, is this recognized that classes for "broken caps" have been instituted at the principal Canary shows, which seems to be equivalent to offering a premium for spoiling one of the most attractive features of this favorite variety. The spangle is important, no doubt, and the body-color no less so, but the cap ought not be neglected either, and breeders will be well advised to cultivate it more than has appeared to be the case lately.

The greatest drawback in breeding Lizard Canaries is that the perfection of the plumage only lasts for one year. In their nest-feathers the young birds are not spangled at all, and but for the characteristic cap (yellow or buff, as the case may be) could not be distinguished from ordinary green Canaries. But with the second change of feathers the spangle makes its appearance in all its glory, to deteriorate at every successive moult until the birds once more, in their maturity and age, revert to their original appearance. The Lizard is rather loose-feathered, too, and should on no account be handled, or it will be very apt to lose an essential part of its plumage from wings or tail or shoulders, which would be fatal to all hope of success on the show bench.

Some breeders give cayenne pepper and other color-food to their Lizard Canaries, but it seems a pity to do so for the reasons already stated, and it is to be hoped that the practice will be discontinued.

Some judges attach most importance to the cap, others to the distinctive spangle, and it is rare to find a bird possessing both distinctions in perfection; still it is a standard that might be bred up to, and would not be more difficult to attain than it is to get other points not only in the various breeds of poultry and pigeons, but also in the case of the birds under consideration.

A word or two with reference to the mating of Lizard Canaries will bring us to the conclusion of the part of the subject. Many fanciers do not begin to breed from them till they are three years old. In the first year, it is said, the birds are immature, and their offspring lack the distinctive characters that mark the adult or perfect Lizard; and in the second they are in their prime, and too valuable on the show bench to admit of their time being wasted on a task that can be better accomplished later on.

Some advise pairing a yellow-capped cock with a silver or mealy hen; but this is a mistake, for there is no proverb the truth of which is more incontestably established than "Like produces like." Therefore if jonques are wanted, jonques must be mated with each other; and to obtain buffs or silvers, these should be paired together: the result in both cases will be satisfactory; but to put two opposite poles together is to court defeat and disappointment.

Although necessarily more or less inbred, probably from their first appearance, the Lizard so far has shown little or no sign of deterioration, either in appearance or stamina. As a rule, it is a hardy bird, and with ordinary care will live as long in a cage as any ordinary Canary.

For many reasons, it is better to keep and breed the Lizards in roomy cages than to turn them adrift in bird-room or aviary, in which, mating as they listed, they would quickly deteriorate in one essential point or another.

FLYING ROOM HINTS
By H. Bartsch

As most all young birds are flying now, we must be careful with them.

A good many are coming in their first moult, and those who have all flying, treat them the same. Remember the egg food. Don't skimp on it yet but make it lighter by adding 2 tablespoons of bread crumbs to egg. This is healthier for them all and more easy for them to digest. I put poppy seeds, a trifle sugar and Lawrence's food in just the same, as I did in breeding season, and a dish of rape is in the flight where they can eat to their hearts content. I also have a pan full of gravel they can pick at.

The floor is covered with straw, a thick layer, bathing water and plenty of drinking water and fresh air—is a few more needful things.

I have very good rape, feed very little canary seed now, maybe once a week they get a dish of it and once a week a dish of ground hemp.

And for green food I feed carrots and their tops and dandelion. I generally shift these, one day carrots and tops and next day dandelion, and about once a month celery.

We must feed our young, good but not too much heavy food in a day or don't over feed one day and starve them for two days after, every day enough food.

Treat your old females like your males. Make no difference in your feeding, they are the ones we must depend on for the work after they are moulted, then we can begin to cut down on the food and prepare them for cooler weather, but now they must grow feathers besides eat to live. It has to be nourishing food.

WITH A SMILE

When the blues and glooms assail you,
Knock you down and almost nail you,
When it seems that all hopes fail you—
That you are beaten by a mile,
Can the worries and disables,
They are only myths and fables—
Show your grit and turn the tables,
    With a smile.

When the boat of luck he's rocking,
And the joy of life he's shocking,
You can stop a knocker knocking
    With a smile.

When the wife with sundry tattle,
Shows that she's inclined to battle.
You can easily change her prattle—
    With a smile.

For the fighter or the debator,
For the lover or the hater,
There is no dope that is greater
    Than a smile.

Life gives back first what you give it.
It is just the way you live it,
If it wrongs you just forgive it.
    With a smile.

When the razz is all you're winning,
You can get the jazz beginning,
And set the world to grinning—
    With a smile.

Would you cause good luck to revel?
If you do it on the level,
You can even beat the devil
    With a smile.

                    Leroy C. Henderson.

THE FRILLED CANARY OF THE NETHERLANDS.

A popular breed in Europe but not much seen in the United States. Some breeders in England have shown the birds, but at no time can it be said they were popular. It is a large bird, about the length of a Lancashire, with a semi-upright position. It is of the Yorkshire type, but unlike the Yorks in the matter of feathering, being frilled on back of head, shoulder, sides, and breast with long, soft leafy feather.

The breeding process is practically the same as with other varieties, yellow to buff, with an occasional doublebuffing to keep up size, substance, and length of feather, generally using a two or three-year-old male bird with one-year-old hens. It is necessary to have feeders for this variety, as the parents are notoriously bad feeders.

These young birds when reared, if intended for show purposes, will require a lot of training. Open wire cages, similar to the Belgian cages, are generally used. When the young are about eight weeks old and well on hard seed diet they must be run in to the show cage and get accustomed to the cage being handled in order to give the birds confidence when approached by strangers. When the birds get accustomed to their surroundings, lift the cage and scratch the bottom of the cage gently to attract the bird's attention; like the Yorkshire, the bird will then stretch itself out to full length and get into position; a little practice every day will soon steady the birds.

They are a breed which requires considerable attention during the moult although there is no color-feeding to trouble about. They will need a liberal diet, for they are a heavily-feathered bird, and must have plenty of good nourishing food. The stock food should be best Spanish canary, hemp, linseed, rape; a little Chemical Food should be added to the drinking water, and cuttlefish bone scraped over the egg-food or kept hanging in the cage.

Seeing the bird is fond of bathing, the bath must be hung in the cage daily, unless the weath-

The Scotch Fancy Canary

The Belgian Canary

THE SCOTCH FANCY CANARY.

A WINNING BELGIAN.

er is very cold. They can be handwashed for show purposes, but as there are so very few shows which cater to this variety they will not require so much attention in this respect as the Yorkshire or Norwich varieties.

Two of the most "nervy" and most difficult to train of all our exhibtion breeds, are the Scotch Fancy and the Belgian Canary. Although in many respects these two varieties are similar, still to the experienced fancier, their differences in make-up are quite pronounced, and it would be, therefore, to our advantage to consider them separately.

Let us look at the Scotch Fancy to begin with, and we will find that it is a bird of peculiar shape. The head is small with a keen bright eye. The neck must be long and thin, set into the shoulders which are prominent and well filled in. The body must also be long and rounded, with long wings carried close to the body, but not crossing at the tips. The tail, in keeping with the rest of the general make-up of this bird, must be long and tightly packed, as in the case of the Yorkshire. The shape of this long and fine drawn bird is that of a crescent, or resembling the formation of the moon in its first quarter.

It has long been known as "The bird of Circle," and this term well describes the bird. To train the Scotch Fancy for exhibition is a task that requires a great deal of patience and kindness on the part of the owner of the bird, for it is an extremely nervous bird, and if once handled roughly in infancy it is then a very difficult matter to regain the bird's confidence.

At the early age of two months, this bird must be run into show cages at regular and frequent intervals not less than two or three times per week. The confidence of the bird must be gained, and the bird brought into its correct position by the handling of the cage always at the bottom, and by light scratching bottom of the cage to attract the bird's attention. The scratching can be done either by the finger nail or a small training stick made for the purpose. With this training you will gradually see the pupils improving, and they will draw themselves into position on each time that the training or show cage is used. The head and neck will be stretched out and curving downwards, while the tail is pulled under the perch, and projected in a forward manner, which, of course, gives the effect so much desired. The graceful semi-circular formation.

There are comparatively few breeders of this class of bird, and I believe the reason is the difficulty in breeding up to the high standard necessary to achieve success on the show bench in anything like keen competition. A show specimen Scotch Fancy must be nearly correct in all points, and a bird with a heavy head or thick neck has little or no chance of winning. Hens of this variety are, as a rule, very indifferent feeders which makes it necessary for the owner to keep a reserve stock of common bred hens but of a good feeding strain, if you are to accomplish anything like success in the breeding room. To those who think that they would like to attempt the breeding of this fascinating variety, I would advise giving lots of room in the way of breeding cages and particular attention must be given to nesting receptacles. The young birds grow to length very quickly, and when feeding, stretch themselves up to such an extent that unless a deep, roomy nest pan is supplied, the feeding hen has difficulty in passing the food into the mouths of the young birds.

The same attention to detail in the mating of these birds is identical to all other breeds which are produced for exhibition work, and are judged for all points with one exception, and that being the song. Length, type, color, quality of feathers, and general make-up being the points to consider, and as far as color goes, yellows should be paired to buffs if the best results are to be obtained.

This is the only variety in which the term "variegated" is not used to describe a bird which is marked with green or dark feathers, and a Scotch Fancy of this class is known as a "Piebald."

Let us now look at the other variety, which is known as the Belgian Canary. As its name implies, this bird is a native of the country from which it takes its name, although now I venture to say, that as many good Belgians are bred annually in Great Britain as on the Continent. This bird, like the Scotch Fancy, is also of a particularly nervous disposition, and one that has to be handled with the greatest of care if we are to have it in the condition and state of steadiness which a good judge so much enjoys seeing in this variety.

The general details of the Belgian are so much alike to the Scotch Fancy that it is unnecessary to repeat them here, excepting one or two fea-

tures. In posing for exhibition the Belgian does not pull the tail under the perch as the Scotch Fancy does, but appears in practically a straight line from the top of the shoulders down to the tip of the tail, and that line in a perpendicular position. The shoulders are more pronounced and the head and neck appear to project almost in a horizontal position from the shoulders. The Belgian Canary lays claim to the title of "King of the Fancy" and rightly so, for a bird of this variety, true to type, and containing the all round quality that a winning Belgian must possess is truly a wonderful and beautiful creation.

These birds are extremely delicate and cannot stand the exposure and knocking about that many other exhibition varieties have to put up with during a long and trying show season.

The show or exhibition cages for both breeds are all wire, and similar in shape to the regulation Border Fancy Cages, but slightly larger. Many years ago it was customary for exhibitors of both the Scotch Fancy and Belgian Canaries to adopt a particular style of decoration for their cages, and many beautiful and costly works of art were used in the staging of their birds. In late years, however, an attempt has been made by the Specialists Clubs to adopt a uniform type of cage, and this has to a large extent dispensed with the fancy cages of polished mahogany, inlaid with "Mother of Pearl," polished brass, and other decorating agencies. The accompanying illustrations will give a better idea of what these two varieties of birds should appear than any words which I might write would convey.

Any fanciers who wish to enjoy the pleasures of establishing a strain of high class Scotch Fancies or Belgians, should begin by securing breeding stock of the highest possible quality, and as free from faults as it is possible to procure.

ROLLER CANARY CONTEST CAGE

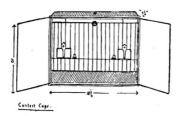

Contest Cage.

The above picture shows a very popular contest cage for Rollers. It is known as the English type, with sliding tray. The shutter permits darkening down. These are made to fit into a cabinet for shipping or traveling, making a splendid arrangement for one or two collections of birds.

The Hartz Mountain, Golden Opera, Grand Opera, Chopper and Warbler

THE HARTZ MOUNTAIN, YORKSHIRES, BORDERS, NORWICH, CRESTS AND OTHER TYPE CANARIES ARE EXHIBITED AT SHOWS AND JUDGED ACCORDING TO THEIR STANDARDS

Owing to the fact that I have dealt considerably with the Roller Canary on the show bench, I do not wish to lead the readers or fanciers of other than rollers to believe that the other breeds of canaries do not have their place on the show bench, and are any less important than the rollers. As a matter of fact the type birds in England and even in many shows in the U. S. when exhibited, out number the Rollers and have just as many faithful admirers, and certainly there is more profit to be made in rearing the most popular type sold in the pet shops throughout the country, as they can be sold at 5 or 6 months of age without any training. There are many more canaries other than rollers owned in the U. S. and they are just as important in the homes and are as prolific and admired as greatly as any roller. Commercially speaking the yellow birds are in demand far in excess of the dark birds, the free singing hartz bird with the mixed song is the ideal bird to raise for commercial purposes, even though personally the author much prefers the patiently trained roller.

THE HARTZ MOUNTAIN CHOPPER OR OPEN BEAK SINGER

Regarding this most popular species of Canary which is often called Hartz Mountain Roller, the Golden Opera Roller, the Capanini, the Living Music Box Radio warbler Serenader, and various other nomde-plume's. They are very hardy and prolific, are free singers and often obtainable in dark golden color, they have the ability to mimic almost as well as the roller, but cannot acquire the soft sweet rolling musical tours of the Roller in same tones. They are mostly open beak singers and have higher pitched tone rather brassy or sharp; they are the loudest of all singing birds, and are favor-

ites of thousands. The Hartz Mountain have been crossed with the Rollers but invariably the young have the short, jerky or choppy notes in the middle or at the end of their song, some of them have rolls of the Rollers but of a different kind of a roll. They are admired by thousands and to those that wish loud jolly singing they have no equal. They are tireless singers, very companionable and the liveliest of the Canary tribe, the difference in a so-called Hartz Mountain and a Roller is immediately distinguished by the short chops and the open beak with the loud bells pouring forth. Even the half-breeds are easily detected as the grounds tones are different being much softer and sweeter in the Rollers and the rolls much longer ordinarily, the females of this type are usually excellent feeders and are often used as foster mothers when raising Roller Canaries.

The Hartz is very popular in the United States, but many of the better educated in art and music of late years prefer the Roller and the great popularity of the loud singers may not continue in the years to come. For those that prefer color, these are an ideal bird as they are indeed most lovable pets and charm thousands with their wonderful song interspersed with the song of the wild birds. It is not possible to train them with a Roller teacher they have a much louder voice and are more vigorous than the average Roller; they do of course pick up some of the notes of the Roller but cannot deliver them in the same pleasing manner. It is not advisable to cross them, no more than one would cross two different species of dogs of thoroughbred lines. There is of course no harm, but if you wish the soft Roller get one which has a variety of changes, they often sing fourteen different tours, which is impossible with any other kind of birds. If you wish the jolly rickling rollicking song of the Hartz, get one of this breed, but keep them pure in blood lines, which is best in any case. The Hartz Mountains have been bred for hundreds of years and the first Rollers were called the Hartz Mountain Roller or German Roller. They were not of as fine a quality as the St. Andresburg Rollers, they bred the Hartz for color and vitality principally while the old painstaking Germans in their thoroughness developed the wonderful music box the Roller Canary and have bred for long distance rolling with many changes in tours regardless of color. In size they are about the same, likely most Rollers are a trifle smaller. If your bird is an open beak bird, that is, sings with beak opened and has short harsh jerks or chops or Gee Gee or Zit, Zit, it is a Hartz Mountain. In both species we find the singing females, but never do they in song quality compare with the males.

Bird stores do not seem to get enough of these "purveyors of cheer" as they are known to supply the demand which has increased to public places such as theatres, restaurants, etc.

The White Canary

THE WHITE CANARY has now become very popular, and the demand so great that more and more breeders are becoming interested in them.

Their food and care are identical to the other canaries given here. They have been developed or created from careful line-breeding to breed out the yellow and yet retain sufficient vitality. They are now found among the Rollers and open beak singers.

The White Canary has come to stay. I can remember them being bred occasionally by individual aviculturists 20 years ago, but through the lack of knowledge by their owners they failed to reproduce white in their off-spring and so eventually they died out. About 1920 some of these birds were exhibited at the Crystal Palace show in London, England, and were greatly admired.

At the present time there are quite a few on the market, the most of them coming from Germany, and to which country we must give credit for producing these pretty birds in sufficient numbers to be able to place them on the world's market.

I have seen them on different occasions, not pure white. Some are of a creamy shade, and others are of a dirty white. We have them at the present time that are pure white, excepting about half of one inch on the flights, and which shows a tinge of yellow. These birds are supposed to be the best of the whites of to-day. They won 1st and 3rd at the Crystal Palace Show in 1926 and again won 1st and 2nd in 1927.

An experiment several years ago in trying to produce white canaries at the end of five years was rewarded with a nest of four birds almost white, two being black and white, but all had a tinge of yellow on wings and rump. I would recommend anyone who intends to breed these pretty birds to get the purest whites and most typical that they can get, whether it be Border Fancy, Yorkshire, Norwich or Roller type, there are a number of each variety being bred, but the Border Fancy are nearest to the correct type. At present we have many fine white Canaries.

Now, there is no more difficulty in breeding good white canaries than there is in any other variety. The feeding should be as follows: The staple diet should be good plain Canary Seed with a little German Rape every other day, and a little mixed seed twice each week. Fresh green food can be given every day. When rearing young the usual egg-food should be given whether it be egg and biscuit or cod liver oil food. They should be fed at this time like any other canaries. The object that several breeders have in view at the present time, is to produce an even marked strain of birds, that is, birds marked with a ring around each eye, to resemble a pair of glasses, and marked like this are in great demand in Europe at the present time. Here we have another field for the experimenter, that is the creation of various colors. From the whites they have produced black, blue, and fawn. The blacks at the present time are not the jet blacks that we would like to see, but more of a greenish black, but this will be improved in time, and by careful and selective breeding. The blues are also a long way from what is required. The present blues are a slate blue. This color also will be greatly improved in the next few years. I have also seen advertised "Red Canaries" but I am unable to say at the present time whether they are genuine canaries, or only color fed whites, but even if they are color fed whites, they must look very pretty indeed.

We have the White Rollers, these are as popular as the other rollers and as an average are of equally good quality. We also have the White Yorkshires, and a more beautiful bird, I have never seen, this is truly an aristocrat. Also we have white BORDERS, one of the most popular of the Types, the "Wee Gem" term used for Borders in a white is a darling. Whites are very beautiful they have gained in favor and are permanently established and no mistake will be made when turning to whites. There is now a club of White Canary Breeders and Fanciers in the U. S., members from Portland, Ore. to N. Y.

29

Color Breeding of Canaries

Producing the Cinnamon, Fawn and Blue Canaries

There is a fascination about breeding canaries in the various colors in which they are now being produced far greater than that which is found in ordinary canary breeding.

While still in its infancy, the art of color breeding of canaries has greatly increased during the past few years until there seems to be no limit to this fascinating study. Throughout the land we find people are becoming more and more interested in the beautiful colors that are now being produced. Color breeding certainly helps a breeder to sell his birds, and at a higher price. If you were able to attend the various bird shows you would notice an increase of interest and sales of birds in the beautiful colors in which they are now being bred.

The possibility of producing new colors without hybridizing has already been demonstrated, for we already have white canaries, orange-red, blue-gray, grass-green, cinnamon, silver, fawn, orange, and all shades of yellow, as well as combinations of some of these colors. The possibilities of new colors yet to be produced adds still greater interest in this already fascinating study. Truly, as one prominent breeder on the Pacific coast has so aptly remarked, "It is a 'New Deal' in the Canary World."

The Cinnamon Canary

The name of this variety is indicative of its color, which is a rich brown or cinnamon, and is in reality a chocolate color superimposed upon a yellow background. The breeding of cinnamon canaries is very interesting because, like the white the possibilities of producing various colors with cinnamon blood are numerous, and no fancier should be without a few cinnamon birds.

Cinnamon blood, however, has its peculiarities; for instance, a cinnamon male paired to a female without cinnamon blood will not produce any cinnamon males; any cinnamons, whether solid or mottled, will all be females. Again, if a cinnamon female be paired to a male without cinnamon blood, no cinnamon colored young will appear. To breed cinnamon male and female young, both parents must have a dominant amount of cinnamon blood, and yet a male bird with only a small percent-

age of cinnamon blood will likely produce cinnamon marked young, but such youngsters will all be females. Such are the peculiarities of cinnamon blood and there is still a large field for experimentation in cinnamon crossing.

Pure cinnamon blood is distinguished by pink eyes in the nestlings before the eyes open, which can be observed through the closed eyelids, although this color usually turns to a garnet shade after the eyes open and before the young leave the nest.

The Fawn Canary

As explained in a previous article, a pure blooded cinnamon male paired to a pure white female will produce fawn. The mating of fawn will in turn produce both cinnamon and fawn birds and they have the same peculiar characteristics found in the cinnamons. A cinnamon male, for instance, will, when paired to a green hen, produce an equal number of green males and cinnamon hens, while a fawn male paired to a green hen will produce green males, cinnamon hens, blue males and fawn hens.

The Blue Canary

The so-called blue canary is not exactly blue but rather a steel-blue in color, or gray-blue, and a very attractive bird. This color may be obtained by mating a green male to pure white female. Blue mated to blue, or blue mated to green will produce both blue and green young, and should one of the birds contain cinnamon blood will sometimes produce cinnamon or fawn.

It is highly probable that a study of the reactions of color in the breeding of the Andalusian blue fowl may give us a key to the production of new colors and even combinations of colors in canaries—especially blue and black. In this breed of poultry pure blues bred together produce one-half blues and one-fourth white with black markings and one-fourth black with white markings. These latter birds in appearance are of a dirty color and referred to as "wasters." Yet they are pure breeds, for when they are bred together they produce all blue. They show no dominant or recessive factors, but the feature of the gametic purity shows here very clearly.

The Perky Little Siskin

For Hybrids and Introducing More Brilliant Color

This dear little bird, the smallest of the Native Finches, is becoming very popular and many who are interested in trying their hand at cross breeding use the Siskin and canary to produce a Siskin Canary Hybrid and are delighted with the result. This little fellow does not resent captivity, but being naturally a bit of a glutton, soon responds to attention, especially if a tid-bit is offered regularly. Since he has a tendency to put on too much weight when in captivity, he should be given a good sized cage where he may have plenty of exercise and care must be taken that he is not allowed to have much hemp or sunflower seed.

Give him the staple foods—canary seed, rape and teazle as well as plenty of wild foods which should be offered in bunches.

The Siskin is inclined to be a friendly little fellow, even in their wild haunts. He is not much of a songster, but is constantly doing his best and sings a little, even during the winter.

In the woods their nest is very difficult to locate, for they build in the very top of a pine or fir tree, hiding their nest smugly among the dense foliage about forty feet from the ground and it needs a sharp eye to detect it. It is not easy to find even when one knows the very tree in which it makes its home. The nest is naturally very small, outwardly constructed of roots, dry grasses and moss, then lined with vegetable down, feathers and hair. The eggs are much like those of the Goldfinch.

Many of these birds are trapped and sold to dealers everywhere and soon find a home with fanciers where they will learn to accept treats from the fingers. We do not see classes for Siskins except at very large shows in England, but occasionally a few specimens are exhibited as a novelty. In selecting these birds for exhibition purposes, you should take into consideration the size, markings and color—the difficulty being in getting all these combined in one specimen, for although the Siskin is small the markings are most important, he should have expansive and dense cap and the wings should be well defined, commencing well up the side and extending to the root of the tail. Both sides should be similar. It is hard

indeed, to find a bird perfectly marked, so you must place a great value on one should you be fortunate enough to possess it. Each color should be rich and clear and not smoky. This bird may be color-fed which is acceptable in contest.

Crossing the Redhooded Siskin with the canary has become a very popular and interesting experiment. Why not try it for a diversion?

It may be best to secure a medium sized Norwich hen to mate with your Siskin in order to produce the size in the hybrid, and if you can, put them through the moult together so that you have allowed them to become friends. Be very careful that the Siskin is not allowed to become too fat because of his tendency to be a glutton, for he will contract indigestion or inflammation or develop a fatty heart (resulting in a gasping for breath and a perceptible, continual lifting of the shoulder or the wing). When such trouble develops, the case is almost hopeless and all the care and remedies are practically worthless. It will be almost impossible to bring him back to normal, so do not supply the seeds in such quantities as to allow the slightest chance of overfeeding.

Be very careful not to be too curious when babies are in the nest, for they will pop out of the nest if disturbed or frightened even when only ten days old. So do not meddle with them at all so long as you see that the hen is feeding them properly. When the hen is off the nest you may see if the young birds are all right.

The nest must be very shallow for the baby birds are so small that it is very easy for the hen to sit too closely and cause them to sweat. Care should be taken also that the seed cups are kept in place, for the young hybrids will bolt through the holes and fatalities will follow. When the babies take to the perches properly there will be little to fear. Let the Siskin and canary stay together during the winter and early spring for best results, for then they will readily mate as soon as the hen is ready. The

(Continued on Page 119.)

31

The Whistling Canary

One does not need to draw upon the imagination when listening to a bird whistle a tune, providing the bird has had the proper training. We have heard all this and more: "Do your birds actually whistle 'Yankee Doodle?'" We have been accused of being a ventriloquist, or having a music box, or small boy underneath the table! We know of birds that whistle the following: "Yankee Doodle," "My Old Kentucky Home," "America," "The Bugle Calls," "Hail, Hail, the Gang's All Here," "Rock-a-Bye Baby," "The Sidewalks of New York," "Pop Goes the Weasel," "Glory, Glory, Hallelujah," "The Whistler and His Dog," "The Old Spinning Wheel," "Good, Night, Ladies," "Rainbow Round My Shoulder," "Springtime in the Rockies," "The Rosary," "Golden Slippers," and a Church Choir that can render "Jesus Loves Me," "Brighten the Corner Where You are," "The Child of a King" and "Silent Night, Holy Night."

* * *

Mrs. Ream write a very interesting story of the training of "Brownie" that whistles "Silent Night, Holy Night." Instead of the meaningless trills and notes of a Roller Canary, he gives a melodious rendition of the famous Christmas Hymn. Brownie whistles anywhere he happens to be. He whistled all the way on a long journey, and when he is released from his cage of a morning he perches on the foot of the bed and whistles, "All is calm, all is bright!" Wouldn't it be inspiring to awaken with that thought no matter how much chaos we are in?

* * *

Helen S. Carlson writes of her whistler and it will surprise you as it did me. She says: "You might be interested to know that I have a common Starling that talks, and whistles the chorus of 'Over There.' He is almost human. I found him deserted by his parents when a week old and he is now three years old. They are very easily taught to talk and whistle, are very intelligent and extremely affectionate. In this state they are not protected, so it is perfectly legal to cage and keep them. 'Chippy' has a large flight, and I think more of him than I do my forty canaries. He eats the same food as the family, even ice cream, so I never have any trouble with his diet."

We sold a pair of birds that caused quite a lot of excitement in the village. "Rin Tin" named himself, because he heard the program on the air featuring Rin-Tin-Tin. This bird would always start his song after he had called very loudly, "Rin-tin-tin." Jenny Lind is his mate, and her owner talks to both birds, well, because they are really members of the family, and why not? Another occupant of the house is Betty, a very tiny puppy. Jenny Lind never liked the dogs as there seemed to be too much attention going that way. One day Mrs. W. held the dog up to the cage and said over and over, "Sweet Betty." Until Jenny thought it must be so, and now she needs no prompting to echo the words, "Sweet Betty," so plainly that one cannot mistake it even if you had not been told.

* * *

Because of the increasing interest in trained canaries, that whistle and talk, there are in existence two Whistling Roller Canary Clubs. One located in Dunreith, Indiana, known as the "Canary Choir Circle," and the other in Los Angeles. These Clubs are devoted exclusively to the breeding and training of Whistling Canaries—birds that are trained to whistle tunes as indicated above, instead of the natural song, though many of them do sing their song, as well as whistle a tune. In December, 1932, Miss Hayes exhibited her Whistlers in Indianapolis, and the following January, in Chicago and Detroit. The Los Angeles Club held an exhibit in January, 1934. This year, there will be Whistlers and Trick Canaries at more than one show, and this is always a very interest feature. The members of both clubs have only the best whistling stock obtainable—birds that are "talented" and that will not only whistle but produce young that can be trained to whistle your own choice of a tune. We are working out a score card whereby these Whistlers can be properly judged at any show. It will bring points of quality of tone, tempo, and whether or not they can render their tune perfectly, and without faulty notes. The training of these aristocrats of the canary family is very interesting and one has a new thrill when the youngsters begin to tune, whistling a few bars of the tune, and learning more each day of training and practice.

America's Latest Creation

The Columbus Fancy

A Most Beautiful Bird With A Very Pleasing Song

THE COLUMBUS FANCY
THE LATEST CONTRIBUTION TO THE
CANARY WORLD

The latest type canary created by Americans

For several years fanciers have been working to create a better singing canary. A better
proportioned, more attractive looking bird, a
lively free singer wearing a stately crown
drawn from the crest bird or old time topknot
bird.

Among those active in the creation and perfection of this new American aristocrat of the
canary family is Mrs. W. A. Finney, a nation-
ally known bird lover with knowledge galore
and a heart that knows no bounds. After numerous crosses and some line breeding in which
the Crest, the Hartz and the Norwich, were
used, the "Columbus Fancy" was created.

While the "Columbus Fancy" is not a large
member of the canary family it is destined to
be a most popular home bird as it is bred for
beauty and song; its length should not exceed
6 inches. Large head crowned with an evenly
rounded crest; short, stocky legs with wide
back slightly curved with a broad, full breast
to justify abundance of melody and vigor. The
members of this family not wearing the crest
are to be called the "smooth head" and not
crest bred as is done with other breeds of canaries.

The many who fancy a crowned or topknot
bird and wish plenty of song and color will be
pleased with this newly created type canary.
They are bred for color and for exhibition and
are not to be shown as colorfed.

Undoubtedly this bird created to gratify the
tastes of many American bird lovers is destined to become a very popular bird, due to
its having been "Tailormade" and we predict
the future bird-shows will find many entries
from this bird whose standard of perfection has
just been perfected.

THE SELECTED STANDARD

A short stout, compact bird not to exceed
5½ or 6 inches. Head large wide and not too
flat on top but nicely rounded in order to carry
an appropriate sized crest; the beak short and
stout; the neck short and thick; the breast
broad and full; the back wide and slightly
curved outwards; the legs short and stocky
looking; the wings and tail neatly made and
well carried. Wings just to meet at the tips
and carried close to the body. The crest should
be more the shape of that of the Lancashire,
coming down well on the sides and finishing
off at the back of the head in a nicely creased
or hood-like effect with closely packed feathers
which should be longer than the ordinary plain
head canary of any type. Call the smooth head

bred from this mating a "smooth head" and
not a Crest Bred. Say rather a Columbus
smooth head and not plainhead as the term
plainhead implies no crested parents for generations back. Clear body with dark crest and
evenly marked wings and tail are considered
very desirable but type as in all other instances
is always to be of first consideration. Breed
for color, as no small compact bird is improved
by color food.

Color; bright, rich and level, through-
    out, natural color ....15 pts.
Short body or shape; beak short and
    neat, bright in color; head round, full
    and neat; neck thick and heavy;
    body short and chubby with wide
    back well filled in; well rounded
    chest. Crest shall be in proportion
    to the size of the bird, well filled in
    and without splits. In the back the
    feathers should taper off into the
    back of the head and neck ....30 pts.
Feather; soft and silky and of natural
    color, tight and compact ......15 pts.
Wings and tail, short, compact and of
    good carriage ....15 pts.
Size, well proportioned not to exceed
    5½ or 6 inches ....10 pts.
Legs, stocky and well set back ...... 5 pts.
Condition, health, cleanliness and sound
    natural color feather ....10 pts.

     Total   ....100 pts.

THE PRAYER OF A CAGED CANARY
By Chas. Crosby

When I settle down to sleep,
My little cage from draughts pray keep,
In darkened corner snug and warm,
Secure from mice and all alarm.

And in the morning when I wake,
If my small home quite neat you'll make,
With perches clean and sanded floor,
My hymn with gratitude will soar.

Fresh seed and water are my wealth,
A bone of cuttlefish my health,
With bit of lettuce, apple sweet,
Or orange as occasional treat.

My bath I covet, but, pray try
To shield me from all draughts till dry;
Yet place me not in sunshine strong,
'Tis rather trying all day long.

Nor hang my cage too high above;
Bring me more close to those I love,
To be where I can always greet
Your kindly words with singing sweet.

CINNAMON S
A POPULAR TYPE

The Cinnamon Canary.

This can scarcely be termed a distinct variety. It is rather a "sport", for it is met with in every known breed, except the Lizard, and has undergone many alterations, not to say transformations, since it first appeared, and not always for the better.

Originally the Cinnamon was self-colored—that is, had no yellow or dark patches on it, and was then a handsome as well as a curious-looking creature; but of late the peculiar dove or cinnamon tinting has been confined to a small patch round the eye, the secondary wing-feathers, and sometimes the flanks and the tail, the remainder of the plumage being either buff or yellow.

In our opinion, color-feeding ruins a Cinnamon Canary, for it turns the delicate dove-color of the natural or unsophisticated bird to a somewhat dingy brick-color, dashed with red and brown.

Some of these birds are crested: most of them belong to the Norwich type; but some to the Yorkshire and other varieties. Where a Cinnamon wears a crest, that should be as dark as possible; it is sometimes met with nearly black.

Paired with an ordinary Norwich, very pretty birds are sometimes produced by a Cinnamon mother; thus, we have seen some that were a dark green on the back and wings, and had all the under-parts a bright golden yellow.

Notwithstanding that the Cinnamon, when purely bred, has pink eyes, showing that it is neither more nor less than an albino, and, consequently, had better not be exposed to too strong a light (which half blinds it), it is by no means delicate, but, on the contrary, full of life and energy. The cocks are good and loud singers, and we have known of some whose

energetic performances caused a blood-vessel to give way in the brain, in each case the bird dropped as if struck by lightning in the very climax of its performance, from apoplexy.

Mules between the Cinnamon Canary and the Gold-finch or the Siskin are usually light-colored, as the albinism of the hen overpowers, so to speak, the influence of the darker-plumaged cock, and a perfectly "clear" bird is sometimes the result.

Do not think of crossing Cinnamons with Rollers or Hartz Mountains. You lose entirely the song that has taken years to produce. The Cinnamon is purely and simply a chopper, commonly termed and as for sweet song, cannot be compared with the real song birds. Their song is jerky, choppy and shrill. Many people have what they call Cinnamons, so called on account of their color in plumage, resembling Cinnamon, but in reality they have a sport Cinnamon, unless they have pink or red eyes.

It is always best to keep any species pure in breeding. No advantage is to be gained in crossing any two breeds. We have heard of some dealers advising some to cross a Roller and a Hartz Mountain. This loses all of the main points created in the Roller by hundreds of years of breeding. To those that have and prefer Cinnamons, if they be real or so-called Cinnamons, my advice is to breed them pure to color and not inter-breed them with any other species of Canary. The color of Cinnamons on any bird does not signify that it is a Cinnamon.

To breed Cinnamons it is necessary that both parents should possess Cinnamon blood. The variety has been used for a number of crossing purposes, especially for quality, and it is an old saying that the Cinnamon can be grafted on to any stock, but nothing can be grafted on to the Cinnamon. If you want to produce Cinnamons you must use a Cinnamon cock paired to a Cinnamon hen, or a pink-eyed hen carrying Cinnamon blood; otherwise the produce will be somewhat mixed.

Space will not allow me to go into details of all the puzzling and interesting results of indiscriminate crossing with non-Cinnamon-bred birds of Norwich type, but one point stands out clear and distinct—that to produce Cinnamons of both sexes you must use a Cinnamon cock mated to a Cinnamon or Cinnamon-bred hen.

In no variety of Canary is it so essential to know the pedigree of your stock birds. If this is not attended to, you may find self-Cinnamons, Greens, and Cinnamon-marks amongst the progeny. I have known of cases where birds bred from a pair of Cinnamons were Cinnamons until the following year's moult; after the moult they were only Cinnamon-marked on wing, and the second adult moult left them clear birds.

As an exhibition bird they have many desirable characteristics. Like their green brothers, they do not require much handling. They stand the knocking about on rail much better than some of the light-feathered varieties like the Borders or Yorkshires. They are fairly hardy, and at shows where no classes are provided for Cinnamons they invariably come out well in the variety classes.

CANARY BREEDING
GENERAL SUGGESTIONS

COST OF REARING CANARIES IN THE U. S.

For years I have listened to people rave about the high costs of rearing their birds, and regretting the cheap price they have to sell their birds for, still having in mind the high prices we were able to receive for our birds a few years back, I recall when Fank Zager sold six canary birds for $1000.00 and when I sold the four concert birds I sent entour to most parts of the U. S. to James Durkin of Spokane, Wash., for $600.00, I have sold many birds for $25.00, $35.00 and $50.00 each, but they were real trained rollers, contest winners and famed. The cost comes in the time, care and keep in training the Roller, but if you breed, say two hens to one male as described elsewhere in this book, buy the popular kind of sale birds that can be sold at five or six months of age and you can make good money selling them for the wholesale prices asked for the Imported birds all of which must pay 50 cents duty. It does not require any sacrifices to rear birds now. The undesirable work of mixing the egg-food is eliminated now, it being possible to buy just as satisfactory nestling food of several makes at a cheap price, the great cost comes in EXTRAVAGANCE, WASTE. I have seen cages with half of the seed on the cage bottom, you only kid yourself, they can't fool the bird, you only kid yourself, they are either overfed, or the seed or food is old and musty and you miss much saving by not feeding the green food found in everyone's back yard. Canaries are not hogs, should not be made fat, a tablespoonful of seeds daily, a treat cup full of rich food is enough.

KILLING A BIRD WITH KINDNESS.

Many bird owners who actually love their pets kill them with kindness by feeding dainties which upset the digestion, and ultimately death is the result. Never give your bird cake, pastries or table delicacies, (tit-bits of the right kind are all right.) DO NOT place in a bird's cup the full portion of its daily ration, unless it is necessary and you are to be away, it is natural that the bird will throw some of the seeds out on the bottom of the cage looking for the seeds he likes best, food if eaten from the bottom may cause serious sickness. NEVER, never pick up and feed green food that has dropped on the bottom of the cage, green food spoils quickly and if eaten after being soiled is very bad.

CARE OF THE TUTOR OR SCHOOLMASTER

The purpose of the tutor is to teach your young birds, they being mimics, and if you ar-range them as described elsewhere in this book (see index) they will mimic their teacher, hence do not permit the teacher to oversing, keep him fresh, place him in a darkened cabinet after a singing spell of an hour or so. If the tutor is permitted to sing continuously he will become faulty, sluggish and bad in total value, the young birds will mimic him exactly, hence it is advisable to keep him at his best in song, vigorous, mellow, sweet and soft.

THE ROLLER VERSUS THE HARTZ MOUNTAIN FOR QUICK SALE

You may love the Roller's song, with the beautiful hollow-roll and deep bass, and the glucks and water tours; and in making your choice selections you do not allow the color of the bird to influence you—but listen to the quality of the song, the variety of the tours alone.

Your artistic ear may influence you to resolve to raise nothing but Rollers, but if you are interested from a commercial standpoint, then you must submit to the opinion of the general public and specialize on the color of the bird as well as its ability to sing loudly. Raise the deep yellows with the mixed song.

These loud singers are oftentimes called "choppers" and sing with an open beak, sometimes called the Hartz Mountain or Golden Opera—in fact many different names are given the large, yellow, vigorous canary and they sell readily. The department stores are anxious for them—the Pet Shops cannot get enough of them.

These loud singers may be registered and are pedigreed the same as the roller and the type birds; their jolly song and brilliant color excel when it comes to sales in the Pet Shops, therefore, think well and consider what purpose you have in mind before mating your birds. And I believe that for the same investment, your birds will show a greater profit to you than the same amount invested in poultry, rabbits, or pigeons; in fact a good business can be developed from raising canaries, when you have established a market for your birds.

One point in favor of the yellow bird with its loud song is that no training is necessary to bring them into full song and furthermore they are ready for the market at five or six months of age, while a roller could hardly be ready until he is ten or twelve months old, say nothing of the time and care taken in the training.

35

GETTING YOUR FEMALES READY

No set rule will suffice for all localities and conditions, the different climates and conditions must be considered, therefore I shall write of my condition at Louisville, Ky., although I have raised canaries in Texas, California and Chicago. About the first of February I begin to get busy with our females to get them in shape for breeding. Some breeders like myself, have their females in cool rooms, not too cold of course, but say a few degrees above freezing. But first of all, lest we forget, they must have a good sized place to fly in, in order to keep their blood in good circulation. A cool room and small quarters will never do. You will then get sick birds. Females should have a good sized cage to fly in. It makes them hardier and healthier birds and more active.

Now the feeding for birds kept in cool rooms. Give plenty of good rape seed, all they want to eat, in dishes or bowls whichever you have. In another dish put canary seed, not too much of this. One medium sized dish to fifty or seventy-five females, and in another dish put some steel cut oats, about the same amount as canary seed, but don't feed steel cut oats every day, say every other day or twice a week, is sufficient feed, according to the temperature of the room. If it is very cold, feed more often, if milder weather feed more sparingly, as steel cut oats heats, as your females want heat for their bodies when it is cold, but if you feed too much oats in milder weather, you will get your females in heat before it is breeding time.

Once in two weeks you can give them a dish of whole hemp to eat, it passes time for them to break the hard shell and that makes their bills and jaws stronger.

Once a week I give them a light egg-food. Two tablespoons of bread crumbs to one egg. Cook number of eggs according to your flock of birds and don't forget poppy seed in your egg-food.

Now for green foods, I feed lettuce, celery and apple, when I feed egg-food, and once in a while carrots. It is pastime for the females and keeps them busy.

I, at present have a good sized piece of bacon fastened to a post where they can help themselves. It keeps them from pulling each other's feathers. But I don't feed it continually. they get it once in a winter time, I don't place it in breeding cages. Some may, but I prefer not to. Females that go through this treatment and are lively, are pretty sure to prove good mothers. Those that sit puffed up and act sickly are not forth their feed, because they won't amount to anything, only a disappointment to you. A sickly female is of no use to anyone. There is enough disappointment in the breeding time anyway without keeping sickly females to breed with.

As to water I would not advise anyone to give the icy water right out of the faucet. Add a little warm water to it, it is better.

Keeping your females in a warm room you have to feed more sparingly on the heat food such as canary and steel cut oats. If your room is heated you need not feed for heat producing foods so generously, feed egg-food once a week, but be careful about bringing them into heat too soon.

BREEDING TIME

With the coming of warmer weather, the end of March or the beginning of April, the fancier starts his breeding operations. The hens are going actively about in their quarters. When they begin to carry nest-building material in their bills and deposit it carefully and mysteriously in the corners of the cages it is a sign that the nesting time is at hand. After a few days the nests are almost completed and now the breeder must daily examine the hens to determine if breeding maturity has arrived, so that she can be placed in the cage with the male, both new to the cage. In examining the bird, blowing back the feathers, the breeder will find that the anus, before the first laying, is somewhat longer and seems thicker at the bottom. But the proper sexual condition has not yet arrived and it would be a waste of time. It would only result in biting and fighting. But as soon as the anus of the hen has lost its normal form, when it has become swollen and extended, then it is time to put them together. A few days after the first sexual act, if it has been successful, the first egg is laid. The other eggs follow daily, being laid at the same time of day as the first one, that is, if the laying process is normal.

In order to have all the eggs hatch at the same time you must remove them as soon as they are laid and put them in a receptacle of sand or other soft material. Keep the eggs from each nest separated from those of another nest. In handling the eggs great caution is necessary. They have thin shells and are very sensitive to pressure and jars. The least shell fracture makes them unsuitable for hatching owing to the entrance of air. Leave a nest egg in the place of the first three eggs removed. One artificial egg is enough, you do not need to add one for every additional egg laid. When the fourth egg has been laid put the other three eggs back in the nest and the incubation period starts. Should other eggs be laid they will generally hatch at the same time as the original four. Incubation usually lasts 13 days, and on the 14th day, reckoning from the first day of incubation you can expect to find youngsters in the nest. The daily supervision of the hatching hens is best done when they have left the nest to feed. In general they must be disturbed as little as possible. The taking of the hens from the nest while hatching, or even after the young ones have arrived, is to be condemned. They become shy and fearful, and are apt to abandon the nest for good. On the hatching day many beginners cannot control their curiosity. They want to see the youngsters and disturb the mother at the very time when it is essential that she should not leave the nest. On the morning of the 14th day you need only to glance at the floor of the cage to see if any egg shells are there. If none are there the young are not yet hatched. So please restrain your curiosity, the birds resent any interference and may go on a strike. If the eggs are fertile and everything else in order, the results will be satisfactory.

When the hatchlings are in the nest see that all egg shell particles are removed, as they may cause injuries to the young. This can be done while the hens are feeding. It is also possible that the half of an egg shell may encase itself over an unhatched egg and make its hatching impossible.

The little nestlings present a tiny, naked and unimpressive appearance. They are very delicate with a relatively large head and beak. At first the fine down visible on their backs is stuck to the body owing to the moisture. The influence of the heat from the mother bird dries it and in a very short time it appears as a delicate, faintly shining formation.

The youngsters lie in the nest in a heap, close together, one neck over the other. If at the least jar to the nest they raise their heads, and the wide-open beaks show a flesh-red throat, then all is well. If this is not the case, if they lie in the nest at all angles in a pale, withered condition, then something is decidedly wrong. Either they are afflicted with hereditary weakness or insect parasites, the worst enemies of nestlings, are at work.

LINE BREEDING

About the end of March or the first week in April is quite early enough to start breeding operation unless the stock is in a very forward condition, and the room of an even temperature. Of course different climatic conditions and heated homes must govern this. If the room is not heated, or is outside or in an exposed position, the latter date is quite early enough; earlier attempts are frequently attended by disastrous results, owing to sudden fluctuations of temperature or the prevalence of keen, cold winds. In such cases egg-bound hens and clear eggs are the usual result, and trying to advance a week or two may mean that you are thrown back a month.

As mentioned previously, see that your birds are fit, and to get them fit you must be fairly generous with your diet. Give your birds some egg food, if you have only a small stock of two or three pairs you can use half a hard-boiled egg at a time. Take a fresh egg and boil it for thirty minutes (this is best done overnight). When cold, cut the egg in half, leaving the unused half in the shell, and if this is placed with the cut end on a plate it will keep quite sweet and fresh for a day.

When one understands the fundamentals of breeding it is most surprising what can be accomplished by scientific matings. Family characteristics or peculiarities can be fixed to a surprising extent so that a whole strain will possess in time some special feature that marks the line of blood. While like produces like in many instances it must be remembered that characteristics must be fixed to such an extent that their dominance takes an aggressively pre-natal form; and the regularity of the appearance of a character in a dominant form can usually be relied upon.

In breeding generally you are confronted with many characteristics such as form, color, size, etc. In the subject under discussion we

are taking tone, which might be termed an invisible characteristic, that is, something that cannot be seen but is present in sound and can be perceived by hearing.

In attempting to produce a strain for tone one must naturally select a male that is above the average in its purity of deep round notes in all ranges. Next to find a mate for this male you are obliged to select a female by its call note (sweet, sweet, sweet). Putting several females together and noting their respective calls you will soon notice a variation in tone. The female with a deep round plaintive call should be a good selection for your male. Assuming that you get results from this pair in the form of good singing males, you must not expect immediate results in tone if you do not know your blood lines, for it must be taken for granted that the male bird may not be a dominant male in tone quality. Though the first progeny may not show equal quality of voice still they are valuable in your next matings in that they are much more likely to produce young of good tone—if you breed them in line to their parents, by taking the females to the father and the sons to the mother. To make the subject simpler we will leave the mother out of the discussion and breed to the father only. Taking the female progeny, his first daughters should contain half of his blood. Mating one of these back to the father the second season will produce young which have three-quarters of the father's blood. Taking one of these grand-daughters back to the father again will produce birds having seven-eighths of the blood of the father. As you have progressed you have been noting the tone of the male progeny in particular which should be ever getting more like that of the original male; and at the time of the third line of progeny you have a decided strain which having so much of the father's blood have his likeness in various forms and should have in particular his voice qualities, for this is what has been specially bred for and sought.

In making a strain it must always be remembered that the first selection above all others is that of vigor, without which you are building without foundation. On all phases of inheritance, vigor must be pre-eminently dominant for without it a strain must end disastrously sooner or later.

Take any factor or group of characters you may wish and breed in line these dominant, but never overlook the fact that vigor is the key to success.

When the pairs have settled down in earnest and the hen has got the nest to her satisfaction, it is much the best plan to remove the eggs as laid, substituting dummy eggs, until the third egg has been laid. The eggs can then be replaced in the nest, and the fourth egg will probably be laid next morning.

To prevent confusion each cage should be numbered and a shallow tray or box with division, (an old egg carton), numbered to correspond with the cages, should be used for keeping the eggs until ready for setting. If the cages are labeled, mark on the label the date the eggs are replaced and the date they are due to hatch, counting thirteen days forward.

Before replacing the eggs give the nest a dusting with some insect powder, more especially during the middle of the season, as nothing disturbs the hen during incubation so much as the troublesome red mite; many good nests have been ruined through these pests.

Many breeders make a practice of examining the eggs halfway through the term to see if they are fertile. The only thing to be gained by this is that if any are clear they can be saved by taking the nest away and getting ready for another round.

I prefer to leave the eggs alone, as many little accidents happen, especially if the breeder is a "horny-handled son of toil" and his fingers are not super-sensitive. Also, when the eggs are hatched, if there is one unfertile, I prefer to leave it in the nest; it acts as a cushion for the youngsters and frequently prevents heavy feathered hens from sweating the youngsters to death.

If an egg meets with an accident, say a puncture from the claws of the hens (by the way, it is always wise to trim the claws before letting her settle down to sitting), do not throw the egg away, for if the shell only is broken and the inner membrane is intact, a small piece of stamp edging or thin greaseproof paper may be fixed over the crack or puncture, and if this is touched over with a little white of egg and allowed to dry before being replaced in the nest then the egg will hatch out all right.

The day before the eggs are due to hatch, if the weather has been very cold and keen winds prevalent, it is sometimes advisable to take out the nest and dip the eggs in warm water. This tends to soften the lining of the shell and enables the young to break through easier; there is then less fear of chicks being dead in the shell. The Canary egg being so frail, one cannot render the same assistance as in helping out the chicks of fowls which is sometimes necessary.

It is not always advisable to let the cock remain with the hen during sitting, some hens give better results if left alone, and if running two hens with the one cock it will be necessary to transfer him to No. 2 when No. 1 hen has completed her clutch. Then by the time No. 2 has gone to nest the first hen will be about due to hatch, and he can be put back to assist in feeding the first nest of youngsters. The hen during sitting may have a little egg-food two or three times a week with plain canary seed in the box.

The night before the young are due to hatch a little egg-food must be given, but yolk only is best for the first few days, adding the whites later. A little green food in the wires will also be wanted.

Provided the hen settles down at once after laying her third egg, and sits closely and the weather is warm, the young birds will hatch out almost exactly to the hour at the end of thirteen days. But if, on the other hand, the hen has been restless and the weather cool, the young chicks will not make their appearance until the fourteen or even the fifteenth day. In any case do not interfere with the eggs, if they appear to be fertile, until the fifteenth day, for any attempt to assist the process of hatching by breaking the egg, even at the last moment, will possibly have a fatal result. Be patient and leave things to Nature—and the hen.

Although the newly hatched chicks do not require any food for the first twelve hours, it is as well to be prepared in case the hen thinks otherwise. On the morning of the fourteenth day, therefore, put a teaspoonful of freshly crushed hemp, some rolled oats and a sprig of watercress in the cage. Put some egg food in three days. For the first few days the hen will generally prefer to feed her young with these foods; use the egg food, a half teaspoonful of this may be offered two or three times daily.

When a hen has laid and started to set, the male should be put in a cage by himself for a day or two, and then mated with another hen in the same way as with the first hen. If the hens are in proper breeding condition this method will prove very satisfactory. Another method is to have two hens in breeding cages for the season and change the cock from one cage to the other each day about dinner time. If both hens are anxious to nest, their eggs will usually be fertile. The hens are allowed to feed their own young birds when the male has not been with them all through the season, usually three nests each, the male being kept in his own cage from the hen that starts to set until the other is ready to nest.

BABIES IN THE NEST

Up to the age of 8 to 10 days, the youngsters are in the nest with closed eye-lids, though not blind as some mistakenly assume. After this period you will notice the eye-lids gradually opening.

If the breeder has always supplied the nesting hen with the foodstuffs essential to the health and growth of the youngsters, if the nests have been kept free from insect parasites and if the mother hen does its duty, then the little ones will progress rapidly. You can almost see them grow. Under these conditions the breeder will be able to attach the rings to the feet of the youngsters when they are from 7 to 9 days old. At about this time also the parent hen no longer removes the excrements from the nest. The young ones deposit their dung on the edge of the nest. Until this stage has been reached, that is, at 7 to 9 days, the mother loving hen, intent in keeping the nest clean, is apt to regard the glittering rings as something not belonging in the nest. Many hens will try to remove the rings from the feet of the youngsters often causing serious injuries to the delicate, undeveloped legs. If she cannot do this she is likely to throw the young out of the nest. If the breeder does not notice this at once the youngster is lost. Not all hens are so cruel, but precautions must be taken. The rings must not be attached too soon, nest conditions must be right. Some hens can never get used to rings in the nest. In that case covering the rings with some substance may help. It makes the rings less conspicuous.

At the age of 16 to 17 days the youngsters are covered with feathers and are then very apt to show a desire to leave the nest. In my opinion it is too early to allow them to do this. I maintain that the longer they can be kept in the nest to obtain a fuller development the more resistant to adverse influences they become and are thus more valuable to breed from in the future. Experience has shown that a longer stay in the nest means a greater vitality. But it is not easy to keep these lively youngsters, almost ready to fly as they are, in the nest. In order to accomplish it you had better partition the nest from the rest of the cage with wire screening, so that the hen will be compelled to feed the young ones through the meshes in the wire net. This also has the advantage of keeping the hen from proceeding to another laying, as she cannot reach the nest.

When the youngsters are 21 days old the growth of the plumage has made further progress. The tail feathers have reached a length of an inch. This is the proper time to take the young ones from the nest and put them with the mother hen in the brood cage. The nest box is taken down or removed and prepared for the next brood. It must be thoroughly cleaned, supplied with new lining and the whole outfit disinfected to prevent insect trouble.

In their new home the youngsters do not feel at home at first. But before long they sit on the perch, at the start somewhat fearful and ill at ease, beside the mother, who looks over her brood with justifiable pride and shows her affection by almost continuous calls. At the age of 28 to 30 days the youngsters have their full plumage and the remaining down remnants on the head rapidly disappear, indicating the complete independence of the young bird. They are now removed from the brood cage and go for a short stay into a flying cage. From there they are put into the flight cage where they remain until the young males are ready for individual training cages and the young hens are put into their winter quarters. When you take the youngsters from the hen the tails must be more than merely forked, they should present a smooth, complete form, just as in the old birds. If the tail feathers are somewhat dilapidated as the result of the attentions of too affectionate mothers, you can determine the age of the birds, with a little practice by the firmness and length of the wing feathers. Torn out tail feathers grow again in a few days but torn out wing feathers are not renewed until the big moulting.

Now a few pointers as to the arrangement of the plumage. The first wing feather is always shorter than the second, but the latter must correspond in length to those of older birds. The feather quill must be no longer soft, but of normal form and firm consistency. When six weeks old the young birds will have new small feathers appearing on their abdomen, and these so-called cover feathers indicate the beginning of moulting for the youngsters. The renewal of the first plumage does not begin before the middle of June. The oldest of the young birds will have an entire new plumage by the middle of August. This change of feathers affects only the small down or cover feathers. Wing or tail called flight feathers are not renewed on the youngsters during the little moulting. The complete moulting takes place only in the following year. The small, or little moulting, if it runs normally, lasts 6 to 8 weeks. It does not put such a strain on the birds and ends with the renewal of the head feathers.

It might be thought that the canary goes through a long period of youth. This is not exactly logical when you compare it with the age a bird can attain. It develops rapidly and comparatively long is the time during which it is possible to equal his parents as to performance.

TIME REQUIRED IN HATCHING EGGS

I recommend removing the eggs from the nest as laid with the aid of a small spoon, place one (no more) artificial eggs in the nest and each day for three days remove an egg, unless the hen happens to lay alternatingly, which tells you something has not been all as it should have been, on the fourth day replace the three eggs, then on the morning of the fourteenth day you may look for the young, if the eggs are to hatch. If the hen has laid more than four eggs the later laid eggs may hatch a day later, it is best to have the baby birds all of same day hatching, not one, two or three days older than the others in the nest.

YOUNG BIRDS

Your young ones that are doing for themselves will need cracked hemp after they have been weaned a couple of days. In spite of many criticisms the ordinary hemp will answer the purpose very well, and the young canaries soon learn to pick up the particles of kernel from the shell. Don't forget to give these youngsters milksop for the noon feed. This has a grand effect on the assimilative organs. It is restive for the stomach. It is a food which requires very little effort on the digestion, and is a good preventative of that bad complaint, indigestion in young canaries, a complaint very often mistaken for inflammation of the bowels.

At five weeks you can sprinkle a little rape seed over the canary seed in the seed boxes, and they will begin to eat this; then they gradually get into canary seed also. At six weeks they will be on hard seed, and the soft food can be reduced to one small teaspoonful per bird per day. Do not withhold the soft food altogether, as some advise, but keep it at this quantity through the moult. Getting young ones on hard seed has a misleading meaning, and is often wrongly interpreted. The correct diet at this age and older is three parts canary seed to one part of rape, a small teaspoonful of soft food, varied occasionally with a little crushed hemp. A little maw may be sprinkled on the soft food, and the rape may be boiled for a change. Green food such as dandelion, watercress, lettuce, or any of the seeding weeds, should be fed every day.

When about four weeks old gradually reduce the soft food and increase the seed until the birds are entirely on hard seed diet. Some breeders do not put water in the cage of the young, but only give it at stated times, as an unlimited supply of water sometimes causes bowel trouble through excessive drinking.

When the birds are thoroughly on to a seed diet, and are getting fully feathered, they may be transferred to a good, roomy flight cage, where they can exercise and develop their frames. Here again the double breeding-cage comes in very useful, for with the slide removed you get a three-foot flight cage, with room for ten or twelve birds.

Give them the best canary seed. Turkish canary, when procurable, is somewhat thinner in the rusk and more easily cracked than Spanish, and I found the young get better away on Turkish on this account. They should also have an occasional change of mixed seed.

Hang on the bath on nice bright days, but remove it at mid-day; otherwise some might be having a dip in the evening and roosting before they are dry, thus bringing on a chill.

NON-FEEDING MOTHERS HEART BREAKING

I cannot recall anything that has distressed me so much as the action of some of my "mother canaries". Sometimes a mother will not start feeding her babies, some feed for a few days, sometimes a week or ten days and then suddenly stop feeding the babies all together, this is often caused by the person tending the birds, it is likely nauseating and has been caused by feeding too much of rich egg food after the plain foods during incubation. If you in your generosity have supplied a surplus of rich egg food for a day old brood "which cannot consume a teaspoonful between them" this has been an inducement for the mother bird to gorge herself on the generous supply of new food. For the first few days the supply of egg food should be fed sparingly, do not overfeed. If a mother bird seems to be lagging in her duties in feeding do not stew, become excited, now is the time to use good judgment. Sprinkle some maw, or poppy seed on the egg food, then next time a pinch of sugar, or a little crushed sponge cake or bread biscuit a little sweetened, a little scalded crushed hemp seed at this time is often splendid in re-invigorating them, of course feed green food sparingly, but often, change kinds often, do not worry if the hen seems to feed entirely on green food, this will work out o. k., the main thing is to bring the mother back to her maternal duties. It is a good plan to dissolve a crystal of sulphate of soda in the drinking water for one-half of each day for a few days, this often ends the non-feeding term, a bath in slightly salty water made from table salt is very invigorating to the mother bird if she will bathe. Occasionally you will find a hen that begins to roost on the perch when her babies are only a few days old and without feathers to keep them warm. Every effort should be made to induce or force her to go back on the nest, first make sure the nest is not infested with mites or that too much mite powder has not been put in and around her nest. If she insists on roosting on the perch, remove the perch, if she goes to the other one remove it, in the majority of cases she will prefer the nest to the bottom of the cage, be sure to replace the perches early next morning. Always notice the toes of the young when they first leave the nest, many a slip claw is corrected by this early inspection.

NESTLING MOTHERS ON ROOSTS

If a hen with a nest of young begins to roost on the perch when her babies are a week or ten days old, it is likely she is beginning to make plans for another nest before her babies are old enough to leave the nest. It is therefore a wise policy to give her a small crystal of soda in her drinking water each day for three or four days, this will cool her off if she can be cooled off safely, otherwise it is advisable to supply her with another nest, otherwise she may pluck the feathers from her babies. Be sure to supply some nesting material, (I make mine from small squares of boiled, washed burlap sacks cut about 2 in. square and loose, beware of lengths enough to entangle her, or the young. Should the mother have started to pluck her babies I have found by supplying some light colored pigeon or poultry feathers, removes the mother's desire to pluck her babies. This in a few instances has failed however, once the mother has started to pluck her babies while in the nest. I have had to place the mother in a separate cage side by side, she would then feed through the wires, also the male may feed the babies, I have used the foster parent plan in some cases, I have raised so many birds by hand that I always plan to avoid the hand raising, unless for a day or two to gain strength.

A very splendid thing is to have one or two large flower pots near by a window and dump your water and waste seeds into them, when they sprout this is excellent green food and saves the seed you would otherwise waste. Sprouted seeds of any kind are excellent and economical and can be had all winter long. Rape seed sprouts are best and easiest to provide.

CANARIES LOVE MEALWORMS

About twice each week, place a dish of mealworms, mixed with some dirt (which has been baked to destroy any insects, etc.) in each cage, and your birds will soon grow to love them. They are clean and a good food, since they live on whole-wheat bread and milk.

Better feed the small, or half-grown ones to canaries and finches, because the skin of the full grown worms are too hard for the smaller birds to digest.

Do not feed too many at one time, and better watch that each bird gets his share, and not some glutton getting too many, which might prove disastrous.

THE ROLLER

The ROLLER CANARY, so called on account of its rolling or connected song with beak closed bridging its tours from one to the other perfectly. The ROLLER is known as the GRANDEST LIVING NATURAL SONGSTER. They are simply a living Music-box and their soft sweet musical rolls will delight the hearts of all who love music or nature. The Roller is without an equal as a song bird. It is fast becoming the most popular pet or companion known to mankind. The better quality of Roller will sing from ten to fourteen different tours or changes. Each note or roll is called a tour. They are perfect pets and most lovable companions.

THE ROLLER CANARY

Presuming you are desirous of adding a little to the finances, and wish to breed for profit as there is always a market for your birds.

We will first consider this variety from the marketable point of view. The great majority of Canary keepers—that is, people who want a Canary for a pet—require the singing qualities as the first and foremost point of excellence; color, quality, size or shape practically count for nothing, their chief stipulation being "It is a nice singer"? They don't want one that brings the house down, but a nice soft-voiced songster.

It is surprising that there is such a large proportion of Roller Fanciers who do not seem to understand the difference and why between the Glucks and Seifert strains of Roller Canaries.

First—What is a Glucke and from whence did it come? Where did Seiferts come from? The reply to these two questions is but a single answer for they are both Canaries, having developed from a common source, nature's variation giving us two branches of a breed that differentiate in voice, one with the ability to express the Glucke tone and the other minus that accomplishment.

The same variation in voice is to be found with the common domestic Canary. Any observant listener will note that some domestics have a decided Glucke tone in their song while others do not give any resemblance of it. From the domestic was developed the Roller by careful teaching. The Roller song has long since become an acquired character. It is reasonable to suppose that the Roller Canary was originally suggested to those early German

41

Pioneers of the breed by a domestic acquiring a longer roll than is usually heard in the common canary song, with the result that development of rolling tours has given us our wonderful bird, the Roller, the delight of thousands of humans throughout the globe. Among the Rollers there are the usual varying factors of nature, including that of voice. It is said that Volkman Bros. of Germany created the Glucke, and Seifert of Dresden the Seifert; but they did not. To them however, must be credited their perception and **ability of segregating the respective strains and breeding them to a pure state.** In producing any living thing in animal or vegetable life, variation is the greatest problem, so that to attain a strain of Seiferts which would repeat each season in all their purity would take several years of close line breeding. With the many fanciers who are mixing various Seifert blood lines each season it is not surprising to hear them say that their Seiferts sometimes sing Glucke. And so with Glucke birds. With the mixing of the strains there should be created birds which cannot express Glucke because they have reverted to the Seifert voice. One might get a young Glucke bird from Glucke parents of unestablished strain and it is likely to be a "Seifert" in throat formation, absolutely physically precluded from singing a Glucke note. Without keeping strictly to blood lines one might easily breed a proportion of the progeny that will revert to the other strain. Yes, the progeny of Seiferts may sing Glucke tours and especially if in hearing distance of a Glucke strain may never express Glucke tours because they are physically unable, irrespective of the presence of a good Glucke teacher.

Regarding the Roller Canary. Was there ever an object so popular and yet less understood? Was there ever a fancy for which there were so many fanciers, who were so eager to study? That the problem is so difficult to conceive there is little wonder. Assuming that the song information was plainly written and described, there is much excuse for the many who are slow to comprehend. The subject of the tours of the Roller canary seems difficult mostly because it requires thorough discussion and classification; and this is seldom done by writers and less by readers. The main problem which is the cause of observing the subject is that very common factor variation. Did you ever pause to realize that the Roller Canary is no different in its inheritance to man? Does not one human sing deep bass, another light bass, another deep baritone, another light baritone, another tenor and so on? This voice problem is a matter of register and confounding to the novice who does not know whether a "tenor" bird is singing schockel because his deep voiced bird is singing his hollow bell in a very similar key. Then there are other factors to be taken into consideration, for do not birds vary in other matters as do humans? Some Rollers are more intelligent than their dull witted brothers, others vary in temperament and are consequently different in disposition. Again you have the vigorous bird who sings in a different style to this weak chested neighbor.

Then comes the difference between an intelligent well-trained Roller and one which has had very little chance to assimilate the tours correctly. Strains of different delivery help to swell the problems of misunderstanding. Is it any wonder then that there are so many people who are well versed in the tours of that wonderful pet, the Roller Canary?

The development of the different song tours begins as soon as the young cocks are in the flight cage. The cocks start when they are six weeks old, and in some cases even earlier. In the elementary stage only a gentle twittering is noticeable, which, however, day by day becomes louder and stronger.

The young bird's first moult does not hinder him in this. He practices daily with diligence, and makes progress, and even in these early days, while the birds are still in the moult, one can already distinguish plainly in some of the more forward birds certain tours in their song. See explanation of song.

SONG OF THE ROLLER CANARY

We may say that the song of the Roller Canary is inherited rather than acquired. The germinal variations of the song have been developed by selective breeding and artificial selection so that it is fixed, and the roller will now sing all of the tours that belong to his particular family or strain, but not without faults, without having heard any other bird. This has been a much debated subject during the last few years as I well recognize, from my own personal experience and the actual experience of several very reliable and thorough breeders the above claims have been substantiated positively, yet I recommend a tutor or a schoolmaster (as many call them), this inspires song, hastens the perfection and development of the song.

The various names of the tours, or song passages of the roller's song are derived from the sound they resemble, such as Bell Gluck, Gluck Roll, Gluck, Water Gluck, Hollow Roll, Bell Roll, deep bubbling Water Roll, Flutes, etc., most of the passages are produced with the beak closed, only when singing flutes and bells does the beak open, or with faulty notes.

A DESCRIPTION OF THE SONG PASSAGES IN SIMPLE FORM

In the present day song of the Roller Canary, we have birds that go through their song in a very high pitched tone. Others have a medium pitch, and thirdly we have birds which sing in a very deep tone from start to finish. We may therefore classify the melody into three divisions as follows:

High Pitched Tours .... Fair
Medium Pitched Tours .... Good
Deep Pitched Tours .... Very Good

HOLLOW ROLL

This tour or roll has been termed the basis of the Roller's Song. While being the most beautiful it is admitted that without it the bird would lose much of its popularity. Hollow Roll is sung in several different ways. There is the straight H. R., Falling H. R., Rising H. R., Rising and Falling H. R., and Bent H. R. The Hollow is founded on U, O, N, A.

Some birds have the habit of commencing their song with a thin Bell Roll coming down gradually on a straight Hollow Roll, and this is often assumed by experienced Fanciers to be a falling Hollow Roll. The quality of the tour consists of the purity of the vowel, and the enunciation of the r-r-r-r-r. The best ground tones are U and O. Vowels A and E are of less value, sounding hard and inclined to be nasal. In this case the tour is generally sung with the beak open. To deliver a good Hollow Roll the beak must be perfectly closed, and the bird in most cases will almost sit on his perch with his head bent forward. The next tour is Bass or "Knorre" as some prefer to call it. This is a very valuable tour and no breeder should think of using birds in his stud unless he has a first class Bass in his birds. I would much prefer a stock bird with a first class Hollow Roll and Bass and which was not without faults, than I would a full variety bird with thin weak tours especially in H. R. and Bass, and which was without faults. Bass, the same as Hollow Roll, is delivered in several different ways and is the foundation of the song as previously explained. The best ground tones are O and U and the less valuable are E and A. The consonant of this tour is r of a double or treble force (rrrrr.) The kind of Bass that is not in much favor at the present time, but which was looked upon as being the best twelve or fifteen years ago, is what I term the Dry Bass. This kind of Bass is easy to recognize. It is hard and flat and is sung on the "a." The sound produced by tearing a piece of paper in two is somewhat similar to dry Bass. Another kind of Bass that is very much favored in England, and which I myself favor above others, is what I may term the Bass Roll. The consonant r and vowels o and u should be equally balanced, that is to say that neither the consonant or the vowels should predominate. They should be equally knit together thus forming a good deep bass roll, and the tone sounding a kind of undercurrent. This has been described by some Fanciers as a Watery Bass, but it is nothing of the kind. A Bass Roll sung on the consonant and vowels I have stated will be sung with the beak firmly closed. A watery Bass would be sung with the beak open, and thereby making a hissing sound almost like a Hard Water Roll, but in the Bass key. The best and most pleasing Bass of all and which I would recommend every Fancier to have in his stock is the Hollow Bass. It appears to be much deeper than all of the other varieties of Bass, but when rendered correctly it can be heard with ease all around a large room. If a person was facing a bird singing a good Hollow Bass, he or she would imagine there was a bird singing Bass behind them. Birds like these possessing other tours equal in comparison are to my mind "World Beaters." A good Hollow Bass almost spells the word TONE.

SCHOCKEL

The ground tones of Schockel are the same as Hollow Roll. O and U also A and E. The consonants are H and L. In Schockel the purity of the vowel is the measure of quality and the consonants are of less importance. This tour originates in the breast of the bird, thereby causing a slight vibration of the body which is most noticeable with beating of the tail. The best Schockel is sung thus: hu-hu-hu-hu-hu. The beak is closed. If the beak opens slightly with each beat it will sound thus ho-ho-ho-ho-ho. The vowel in each case being predominant. If the beak is kept open throughout the run in Schockel the vowel A and E thus being predominant it will sound nasal and harsh and of no point value.

HOLLOW BELL

Hollow Bell is rightly described as a sister to Schockel. The most noticeable difference being that instead of the tour originating in the breast, Hollow Bell originates in the throat of the bird. It is brought easy and without exertion and therefore there is no vibration of the body. The ground tone is U and the consonants are L and H, thus lululululu or huhuhuhuhu. Its composition is therefore quite simple. The quality depends upon the pure U with a soft L and H. The L gives the song a delightful lulling lullaby effect and is a better tour than Hollow Bell sung with H. This tour becomes faulty when the A and E vowels appear being harsh and nasal.

WATER ROLL

The best way to distinguish a water Roll is to place a thin tube into a bowl of water, and by blowing down the tube and at the same time raising and lowering the tube, the effect thus produced will give you a good description of a good and valuable Water Roll. Now by raising the tube to the surface of the water, and by blowing as hard as in the first case, you will produce a weak splashing sound, which will closely resemble a Water Roll of hardly any value. Further a tour so produced is a dangerous tour to breed from. The first description would sound on the vowel U and with the consonant B and L or D and L softly intoned, and with the beak quite closed. In the second description it would be sung with beak wide open and would cause a hissing sound to be produced.

GLUCKE

In describing this tour I want to try to illustrate in the simplest manner possible, so we will take a circumstance which I believe will be the most common, and which no doubt will have been experienced by every reader. You have all visited or possibly owned a Poultry Farm or Chicken Run. If not then visit one during the chicken hatching period. Look out for a mother with her brood of chicks walking about the yard. You will notice that she commences to scratch up the earth until she finds something suitable for food for her brood. She then calls her chicks in rather a quick GLUCKE-GLUCKE-GLUCKE — GLUCKE When the chicks have eaten up the food the mother will set off to look for more, and at the same time she will repeat GLUCKE-GLUCKE-GLUCKE—GLUCKE. This time with a far more pronounced tone and much wider beats or divisions between each GLUCKE. In this description you will have the best idea and the nearest to a real definition of the GLUCKE TOUR that I can give you. Of course you may listen to hundreds of Glucke Rollers, and then not hear it brought with the same deliberation and spacing that I have described, but nevertheless there are birds that do sing it that way and at most of the Contests.

In Glucke the best ground tones are U and O, and the faulty are A, E and I. The consonants, RE, GL, KL, BL, glucke-glucke-glucke-glucke—glock-glock-glock, bluk-bluk-bluk, etc. The tonality in the deeper kinds of glucks are better when the syllables are more distinctly divided, that is to say those with the longer beats between each glucke. If the consonants are brought too closely together, the ground tone is at times smothered and causes a clattering effect. If on the other hand the ground tone is predominant, the tour becomes deep and full and this is termed Hollow Glucke and it is very charming to the ear. A fancier who is thinking of starting with Glucke birds, must be sure to commence with birds that sing the Hollow Glucke because the Glucke Tour will, unless under expert management, begin to deteriorate sooner than other standard tours.

Some judges say that Glucke Roll should be dry, and others say that if there is a watery intone it is still Glucke Roll. Others hold the opinion that the L consonant causes the watery effect and that all tours with the consonant L are watery. This I am sure is quite wrong because Hollow Bell, Schockel, Bell Roll and Bell Tour have the consonant L and there is no watery effect in these tours. Glucke Roll is simply a Glucke sang at a very high speed and to give my readers an idea how to detect it, I would ask you to repeat the word glucke as fast as you can. You will notice that you will very soon be attempting to say glucke while your tongue is touching the roof of your mouth, and thereby forming the letter L. The word that you would be saying would be gluckl —gluckl—gluckl. The L in each glucke thus filling in the beat and consequently causing a rolling effect. A bird, of course, would sing the tour very much faster than a human being, so that it would be impossible to detect a beat between each syllable. Much force is used by the bird in the delivery of this tour and in some cases the letter G in glucke is omitted and therefore the tour would sound like lucklluckl-luckl, etc. Thus the consonant L combined with the vowel U would have a watery effect and would sound like a Rolling Water Glucke, and would therefore come under the column allotted to Water Glucke. Good ground tones in glucke roll are U and O, and the bad are A and E which is nasal, being sung with the beak open. Good G. R. will be sung with the beak perfectly closed.

If a beat is detected between each syllable it is a Glucke and not a Glucke Roll. Birds those in competition against them have held the same opinion and thought it to be glucke owners have thought it to be Glucke Roll, and have often been awarded Glucke when their roll. If the bird in question has beaten their own, they will often be heard to say that So and So's bird got so and so for Glucke and it does not sing it, and thus unintentionally casting a reflection upon the work of the judge.

BELL GLUCKE

This tour, when properly sung, is a wonderful thing and sounds really charming, but it is at the same time a very dangerous tour to have in your birds. It is often spoken of as a curse in the Roller's make up. How many of my readers have entered a show room when a Roller contest has been in progress and heard sounds such as clack-clack-clack, tut, tut. tut. These sounds are faulty gluckes and often deteriorated bell gluckes. Some are comparable to a Blacksmith striking his anvil, and you cannot get it out of the birds unless you take off their heads. Further you cannot beautify it by getting fresh blood, for it simply goes from bad to worse, and many a likely winner or tutor has become spoiled by developing a faulty bell glucke. We have to recognize the tour because it has its allotted column in the song standard. Bell Glucke as the name implies is higher up the scale than Glucke. The ground tone is U and an I accompanying thus glui-glui and which gives it a double effect. It is the I which gives it the bell-like song.

WATER GLUCKE

The sound of Water Glucke is similar to the sound produced by a drop of water falling into water and with the echo of the rebounding drop. If any of my readers get six small pebbles and drop them in very quick succession into a pail of water, the sound produced will convey a good impression of a good Water Glucke. Another pleasing Water Glucke is what is described as a Gurgling Water Glucke. A good illustration of this would be to fill a bottle with a rather wide neck full of water. Turn the bottle completely over and let the water gurgle backwards and forwards in the neck of the bottle. The sound so produced will be very similar to a gurgling Water Glucke. Water Glucke is often described as a double Glucke, because you get the deep U sound with the I on the after-beat and with the consonants bl and gl thus sounding (bluik-bluik-bluik-bluik) or (gloik-gloik-gloik-gloik) the latter being of the most value. Another pleasing Water Glucke generally called the Thumping Water Glucke is produced when the bl or the gl are very pronounced and the I being almost absent. It is becoming quite common for this tour to be awarded points for Glucke, especially when a bird brings a nice soft Water Glucke then to follow with a slow thumping W. G. I might add that this change is very misleading, even to well experienced Fanciers, and the circumstances mentioned have often caused discontent amongst Exhibitors. So much for Water Glucke.

Another Water Tour which has found favor during the past few years is the **Deep Bubbling Water** Tour, and which is marked upon the standard as D. B. W. T. It is one of the most difficult tours to recognize. The effect produced is a very deep bubbling water in the bass key. Some people are under the impression that it is a Watery Bass, but whereas a Watery Bass is sung with the beak slightly open, the D. B. W. T. is sung with the beak closed. To produce the sound nearest to D. B. W. T. fill a narrow drinking glass with water. Place a thin glass tube into the water and until it touches the bottom of the glass. Now blow gently into the tube and you will note that two distinct sounds are produced. One from the bottom of the glass and the other from the bubbles rising to the top of the water. The sound at the bottom of the glass very closely resembles Deep Bubbling Water Tour.

BELL TOUR

Several years ago it was considered almost a crime to win a prize with a bird singing a Bell Roll or a Bell Tour. I have known Fanciers who were mad on breeding for purity, remove their birds away from those singing Bell at the shows, and this applied even if the birds singing the Bells happened to be the winners, and the same Fanciers would take away the credit from those successful Exhibitors who had won with birds singing Bells, but how times have altered, during the last few years we have several "purity fiends" who will use a tutor now singing Bell Roll and Bell Tour. Why? Because a breeder now has to get as many tours in his birds as is possible. Competition is so keen. Very often only one point variation will remove a bird from FIRST to SECOND PRIZE.

At the same time a Fancier has to be careful not to breed faults as well as extra tours and which is often the case in some strains. So to come to the point let me say that to have your contest birds sing Bell Roll or Bell Tour will add a few more points to your scores, and providing these tours are not Harsh, Nasal or Sharp they will add to the beauty of the Roller Song.

Some Bell Rolls sound similar to a rather high pitched Hollow Roll on the French Vowel "ü" and the consonant "r". The consonant must not predominate over the vowel if both are blended evenly it will add to the beauty of the tour.

A Bell Roll with the "r" and the vowel "i" will give a higher sound, especially if the vowel predominates. In that case the beak will be wide open causing the tour to sound harsh.

Bell Tour is sung in the same key as Bell Roll but in this case there is no rolling effect. being minus the consonant "r" there being a distinct beat between each syllable, sounding almost like a high pitched Hollow Roll.

BELLS AND FLUTES
IN THE ROLLER SONG

There are a great number of people of the Roller Fancy who have a wrong impression of the Bell Tours and the Flutes, believing that a bird which sings his Bells or Flutes is a worthless specimen. Breeders receive inquiries, which are not uncommon, for "birds that do not sing Bells nor Flutes." Such demands, though well meant, do not reflect an intimate knowledge of the Rollers' song, nor the judging standard. Most all birds sing the Bells, and all do in time. These high tours denote vigor and health and a virile breeding instinct. True a competition Fancier likes a bird of refinement, and some maintain that a Bell singing Roller shows lack of quality, quite forgetting the standard which was compiled by the world's best judges, includes the Bell Roll and Bell Tour. These notes are the natural repertoire of a Canary, and therefore it is natural that they should be expressed. This is just where good breeding and above all, good training comes in. The alert and observant breeder and trainer is ever on the lookout for these high tours, not that they may be eliminated, but that the young birds may be tutored to control themselves from rendering bells in an over exuberant manner. It is true that most faults emanate from badly rendered Bells; but a bird that is tutored to modulate his Bell Roll and Bell Tour is a bird that will gain up to four points in his song score, thus putting him that much further ahead of his competitor. Yet, it is far better to accept the Bells as natural notes of a Roller's Song and see that you train the bird to modulate by operating a good song cabinet. True, a whole Aviary, under a good teacher, can be trained to avoid the bells most of the time, but NOT ALL OF THE TIME. The presence of females within calling distance is greatly responsible for birds sounding their high tours in an endeavor to attract feminine attention. Keep the females far away from the contest singers if you do not wish Bells to come early.

FLUTES

There are a number of fine flutes. While some may be very badly rendered occasionally; or a bird may develop a habit of singing incessant flutes in a Chee-Chee-Chee manner, bad training and the breeding instinct are frequently responsible for bad flutes. Flutes are called for in the standard and allowed no less than 6 points if perfectly expressed. Good flutes go a long way to perfecting a fine singer. All Rollers sing Flutes.

TRAINING THE ROLLER

The training of the Roller Canary is, of course, a most interesting process, and occupies about three months; breeders are not all alike in the time they take to train their birds. They vary, either for set purpose or by reason of different methods and conditions. One will cage off early from the flights, while another will delay the operation; or it may be that the birds are backward, either by nature or by reason of the lack of continual, steady tuition through the available schoolmaster going off song in the moult and no substitute being forthcoming for some time, no phonograph record having been provided.

It goes without saying that the longer a young bird can be kept in the flight the better chance he has of coming safely through his first moult; of expanding his frame, and becoming a robust youngster.

The tutor is kept near the flight in a cage and songbox by himself. If a youngster becomes quarrelsome, or if he develops sharp or harsh notes or frequent high calls, he should be taken away. To minimize these troubles, or to prevent them, it will be found effective if the flight is shaded, either by curtain or by darkening the room.

Some cage off the cocks almost as soon as the sexes are discovered; others cage them off as soon as they show livelier attempts at song (cocky). The birds are put into small wire cages, and the cages are placed in boxes or cabinets provided with doors. These cabinets almost exclude the light, some entirely so, and the birds are ranged so that the tutor is in the center.

When you have your young birds through the moult, place the young cocks in the cages, being careful to place the ring number on the cabinets, for this will enable you always to find any particular bird by referring to your stock book.

After placing the cages in the cabinets, leave the door open at first to make sure they find their feeders and drinkers, and let the doors remain open for at least two days. On the third day close one door, and the following day partly close the next door, and the succeeding day close all up.

Be sure you have plenty of fresh air in the room in which you are going to keep them. Open the cabinets, and give fresh food and water the first thing every morning, and leave the cabinets open for an hour. Open the doors again at noon for half an hour, and then close until evening.

When you hear one or more of your young birds singing in the darkness open the doors immediately, and let them sing their song. Listen critically for any bad faults, and when they are finished close the doors.

It is asserted in some quarters that birds from their earliest youth, even as nestlings, acquire already from the tutor the form of their song, but upholders of this theory seem to lose sight altogether of inborn tendencies.

If this were so, it would be needless to concern ourselves about pedigree and inherited qualities, and all we need trouble about would be to look out for a good tutor.

Now, whereas we know that we can only produce birds of high quality from high-class breeding stock, no one can correctly assert that the youngest birds, nestlings, even, take up the song of the tutor. It is well known that the father is the best tutor, a fact in favor of my point, for the birds in time will bring out their song, an inherited one.

Hen Transmits Song

There is another example of song inheritance—namely, in the case of a hen of a strain representing a variation from the breeder's style of song being crossed with his breeding cocks. The hen transmits, in part or in entirety, the new style of song, etc., so the hen cannot teach the cocks to sing; the breeder puts them under a good tutor, maybe their own father. It will then be found that they have not only learned what their tutor has taught them, but also the pedigree tours of the mother, although they have never heard them.

If the mother be a very fine strain, and the young cock develop the fine tours inherent in her, in the absence of any performance thereof on the part of the tutor, it will be evident to the breeder that the birds needed no special tutor, but, nevertheless, were very good in their song.

These facts have also been further verified in the case of a breeder giving to another breeder eggs from a nest in exchange for a nest of his own, the respective strains being foreign to each other.

Now, if the youngsters hatched in the strange room from a good Bass or Schockel strain, tours not in the repertoire of the birds in this new home, they will nevertheless, when the autumn comes, bring out their Bass and Schockel, even though they have had no tutor to help them.

It is thus shown that on the surface of things no tutor is necessary, yet from what follows it will be seen that, in order to obtain the best from a bird, it is necessary that they should be coached by capable tutors.

For be it noted that the fundamental tours of a Canary's song are not the only elements of a good performance, but what constitutes beauty is the order of sequence of the tours, the manner in which they pass one over the other, the bridging over, as it were, to modulation, and the general connectivity, for it is all this that goes to make up a fine song and enhance its value.

Mark well, absence of faults or of faulty delivery does not indicate value, but what does is method and style of delivery.

Now, these special attributes are learned from the tutor if the young birds are fortunate enough to be brought into contact with one. I fear that it is through the scarcity of tutors on the one hand, and the excessive number of scholars on the other, that generally so few birds in the many breeding rooms every season turn out first-class songsters.

When a large number of young birds are on the racks, and the tutor is leading, it is not possible to give them a proper hearing, so much does their warbling drown the song of the old birds. It cannot therefore be expected that one single youngster is capable of taking up the song of his tutor when these tours of a quality so necessary for him to study are overborne by the efforts of the large number around him. The result is that, though the tutor plods on, his efforts are lost, as not one single cock hears him properly.

If, in order to surmount this difficulty, several tutors are placed among the birds, their song will, of course, dominate. As the tutors do not sing the same at the same time, but change about, one singing this tour and another that, the result is that the youngster is at the same disadvantage, as the individual tours are lost to him by reasons of the strong volume of sound with, to him, the confused interchanges.

This explains the generally indifferent results of large breeders, notwithstanding their care in providing their birds with good tutors. In the smaller and very smallest breeding rooms there is often a surprisingly large percentage of cocks which develop into first-class songsters in cases where they are placed under a really good tutor.

These youngsters have been fortunate enough to have a first-class bird to listen to, and also benefit by, for although they are with others on the training rack the school is such a small one that their united efforts do not drown the effect of the song of the leader, and thus all times of the day he is able to lend them direction and support.

Now, if a breeder has a large number of young cocks to train he should not allow more than ten to fifteen for one tutor, and each flock of this number must be kept entirely separate; that is to say, staged in separate rooms, for if these flocks are kept in the same room the crossing of the tours, both in old and young will damage the song.

The system of separation into isolated rooms brings the plodding fancier up against difficulties; he may be able to manage in different rooms so long as the warmer weather lasts, but when winter approaches there is the question of temperature, and for the sake of the birds, which, compared to his hens, are inactive, confined to small cages, he may be compelled to bring them all into one confortably warmed abode.

The result will be that the advantage he has gained will be lost, for the birds, although well ahead in tours, are not yet fixed in song, and will consequently vacillate and change about.

The imitative faculty of the Roller is remarkable; for instance, time after time we found that, in the case of a year old cock,

which has been used to breed with during the summer, if when he drops into moult he is placed alongside a cock not moulting, he will take up the new song, so much so that you will often not be able to distinguish one from the other.

In some experiments of our own, some moulting cocks in a flight were set apart in a quiet room, and here, a small company, undisturbed, they entirely forgot their own song and acquired that of the bird placed in their hearing. In these cases it was a question each time of a beautiful bent, rich song which seems to have been especially attractive to the musical sensibility of the moulting cocks.

In conclusion, if a breeder wishes to obtain the greatest number of good birds (and who does not?), and if he lacks a sufficient number of separate rooms, and perhaps of tutors also, let him take the youngsters bred from his best cock and put them together with him in a room apart, or, failing the parent cock, then some other first class tutor.

He may thus reckon on obtaining a small output of good birds; he can then let the general stock be trained in the ordinary way with several tutors if numbers require it, separating out eventually those birds which are of exceptional promise. If a special room is necessary for the throw-outs, how much the more important it is that the young birds of high promise should have one.

About the Schoolmaster

For a tutor a quiet, slow songster is better than a bold, racy one; a bird weak on his upper tones is better than one who may sing clear but high, and the bird that starts on his lower tours, bass for preference, is better than one who starts on his higher tours.

A bird with faulty high tour or other faults is often good to breed with, coming of good stock and pedigree, but for a tutor he is no good. The tutor should be the best your purse can afford; many fine birds can be bought at their proper value from well-known breeders, but if you limit them to a low figure you cannot expect to get the quality here required.

The very best are priceless; they are very rare, and the owners keep them. They may sometimes be picked up at shows, but many breeders will not risk sending out their very best for exhibition.

High class birds, however, may be had from fair-dealing breeders or stores, which, if not of the very highest category, are of close blood relationship to these supreme songsters, and will therefore not only train well, but will breed you first-class birds, and so put them on the right road to excellence.

If your first season does not come up to expectations, remember it is the second season that generally counts; you cannot estimate what you possess until you know the quality of the grandchildren. Perseverance, patience, good judgment, and an attentive musical ear; these are the attributes necessary to a Roller breeder.

My final word as a plea. If you use the song box, take the cage out at least once a day for an hour, and so give the bird an airing and encourage him to hop about and preen his feathers; make his little life a happy one, give him all the liberty and enjoyment you can.

It is generally conceded that when the bird has recovered his song after the second moult that song is fixed for good. There can consequently be very little reason why the older birds should not be permitted to enjoy more light and liberty, and live to a good old age.

What are the qualities I must seek in my choice of a Schoolmaster? Upon this hangs the result of our breeding. After careful, judicious pairing of our birds we may by inattention to this vital question spoil our labor by damaging the song through faulty selection of a tutor.

To my mind, it is immaterial how a tutor commences his song, so long as it starts with a good tone. Some think that a start on the Bell tours may damage the young cocks by encouraging them to sing only light stuff. This, however, will not occur so readily as in the case of a tutor starting on deep tours, and finishing up with Bell tours, which linger on as if they never wished to finish. Under either such tutor you will always get birds which will start with Bell tours.

No doubt exists of the necessity for a tutor in order to educate young birds, although ideas crept up here and there to the effect that education may be brought about without the schoolmaster. These ideas arise from the fact that, in the first place, the bird possesses certain inherited tendencies, and secondly, he will sing his inherited song without ever having had a cock to guide him: for instance, if in his earliest youth he passes out of the breeder's hands into those of a person who keeps him in absolute solitude, leaves him entirely to himself, and so permits him to develop his song.

One can take up an attitude on both standpoints, and correctly so; namely, "breeders need no school master for song development", and, contrariwise, "breeders are bound to have schoolmasters if they wish to develop their song."

Pupils With Faults

Keep open a keen ear, remove the high-pitched offender; if a bird seems inclined that way, put him into a dark part of your rack. If really bad, he must come away altogether in a day or two; they pick it up in no time, as faulty tours, especially high bell and, in fact, all high notes are easier for them to imitate than the good deep ones.

Sometimes a bird may not be satisfactory for other reasons, as time goes on his style of delivering may not suit, or he may sing a good tour, but repeat it too often, and so cause

it to predominate in the others. The bird should be taken away; he may improve by isolation or placing near another, apart from the rest. Sometimes you may have taken a bird away, and may find later on he may go back, but when once he has high bell there is little hope of him being any good in the school.

Keep the best songsters nearest the tutor until they are well advanced. Should your tutor fail you by moulting late, or start early with a long moult, you may find one or two of these youngsters very useful until he comes round again.

When the song has fully developed, study your pedigree, find out the lines of your deepest and purest birds, and mark your hens, so preparing for next season's breeding. Choose your show birds, transfer them to the standard show cages about three weeks before the show, and train them to sing readily to the judge; shift them about the rooms, take them with you to a friend's house, open them out on the table with a sheet of paper before you as if you were judging, etc., etc.

Don't neglect the training of any kind that appears likely to make a specimen. This should be transferred to a show cage almost every day and put through his paces. Have plenty of patience with them. Don't start knocking them about because they happen to be wild. Canaries are like mules and kicking horses. It's patience and kindness that tame them. The commoner looking birds that have no pretentious looks may be turned into a roomy flight where they can have exercise and baths and gain strength. But show birds must be kept in small cages or they will become wild.

This experiment you can also practice with a few young cocks if you want to introduce a tour or a new style of song. Of course, this applies only to a man with plenty of young cocks, but it is worth trying.

There are no end of little details to write about the different ways of training, but I have just given you a few of them.

As your birds progress in song you must begin handling them, by which means you have to take several of them into another room and put an old one among them. He will start the concert and by this means you will get them to sing anywhere and in other surroundings, which will come into your good when they are judged later on.

The first of the notes which strike the ear as disagreeable are the faults in the song which later on, when the bird is fully developed, make it necessary to isolate him from the general company. Quite early we may hear sharp flutes, for these are the first to break in upon the soft warbling. After this we get a lengthy bell, which gradually becomes longer in delivery and harder, if not finally quite sharp.

GENERAL TOPICS

Canary Breeding Suggestions

There are many breeders who have devoted years of study to the perfecting of their studs, and they now have birds better in song and stronger in stamina. Get in touch with some reliable bird store or dealer and if possible see the stock and hear them for yourself. If your funds permit, get, say, two cocks and four hens, unrelated for preference; run each cock with two hens. If you can manage to get both of the first pairings to go to nest about the same time so much the better, for then, in case of any accident to either pair, the eggs, or young when hatched, can be transferred to the other pair. Also it saves trouble in making up egg-food, etc., for it is just as easy to make for two nests as for one. Try and work your arrangements on these lines throughout the season if possible.

Take Care, and Time

Having settled these initial difficulties and procured the requisite stock of birds, one will naturally be anxious to set them up in housekeeping. Here, however, one cannot too thoroughly absorb and digest the wisdom of "More haste, less speed." Putting the birds together before they are in the proper condition, and stimulating them into condition too early, are doubtless the cause of more losses and disappointment than all other causes put together.

When kept under normal condition and not stimulated by the too free use of rich oily seeds, the bird will not, as a rule, show signs of desiring to go to nest until about the middle of March, which is quite early enough to begin. But when the operations are carried on in a heated kitchen it is not always possible to restrain the birds so long. The most that can be done in these circumstances is to limit the diet to a staple of canary seed, with a pinch of niger twice a week for the hens, teaspoonful of rape twice a week for the cocks, and a little bread and milk once a week all round. Green food or a piece of apple or banana should be given two or three times a week.

Then when the birds come into breeding condition it is better to take the risk and mate them. If the day and night temperature are fairly equal all will probably go on well, let the season be what it may. Indeed, it is almost invariably in a warm kitchen where fires are left burning at night that one hears of unusually early young being reared. But the breeder who keeps his birds under different conditions, and in unheated rooms must not be deluded into trying to emulate the example of early mating and put birds together too early, or he is practically certain to meet with grievous disappointment.

Food When Prepared for Breeding

Birds being prepared for breeding may be given a more liberal diet by adding a fourth part of summer rape to the staple food. Next, make a mixture of equal parts of hemp, maw, niger or thistle, and linseed, and give a small teaspoonful of this mixture to the cocks every second day, and to the hens twice a week. A teaspoonful of egg-food or crushed biscuits should also be given to the cocks twice a week, and the hens once a week. A spray of green food should be given daily when the weather is favorable for gathering. Do not, however, give greenstuff that is gathered in wet or frosty weather, unless it has first lain indoors for an hour or two; better still, do not give it at all.

While the birds are being brought into condition the breeder should take the precaution to overhaul the breeding cages in a final inspection. See that all the fittings—seed and water vessels, egg drawers, sand trays, etc.— fit securely in their places, and yet slide in and out without jamming; that the perches are firm and secure; and a piece of cuttlefish and nest pan firmly fixed in place. The position I like best for the nest is on the back of the cage, midway between, and on a level with, the two upper perches, because the hens generally prefer the little extra seclusion which this position affords, and also bcause the nest will hang more free of the perches. When it is hung on the side of the cage the perch is usually quite close up to the front of the nest and is apt to tempt young birds out of the nest too soon. The only objection to the nest being at the back is that one cannot peep into it so easily, which is, perhaps, a point in its favor after all, as the novice should cultivate from the beginning the habit of interfering with the birds as little as possible.

Selecting Breeders

The most popular method of breeding, and one generally used, is to put the pair together, and let them settle their household affairs. Good results have been had in this method. However, the most scientific way, and one generally used by professional breeders, particularly when one is breeding for special purposes, as follows:

While the birds are being prepared for mating it is well also to utilize the interval by going carefully over their good and bad points, and come to a decision as to which birds shall form each pair. It is not the purpose of this work to enter into the pros and cons of pedigree breeding, or the cultivation of fancy points. There are, however, just a few general principles which it is better to keep in view from the very first start in the art of breeding canaries.

The chief of these may be roughly divided into two classes: (1) That two birds both possessing glaring faults, and especially the same fault, or any point it is not wished to reproduce in the young, should never be mated together (2) that two yellows, or two buffs, should not be bred together. Of course these, and particularly the latter, are but broad, general principles from which the experienced breeder deems it advisable at times to deviate, but all such considerations come merely within the scope of the fancier who has passed the stage of learning to breed and rear a bird of some kind.

JUDGING ROLLERS

It may be of interest to some to know exactly the conditions under which Rollers are judged in this country. The majority of fanciers have never seen—nor are ever likely to see—the actual judging, for it is an old established rule that "no person, unless officially employed, shall have access to the judging-room during judging." This rule was framed to prevent collusion and favoritism.

The ringing or banding of the young birds was made compulsory for all exhibits in the young birds classes so as to enable the show officials to check the actual owners and breeders, preventing the "borrowing birds" for exhibition.

Another safeguard is the rule that all birds must be shown in "the adopted show cage" preventing any favoritism on the part of the judges. Every exhibit is placed before the judge in a cage that is similar in every detail to every other cage in the show. The slightest variation in construction or color is liable to lead to immediate disqualification. An illustration of this official show-cage is given herewith.

The interior is colored with the standard sky-blue enamel, and the outside of the cage and shutters painted black.

The list of the Exhibitors' names is held in strictest secrecy by the Secretary, and until all the birds have been examined, even the Judge is quite unaware of the owners of them. Only the numbers on the cages are taken into account in the allocation of the awards. Indeed, so scrupulous are these exhibition rules, that it would seem absolutely impossible for any fraud in the nature of collusion or favoritism to take place at a Roller contest. With these observations we will now pass on to the actual method by which the birds are examined and the awards given.

Adjoining the large public showroom where the exhibits are staged by the show manager and his stewards, are several smaller rooms which serve as judging rooms. The judge has a room to himself, and it is usual for one or more of the club officers to serve as attendants to carry the birds to and from the judging room.

The Judge takes his seat at a table in the room, and with his "judging sheet" laid out before him, calls for the first batch of birds. The attendant places the birds before him, opens the shutters, (if using cages with shutters), and standing back of the cages so that any cage door may be closed from behind without disturbing the bird at a word from the judge. In this way each bird may be heard individually until the judge has heard all of that team.

The attendants continually pass back and forth between the showroom and the judging room, replacing those exhibits which have sung by those in turn to be examined until the whole has been judged. At the end of the day's work the judging sheet is handed to the Secretary of the Society, and the numbers of prize winners are noted and awards made accordingly. In case of no song, the bird is given a second trial. There are classes for young and old birds. All entries are placed four in an envelope and sealed and numbers alternated or mixed to avoid any favors being given.

For the benefit of those interested we are showing below the song standard used by the I. R. C. B. A. and The American Ass'n.

INTERNATIONAL STANDARD
Points to Count

	Up to
Hollow Roll	10 pts.
Koller	10 pts.
Bass	10 pts.
Glucke	8 pts.
Glucke Roll	8 pts.
Water Glucke	8 pts.
Hollow Bell	6 pts.
Schockel	6 pts.
Water Roll	6 pts
Deep Bubbling Water Tour	6 pts.
Flute Notes	5 pts.
Bell Roll	2 pts.
Bell Glucke	3 pts.
Bell Tour	2 pts.
General Effect	10 pts.

Total of points to count ....100 pts.

POINTS TO BE REDUCED FOR FAULTS

	Up to
Bell Glucke faulty	3 pts.
Aufzug, Hard	3 pts.
Flutes, Sharp	6 pts.
Nasal Tours, Bad	6 pts.
Faulty Bells	6 pts.
Schwirre, Hard	3 pts.
Schnatter	6 pts.
Ugly Interjections in the song	6 pts.

Total points to be deducted ......39 pts.
Penalty for Zitt or Chop—Expulsion from the contest.

The American Canary Judges Association has adopted the following Song Standard, for use at song contests where certified Judges, members of the American Canary Judges Association, officiate.

AMERICAN SONG STANDARD

Hollow Roll	to	10
Bass	to	10
Glucke	to	9
Water Glucke	to	9
Schockle	to	9
Glucke Roll	to	6
Hollow Roll	to	6
Water Roll	to	6
Deep Bubbling Water Tour	to	6
Flutes	to	6
Bell Roll	to	3
Bell Tour	to	3
General Effect	to	6

Penalties for Faults

Bad Bell	to	6
Bad Flutes	to	6
Faulty Glucke	to	6
Aufzug	to	3
Bad Water Tours	to	6
Bad Bell Glucke	to	6
Ugly interjections	to	6

Breeding and Raising Canaries

FEEDING TIPS, ETC.

This is notoriously a thorny subject, but I shall endeavor to give each method a fair consideration without prejudice or feeling whatever. Perhaps I had better have said "soft food," since one small section would discard egg in all forms from the bird's diet. I will consider the latter aspect first and say at once that their objections to egg are based on facts which have been proven by scientific experimentation. Briefly, the objections are that egg is one of the best media for cultivating the bacilli which causes that terrible scourge of the bird breeder, septic fever. So it is during the breeding season, when the resistive powers of the birds to disease are lowered, that the septic bacilli, is so favorable a breeding ground as a constant supply of hard-boiled egg, are quickly bred to an unusually dangerous degree of virility.

To Rear Without Egg

To remedy this we are told that egg should be cut out of the dietary. The simplicity of the remedy cannot be gainsaid. But there remains the question: Can we rear the same proportion of young from a given number of birds quite irrespective of size and quality of young without egg as with it? My own experience gave a negative reply, although I had experimented and fully proved the possibility of rearing Canaries without egg in any form long before the no-egg theory was publicly mooted. Thus, of its practicability in rearing high-class birds I have yet to be convinced.

However, I shall leave the breeder to settle the matter himself, and if he wishes to go in for the no-egg method he may supply either of the following foods instead. First, in addition to the usual seeds, give a daily supply of crushed biscuit slightly moistened, and in a separate vessel a liberal allowance of cracked hemp, with which may be mixed a little dried fruit. When young birds are four or five days old one may begin to add a little soaked rape seed to the biscuit food, and also give a daily supply of green food. One must bear in mind that soaked rape rapidly turns sour, even in a moderate temperature; therefore it must be prepared fresh every day—twice each day would be better—and only sufficient be given to last the day. If any is left at night it should be thrown away and the egg drawers washed before putting in the supply for early morning feeding.

Another method is to use "prepared seeds" as a substitute for egg-food. This, as its name implies, appears to be composed entirely of seeds and vegetable compounds, and only requires moistening with water. All the shells or husks of the seeds have been eliminated. Perhaps the most satisfactory of all the no-

egg systems is to employ crushed puppy biscuit as a substitute for egg and biscuit. Either cod-liver oil or cod-liver oil and malt brands which do not contain meat are the proper brands to use. When crushed finely and slightly moistened with water they form a really excellent and wholesome soft food, and there is no reason whatever why they should not rear strong, robust birds just as well as the orthodox egg-food. Indeed, they have been used successfully for many years past by numbers of amateur breeders.

Again, scalded chicken meal will provide a very efficient food for rearing young Canaries. To prepare it, the required quantity of meal for one feed should be placed in a cup or basin and just enough boiling water poured over for it to absorb in the process of scalding, cover with a saucer and allow it to stand until cool, then stir with a table fork and if necessary add a little dry crushed biscuit to bring it to a crumbly, moist state. A slight dusting of sugar may be added to the whole, but is not essential.

The fact remains, however, that practically all the principal breeders and exhibitors cling to the old method of egg and bread crumbs, or depart from this system only so far as to substitute crushed biscuit for the bread crumbs. But the general consensus of opinion would probably be in favor of crumbs of bread. The heads of the Fancy, so to speak, do not seem to be troubled with visitations of septic fever to any greater extent than their humbler brethren. Of course, the explanation doubtless lies in the fact that these "leading lights" have immense advantages over the average amateur in the way of hygiene and healthful surroundings for their birds.

A Middle Course

But to steer a middle course between the egg and no-egg systems is a rather easier matter, and in most hands the method will succeed very well so far as concerns quantity and quality of results. This method consists in substituting the preserved yolk of egg, which is sold under such divers names as preserved yolk of egg, desiccated egg, preserved egg, egg flake, and several others, for the orthodox hard-boiled yolk of fresh eggs, and adding thereto the usual quantities of crushed biscuit or bread crumbs.

A very good food which can be mixed in sufficient quantity to last a week may be made by crushing a pound of ground bread and adding half a pound of preserved egg flake. Thoroughly mix all together and pack dry in a clean tin, or earthen jar with a close-fitting lid or cover. It will keep in perfectly good condition for a long time if kept in a cool, dry place. When required for use simply take out the required quantity and slightly moisten

51

it with a few drops of water, or crumbs of stale bread that have been soaked in water and squeezed nearly dry. Blend with a fork, and it will moisten the whole sufficiently.

Of course, this food may be prepared in greater or less quantities by adhering to the same proportion of two parts crushed biscuit to one part of egg; but it is best to prepare only sufficient at one time to last a week or thereabouts. Further, any other kind of plain biscuit, or even mixed broken biscuits, which can often be bought very cheaply, may be used instead of the maizena, but the latter are as good as any, and much better than some other kinds, so that one is pretty safe in using these only.

I now come to the almost universal system, of feeding hard-boiled fresh egg and bread crumb, or crushed biscuit. Bread crumb is still the favorite with many of the most successful breeders of our day. That the danger from septic infection is real none need deny, regardless of the fact that probably ninety out of every hundred Canaries reared are brought up with the aid of hard-boiled egg. Therefore it would seem that in the present state of our knowledge we cannot do better than adhere to that course, taking care to use all the safeguards available to avert the risks of infection.

It now only remains to give the proper mode of preparing egg-food for use, and to point out the principal dangers connected with its use. First boil the eggs for thirty minutes, remove them from the water, and lay them aside unbroken until quite cold, which may require an hour and a half or two hours, as the yolk retains heat after the shell feels cold. If one is pressed for time in the morning, one should boil the eggs required for the morning feed before retiring at night, and lay them aside unbroken when they would be quite ready for use when one arises. Hard-boiled eggs, when the shell is uncracked keep good for a considerable time.

Break open the eggs, remove the yolks, and, together with a little dry powdered biscuit, place them in the egg sieve and press all through the sieve into a basin with the back of a spoon. Stir it with a fork, and if not sufficiently granulated add a little more dry crushed biscuit, and repeat the process of pressing it through the sieve. Stir it in the basin with a fork until it is all a finely granulated mass. Then grate about twice its bulk of bread, about two days old, by turning the egg sieve over and rubbing the bread through. This is supposing that one has a combined egg sieve and bread grater in use; failing this, one must use an ordinary grater such as is commonly used in culinary operations. But providing the bread is in the proper degree of staleness, these articles are not altogether indispensible, as the bread can be rubbed into crumbs between the fingers just as well as with a grater. Having made a sufficient mass of bread crumb, add it to the egg in basin and again thoroughly mix and blend all together with the fork. Do not touch the egg with the fingers nor try to mix the ingredients by rubbing them through the fingers, as it tends to make the egg sodden and sticky. A fork is by far the best and simplest implement for mixing purposes. One now has a good wholesome soft food ready to serve out to the birds.

Some fanciers add a sprinkling of maw seed, sugar, rice powder, crushed linseed, and other things just to suit their individual fancy, or to try to induce the birds to eat more of the soft food in the hope that they will in turn "feed" more of it in due course to the young. Such a plan will succeed fairly well with some few hens who are not the best of "feeders," and requires the egg-food made to suit their taste in order to induce them to partake of it freely; but with good feeding hens the simple egg and bread crumb mixture is quite the best until the young are at least five days old, when a little soaked rape seed may be added, and the proportion be gradually increased from day to day until it forms about one-third of the bulk, beyond which limit it should not go.

When crushed biscuit is used instead of bread crumb, one of the small mills which may be adjusted either to crack hemp or crush biscuits to powder will be useful. If one has to cater for many birds it may be looked upon as a necessity, as the crushing of biscuits and seeds will make quite a considerable inroad upon one's spare time unless this mechanical aid is available.

Having now gone into details of several methods of providing food for rearing the young, I wish it to be understood that every reference to "egg-food" in this work (unless specially mentioned to the contrary) will refer to egg-food made with egg and bread crumb or crushed biscuit. I should at all times prefer crumb of good bread.

Yolk, or Both Yolk and White

One other point in connection with egg-food may be mentioned. It is as to whether only the yolk of the eggs, or both yolks and whites, should be used in making the egg food. As with practically every other point opinions on this matter differ considerably. Some breeders use the white as well as the yolk with very satisfactory results, whilst others find but indifferent success from this method.

It is not improbable that this lack of success may be to some extent due to the fact that the whites are not so easily broken up and granulated, so that unless the food is carefully prepared and more time spent over the mixing it is never so well blended together as when only the yolks are used. This is only an off-hand theory as to the reason why some succeed whilst others fail when using the same food.

My opinion is, that providing due care is exercised to see that the whites are well granulated and thoroughly blended with the food, it is perfectly safe to use them after the young are from five days to a week old. For the greater parts of the first week it is quite the best way to use the yolks only and throw away the whites if no other use can be found for them, but after that time such waste is by no means necessary.

It will be noticed that in the instructions about the mixing of egg-food, no mention is made of the addition of any kind of moistening fluid. Lest this point should be misunderstood it may be advisable to say that no such addition is necessary. There is sufficient natural moisture in the egg and bread when blended together to bring it to a very nice degree of crumbiness for the birds. When ready to give to the birds the egg-food should contain no superfluous moisture than can be detected by the eye; and if a small quantity be pressed together it should, immediately as it is touched, readily fall into a mass of loose crumbs again.

Different Ways of Using Egg For Food

If the breeding stock is larger, and the breeder is pressed for time in the morning, larger quantities of egg food will be required. It is then best to prepare it the night before, and the best method of keeping it sweet and fresh is to thoroughly mix the egg or eggs and cracker or bread, whichever is used, and put the food so made into a screw-top or lever-topped empty fruit jar which has been thoroughly scalded out; in this the food will keep beautifully fresh for a couple of days.

This saves a lot of time and worry in preparing for every morning and evening meal; a few minutes' work will soon see all the stock going with fresh supplies, especially if the breeder keeps a double set of egg-dishes and a dish of water in his rooms, for the dishes can then be put into the water in the morning and be ready for use again in the evening and there will be no fear of any stale food being overlooked.

Some breeders use only the yolk, others use both yolk and white. For breeding purposes and when the birds are feeding the young, I use the whole egg, for moulting and general feeding I always use the entire egg, shell as well; this latter I pulverize into powdery state and mix with the egg and biscuit.

For the purpose of conditioning, the yolk only is to be used. Separate this from the white and press through a sieve with a knife; add some bread and cracker or a sweet biscuit (this needs no sugar added to it). Thoroughly mix together, add a little maw seed to it, and give some of this every morning. If the breeder is at home during the middle of the day another supply can be given then, or if away all day it must be given in the evening. All left over from one part of the day must be thrown out and a fresh supply put in, as in hot weather it soon gets stale.

In the early part of the breeding season watercress is a good green food to give, but let it remain overnight in tepid water to be sure of being clear of any frost. Later on, fresh groundsel or young dandelion leaf may be given. Later still, lettuce leaf is a good change, also sweet apple and celery tops. A few days of this treatment will work wonders in bringing forward your stock; the hen will be calling and plucking at her tail feathers, carrying feathers in her beak and showing signs of wanting a nest. When these symptoms appear then is the time to run the male bird in with the hen, and in a day or so put in the nest-pan and some nesting material.

Nests can be purchased free of linings fixed in: all will require lining. The hen may probably spend some time in making and unmaking her nest, but will eventually settle down to business.

For the position of the nest I generally use the left hand end of the cage; then if the hen is of a very nervous temperament a piece of brown or white paper placed over the wires gives her the seclusion desired. I like the edge of the nest to be about an inch above the perch so as to enable the parents to feed the youngster more easily than when the nest is level with perch.

If the nest is fixed at the back of the cage the best position is between the two perches; this enables both parents to feed at the same time. Never put the nest right up in the corner of the cage or too near the top.

I have had hens which would persist in laying the eggs on the bottom of the cage and would not go near the nest where I had fixed it. If the hen will not go to the nest then the nest must go to the hen, so the nest was taken down and placed on the floor and remained there until the young were hatched. It was then put in its proper place, and all went well.

Reverting to the methods of rearing, the majority of breeders use egg food, and without doubt, if the hens will feed their young with this nourishing food there is nothing more suitable. Others, who have not the necessary time to spare in providing and preparing the usual egg food, find it more convenient to use an egg cake preparation. This is prepared and given as follows:

One pound finest ground whole wheat meal made into a stiff dough with as many fresh eggs as the meal will absorb (6 to 8 eggs). Use no water. Bake in a slow oven for three hours. Cut up into small pieces and replace in warm oven until all moisture has gone. Keep, after grinding to a fine powder, in an air-tight tin. When feeding, take five parts of the egg cake, one part of maw seed, one part of sugar, and moisten with boiling water. This will keep fresh 12 hours. The powdered egg cake if kept as directed in a tin and in a dry place will keep indefinitely.

Take 12 raw eggs, 1 qt. sweet milk, mix well, take all the ground bakers bread it will absorb, bake a cake dry and grind. Mix 1/2 teaspoon malted milk baby food to 2 tablespoonfuls of cake.

There are also several other soft foods such as the various cod liver oil food and biscuit preparations, which may be used. I have also heard of ordinary sponge cake being successfully used. It may be added that one of the main secrets in feeding these soft foods successfully is in the mixing; they should not be made too sloppy, but of a crumbly consistency.

Although the egg food system is the one generally used there are many breeders who experience the greatest difficulty in getting their hens to rear their young chicks on it. The writer himself, some years back, lost several nests of valuable young birds, in attempting to force the hens to use egg food in spite of their evident antipathy to it. Although as a general rule, Roller hens are excellent feeders, some hens do not care for egg food, and rather than give it to their broods will let them starve. Such, as I have said, has been my own experience.

An alternative system of rearing can, in

such cases, be used. Freshly crushed hemp seed, rolled oats and watercress is given from the first daily, and given without stint. Seldom will a hen refuse to use this diet for the rearing of her brood; in fact, those hens which may be very indifferent feeders with egg food will generally prove most energetic and excellent feeders with the crushed hemp and watercress. Along with the hemp it is as well to offer a little soft food in the shape of milk sop or moistened biscuit.

Not only is this hemp seed method generally quite satisfactory and successful, but it has also the advantage of being much more economical and much easier to work than the egg food system. Care must be taken, however, that when once crushed, the hemp seed must not be left in the cage for more than a day, as the exposed kernel is liable to become rancid very quickly in warm weather. It is advisable to give the hen about a tablespoonful three or four times a day.

In many respects it is an excellent plan to fix the hours of feeding; indeed, regularity in this matter is regarded by many authorities as of greatest importance. The egg food should be given to the birds at 7 A.M., at midday, 4 P. M. and 7 P. M. daily. I also recommend that a seed mixture of 2 parts rape, 1 part Canary, and 1 part groats should be supplied to the hen for feeding her young, and that maw seed must be given with the egg food every other day or separately. In addition, I recommend that crushed hemp be supplied every afternoon, and when the young are on the perches soaked rape seed with egg food is to be given.

When all is going well the young birds will be seen to increase in size and strength from day to day, and their vocal efforts when requiring food, or while being fed, will proportionately develop. Do not, however, let anxiety prompt you to be continually interfering with the nest and looking into it. At a glance every morning and night, just to see that the birds are all safely in the nest, be sufficient. It should not be necessary to touch the nest to accomplish this if one watches for the birds as they rise up to be fed. Avoid all interference that is not absolutely necessary.

Another type of hen will sit comfortably on the nest continually calling to the cock for food, but rarely passing on to her young any of what he conveys to her. Such a hen will often be roused to a sense of her duties by taking the cock away and placing him out of sight and earshot. Then she is compelled to leave the nest for food and water, which not only gives the young brood a refreshing breath of air, but the effort of procuring her own food helps to arouse the maternal instincts. When she returns to the nest of gasping young, unless she is an incorrigible, she will be almost certain to give them at least a little bit, which will have the wholesome effect of making them beg vigorously for more; and then by degrees in a day or two she may perform her duties with much satisfaction.

In these cases a variety of food is also advisable, the object being to tempt the hen to feed freely herself, and thereby increase the chances of the young coming in for a greater share. A little green food and cracked hemp (the seed should have only the husk cracked so as to leave the kernel nearly uninjured) should be given from the first—a young lettuce leaf is pre-eminent over all other green foods in such cases as these, and will induce a hen to feed the young when nothing else will.

On the other hand, I have found dandelion decidedly aggravates the trouble, hence one of the chief reasons why I strongly advise its rejection entirely during the breeding season. I am well aware that many whose opinions are entitled to every consideration differ from this. Now and again one will find a hen that will feed the young solely on some particular food—sometimes it is green food, or it may be cracked hemp. But whatever it is, a supply of that food must be given. It is remarkable how some hens will bring up young apparently on green food alone.

Many other plans and nostrums have been put forward from time to time to cure the non-feeding hen; such as placing a cube of common salt between the wires for the birds to peck at, or adding sufficient to the water for one day to make it taste slightly of the salt; or adding sufficient Epsom salts to the drinking water for a day to make it taste slightly of that drug—all of which are harmless enough to warrant a trial in very bad cases.

But little must be expected from these crude methods. The only real "cure", if such it can be called, probably lies in the proper feeding and management of the birds prior to the time the young are hatched.

It has been suggested that non-feeding is probably due sometimes to the hens getting bilious and surfeited by the sudden change from the diet given during the period of incubation to an unlimited supply of rich egg-food when the young are hatched. While not disputing the possibility of such a thing happening, I would point out that in such case the indiscretion lies in the fancier's own judgment. An unlimited supply of egg-food should not be given suddenly as soon as the young are hatched, neither should pure yolk of egg without any mixture of bread be given for the first few days, as others suggest as a possible cause. If the instructions given elsewhere are adhered to, both these errors will be avoided.

Very good results may be obtained in some cases by this simple treatment if it is begun as soon as the hen is seen to be neglecting her duties, or, rather, not beginning them. Give a small piece of bread soaked in cold milk—not boiled—fresh two or three times a day instead of the usual egg-food, and supply a saline bath. Prepare the latter by dissolving a dessert spoonful of common salt in a pint of water and give from a spray, just sufficient to bedew her plumage, when she will probably enter the bath and complete her toilet.

Whether this bath possesses any really exhilarating influences for canaries, I do not profess to say, but it certainly will often serve to brace a hen so that she is quite brisk about her maternal duties. Altogether, this last-named treatment I consider far the most satisfactory.

The increase in the food supply and the inclusion of a supply of soaked rape seed (either given separately or mixed with the egg-food), from about the fifth day, has already been pointed out. It cannot be too strongly impressed upon one here to take note of the egg-food, should the rape be added to it, as during fairly warm weather a very few hours will suffice for it to turn sour.

Steeped Rape Sprouted Seed

A very good plan is to place a sufficient quantity of rape seed to last two or three days in a mug or basin and fill up with cold water. Each day the whole contents may be poured into a sieve, the seed returned to the vessel, and a fresh supply of water added. In this way the seed will keep perfectly sweet for some days and if it begins to sprout, it will be no detriment whatever. It also has the advantage of being always ready for use, as it is only necessary to ladle out the required quantity at any time with spoon, drain off the water, and drop the seed in a towel.

Feeding Nestlings

When the hatching process is completed one should begin to supply egg-food to each pair as occasion requires, beginning with pure egg yolk, and gradually bringing them on to the ordinary egg-food by the third day. For the first three days let the usual seed diet and egg-food suffice. Give the latter in small quantities, and give a freshly prepared supply, whenever possible, at least three times each day. Do not try to economize by mixing any that may be left over with the freshly made supply. This is certainly the very worst kind of false economy. Throw away all that is left, and wash out the egg drawer before giving the fresh supply.

For the first two or three days half a teaspoonful at each meal will be sufficient; but one must use his own discretion, and not adhere to any hard-and-fast rule as to quantities, some birds consume a far greater amount of egg-food than others, and it is a safe plan to endeavor to regulate the supply so that the quantity given is just cleared up before the time to give a fresh supply. It is not really difficult to manage this, by noting the condition of the egg drawer for the first few days, and increasing or diminishing the supply as seems necessary.

When this plan is properly carried out the birds are keener to feed than when surfeited by having an unlimited supply of egg-food always before them; they will nearly always set to work to feed the young as soon as each fresh supply is given. The method certainly demands strict regularity in the times of feeding, but as this should be a cardinal virtue with every breeder, it should be no real obstacle and the advantages gained by the method are very great.

Feeding Tips

An old-timer's tip, given to me many years ago when first keeping exhibition stock, was to use up the entire egg, powder the shell after removing the membrane, thoroughly mix with the biscuit, and then chop up the green food and mix it with the egg instead of giving it separately.

I have found hens feed better when this has been tried than when the green food has been given separately. Sometimes, instead of using the egg shell, I have scraped some cuttlefish bone over the food. Sweet apple ground up with egg food is splendid also and 1/2 teaspoonful of malted milk baby food added to one egg and bread is good.

Do not disturb the hen when sitting; some are very nervous in this respect. Also do not be over anxious to peep into the nest when hatching is due; leave the birds to themselves. If you find the hen off the nest, well and good, but do not drive her off to satisfy your curiosity.

When All Goes Well

If all continues to go on well and the hen feeds the young satisfactorily, give her a bath on the third day after hatching, and continue it daily afterwards. Begin also to give a little green food, commencing with a small leaf of lettuce, or spray of watercress or chickweed, and gradually increasing the quantity given from day to day until what is considered a fair allowance is reached.

The amount of egg-food must also be gradually increased as the needs of the growing brood become greater, always endeavoring to keep it within the limits already pointed out, and giving it fresh as often as is convenient. To digress for a moment; in saying this, one must not imagine that by mixing a sufficient quantity of food in the morning to last through the day and serving it out in small quantities at intervals, one is properly carrying out the principle of giving fresh food two or three times a day. This is by no means the case, and simply amounts to giving fresh food once a day and no oftener. Properly to carry out the principle, only sufficient food should be prepared each time to supply the needs of the birds at each serving. If you require more than one egg a day—and the food should be kept on ice or air-tight to keep fresh, and the remainder of the eggs required for the day's supply should remain unbroken until required for immediate use. Thus, although one may save time by boiling all eggs required for a day's use at one time, one must not try to economize further by also mixing a sufficient bulk of food to last a day, during the very hot weather.

After the first three days the increased demands of a healthy brood of young will soon become apparent if the parents are fulfilling their duties properly and the supply of egg-food will soon need to be doubled and trebled. A little cracked hemp should be given in a finger drawer on the third day, and a moderate supply of this should be continued afterwards, cracking it freshly each day (a small matter when one has a mill), except in the case of hens which start nesting again before one brood is able to leave the nest when the supply of hemp should be withheld until the young are at least a week or ten days old. It is also important to see that the hemp used is of good sound quality, having a milkywhite kernel, full of natural oil when crushed. Hemp seed with discolored brown kernels, or with a large proportion dried up in the husk, is unfit for feeding Canaries either young or old, and is frequently the cause of young broods being lost. From the fifth day onwards a proportion of soaked rape may be added to the egg-food.

Under this regime the brood should thrive and flourish apace, and be able to leave the nest from the eighteenth to the twenty-first day after hatching. In practice, however, things do not always follow this ideal path, but are all too apt to divert from the straight course at many points and land the erstwhile hopeful owner into a veritable slough of despondency.

From the time the young are hatched until they are quite able to take care of themselves in the nest, one should make a point of taking a glance over the cage floor every morning and night, and try to get a glimpse of the birds' heads as they raise them when gaping in expectation of being fed, in order to see whether a chick has been dragged out of the nest or has died within it. In the latter case it must be removed at once before it becomes offensive.

It sometimes happens that chicks are found on the bottom of the cage, having been accidentally dragged out of the nest in the claws or among the feathers of the hen when she left it for food, and when this occurs the chick is almost invariably totally ignored by the parents as soon as it is out of the nest. Should the youngster still be fairly lively when found, hold it between the palms of the hands and breathe upon it between the thumbs for a few moments until it begins to feel a little warm; then gently replace it in the nest with the others.

But should the chick appear cold and lifeless, do not jump to hasty conclusions and throw it away. Place it between the palms of the hands as before, and hold it in this position before a fire (as near the fire as can comfortably be borne by the hands) and every now and again breathe vigorously between the thumbs on the bird. Many a chick that is apparently quite lifeless will be resuscitated by ten or fifteen minutes of this treatment. If it shows signs of life let it get thoroughly warm, and place it in the nest with the others. Next morning it will often be impossible to distinguish it from the rest of the brood.

In cases where young are being continually dragged out of the same nest, it is a good plan to catch the hen and examine her claws to see if they are overgrown, as this is frequently the real cause of the mischief. If this appears to be the case, carefully trim the claws to a reasonable length, but be careful not to go too close to the red vein which runs down them, and so make the claws bleed. The vein can be plainly seen on holding the claw up to a good light. It must also be understood that catching the birds and performing any kind of operation is to be avoided as far as possible at this time. It is only in case of extreme necessity that they are recommended.

Occasionally this trouble may be due to a habit some young excitable hens have of flying off the nest direct on to a perch instead of rising and hopping carefully on to the rim of the nest pan before taking to the perch. When a hen is seen to leave the nest in this manner it is well to note how the pan hangs in relation to the perches. Probably the rim of the nest will be on a lower level than the perches, so that the latter can be seen by the hen as she sits on the nest, and tempt an excitable subject to take a flying leap to them.

If this is the case the nest pan should be raised until the rim is slightly above the level of the perches, so that she cannot see them until she stands up to look about her. This simple adjustment will often prevent the young or eggs being dragged out of the nest accidentally.

Another trouble that may come early in the experience of the breeder is that hens after laying and hatching satisfactorily will refuse from the first to feed the young. In some cases, particularly with young hens who have their first brood of young it appears to arise from sheer nervousness, and keeping the hens as quiet and secluded as possible for a few days will often have a good result. Frequently, however, with such hens the first brood is lost, but they should be given another chance, and with future broods will often make very good parents.

Having now considered that type of hen which does not really commence to perform her maternal duties, I may go on to another type which is, perhaps, even more disappointing to the beginner, because her conduct fills him with high hopes at the beginning, only to dash them to the ground a few days later. This type of hen begins to feed the young and continues feeding satisfactorily for three or four days, or perhaps, a week, when she gets affected with the trouble popularly known as "sweating," from the fact that the plumage on the hen's breast and abdomen, and also the down on the young birds, is often damp and moist, as though with perspiration. In some cases at least this appearance is believed to be due partly to the unduly water evacuations of the young—a sufficient proof that the health of the young is also at fault.

In the great majority of cases, however where the birds were in good health and condition before starting to breed, this trouble, doubtless, arises from surfeiting the birds with too great abundance of egg-food, green stuff, and other varieties of food, as soon as the young are hatched, in the hope that the more liberal and varied the diet the better they will feed the young. This is a very mistaken idea, and although it may answer in some special cases, as when the hens require some coaxing in the greater number of cases, defeats its own end by upsetting the birds, coming, as it does, quite suddenly after the very plain diet which should suffice during the period of incubation.

When the birds are treated as already described during the first few days after the young are hatched the latter cause will be removed and consequently "sweating" should be comparatively uncommon. It may not yet be sufficiently well known that a frequent cause of hens "sweating" the young is believed to be due to a non-virulent type of septic bacilli, and hence somewhat akin to septic fever. Remedy, in this case, there is none; and prevention, as previously pointed out, lies in sacrificing the use of egg as a portion of the diet.

The eating of food is necessary for but one natural reason. To supply necessary nutritive values to the body for its construction of tissue, all tissue wears out and must be refurnished.

Good sound food (seed) will furnish the

principal of this diet at a minimum of effort on the part of the digestive organs and by so doing, sets up a storage of vitality in the bird's body. Neglect this proper diet through the feeding of unnatural stale or low grade food and the organism of the bird becomes overworked in its effort to abstract the required nutritive qualities from this devitalized food, resulting in a continued sapping of the vital force this process of non-replenishment of vitality and withdrawal of stored-up vitality very soon reacts on the constitution of the bird, for in a very short space of time we have but a shell of its former self and then another bird passes out.

What is one man's poison is another's meat, is also very true in bird life. We should consider this when preparing our birds for the breeding season. Some come into this condition naturally. Should we over-condition them with conditioning food, we simply train them for the fighting game, rather than for the time of love and family cares, this over-conditioning is a case of nerves, resulting from the high state of breeding desire, causing the nerves to become highstrung and on edge, this results in the abandoning of nests, eggs and young. This over-conditioning is more likely to occur during hot or muggy weather than at any other time. Nature provides natural heat during the summer months and it is unnecessary for us to overheat their blood by feeding heating foods at this time.

SEED

Scientists have drawn up many charts showing the elements found in foods, let us use them as a basis for all dieting, remembering that none of these food elements can be eliminated without detrimental effect to the body.

PROTEINS—The protein or albumins being the nitrogenous elements of food, must be furnished in sufficient degrees so as to build and repair the cells, a deficiency of same will account for loss of weight as well as thinness of voice. An over-production of proteids produces thickening of the blood, and consequent putting them on of flesh, which will lead to liver and heart troubles, and then again the excess of nitrogenous foods causes stagnation of circulation, being thus converted into a poisonous product of waste, which eventually impregnates the entire body, producing the final state—Death. It is obvious that the remedy for this condition is "Go short on such feeding." You will then notice a rapid recovery of the patient. The following will show percentage of proteins—Canary 14, Hemp 16, Niger 17, Maw 18, Rape 20, Linseed 25.

CARBOHYDRATES—Consist mostly of starches and sugars, but contain no nitrogen, it is readily seen that they are not builders of cell protoplasm, they do however contribute bodily heat, replace fatty tissue and produce energy, they too, can be used in excess and thus produce liver and heart trouble. The following will show percentage of carbohydrates. Rape 10, Maw 12, Niger 15, Hemp 16, Linseed 18, Canary 50, Millet 60.

HYDROCARBONS—Are the oily or fat producers and somewhat similar to Carbohydrates. They must be used with discretion, more especially during warm periods and when feeding young during that period. Starchy foods are a necessary food mixture in conjunction with the above. Following, is the percentage of hydrocarbons in these foods, Canary 5, Millet 5, Hemp 30, Niger 30, Linseed 40, Maw 40, Rape 50.

WATER—Water, which is absolutely essential for the maintenance of life, is always found in natural seed, although same appear hard and dry, moreover this water is most pure, not being laden with deleterious matter, which in most cases of water supply, has been unprotected from contagion. As stated in the writings of Richard Morse, F. L. S., F. R. H. S. from which I have gathered information and knowledge, we are further informed that the higher the percentage of water in a food the less the quantity of other essential constituents, and as a general rule, foods containing a large percentage of water, seldom are very nutritious and can not take the place of more solid food materials which may contain a goodly percentage of proteids, in other words, foods containing as much as 90 per cent water contain but 2 per cent of body building or heat supplying elements. Such foods are therefore very low in nutritive value. In the feeding of such foods, body building or heat forming foods should be used in proportion to elements needed and also used according to weather conditions. Hen's eggs are generally supposed to be very high in percentage of nutriment, but contrary to this belief, they are a most expensive food, containing no less than 73 per cent of water, leaving the nitrogeneous elements at about 12 per cent. We can therefore see that the seeds in common use are of more nutritive value to the birds than eggs. A good food ration to my way of figuring, consists of natural seeds, soaked also partly sprouted, and egg food, this ration being used mostly in breeding time. Water is represented in percentage as follows: Niger 8, Rape 11, Hemp 12, Millet 13, Barley Meal 14, Canary 14, Maw 14, Beef or Mutton 72, Eggs 73, Dandelion Leaves 86, New Milk 87, Lettuce Leaves 94.

Necessary Salts

NUTRITIVE SALTS—Most of the body ills known as disease, results from a disordered blood, and the basic cause of such ever present malady is an insufficiency of nutritive salts in the food. It is these salts, potash, lime soda and magnesia which are contained in varying proportions in green foods and seeds, which make all the difference between digestion and no digestion. The absence of the above salts must result in lack of vitality, strength, and finally in death. Do not neglect to feed your birds green foods at all times, and remember that soaked and sprouted seeds are most beneficial.

VEGETABLE ACIDS—These acids are not necessarily a food. The chief acid among such is Malic Acid. It is found in considerable quantities in certain fruits, especially in apples and pears. Other acids are, Citric and Tartaric acids, mostly found in fresh fruits and green foods, and undergoing a chemical change within the body, through the formation of carbonates, exercise a powerful influence towards the healthful alkalinity of the blood and other essential fluids.

FIBRE—Practically all foods contain varying proportions of matter called Fibre. The food values of such is of no relative value but may have some value as a stimulant to the bowels in their natural movements.

VITAMINS—These are known to exist in a large number of unspoiled natural foods, such as greens, grains and fruits. There are an absolute necessity in all diets, and when omitted, disease will be the result. Beri-beri, being most noticed, and unless vitamins are present in later feedings, death will end the life of the victim.

Let us therefore use judgment in all relations with our pets, remembering that nothing can be expected from them, unless we supply the necessities for giving. This applies most strongly in relation to song, color, and reproducing of young.

LANCASHIRE COPPY
and PLAINHEAD

BREEDING SUGGESTIONS

The breeder who wishes to raise good-sized birds (of good vitality and stout in body) must not expect to do so by mating together two puny, undersized specimens. He must have plenty of size to begin with in one, if not in both. Similarly, if he desires to breed clear birds, he cannot expect them to be produced (except an occasional sport, as it were), from the mating of heavily marked or green birds.

In selecting the breeding stock one should mate a yellow with a buff, and refrain from "double-yellowing," or "double-buffing"—which means mating together two yellows or buffs, as the case may be—until some experience has been gained. In a general way the yellows give color and quality of feather; the buffs size and substance of body and profusion of feather. It will also materially help to keep up the natural depth of color in the young if one of the parents is a·variegated bird. It should be known that the real source of all natural color is the green, but beyond mentioning the simple fact I need not touch further upon the subject here.

In yellows, although the depth of color may vary in tone from pale lemon to a rich orange, the color is continued right to the edge of the web of the feather, whereas in the buff the yellow color stops just short of the edge, leaving a narrow margin of white around the edge of the feathers, which gives a frosted appearance to the bird's plumage, as though its yellow color was dusted over with white powder. This buff plumage is also called "mealy."

Color has no bearing when mating Rollers for song.

The hens should be placed in their breeding quarters, the latter fully equipped for breeding, with the sole exception of the nest, which must be withheld until the birds are properly mated and ready to begin nesting. The cocks should be placed in separate cages and hung beside their respective partners, in full view of each other, and in such a position that the cock can feed the hen between the wires when so disposed.

One of the advantages of using a double-breeding cage for each pair is that the hen may be placed in one compartment and the cock in the other, with only the wired partition separating them. When the birds have been kept in this way for a few days, and the cock is seen frequently calling the hen to the wired slide and giving her food, it is only nec-

essary to take out the slide and allow them to begin nesting.

On the other hand, when single cages are used, it is always advisable, and often quite necessary, to place the cock in a small cage, such as a nursery cage, and hang it on the front of the cage containing the hen for a day or two before finally putting them together. Serious quarreling often results by introducing them to each other too suddenly.

Except under such special circumstances as previously pointed out (where the birds are kept in a warm location) the latter end of March is quite early enough to carry out the work just described, and the last few days in March or first week of April will be early enough finally to put the birds together. But personally I have had satisfactory results in May but the climate must be considered. This leaves an interval of about ten days during which time the birds should still be given the more generous diet already advised. A small leaf of dandelion daily will be of great value, and a pinch of niger or thistle seed every second day given in the finger drawer, to the hen only, will be invaluable as a preventative of egg-binding.

If all goes well, not many days should elapse before they are ready for mating. But whether the period be long or short, it is not only advisable to run them together as soon as they reach the proper condition, but it is also essential that they should be kept apart until that condition of fitness is arrived at. No good will come of putting together birds that have no desire for mating, although so often done.

Signs of Breeding Condition

But how is the beginner to know when the birds are in the proper condition? Given birds in normal health the signs are not easily mistakable. And here let me say that one of the most vital principles that lead to success in breeding in the early days of one's connection with the hobby is rigidly to weed out and reject weakly, unhealthy stock birds. To return to the subject of mating. When the cock is seen frequently popping down to the wires next to the hen's compartment and calling vigorously to her, and giving her food out of his beak, filling up the remainder of his time singing violently to her, he is in the proper condition for mating; as also is the hen when she is seen traveling about the perches restlessly and excitedly; and responding quickly and freely to the "calls" of the cock, and occasionally pulling at a beakful of her breast feathers, which she may make some pretense of carrying about and placing in the nest pan or upon the end of a perch. At this stage she is apt to steal a few feathers from the cock bird whenever she gets an opportunity to grab a beakful of his plumage.

It is now that just a beakful of nesting material, or even a single feather, or a bit of partly ravelled string tied on the wires, is sometimes useful to prevent her plucking her mate or herself. But when both birds exhibit the symptoms just detailed no time should be lost in putting them together—they will doubtless begin nesting at once.

In some cases it is quite as harmful to keep the birds apart when they have arrived at a "ripe condition" as it is to mate them before they are ready. Whereas, if they are put together at the proper time, excepting, perhaps, in odd cases, which only go to prove the rule, all else will follow as a matter of course, and the birds will frequently be sitting upon their first nest of eggs at the end of a fortnight from the time the slides were finally withdrawn.

The breeder who is only breeding for the ordinary singing Canary to "keep the pot boiling" should find out about the finer song points. First of all master the rudiments, and then launch out into the higher grades, and if you then feel sufficiently satisfied with your efforts by all means take on the more valuable strains, only first learn to walk before you run. Whether you go in for the "Moderates" or "Classics," get the best you can afford to get; the food bill will be just the same.

Another word of advice. Don't be tempted to cross-breed with any other variety; if you breed Rollers breed Rollers. A cross with other varieties does not improve the Roller song; in fact, I should not advise you to keep any other variety in the same rooms.

REDUCING FAT BIRDS

Every breeder should now inspect their females, examine them to ascertain their condition. There will be some too fat, some bowel inflammation, some with black breasts. You can't be too careful when selecting and examining your breeders. Too fat females can be reduced with green food, apples and lettuce, but best not to discontinue egg food entirely. Feed egg food twice a week at least. They should have a bath daily. If convenient a large room or flying cage will assist materially in reducing their condition and rounding them into condition. Birds with black breasts will hardly get into breeding season without some months and have good results. They are in bad condition—blood weak, liver hard, or their digestive organs do not properly function. Generally this kind of a bird will have clear eggs. However, should some of the eggs hatch the young usually go West for failure of the mother to feed or other causes.

If you continue to feed rich food the next malady from which your birds will suffer is Gap. Should you find a hen on her nest breathing heavily and puffed, they are feverish and generally open their beaks. When dis-

covered be sure to remove this bird AT ONCE. Give her a good examination, place her in a large flying cage where she can get plenty of exercise. Must be kept spotlessly clean and free from Canary seed. Put in fresh supply of clean gravel. The temperature of the room should be 60 to 70. Feeding such birds should be as follows:

Sweet Dutch rape, sweet or baked apple. Boil an Irish potato in salt water. After it has cooled mash fine; then take a raw carrot, grate finely and mix two parts potato, one part carrot. This should be fed fresh daily. Be careful not to allow to sour. This is death to your bird—feeding sour feed. Change the drinking water twice daily. Keep a close watch on the bird's droppings. When thin and watery place to themselves. This is very contagious. We have known of entire flocks being lost, so beware. There is less disease among canaries than among chickens, rabbits, etc., but unless you use precaution and common sense it is likely you will have an expensive experience. When this bowel inflammation has set in the bird must be treated with special care. Green food, apple, lettuce or baked apple should not be fed. Birds so affected should have a little canary seed, steel cut oats and a little egg food.

The cage or container of all such birds should be cleaned out daily and fumigated and scalded. The temperature should be 75 to 80, if possible. Drinking water should be a teacup of water with a tablespoon of rolled oats brought to a boil; allow to cool, strain and give to bird as drinking water. Give the bird a few drops of port wine in its water; this is a splendid tonic. Special care should be given the bird as it is likely to develop Typhus Diarrhoea (Roteruhr). Very few birds are saved from this disease and none are worth their care and feed after having had it. Each cage having been inhabited with a bird having this disease should not be used again until it has been scalded with lye water and disinfected. I know a breeder who lost over one hundred good birds from such a disease and by not thoroughly disinfecting the cages. Young birds cannot be saved from diarrhoea; feed and care for them according to the information given in this Journal.

Cause of Eggs Not Hatching

Failure of eggs to hatch is invariably caused from lack of condition, and seeing that the hens have laid and set. The more vigorous condition the male bird is in the more likely are the eggs to be fertile. The only thing that can be done is to separate the birds until you are able to see by their actions that they are wanting to mate. The hen should be calling and the cock bird in full vigorous song, especially when his cage is placed in view and close to that in which the hen is kept.

Nesting Material

For nesting material, there is nothing much better than short strands of burlap sack or the little bundles of cow-hair sold in the shops; but care must be taken to stove or thoroughly bake them before putting them at the birds disposal, for the double purpose of killing any red-mites that may happen to have invaded them, and for destroying any germs of disease they may have contracted in the shop whence they were obtained.

If, however, a fancier has no liking for these useful bundles of nesting material, he can supply his birds with a little fine hay, some short horse-hair, and a few little feathers. Some hen canaries are very clumsy, and seem to be quite incapable of building themselves a nest, no matter what kind of material is placed at their disposal. Either they will push all the stuff to one side, or pile it up so high that the eggs are apt to roll off when laid; or they will put the lining of the nest in, and pull it all out again many times over.

Separating the Sexes During Incubation

If the cock, as sometimes happens, seems disposed to interfere with the construction of the nest—and some males are very tiresome in this respect—he will have to be removed from the society of the hen, or hens, except for a little while every morning, when the partition that separates them can be opened, and the gentleman allowed to enter. But even then he will have to be watched, and prevented from interfering with the nest. As a rule, the cock canary does not touch the nest, and need not be separated from the hen while it is being built; in fact, the less the birds are noticed and interfered with the better.

BANDING BIRDS

Closed leg bands or rings on a Canary are certainly an asset for the owner. The year hatched is very plainly stamped on the band, thereby giving the age of the bird. The bird's age has long been a mystery. There is no definite time to ring your birds but usually five to eight days of age. There is a difference in the size of closed rings. The smaller rings must be placed on at from five to eight days old. This is not hazardous, and is often done. The placing of rings on your birds is a simple process and requires no experience whatever. Very seldom is there any ill effects from ringing your birds. Take the chick in your left hand with tips of thumb and fingers free to hold the leg and foot. Some sprinkle with talcum powder; some use vaseline; many use nothing, some wrap thread around toes and run thread through band. In any event have leg clean and dry when placed back in the nest. Now place the hind toe back against the shank of the leg, and the three front toes straight out and close together. Now place the three out toes through the ring and pass the ring out over the foot back, screwing or turning as you slip band on, and pass the hind toe which is against the leg; when the ring passes the end of the toe it returns to its normal position and the ring cannot slip off. Now make a record of the ring number and nest and parents.

DIARRHOEA

If the birds seem to have the dreaded diarrhoea dealt upon in another part of this book more fully, just give some carbonate of bismuth on some fresh milk sop twice or three times a day. Remove other foods. Give about 30 drops of ordinary chalk mixture daily for three days.

Diarrhoea, in nesting hens especially, is very annoying, although not serious. The cause usually is from stopping the feeding of rich food too suddenly. The hen should be weaned from egg food gradually after she begins to sit. Give her a small taste of egg food for several days; then every other day for a week. It can be cured by giving a mild dose of salts for a few days and milk sop sprinkled with powdered arrow-root. Many hens contract this at every nesting and should be watched, and the cause removed. Should you have a hen that persists in laying from the perch instead of the nest, remove the perch at night before she is expected to lay. This will usually cause her to lay in her nest. If you pump a hen too much in the matter of laying, you are sapping her vitality. Three clutches is sufficient. If a hen has started plucking her young, nothing can stop her so long as she can get to them. Remove the birds and hang a bacon rind in her cage. She will possibly forget it before next time. If too young to remove, a piece of white, wooly string tied to the wires will find her plenty work, and often will detract her attention from the young.

The only time when interference with the eggs is necessary is in the rare instances when the cock evinces a disposition to meddle with them. Then, indeed, it will be safer to take each away as soon as it is laid and to introduce one of ivory or bone in its place, doing so each morning, until the hen has laid her last egg, and settled herself down to her duty. The artificial eggs should then be taken away, and her own eggs restored to her to incubate in peace, in the absence of the cock, placed elsewhere.

As a rule a hen, even when the pair agree, will not trouble herself about the removal of the cock once she has begun to sit, and he may then be transferred to another cage and put up with another hen. But should she appear to miss him, and become restless and inattentive to her duty, it will be safer to return him to her society, even if he be suspected of cannibalism, and to let the eggs take their chance; he may behave all right, and not interfere, but if the mother should, in her restlessness, let them get cold, the eggs would of course be lost.

Not very many cocks, however, meddle with the eggs—some cock canaries are apt to be troublesome in this respect, and when one of them is to be the father of a brood, both watchfulness and care will be necessary, or the hatching may come to naught.

When all the means I have gone into for keeping a hen at her maternal duties, including the removal of the cock, have been exhausted without success, there remains the last hope of saving the young by transferring them to a foster-parent. If the young being neglected are from valuable stock there is, of course, little compunction in disposing of a nest of common stock belonging to good feeding parents, and substituting the better-class young for them. As with making a new nest, it is best to make their transference in the evening, and when doing so, if the young appear weak through lack of food, place a little fresh egg-food in your own mouth to warm and moisten it, and give each youngster a cropful off the end of a toothpick before placing them under the foster hen.

When contemplating an exchange of this kind, one should endeavor to fix on a brood of young of about the same age, or a day or two younger than the brood that is to replace them. If one wishes to give the common young ones a chance they may either be distributed among other hens who have small broods about the same age, or given altogether to the "sweating" hen and be partly hand-fed, in which case there is just a chance of the hen pulling herself together and resuming her maternal duties with tolerable satisfaction after a few days.

On the whole, however, when a hen persists in "sweating" and does not respond to such treatment as indicated above, it is a much better plan to turn her into a large flight, where she can have abundant exercise for two or three weeks before mating her again. In the interval devote your attention to bringing her into a good, sound, healthy condition on a plain seed diet, with daily baths and strict attention to cleanliness, and if she is in poor condition of body, a little bread and milk daily instead of egg-food. On the other hand if she seems in an over-fed condition, supplement the seed diet only with a liberal allowance of green food; with an occasional small pinch of Epsom salts in the drinking water. In two or three weeks such a hen may be mated up afresh if she seems in breeding condition, with a fair chance of better success.

Complaints reach me regarding young ones coming out of the nest before their time, say at 16 days, or even at 14 days. These, when put back again in the daytime, refuse to stay in, and often as not if a solitary one has come out and an attempt is made to return it, the whole brood is flushed. Therefore, I have found it a good plan to leave it in the bottom of the cage until dusk, when they are all asleep, then get hold of it gently and quietly, and put it back in the nest without any disturbance. On several occasions I have done this successfully this year.

When a hen has a brood a week or more old, a bath is a most refreshing thing for her. Give it to her in the middle of the day when the sun is shining.

All may go well until the young are ten or twelve days old, by which time the quills of the future feathers should be well developed. From this time onward until the birds are quite able to do for themselves, another trouble is likely to beset the breeder. The hens, even though feeding and brooding the young as well as one could wish, will sometimes commence to pluck out their quills or immature feathers.

This is always a serious trouble, not only on account of its baneful effect upon the growth and development of the young, but in that it is often quite impossible to cope with it. Feather plucking, as it is called, may either arise from a desire on the part of the hen to begin nesting again, or, as sometimes appears, from sheer depravity or viciousness on her part, for the trouble is nearly always confined to the hen.

In the former case, provided she is a hen one knows will feed and rear her young without the cock, he should be removed (as before described), and this is usually all that is required to overcome the difficulty in these cases.

When the hen begins to pluck the quills or feathers out of the young, and yet does not appear anxious to begin nesting again, little can be done to prevent her unless the young have reached a stage when their bodies are fairly well clothed with feathers, so that they are able to do without the hen sitting over them during the greater part of the day. If the plucking becomes really serious at such a stage in the development of the young, and one has ample opportunities for transferring the young to more careful parents, this is really the best and most practical course to pursue, carrying out the exchange as aforenamed, with the exception of giving no young of any kind to the offending hen.

One thing I may mention before going further. At the very commencement of plucking always examine the nest carefully to see if red mites are at the root of the mischief. If a wooden box is used, unhang it, and examine the back and the part of the cage against which hangs for colonies of red mites. If they are found to be the cause, the remedy is sufficiently obvious.

Dip in kerosene and linseed oil—half and half or scalded in hot water and then make a new nest in a clean box or pan, dust the bottom of the box freely with insect powder before putting in place; also dust a little around the sides after the nest is made, and place the young birds in the clean nest.

As soon as the exchange is made, burn the infested nest, and plunge the box or pan into boiling water for a minute or two. Above all, do not make the mistake of transferring the birds to the clean nest, and then allowing the infested nest to stand about in the room while some other task is being done, thus allowing a goodly number of its tenants to quit, and locate themselves elsewhere in the room. After giving a clean nest it will be advantageous to give the hen a few baths in which a little quassia extract has been dissolved.

Should the plucking commence when the feathers of the young are well through the quills so that they do not require the constant brooding of the hen, the nest box may be removed and placed in a nursery cage from which the perches have been removed during the greater part of the day. The nursery cage, which is simply a small open wire cage fitted with hooks for hanging it on the front of the breeding cage so that the old birds can just comfortably reach the young through the wires when they gape for food, but cannot easily reach them when they are lying snugly in the bottom of the nest.

Then a small piece of partly ravelled string may be tied to a wire of the breeding cage in some place a little away from the part occupied by the nursery; or a few short pieces of soft hay may be thrown inside for the hen to amuse herself with. This will often counteract the propensity to pluck the feathers out of the young.

Hens in a Hurry

When the youngsters are about three weeks old, keep a sharp eye on "Madam." If the cock has been assisting in the domestic duties she may think it time for another family, and may begin plucking the feathers of the young for nesting materials.

When this happens, either remove the young birds to another compartment, and the cock with them, running him in with the hen for a short time in the morning and evening or hang a nursery cage to the front of the breeding cage, so that the parents can feed the young ones through the wires without being able to get at them to pluck them. This is the time when the double-compartment breeding-cage with a partially wired slide comes in so useful.

After a few days in the nursery cage a dish of egg food may be put in and the youngsters will soon begin to pick over it and feed for themselves. A pinch of soaked rape seed and cracked hemp must be put on the top of the egg-food until the young are practically doing for themselves. Also mix a little green food with the egg for a few days.

It is not permissible to recommend any special brand of color food, but get the best; it is cheaper and usually gives better results than cheap or home-made mixtures. Your bird store sells fresh stock.

When the color-feeding is well advanced, any birds which show signs of becoming show specimens should be put aside, two in a cage, and a bit extra care bestowed on them in order to get them through quickly for the early shows, which generally commence in October. Here the early bird catches the judges' eye and comes home with the first prize ticket on its cage.

A bit of extra care is also required during the early days of the show season, and the spray bath must be used for a time or two, or the birds will soon get soiled in plumage. It is not advisable to resort to handwashing if it can be avoided, so cover up the cage at nights or while sweeping up the floor of the room. Also give them a bit of egg-food on returning from the shows, and a tonic in the drinking water. If any seem suffering from cold or exposure, keep them in the living-room over night.

Preparing for the Second Round

If the first round has proven satisfactory and the brood is going on all right, the next round can then be proceeded with, the same routine being followed right through. Before commencing operations, however, endeavor if possible to give the cage or cages a thorough cleaning; soak the perches in hot water with carbolic in it, scrub the sand tray, and give all the corners and crevices (if any) a good bath with kerosene, and then, if possible, leave the nest materials and give a new lot. Outside nests are better.

If the young are separated but not quite doing for themselves, let the cock bird attend to them during the day, running him into the hen's compartment in the evening. But if the young are well on the seed; leave them to themselves. The weather now being much warmer, a little more green food can be given, but if the hen has fed well on any particular food the first round let her have the same kind again.

When the early nests have gone on all right, it is possible to manage a third round, and get them reared by the end of July or early August, but it is not advisable to prolong the breeding season beyond that time as the parent birds are beginning to moult. The young birds frequently get neglected before being able to leave the nests, so very little may be gained by prolonging breeding beyond the July round.

I find it is always wise to give the old birds a little rest before the strain of the moult overtakes them, and a few days in the flight cages does them good. Hang on the bath, and give a tonic in the drinking water daily. Turn your double-breeders into flight cages by removing the partitions, and let the young birds have as much exercise as possible.

Do not overcrowd, and keep a look-out for any ailing ones or any which do not seem to be making progress. Cage these up away from the others, and give a bit of extra diet in the shape of egg food and soaked rape seed, and they will then have a chance of making progress more quickly than when kept in larger groups. Some birds are very shy, and others are somewhat domineering, and the weaklings get pushed aside, and do not get their fair share of food.

When the young have reached the age of ten days the edge of the nest will be very thick, and will require changing. Have your duplicate nest exactly like the old one, and ready to put in; lift the young into the new nest, and replace the nest as quickly as possible.

If the old nest has been kept fairly clean it should be left alone. I had the misfortune to have some hens refuse to go on to the new nests provided. The best plan, therefore, is to try the change and watch if the hen approves of the new nest; if so, well and good: if she objects, get the old one back again quickly.

Another plan when plucking occurs at a later stage, when the young are able to get on the side of the nest, or perhaps, have left the nest altogether, and the cock has been left with the hen during hatching and rearing, i' she does not appear bent on nesting again at once, and the cock is a good feeder, is to take the hen away and leave the cock to finish rearing the young. If the double breeding cages are used it is only necessary to shut off the hen by herself in one compartment until the young are old enough for the process to be reversed —i. e., to shut the young off by themselves and leave both parents together in the other compartment, when they may begin nesting again as soon as they feel so disposed, and will still go on feeding the young through the wired part of the partition.

In all ordinary circumstances when the cock has been removed at the commencement of incubation the best time to return him will be when the young begin to come out of the nest and pick at the egg-food. At this time they may quite safely be transferred to a nursery cage for the parents to complete the rearing should the cock adopt a spiteful attitude towards them on his return to the hen. If a saucer of egg-food is kept in the nursery cage the young at this stage will quickly learn to help themselves, and what assistance they will get from the parents will prevent them starving.

A Watchful Eye

But even when all goes along smoothly and none of the foregoing troubles arise, one still needs to keep a watchful eye over the birds and their surroundings, besides adhering to the routine work of supplying fresh food regularly, and at as frequent intervals as can be made to fit in with one's ordinary avocation, keeping the cages and all appliances scrupulously clean and free from everything in the shape of stale, sour, or decaying scraps of food, and seeing that insect pests made no headway.

This latter is an important item; and even though one should fail to discover a single mite in the cages, it is always the safest plan to make it a point to touch the corners of the cages inside, the joints of the doors, the ends of the perches, and the grooves in which the partition slides with a brush dipped in fir-tree oil or some other insecticide at each weekly cleaning. Occasionally the back of the nest box, if a wooden one, or the bottom if an earthenware pan, may be brushed over with the same liquid. The importance of persevering with these precautions will be obvious to all who have had the misfortune of witnessing the alarming increase of the red mite pest during warm weather once they put in an appearance and it is only strict attention to preventative methods as first indicated that will prevent their appearance.

Mites in Nest

The nest is often a breeding ground for mites, and as it is also apt to get soiled by the birds and present an unsightly appearance when the young are about a fortnight old it should be replaced by a new nest in a clean pan about this time, the soiled nest being burned at once, and the box or pan dealt with in the same manner as an insect-infested nest.

To Feed or Not to Feed

Some years ago I set aside fourteen birds to test; seven of these were to be non color-fed and the other seven to be color-fed. The housing conditions were exactly alike, the only difference being the addition of color to the egg and biscuit given. Out of the seven non-fed four "went west," and the remainder lingered in the moult over three months, while the color-fed birds all came through in perfect health and condition. However, it is not my intention of going further into the pros and cons, and the matter is entirely in the hands of the breeder. In breeding Rollers color feeding is not necessary and seldom practiced.

If color-feeding is decided upon, then the young birds may be put on to the feed at ten weeks old, before they begin to show any signs of new feathers. The egg and biscuit is prepared in the same manner as for rearing purposes, but a little color-food tasteless red pepper is added and thoroughly mixed with it.

Only a small portion should be added at the first, in order that the birds may get accustomed to it.

Some breeders remove the seed box entirely until the birds get thoroughly on the food; others take off the box during the day and put it back for an hour or two in the evening, but once they have taken to it there will be no need to remove the seed. With old birds it is best to put them on to color as soon as they have finished the breeding operations, in order that the coloring matter may be well in the system before they commence moulting.

Economizing Time and Material

I always mixed the egg and biscuit overnight and let it stand in the lever-top pickle jars before mentioned until next night, but I gave the contents a good shaking up before giving to the birds. This method I found much more effective than giving the food freshly made; the egg and biscuit had become thoroughly impregnated with the color, and a more even color in the birds was the result. Not only that, but less pepper was used, the method economized time and material, and gave more effect. A single egg (yolk and white), made enough for a couple of days' feed for about sixteen birds. I used to add a little moist sugar when mixing, and also sprinkle a little maw seed over the egg pan.

As a tonic for use in the drinkers, I put a few drops of syrup of buckhorn into an empty medicine bottle filled up with boiling water. Let it stand all night, shake up, and fill the drinkers in the morning. Towards the finish give some tincture of iron in the drinkers; this helps to fix the color.

Birds must not be exposed to a strong sun while they are being color-fed, and for this reason the cages are usually screened with a muslin curtain, but if the windows of the room are screened it is not necessary to screen the cages.

It is best to keep the birds on color for a few days after they are apparently through the moult, as there may be some old feathers still unfinished also keep a watchful eye and see there is no plucking going on, or you will have to resume the color-feeding until the new feathers are grown.

The head and neck feathers are generally the last to moult, and sometimes prove very troublesome and slow in getting finished. An occasional spraying with tepid water helps the finishing process. When all the birds are through the moult the owner will feel well repaid for all the extra trouble, and the extra cost will be more than met by the increased demand and money for any surplus stock that is to be sold.

To the non-feeder for color the moulting routine will be the same, by the mixing of the color-food, the natural color of the birds can be much improved by giving nasturtium flowers, marigolds, dandelion flowers, etc., also a little scraped boiled carrot in the egg-pan.

Don't Mix Egg With Water So It Is Soggy

I have seen egg-food mixed with water until it was soggy and sour, and then expect females to feed. They get sick themselves, and won't feed such food to their offspring.

Fresh air is absolutely essential, but draughts must be kept away at all cost, as no bird can last long if subjected to draughts.

Sand and grit are great factors in the lives of birds and a plentiful supply must be within reach of them at all times. There are several kinds of sands such as red, silver, and so on and for small cages these cannot be beaten, if used alternately. It would be quite expensive to cover the bottom of an aviary with this kind of sand, so if possible to procure a good Sea Shore Sand or even a River Sand, either of these will be found perfectly satisfactory, but it is advisable to wash the River Sand well to remove the very fine dust.

In buying drugs and medicines or even such things as Cayenne Pepper, Rock Candy and the like, be sure and get the pure products from a drug store and not the usual commercial qualities as sold at grocery stores.

Packet seeds should be used only when fresh and sold by pet shops, bird supply specialties and not grocery stores or drug stores shelving them. No doubt some of the people who sell these are perfectly reliable, but they never know how long the packets are going to stand on the store shelves and seeds dry out and become not only valueless as food, but are positively harmful as they cause acute indigestion, sore throat, and no end of other troubles.

MOULTING PERIOD

About the middle of July the birds will begin to show signs of dropping into moult, which is the very practical and efficient plan employed by Nature for disposing of the old, soiled, and worn plumage of birds and replacing it with new. In adult canaries this change should be thorough and complete at the end of each summer—that is, the whole of the plumage from beak to tail should be cast off and replaced by new. In young canaries, however, the process may be regarded as only partial, as the whole of the plumage is not changed naturally at the first moult. The tail, and the large quill feathers in the wings—also called the flights—are the parts that, in the natural course of events are not cast off until the second moult. All the smaller feathers are cast off and replaced by new ones.

I say the flights and tail are not shed in the natural course of events advisedly, because it was once the custom of the expert color feeder to forcibly pluck out these feathers during the time the birds are moulting. The object of this was that the new feathers might be acted upon by the color food, as it is only during the growth of the new feathers that the color can be materially affected by food. Tailing and flighting is a cruel and useless practice, and one that is not now tolerated.

The oncoming of the moult will be quickly distinguished by the effect upon the birds, even before any feathers are dropped. The disastrous and fatal effects which are seen on improperly managed and weakly stock have been already dealt with. Given healthy and robust birds, rationally treated, these baneful effects are very rarely experienced. With this class of birds there is probably a feeling of drowsiness and lassitude, but not of actual illness.

At first the bird may pick over its food without eating much for a day or two then it snatches a few minutes' rest on the perch at intervals during the day, rouses up, stretches its legs and wings, and appears quite itself again for a time; it settles down to roost earlier at night; then it begins picking about the bottom of its cage a good deal without any apparent object in doing so; next it will

be observed frequently inspecting its plumage with a critical eye, picking at a feather here and another there, and giving itself a good shake; finally a stray feather or two will be found in the cage—an unmistakable proof, not that the moult is about to begin, but that it has already commenced and is in progress.

By observing these symptoms from the onset the fancier soon learns to tell with great nicety when the moult will begin. Some of the symptoms detailed above, such as constant picking at the feathers, are very similar to the effects of parasites. Of course, the fancier can easily satisfy himself on this point, but in taking the symptoms altogether it will not be easy to mistake the moult for attacks of red mite; besides, unless the cages are in a shocking condition with this pest, the effects of the latter will not be so noticeable during the day as for an hour or two after the birds have settled down to roost in the evening.

But supposing the fancier is able to recognize the very first indication of approaching moult, it by no means follows that he must wait until these symptoms manifest themselves before the birds are drafted into them. It is sheer folly to place a bird to moult in a cage that is not spotlessly clean, otherwise the new plumage is soiled before it is fully grown.

An excellent tonic to give as a pick-me-up and to put a proper termination to the moulting process consists of half a drachm of ammoniated citrate of iron and quinine dissolved in an ounce of sherry and a teaspoonful of honey added. This combines sufficient aperient qualities to counteract the effect of the iron, so that it is not necessary to follow it with any other aperient. Fifteen to twenty drops in the drinking water is the dose.

Importance of Exercise

It is most advisable to allow the birds the benefit of extra space for exercise in the larger cages until they have commenced to cast off their feathers. Then all the most typical specimens, and such as appear likely to make birds fit for exhibition, should be drafted into the moulting cages in twos and threes. They will invariably be found to feed better in this way than when caged up separately, because the birds will take to the soft food far more freely when two or more are together than when alone.

At the same time, one must not go to the other extreme of putting too many in each cage, or quarreling and, perhaps, feather-plucking may arise. This feather-plucking is a danger for which the breeder must keep a sharp look-out all through the moult, and if it occurs the culprits must be discovered and immediately removed and caged alone, otherwise the plucked birds will probably come out of the moult very uneven and patchy in color, and have their show prospects seriously damaged.

A rapid moult is always better than a slow one, and a bird that casts its feathers "all at once," so to speak, will invariably get through its moult better and in finer condition than its fellows who are slowly dragging their way through for weeks after the former are ready to appear on the show bench if required. When the moult progresses very rapidly and the birds are in consequence very thinly clad, care must be taken to avoid cold draughts about the cages.

All the birds may be left in the large cages all through the moult, when they will doubtless derive much benefit from the extra exercise they will be able to obtain, although, as a rule, the moulting season will be rather more prolonged with these birds than with those in the moulting cages.

Fresh Air and Baths

You cannot at any time have too much fresh pure air, but always see that it is not accompanied by draughty cages. The simplest improvised screen of paper or curtains will often divert a current of air going direct into the stack of cages.

The bath also must be given with discretion during the middle of the moult, and not given on cold damp days. This precaution will go far to prevent birds growing imperfect feathers, particularly in the wings and tail, with narrow, dark, thread-like lines across the webs, and which, when held up to the light, are seen to be deficient in webbing where the lines exist. Such feathers are well known to every breeder and are believed to be due to the ravages of red mites. That this is an erroneous opinion is easily proved by the same thing occurring with birds kept under circumstances in which the presence of red mites is known to be quite out of the question. As a matter of fact, the lines are due to temporary stoppages in the growth of the feather, probably caused by a chill, such as a serious drop in the normal temperature, or to a cold bath, which temporarily checks the growth of the feathers.

Toning Down the Light

When the moult has progressed until some portion of the new plumage is expected to put in an appearance, very soon it will become necessary to shut out some of the light. This will be in from two to three weeks after the birds have begun to drop their feathers freely.

It is not by any means necessary to make the room or cages dark, as is sometimes imagined, and in the case of birds that are not being color-fed they may be allowed the benefit of the full natural light if the owner cares to sacrifice a certain amount of tone of color.

For the general stock it will suffice merely to subdue the light by keeping colored blinds—yellow, orange, or red for preference—hung before the windows. The use of Venetian blinds where available would be a good substitute. This will tone down the light all over the room.

But it will still be advisable to hang a curtain of some light material before the cages containing the most valuable birds. The cheapest kind of unbleached calico serves the purpose admirably, and is to be preferred to the plan of covering the cages with sheets of brown paper, which are apt to admit either too much or too little light into the cages. It will be a great convenience to have a curtain made to run on a tape and cover the whole stack of cages; suspend it about two or three inches away from the cage fronts. This method will admit sufficient light for the birds to find their way about the cages and to eat and drink; will allow free ventilation of the cages, and thus avoid stuffiness; and the cover may be instantly drawn across to one end, to leave the cages completely exposed for an hour or so morning and evening, while the birds are being fed and tended.

Further Hints

A few grains of linseed may be given to each bird twice a week from the time they are ready to go into the moulting cages, as it will help to add a nice lustre and finish to the new plumage.

When the moult is quite finished it is a good plan to go over the stock and select all those which have come out good enough to warrant their appearance on the show bench, and cage them separately in perfectly clean cages, covered with some light flimsy material to exclude dirt and dust. By this means the birds may make one, two, or even three appearances in public before going through the ordeal of washing, and will doubtless gain in other ways, as it is only the most accomplished performers that can hope to wash a bird without some loss of the natural tone and bloom of the feathers.

The Influence of the Moult

If, as occasionally happens, a breeder possesses a young cock who, in spite of being a sound, healthy bird, misses his first moult, he will discover that this bird, after a very short course of study, will outstrip all his companions, and bring out his tours like an adult. The conclusion is, therefore, obvious that the moult hinders development of the song. It is a question of duration, that is, whether the bird renews his feathers slowly or quickly, and it will be found that those which have made the most progress in the moult will show the greatest advancement in their song.

Age has nothing to do with it, for birds of the same age who vary in their stage of moult will vary accordingly in their song development, a fact which can be verified during any breeding season, for it will be found that older birds having a long moult are outstripped by quick moulting younger ones. With an even moult all round the older ones naturally are the best developed in body as well as song.

As it is mostly the custom to keep the birds in the freedom of the flight cages during the moult, and to cage them off only after completion, it follows that the song develops while they are already in the flights. So long as loud and distinct notes or passages are not distinguished above the twitterings of the beginner, the birds may be left quietly alone.

In a state of nature birds seldom suffer from sickness or disease, but in captivity they unfortunately are liable to suffer from many of the "popular" diseases "enjoyed" by mankind, and the same numerous quack remedies have had their turn with them.

Firstly, a bird has a good appetite, which is looked upon as a proof of strength and energy, but an appetite alone without proportionate digestive power would be worse than useless. The apparatus of digestion must be first rate. In birds, the gullet is large; in the seed eaters it opens out into a great expansion called the crop (a storehouse). Food is not digested here, but passed into the stomach proper, the first part of which is the proventriculus, the soft foods being digested here, such as flesh foods; corn and seeds pass on to the gizzard, the walls of which in seed eaters are very thick and strong. Grit is swallowed to assist in the work of crushing up the food before it can be properly digested.

The food then passes into the first part of the small intestine (the duodenum), where it is acted upon by the juices of digestion from the liver and pancreas. This completes the work of digestion; the blood is now able to take up the food, which is carried to all parts of the body. The force pump behind this function of conveyance is the heart, and on its journey much of the blood passes through the kidneys, which assist the lungs to expel the waste from the body.

In man, three organs divide between them this work—the skin, lungs, and kidneys; but in birds the skin is not an excretory organ, so the lungs and kidneys have the duty of getting rid of superfluous water.

The kidneys are a pair of three-lobed organs lying flat in the pelvis, of a dark red color. They are very active in excreating urea and uric acid, which in birds is in a solid form, seen by its whiteness in the excreta.

UNSATISFACTORY MOULTING

It often happens that some canaries fail to moult during the autumn, the time every normal and healthy bird should moult, and yet seem to be as healthy and active as ever. These birds are quite different from the birds that are what we term "stuck in the moult" due to being out of condition and become physical wrecks as a consequence, as breeders these birds are utterly worthless.

The first mentioned bird however, will be of the identical value as a stock bird just as though he had enjoyed a perfect moult as is natural for all birds to do yearly.

In the event you desire to use the bird for breeding purposes it should be watched at the beginning of the year and any signs of moulting should be encouraged, NEVER TRY TO STOP A MOULT; but undertake to hasten the moult as rapidly as possible. If they show no signs of moulting by the end of January, it is a good plan to change the temperature of its cage, if now in a heated room remove to an unheated room, and vice versa, but always avoid a sudden extreme change, be sure to avoid any and all draughty places. If a moult due to the change of temperature does not begin at the end of a week repeat the change, that is place the bird back in its former place. Very seldom the change of reasonable temperature fails to participate a moult and a spring moult is usually very rapid and little time will be lost in mating the birds desired, in the event of a failure to start the moult a hand wash in water a little above the usual temperature often will help to get them started.

The so called FRENCH MOULT or "false moult" occurs among birds that have already gone through the normal moult at the proper time, this is frequently caused by cold draughts or extremes of heat or cold, especially during damp, foggy weather, its effect on the early part of the breeding season is disastrous, in this case you must seek and find and remove the cause, after which you should put the bird on a rather liberal diet, adding rape seed to the amount fed to one third more rape, staple seed mixture, and add about 10 or 12 grains of good sound fresh ripe hemp seed every other day, on the alternate day add ten drops of the following mixture to each teaspoonful of the birds drinking water. Two ounces of sherry into which dissolve a dram of ammoniated citrate of iron and quinine, then add a teaspoonful of strained honey, stir until well mixed, or use bird bitters which is of the writers formula.

When the birds are in sound, robust health, it is not often that backwardness in condition for breeding is experienced. The real difficulty is to prevent them from getting too forward before the season is safe. Remember you should not, for good results take more than three nests from any mother. Three is the usual and best number. For show and special breeding I never take more than two nests in a season from any choice mother for preferred matings, two nests from young birds. If more than three nests are taken and this is often done, sometimes more than doubled the result is weaklings, non-feeding mother, short song singers and such like, and the mother is ruined for the next season and mates for all time. If a bird is too forward feed only canary seed for a week or so with green food such as watercress, plantain, and shepherd's-purse, do not feed dandelion which is not to be fed to forward birds, this is one of the best green foods. Dandelion flowers, washed roots and leaves are all excellent for canaries, unless they are in too forward a condition before you wish them to feel safe to start to raising their young, again I suggest in this case a crystal of sulphate of soda every other day for three times, this will help to keep them cool. The best of all is to keep the sexes out of sight and if possible out of hearing of each other when too forward, do not permit the bird to over breed itself or suffer because you have over fed it and caused its forward condition, this is pure criminal.

When your birds fail to come into condition to breed with the approach of spring it is due to some mistake or neglect of the person responsible for its care, do not blame the bird, unless it is not in normal health. The first thing to give them is a mild saline aperient for two days, and then a tonic of equal parts of tincture of gentian and calumba and dilute sulfuric acid five drops, (no more) should be given in each tablespoonful of drinking water every other day until 6 doses have been given, the same time begin a more generous diet of richer foods.

Canaries in their native state do not eat all seed diet. Upon dissecting 914 canaries in the wild, one spring 31 percent of the crops showed vegetable contents, thus you must realize to feed more green stuff from your back yard or the vacant lot, gravel-grit must be supplied daily, or at all times on the bottom of the cage, cuttlefish bone is necessary.

You do not want ham and eggs for every meal, every day, nor does your bird like the same diet at all times, however, canary and rape seed is and should be its main staple diet, or its bread and butter, bread and meat. To over feed is as bad as any neglect in so far as song and breeding usefulness is concerned. Many of the treats, novelties and toys are mere waste and extravagance and works to the detriment of birds often. You can easily tell if your bird is too fat by catching it, holding it gently in your hand and turning its stomach up and blow your breath on its stomach which will remove the feathers and expose the skin, if yellow like butter it is too fat, if red or black consult the question and answer columns of this book in the back and find the condition that suits your bird and you will have the cure, if any.

Two leaves of nice crisp dandelion should be given to backward birds every day, I like to feed the washed roots for a change. If the bird will eat a meal worm occasionally it will be good for it, I have chopped up the meal worms and mixed it up finely with egg-food.

At present you can buy good, satisfactory egg or vitamin foods from different firms. In the wild state the birds enjoy the sun as they like it and thereby get the necessary vitamin D, this is now best supplied in Cod Liver Oil foods, or sundried white bread steeped in warm milk (milk-sop).

Banana, sweet apple, celery tops and lettuce are good treats for the winter when green food is not available. Playthings are not the best, as they keep the birds from singing while so occupied.

Some people believe that bird tonics or bird bitters are desirable for all bird ailments, but this is wrong. Different formulas are required for the different maladies and are available at first class pet shops.

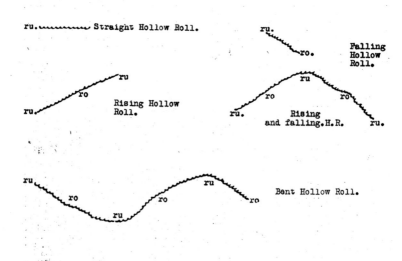

LINE BREEDING

By Judge Arthur G. Griffiths

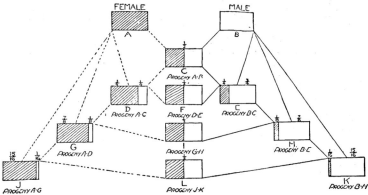

We are repeating above, a chart arranged by Judge Griffiths.

In this chart, Mr. Griffiths, with unusual clarity, sets out what can be accomplished when blood purity, if consistently maintained, and a definite object is sought. Starting with the foundation flock (A and B) the diagram could logically be extended to 25 or even 50 generations and then, by properly mated hens, come directly back to the original proportion contributed by the original matings. It, of course, is most essential that progeny be banded and accurate records kept year after year.

Line-breeding is a science which, up to the present, has been adopted by a surprisingly small proportion of Roller Canary breeders. In the science of breeding, desirable qualities can only be prescribed from one generation to another by a careful system of selection of the breeders that have in them the strongest developed and by the careful breeding of these specimens.

In the case of the Roller Canary breeder the most dominant factor is that of song. Outside of vigor, all other factors are subordinated or overlooked in the effort to produce a bird with a deep, mellow voice. Personally I am of the opinion that the time has arrived when the items of vigor, type, size and color should be included in the score card. In pure line-bred strains these factors can be easily established and controlled, without in the least degree depreciating that of song.

The object of line breeding is to fully establish the prepotency of the offsprings so that line bred specimens are more qualified to reproduce their dominant traits. Line breeding increases existing traits regardless of whether they are desirable or undesirable. Therefore it is most important to begin a strain with the best specimens your pocket will allow.

The special aim in line breeding essentially is not only to hold any superior quantity but by judicious mating of related birds to improve the good and eliminate the bad qualities. Line breeding means breeding in line, or, using the same blood lines for generation after generation without the introduction of new blood which at once discredits your stock and confuses your aim.

Introduction of new blood causes a disturbance of the line, creating variations, usually of a reversionary character.

Line breeding as a science includes only mating related stock and handling the blood lines to the end and extent that it will not reach a state of intensive inbreeding and its resultant bad consequences.

A breeder who undertakes to breed in line must be prepared to keep accurate records of his breeders, year after year, recording the parents so that mating of your stock can be followed on intelligently and the results you are striving for can be gauged accurately.

The foregoing advice is equally applicable either to those who wish to breed for pleasure or for profit, only with this difference—those who can afford to put more cash down at once, and only breed for their own hobby, should get their stock birds from a breeder or dealer who has the best, so as to start from a good foundation and save two or three seasons of experimental breeding. High class Rollers can only be obtained from high class stock, and when obtained they require every care and lots of attention if you wish to keep them right, and that is why I say I don't keep anything but Rollers in the room. To the breeders of other varieties, where song qualities are not a consideration, it is a matter of no moment how many different kinds of song there may be; the chief concern is in the matter of show points.

It is not my intention to go into details of training the young birds now, but in passing I must state that this is a matter of great care if you are desirous of maintaining purity of song. Special song cages are used, and the birds trained to sing in day or night.

I have attended many a singing contest at the big International shows, and I was agree-ably struck with the purity and variety of tone of some of the winners, but I did not envy the judge his task in alloting the various points. He needs the ear of an accomplished musician, the wisdom of a Solomon, and the patience of a Job, a combination rarely to be found ex-cepting in a successful judge of Roller Canaries.

Another Line Breeding Chart

The breeding charts below are presented to better illustrate the subject of line breeding, which is very important in the art of breeding Roller Canaries for song. This chart has been in use for the production of song and the creating of different strains among the Roller birds for years. Very little of it is practiced, however, because of its not being generally known of. It would be impos-sible to create a new strain of song without its use in one way or another, and it should be the constant aim of every breeder to estab-lish a special strain of song in his own birds.

The dark portion of each circle represents the male's blood in each mating of his family during four years of time, providing he lives that long. The white portion of each circle represents the mother's blood during the same length of time. It will be necessary to start with our birds one year old if possible in order to reach the highest percentage of each side's blood in our family before they become too old for satisfactory breeding.

Follow our breeding chart, we mate our Adam and Eve of our new family which we are about to consider. The result is repre-sented by circle No. 3, which means that all birds raised the first year have 50 per cent of Adam's blood and 50 per cent of Eve's blood. From the birds in No. 3 we pick out the best singer in the lot and mate him back to his mother, No. 2. On the father's side we can mate one or more of his hens from No. 3 back to him in the third year, which will produce birds illustrated in circle No. 4, with 75 per cent the father's blood and 25 per cent the mother's blood. In this No. 4 we get singers bringing their song much more like the father's song probably some just as good. The mother mated to her son, in circle No. 3, brings birds represented in circle No. 5, with 75 per cent the mother's blood and 25 per cent the father's blood, which brings birds singing more like the mother strain of song. If there is any difference between the strain of the father and mother it will be noticed now. All birds raised in circle No. 3 can be dropped from our family. We will, the fourth year, mate the best singer in circle No. 5 back to his mother, No. 2, and will get birds represented by circle No. 8, with seven-eighths the mother's blood and one-eighth the father's blood. Also in this same year we can mate a singer from circle No. 4 back to his grandmother, No. 2, and get

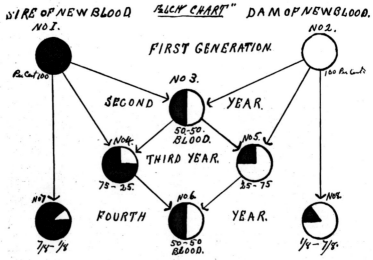

birds with 62 per cent the grandmother's blood and 38 per cent the father's blood in No. 1.

On the father's side mate some of his hens in circle No. 4 back to him in the fourth year and get birds represented in circle No. 7, with seven-eighths his blood and one-eighth their mother's blood. Also mate one or so of his granddaughters in circle No. 5 back to him and get birds with 62 per cent his blood and 38 per cent of Eve's blood in our family.

In this fourth year mating we have a chance to get back to 50-50 blood again by mating singers from circle No. 4 with hens from circle No. 5, which is represented by circle No. 6. This time our 50-50 mixture of blood is very much better than the 50-50 blood in circle No. 3, because the blood is becoming more concentrated or evenly mixed, and in this No. 6 group of birds we may find new notes coming out. Anyway, they will be better singers than in circle No. 3. In all the four years of line breeding we make no thought of plumage. Our aim is to select the very strongest birds we have each year and those that bring the best tone of voice and changes. In the fifth year it is possible to mate singers from circle No. 7 with hens from circle No. 8 and bring birds in the fifth year with 50-50 blood again, which still concentrates the blood more thoroughly and brings new notes in our birds and better song.

We can go on for several years longer, working the same blood backwards and forwards in our family, which would very likely bring out some improvements in our bird's song, but not in size and plumage. So, for the bad results which might creep into our family, it is not advisable to continue further with our Adam and Eve in our chart, but the blood in our younger generations can be still experimented with. Once in three years or so a bird with new blood can be brought in and worked out in the same way.

I have explained this line breeding to show fanciers how foolish it is to buy new blood every year and always keep mating their birds away from the results in song which they wish so much to gain. Every time you mate a bird you change the blood in the youngsters, and after a few years there will very likely be seven or eight different bloods in your birds which bring very poor song.

It will be noticed by the chart that birds of the first pairing in the second year only carry one-half the parent's blood, and then by mating the young in the third year to still another mate of another blood which is outside our family, the young will only carry 25 per cent of the original parents' blood, and still another cross with the young in the fourth year would reduce the blood beyond any value as far as song is considered in the birds.

In-breeding is the foundation of the song, but requires much forethought and study by those most skilled in the work in order to produce the best results. Such work in the hands of those who do not know the different tours might turn out very unsatisfactory. However, anyone with good common sense can raise good birds by securing their breeding stock from a reliable breeder who has established a good

strain and then continue to breed with these birds through their natural life of usefulness.

It is not good practice to mate two all-yellow birds. In the young from each mating of this kind the heads of the birds grow smaller each year, also the feathers grow shorter and thinner, and if carried on for several years they become very brittle, which causes them to be broken off long before it is time to shed them. It is much better to mate the dark birds with the yellow or buff colored, or dark and mottled birds together.

The object of line breeding is to fully establish the prepotency of the offspring so that line bred specimens are more qualified to reproduce their dominant traits. Line breeding increases existing traits regardless of whether they are desirable or undesirable. Therefore it is most important to begin a strain with the best specimens your pocket will allow.

The special aim in line breeding essentially is not only to hold any superior quantity but by judicious mating of related birds to improve the good and eliminate the bad qualities. Line breeding means breeding in line, or, using the same blood lines for generation after generation without the introduction of new blood which at once discredits your stock and confuses your aim. Introduction of new blood causes a disturbance of the line, creating variations, usually of a reversionary character.

Line breeding as a science includes only mating related stock and handling the blood lines to the end and extent that it will not reach a state of intensive inbreeding and its resultant bad consequences.

A breeder who undertakes to breed in line must be prepared to keep accurate records of his breeders, year after year, recording the parents so that mating of your stock can be followed on intelligently and the results you are striving for can be gauged accurately.

LINE BREEDING NOT IN-BREEDING

While line breeding materially assists in making "like produce like," there is ever a chance of a reversionary variation, that is, the tendency to "throw back," usually to a poorer specimen. At the same time progress is dependent on variation, for, whenever a better bird is produced in the progeny, you breed to such birds, and thus on improved variations rests the success of your venture.

Due to the fact that he has been bred in line the "blood" specimen is pure to his quality of song and thus as a line breeder you have every chance of holding the quality and making the good points dominant in the next generation.

On the other hand when out-breeding or breeding with unrelated stock, the good points perpetuated in your "blood" specimens may be entirely lost on his confused progeny. For this reason it is most desirable that the introduction of new blood be avoided by the successful line breeder, as new, unrelated blood means wholesale variation and gets the problem entirely out of control with the breeder only guessing and hoping.

While there is a fixed line of demarcation between line and in-breeding the experienced and consequently the more daring breeders sometimes take liberties by adopting close inbreeding, such as mating brother and sister, but such practice has only a minor place in the general scheme of line breeding, and the novice and inexperienced should avoid any such undertakings.

Line breeding is a most interesting subject, and it is also the only sure way to attain permanent success, combined with the pleasure every one experiences in producing something better than the other fellow. It is not to be undertaken lightly but must become a permanent fixture in your efforts if you are to achieve success in it. You may not at first be sure just what success you have had with it, but there is one sure way to tell when you really desire to know. Enter your favorites at some good show that is being judged by a judge of the right sort, and you will soon find out where you have landed with your efforts. To the real fancier the privilege of seeing his songsters win in a strong class is truly the thrill of a life time. It is a concrete reward for persistently following out definite and established practices in line breeding your birds to higher standards than did your neighbor.

Linebreeding, strictly speaking, means the mating of brother to sister or parent to offspring, but many of our best authorities now regard inbreeding as the mating of two animals which have at least fifty per cent of like ancestry. This does not necessarily mean descent from the same animal however. These same authorities define line breeding as the mating of individuals with not less than twenty-five per cent and not over fifty per cent of similar ancestry, but with a succession of sires that trace to the same individual. The principle involved in both inbreeding and line breeding is the same and the difference that of degree only.

There have been few subjects connected with breeding that has caused such acrid discussion as inbreeding. Much has been said in its favor, much against its use. There have been many laboratory experiments conducted to prove the harm or the harmlessness of it. (The use of the word "blood" in this connection is somewhat misleading and has reference to hereditary material itself).

Undoubtedly there are many examples of linebreeding that could be pointed to among birds, by those who are familiar with the history of the various breeds. The great objective of inbreeding is the fixation of hereditary qualities. This is of great value in emphasizing those qualities which are desirable, but it must be borne in mind that the undesirable ones are just as easily and firmly fixed. It should be quite easy to understand just why this is so, when we recall that by inbreeding we are simply bringing together individuals whose hereditary material is more uniform, and whose characters are more nearly alike, than we do when we mate those not related. In consanguineous breeding, the mated stock, having the same ancestry, would and do have many of the family characteristics in common. These characteristics, shared in common by both parents, are also transmitted by both parents to their offspring, hence, in this way, become intensified and strengthened by the augmenting power of the two similar hereditary forces.

It should always be remembered that linebreeding has no creative power, and by its use we only intensify existing characters, both good and bad. In other words, it is of benefit to the breeder in that it enables us to accumulate the hereditary material of a superior animal in the founding of a family of his breed. The greater per cent of this material assembled in his descendants, the more the offspring will resemble their sire and the more they will resemble each other, and the more likely they will be to further transmit this material to their offspring. In this way the characters with each succeeding generation become more firmly fixed.

In practically every breed of animals or fowl, inbreeding has been resorted to, by the earlier breeders at least, to assure that fixity of type which entitles a class of them to be called a breed, and, where males or females of equal quality to the type of the families within that breed. It should be clearly understood, however, that one reason earlier breeders resorted to its use was their inability to secure elsewhere males or females of equal quality to those in their own stud, and that inbreeding was followed, perhaps largely, because they did not wish to introduce into their stud hereditary qualities that were inferior to those in their own.

It would be very difficult indeed, to overestimate the very great benefit breeders of various kinds of livestock, poultry and pet stock have derived from very close breeding, and those familiar with the history of various breeds of all breeds of birds, pigeons, poultry and animals can name many specimens whose outstanding quality or prepotency was without doubt due to it.

The more closely an individual is inbred, the more nearly his hereditary characteristics or units become homozygous, which results in specimens whose reproductive cells, so far as hereditary characters go, are of one kind, as the tendency is for the heterozygous to be automatically displaced by the homozygous. The closer the degree of linebreeding, the stronger is this tendency. Inbreeding by this very tendency to secure homozygous characters, often brings to the surface latent or recessive characters.

It is quite generally believed by all breeders, and rightly so, that sires whose ancestry are of the same line of breeding, who are therefore somewhat closely related, are much more prepotent than when the parents are of dissimilar ancestry.

There are four forms of inbreeding possible among animals and fowl if we accept the description of the terms as given previously.

1.   The mating of a sire to his best daughter or daughters. This is used when the sire is such an exceptional individual that it is desired to secure as great a per cent of his blood as possible and, if followed up even for a few generations only, will result in animals of but

one line of ancestry,—that of the sire. The offspring, even from the first mating, contains three-fourths of the blood lines of the sire, that of the second mating containing eighty-seven and one-half per cent. It is a well known fact, however, that a sire can be bred successively to his daughter, grand-daughter, and great grand-daughter without his type becoming fixed unless it is fixed in himself.

2. The mating of a female to her best son, thereby increasing the bloodlines of the dam. This is used when the female possesses exceptional merit, and it is desirable to preserve and condense her bloodlines.

3. The mating of brother to sister, in which the bloodlines of the sire and dam are present in equal proportion. This should be used only when the previous mating has been unusually successful, the offspring being superior in quality to both sire and dam and it is desirable to preserve the high quality of the two mated.

First of all I will say that you should never consider the mating of related birds, until you have gone fully into the subject, and only when you have a good reason to consider such a step. I can tell you that in many of the larger studs, excellent results are being obtained by the system known as LINE-BREEDING. A study of a chart in this book will help considerably to simplify matters, and give you a clearer conception of the subject. In following the system of Line-Breeding, we will suppose that your stud consists of just one pair only. Now the first and by far the most important point is to be quite sure in the following information: Both birds, male and female, most be of the same strain. They must be large, strong, healthy stock. The male should have excellent variety. Good tone and a pleasing delivery. He should be in every sense a Tutor and a first class specimen of his strain. The hen MUST BE OF THE SAME STRAIN, but you must make quite positive that there is NO RELATIONSHIP WHATEVER between the male and female, for if there should be any relationship, then the results of the work will most likely prove a failure, and the degree of the failure will depend upon just how close the relationship is. Now in the first season the selected pair are mated together. The young birds should be kept quite apart from any other stock, and the young males trained by their Father. At the end of the season, and when the young males have fully developed in song, you will select from the young stock the two best young singers, and the two biggest and best looking hens. The balance of the young stock can be bred into other lines or sold as the Fancier may decide.

Now in the second season, you will mate the best YOUNG SINGER back to the old hen (His Mother) and on the reverse side you will mate the OLD MALE in turn to the two young hens (Their Father). If we consider the blood of the old male as being black, and the blood of the old hen as being white, you will be able to see that in the progeny from them we will have birds which are bred from

a 100 per cent of black and white blood and these can be spoken of as being 50 per cent black and 50 per cent white blood, or in other words a blend of equal parts of original male and female blood.

Now let us consider just what is done when we mate the young singer to the old hen (His Mother). We are mating a balanced blend of black and white blood to a bird which is 100 per cent white blood, and in mating the young hens back to the old male, we do exactly the same, but in the reverse direction, namely pairing young hens which are a balanced blend of 50 per cent each of black and white blood to a bird which is 100 per cent black blood. Now what do we get in the progeny from these matings? From the young singer and the old hen, we get young birds which are mathematically 75 per cent white blood and 25 per cent black blood. From the reverse mating, the young hens paired to the old male produce progeny exactly the reverse, i. e. 75 per cent black blood and 25 per cent white blood and the following of this will bring us to the end of the second breeding season. In the first season we had only one mating to take care of, and in the second season we had two, so in the third season we are now able to add another mating as follows: The old male (100 per cent black blood) is mated to two young hens produced in the second season and which carry 75 per cent black blood and 25 per cent white or female blood. The old hen (100 per cent white blood) is mated to a young singer carrying 75 per cent white or female blood and 25 per cent black or male blood. The progeny from these two matings will produce young birds which in the first case carry seven-eighths black or male blood, and only one-eighth white or female blood, while on the reverse side we get young birds carrying seven-eighths white or female blood, and only one-eighth black or male blood. Now the third mating in this season is important for it consists of mating Brother and Sister together, but in a totally different way than would be the case if the matings had been undertaken in the second season. This mating consists of pairing a young male 75 per cent black or male blood and 25 per cent white or female blood to a young hen bred in the exact reverse way, i. e. 75 per cent white or female blood and 25 per cent black or male blood. It can be readily seen that in doing so, we do not produce a new line of breeding, for we really bring the percentage of the two bloods back to the 50 per cent and 50 per cent basis as secured in the young birds bred from the old pair in this first season's breeding. We have young birds which are carrying only 87½ per cent of the original female blood. Another line of breeding is the exact reverse, 87½ per cent white or female blood and only 12½ per cent black or male blood. Then we have another line of breeding, which is a 50 per cent blend of the two bloods. We have arrived at the stage where the quality on either side will show itself, or if a 50 per cent blend of the two bloods is going to give us the best song results, the males will be found in the third of center line of breeding as mentioned.

BIRD DISEASES
REMEDIES

What is Disease?

To turn to that part of our subject concerning bird diseases: Disease is a physiological process whereby certain organs have their functions increased, diminished, or accompanied by pain.

In dealing with bird ailments nothing is of greater importance than prompt action—an early application of suitable remedies, in conjunction with the immediate institution of strictly hygienic conditions, where these have not been above suspicion, and the removal of any exciting causes of the disorder which may be found to exist. By this means many a bird will be saved which would inevitably succumb after a few hours' neglect, not to speak of the many that will be relieved of minor troubles which might rapidly develop into serious and chronic illness, with the added risk of spreading infection and contagion broadcast among the stock.

Concerning the isolation of all ailing birds from the rest of the stock, and the quarantine of all freshly-acquired birds, whether healthy or otherwise, the strict observance of these two points would of a certainty prevent a great amount of trouble. When a bird falls ill, it is folly to wait a few days to see how the matter "goes on" before taking steps to isolate it, because during every hour of those few days it may be disseminating disease germs, cultivated probably to a degree of virulence which limits the chances of other birds in near proximity being able to resist attack. In the case of fresh birds being acquired, it matters little that they appear in the best of health and condition, for disease may be active in the system, though it may be many days before it manifests itself in the condition of the bird. Thus if it has been housed among one's healthy stock for several days before it falls perceptibly ill, a vast amount of mischief may already have been done. The moral is obvious: Isolate every bird whose previous surroundings you are not perfectly familiar with, and keep it in strict quarantine at least a fortnight.

As regards all birds, isolate them as soon as they show signs of illness. Do not simply put them in another cage in a corner of the bird room. This is merely "playing at isolation." Keep a cage, or flight, specially set apart away from the bird room as a kind of hospital. A snug corner, well ventilated, but quite free from cold draughts, and moderately warm, is the ideal place. With few exceptions a little extra warmth, save, perhaps in the height of summer, will in itself prove an excellent curative of many of the minor ills bird flesh is heir to. An ailing bird desires nothing better than to "nurse its woes" alone, and the repose of isolation is another important factor in helping it to recover. Keep the bird, or birds, as quiet as possible.

Observe the strictest cleanliness in cages and all food and water vessels, and clean the perches well daily. As a preparatory step towards further treatment, give a mild aperient in water for a few hours and keep the bird under close observation, carefully noting its symptoms when it is at rest. Note in particular if there is any panting or labored breathing, or wheeziness, and the condition of the bowels—the latter point is best ascertained by noting the condition of the droppings and whether the bowels act freely or with difficulty, or frequently or seldom. It is an excellent plan to make a visit at this period to the bird at night, a few hours after it has settled down to roost, and without disturbing it unnecessarily take note of its condition and any symptoms it shows at this time. Such a visit will sometimes be quite a revelation, and provide evidence of symptoms which may have been quite absent during the daytime. Without some knowledge on these points it is by no means easy for the amateur to differentiate between other external symptoms, because when a bird is ill from any cause whatever it usually is puffed out like a loose ball of feathers, which means very little beyond the fact that the bird is feeling out of sorts from some cause or other.

It is generally a safe rule to commence with an aperient in every case, even when the most pronounced symptom is undue looseness of the bowels. It may be that the looseness is due to some irritation of the digestive organs and intestines by something which needs removing before any permanent improvement will take place. Nothing is better for this than five drops of syrup of buckthorn in each tablespoonful of water; practically all birds will take it with the greatest freedom. If a bird shows great thirst, especially if there already exists looseness of bowels, this aperient mixture must not be allowed to remain on so long—two hours may suffice in such cases, the actual length of time depending upon the quantity of water consumed.

It will be noted that it is almost invariably recommended to give all medicines as additions to the usual water or food supply. If only the most ordinary care is used this method is by far the best that can be adopted. Giving medicine direct into the beak is not only unreliable, but in many cases positively dangerous, and particularly so when a powerful drug to which the bird may be very susceptible is one of the ingredients. On account of the difficulty of always gauging the precise quantity of the mixture which the bird will swallow, medicines containing a poisonous drug should never be given into the beak direct unless it be known positively that the particular poison has no specially destructive effect upon bird life. Comparatively few fanciers possess the knack of giving a bird medicine by the beak with certainty. It is granted that anyone may force, or cajole, one or two drops of fluid into a bird's beak, and perhaps insure some part of it disappearing in the direction desired, but the ability the bird will display in frustrating one's object in this direction is worthy of a better cause. But the most serious objection to giving medicine direct in the beak is the disturbance and nervous excitement to which the little patient has to be subjected. This in itself is very harmful, and in a great proportion of cases may do far more harm than the medicine is likely to do good.

We are well aware that the method of adding drugs to the drinking water has been criticized as slipshod and unscientific, but the judgment was doubtless given without due consideration of the fact that we have the advantage of being able to know precisely the quantity of water in a bird's drinker, and, within very narrow limits, the quantity that will be consumed in a day, and that it is only a matter of simple calculation to tell with great exactitude the quantity of any medicine to add, in order to insure the bird consuming a given quantity each day.

One word of caution must not be omitted here. When giving any drugs in the water, particularly those which are strong-smelling or unpalatable, or to which the patient shows an objection, never give them in greater strength than is advised, otherwise the bird will not drink more than it is absolutely compelled to do in order to assuage the pangs of intense thirst, and in some cases it will refrain from drinking altogether, with but one unfortunate result, if its abstention is not discovered in time to avert a calamity. In practically all such cases only a very small proportion of the usual quantity of water will be consumed in comparison with the quantity which would be taken if a weaker solution had been employed. Thus it will be seen that by giving objectionable drugs in very dilute solution a much greater quantity will be consumed than if a stronger solution be offered, which, instead of conferring more benefit than the weaker solution, would merely defeat the object which it was meant to achieve.

In the matter of diet, care must be exercised at this early stage. Until one feels more certain of the nature of the ailment, and has decided on a course of treatment, a quite plain but nourishing diet, easily assimilated, should be given. The greatest care should be taken to ensure the food supply being perfectly sound, sweet, and fresh. Do not omit to examine well every item, to try to discover cause for the illness. Stale, rancid and decaying items of food of any description may generally be looked upon with grave suspicion, as also mould-infested, musty, or weevily and mite-infested seed, etc., whilst the soundest and best of food may be rendered unsafe, or even dangerous, if exposed to visits by mice and similar vermin.

The water supply should be kept quite above suspicion, and the vessels emptied and well rinsed at least once each day. To merely empty away the stale water and fill vessels with fresh is very little better than the dirty habit of adding a little fresh water to the stale that is left in the drinkers. Both practices are thoroughly bad and extremely dangerous to the health of the birds during the summertime, when the weather is warm and sultry. The danger to health is present more or less all the year round, but during hot summer weather the risk of such a water supply setting up an infectious fever is enormously increased. If there is the least doubt about the purity of the water supply, boil it before it is used. This is always a wise precaution in the case of sick birds.

When medicine is added to the water the proper course would be to use only distilled water, which can be bought of any chemist or ice factory or Auto Battery charging plant for a nickle a quart. Ordinary water, even when filtered, especially if it is of a hard nature and contains the salts of lime in solution, may, and often does, quite alter the character of certain drugs when they are added to it, so that in such circumstances much of the desired effect of the medicines may be lost. Filtered water, that has been well boiled and allowed to stand until cold again, is the best substitute the average fancier can employ for the distilled water, and this, fortunately, is easily obtainable in practically every household.

Drugs that are insoluble in water, or have no affinity with it, are of little use given in this way unless an emulsifying or solvent agent can be employed with them. But this is not always possible, and, where convenient, such drugs should be given in some kind of food, or solid or semi-fluid, item of the dietary.

Green vegetable foods, fruits and roots, such as carrot, also need careful surveillance. Of green foods, only those should be used that are clean, tender, crisp, and fresh, and grown on clean ground under wholesome conditions. As a rule quite young growths are not only wholesome but the best for use. It should never be given saturated with moisture, and it is best to gather it in dry, clean weather if possible. If gathered from places to which many other animals have access, however, it is a wise custom to wash it well before use and shake it as dry as possible before giving it to the birds. Watercress, in particular, should only be used when grown under hygienic conditions. All decaying and unhealthy portions, or those which have been nipped by frost, must be scrupulously avoided. Of course, all such foods are dangerous whilst frost is on them. As a rule it will be wise, when looseness is a pronounced symptom, to withhold all green food for the time being.

A supply of suitable sized, clean, gritty sand should be accessible in the "hospital cages." Supply this in a small vessel hung on the cross bar and use clean pine sawdust on the cage floors. The absorbent nature of this is a great help in preserving a clean and sanitary condition in the cages, and if it is frequently removed and burnt it will assist greatly to prevent the spread of any contagion. One point concerning grit must not be overlooked. In the case of many newly-acquired foreign birds, or imported canaries, which have often been deprived of grit for some time, note whether they have gorged themselves with grit by swallowing it too liberally when first regaining access to it. If this has happened, or is suspected, grit of course, must be withheld until the birds have returned to a normal condition. This may always be prevented by giving grit cautiously for a week or two to all birds likely to have been deprived of it for some time.

Lastly, a few words on the subject of fresh, pure air. Remember that a bird will very readily fall sick in a stuffy, vitiated atmosphere; also that it will not readily recover, even with the most skillful treatment, if kept under such conditions. Although it is of the greatest importance to protect ailing birds from cold and cutting draughts, it does not follow that this should be accomplished by shutting them up in a close, ill-ventilated place. Abundance of fresh, pure air should be always assured. Never hang the birds near to burning lights, or above them, nor high up near the ceiling, in all of which situations the worst air in any given room will doubtless exist.

Treatments

In giving a brief summary of the common ailments most likely to be met with among cage birds, we do not propose making any pretence of laying down a set code of symptoms in detail for each particular ailment, for the reason already named in the previous section; that such an attempt would assuredly defeat the end in view, and serve only to confuse and baffle the ordinary fancier, to whom one set of symptoms, with, perhaps, a few prominent exceptions, would appear very much of a sameness with any other. Therefore, where symptoms are given they will be those which are most pronounced and characteristic, and not necessarily the only symptoms that may be present, or appear from time to time, in the ailment in question.

Before going further we would particularly draw attention to a point of some importance in the medical treatment of cage birds. Never use any kind of metal drinker when giving a bird drugs of any description in the water, nor for the reception of soft food in which any drug is mixed. At ordinary times zinc drinkers, or enameled vessels, are perfectly harmless, even if the latter are slightly chipped, and they have the great advantage of being easily cleaned and sterilized. But when a drug is added to the water it will often set up chemical action with the metal and be converted into quite a different agent, which may not only be useless for the bird's ailment, but actually harmful, or even poisonous. A perfectly enameled vessel would serve the same purpose as one of china or glass, but if the enamel is chipped off and only a tiny portion of the underlying metal exposed, it is quite

as dangerous as a naked metal one. It is imperative, therefore, that none but china or glass vessels be used when administering drugs of any description.

Asthma — So-called asthma, which more frequently resolves itself into bronchitis, is one of the most common troubles of small cage birds. True asthma is less common, but none the less serious, and all forms are more or less due to the same predisposing causes, which must be removed before any hope of recovery can be entertained. Impure, stagnant air, alternately very cold and hot situations, exposure to cold draughts, or a dusty atmosphere, irritant gases or vapors, and fumes from burning lights, and overcrowding in small, badly-ventilated rooms, may be looked upon as the chief causes. In asthma there is a spasmodic action of the breath at intervals, generally more noticeable at night. The bird gasps, and evidently finds breathing a very laborious and hampered process. At other times, and in some conditions of weather, the symptoms almost disappear, and may quite do so in the early stages of the complaint, but soon present themselves again if the bird is fluttered about the cage a little.

In bad cases, treatment is more palliative than curative, and such birds should never be bred with. Remove the causes, give a mild aperient every second day for a week, and give a plain and easily assimilated diet. If the bird is not in an over-fed condition a morsel of bread and milk, on which is dropped two drops of a mixture of equal parts cod-liver oil emulsion and syrup of iodide of iron, every second day for a week or two, should prove very beneficial. As regards the general diet, it is best to find out by observation what foods aggravate the condition and omit them in future from the dietary. Ten drops of coal-tar solution—Liq. picis carbonis, B. P.— in the water for a time will do good in many cases. Or try five drops each of paregoric, syrup of squills, glycerine, and tinct. lobel. aether, in the water every second day for a week at a time, omitting it in the alternating weeks. Should this fail, get any chemist to dispense a small quantity of a mixture of two drachms each of glycerine and oxymel of squills, one drachm each of ipecacuanha wine and chlorodyne, and eight grains of iodide of potassium. Give 15 drops of this in the water as often as seems advisable. Stop it for a time if bird appears to get unusually drowsy.

Baldness.—Loss of feathers is due to so many causes that each case can only be dealt with on its merits. It is often due to cold, and recovery takes place during the summer months, or at any other time if the bird is placed in a warmer temperature. At other times it is due to insect pests, when the remedy is to treat as advised under heading **Lice or Red Mites**, as the case may be. If due to apparent skin trouble, the general health of the bird should be attended to, and the bare places smeared now and again with sulphur ointment. Most other cases that are curable will yield to keeping the bird in a moderate temperature, allowing it to bathe freely, and adding a slight dusting of flower of sulphur to a little soft food three times a week for a month, and on the intervening days dissolving as much chlorate of potash as will cover a nickel in each two tablespoonfuls of its drinking water. But all treatment,—expect an increased temperature,—is apt to fail unless it is made to coincide with the moulting season.

Beak.—The mandibles sometimes get more or less broken, from various causes. Whether nature will repair the damage depends upon its position and extent, and somewhat upon the health and vigor of the bird. If the cause of the damage exists in the cage it should be discovered and removed. Painting on the damaged portion a little of the strong extract of witch hazel is excellent, and ensures it being in the best condition for natural repair, if such is likely to take place. Failing this, it may be painted once with Friar's Balsam. If the use of the beak is impaired for feeding, the bird should be caged alone and given sufficient soft food to prevent starvation until the beak is again strong enough to perform its proper functions.

When the beak gets overgrown at the tip, the excessive growth should be nipped off with a pair of sharp nail scissors. It is a very simple operation, and one can scarcely go wrong with any hard-boiled bird having mandibles of practically equal length. With the Parrot family, care must be taken not to shorten them beyond a normal length, and to avoid cutting back to the "quick". Swathing parrot type birds in a towel before operating is advisable. For the Parrot tribe, a good supply of wood to cut up; and for other species, cuttlebone, old mortar or a cube of sugar in the wire will help prevent beaks getting abnormally long.

Bowel Inflammations (Enteritis and Gastro-enteritis).—These two diseases are scarcely worthy of separate description; for in birds it is seldom that one exists without the other. The term "Enteritis" indicates inflammatory changes of the mucous coat of the bowels, and "Gastroenteritis" when both the stomach (or proventriculus) and bowels participate. The inflammation may be primary and independent, or secondary (such as arises in the course of other diseases), or it can be classified as arising from the introduction of ptomaines, by the taking in of thermal irritants and mineral and vegetable poisons as part of infectious and contagious diseases, such as tuberculosis, septic fever, bacteria which produce changes in the liver substance (so indirectly causing the disease), and lastly, a mycotic form arising from the eating of mouldy food, and irritation brought about by the presence of parasites in the bowels. The causes will thus be seen to be numerous, but the common causes may be set down as errors in dieting, want of cleanliness, and alterations taknig place in the food.

Enteritis is a very common trouble in birds, and is often associated with pain. There is redness and irritability of the mucous coat of the bowels, or stomach and bowels, the contents varying much in nature, sometimes being thin and watery, at times stained with blood, or they may be slimy, and occasionally the excrement may consist of blood alone, but more often it is greenish. If a bird so affected is handled, the body is seen to be tense, swollen, and often reddened, the swollen state arising from tympanitis due to the formation of gases within the bowels, the products of decomposition. The bird shows fear and restlessness if much pain is present. The symptoms are very rapid in their onset: the birds go "thick," assume a somnolent attitude, rapidly lose flesh, there is excrement around the vent, and death occurs in the space of a day or two. In cases of a more chronic nature, birds may make temporary recovery, but later have a return of the symptoms and die, much depending upon the age of the bird and the time of the year.

If early recognized, a little scalded bread (or biscuit) with milk may be given, dusted over with bismuth. When pain exists, a few drops of tincture of opium may be given with advantage in the drinking water.

The more chronic form of enteritis is commonly due to local ulcerations of the bowels, tuberculous growths and parasites. In the larger birds, such as the Parrot family, this form is very common. When due to parasites, or worms, the diarrhoea will be found to be intermittent, and if tapeworms, segments of these will be found in the excrement. Here the disease may persist for weeks, the birds losing flesh and in protracted cases becoming almost skeletons. The cause must be removed. If due to tapeworm infestation, areca nut, or tenaline, may be prescribed for round worms, pomegranate root powdered, kousso, or common salt dissolved in the drinking water, the dosage depending upon the bird to be treated. In all cases (from whatever causes) warmth should be insured, as where diarrhoea exists there is always great loss of body heat.

There is no doubt that the trouble with young canaries, soon after leaving their parents, known as "Going Light," is often due to this complaint, and the most likely causes to suspect in their case are stale water or egg food, sour food, decaying portions of green food, overcrowding, and unhygienic cages generally. Any or all of these causes which may be found to exist must be removed with the least possible delay. Besides being kept warm these patients should be put on a diet of bread and milk until recovered. When the acute symptoms have passed, add a little maw seed to the diet each day, and gradually bring them back to the usual dietary. In the drinking water give for one day only ten drops of syrup of buckthorn in each ounce of water, and follow this up with six drops each of tincture of quinine and dilute sulphric acid daily until the acute stage is passed, when it may be given on alternate days for another two or three weeks, on the intervening days giving instead four drops of a mixture of equal parts cod-liver oil emulsion and compound syrup of hypophosphites on the bread and milk.

Broncho-Pneumonia is in all cases fatal. But with early recognition, removal of exciting causes, and suitable treatment this should be avoided.

There is not much interference with appetite, the bird feeding well, but in the intervals between "meals" assuming a listless attitude. In the larger species there will be observed a slight noise of a wheezy character; this is not always perceptible in the smaller birds, but in most there is gaping. Provided the disease does not extend, then recovery occurs fairly rapidly, and there is no recurrence.

The bird should be placed in a well-ventilated room, at the same time insuring warmth. No alteration in the diet is necessary, but a little green food, if procurable, will materially assist in recovery. Give a course of the following medicine: Carbonate of ammonia, 3 grains; tinct. of squills, 3 drops; glycerine, 5 drops; twice daily in the drinking water. This, of course, is for one drinking-vessel, containing one ounce of water or thereabouts. Enough can be dispensed by any chemist to last one for a week, when it should be discontinued. As a recuperative, 4 drops of compound infusion of gentian should be given night and morning, similarly administered in the drinking water. To any one of the prescriptions given above a small quantity of simple syrup may be added where any difficulty is experienced in getting the bird to partake of the mixture.

The chlorodyne and potassium mixture given under **Asthma** may also be tried when other things have failed.

Chill and Colds.—A serious chill is often the premonitory symptom of acute bronchitis or pneumonia, and may arise from temporarily placing bird in a cold draught, or from too vigorous bathing when a serious drop occurs in the temperature of the atmosphere. It is to be avoided rather than cured. In cases of common cold, with slight hoarseness or loss of voice, keep the bird in a comfortable temperature, free from draughts, and other unhealthy influences, give a morsel of bread and milk, with 2 drops of codliver oil emulsion on it, and sprinkled with soft sugar, for a day or two, and add to the drinking water 15 drops of a mixture of equal parts glycerine, honey and lemon juice. A teaspoonful of whiskey in an ordinary drinker full of water will often give immediate relief. For more severe colds add 5 drops each of oxymel of squills, glycerine, ipecacuanha wine and sweet spirits of nitre to each tablespoonful of water for a few days. During the treatment the bird should be kept in a comfortable temperature, free from draughts and the fumes of burning gas or oil stoves. The latter is an important consideration in the curative treatment of all diseases, for the foul air engendered by burning gas and oil is detrimental to the health. A piece of bread scalded with milk, pressed nearly dry, and sprinkled with a little soft sugar, is an excellent food to give during colds and loss of condition in cage birds but it must be given fresh every morning, and what is left removed in the evening. Some birds will refuse it when first offered, but a sprinkling of maw seed, or gold of pleasure, on the top will invariably overcome their prejudices.

Congestion.—A general congestion of the system is not infrequently met with in well-fed birds. They are generally birds which feed not wisely but too well. In many cases the organs of the body are so much packed with masses of fat as to be quite unable to perform their appointed functions. The diet of such birds must be strictly limited. They should also be given ample space for vigorous exercise. Once, twice, or three times a week, according to the severity of the case, add 10 drops of lemon juice and sufficient Epsom salts to the drinking water to make it taste faintly saline. Congestion of the lungs is a far more serious and fatal malady. For information concerning this, see under heading **Pneumonia.**

Constipation.—In cases of constipation a dose of ten drops of glycerine in the drinking water for one day will generally be sufficient, but if this fails, a dose of Epsom Salts should be administered for one or two days, as seems sufficient. This dose should consist of as much of the salts as is necessary to make the drinking water just taste saline. At the same time seed-eating birds should be given a more liberal supply of green food, whilst for soft-billed birds nothing will equal a few spiders, if they can be procured. Some birds object to the saline taste given the water by Epsom Salts, and after one sip are loath to go near it again. In this respect sulphate of soda has a distinct advantage over the Epsom Salts, being just as good in action, and almost imperceptible to the taste. A suitable dose of the powdered form is as much as will lie on a sixpence dissolved in every two tablespoonfuls of drinking water. In bad cases as much as will lie on a nickel may be used; but this should not be left in the cage longer than six or seven hours.

Consumption.—Contrary to general opinion, this is, in the opinion of scientific investigators, one of the rarest diseases in cage birds. In hundreds of cases microscopically investigated by a medical authority, many of which were believed to be tuberculosis, the disease proved to be septic fever, which bears a striking naked-eye resemblance to tuberculosis, and necessitates the aid of the microscope to make a correct diagnosis.

Debility is often due to a progressive weakness probably resulting from confinement and lack of proper exercise for the vital organs. Often there exists no specific disease, when hygienic treatment—plain, wholesome food, plenty of fresh air, and space for exercise—should be all that is required. As a remedy 6 drops of Syrup of Buckthorn in each ounce of drinking water has proved of very great value. Or 4 drops of a mixture of equal parts cod-liver oil emulsion and syrup of iodide of iron given every second day on a morsel of bread and milk will prove of the greatest benefit in most such cases. See questions and answers.

Diarrhoea is a symptom of various diseases and conditions rather than a disease in itself, and should be treated as such. It may arise from a too relaxing diet, damp, frosted, or unwholesome green food, or food that is wholly unsuitable. In such cases a change of diet is essential, and any very relaxing item of the diet, and all succulent green food, withheld for the time being. A liberal use of maw seed will do much to correct this trouble in nearly all birds that will partake of it, and a piece of cuttlefish in the wires for the birds to peck at, or crushed and strewn on top of the food, is also of much service in checking the complaint. The first step in treatment should be to give an aperient to remove any irritating matter from the intestinal tract. Two drops of salad oil direct in the beak, or ten drops of syrup of buckthorn in each tablespoonful of drinking water for a few hours will serve this end. After this add to the water for a day or two 20 drops of whiskey, 6 of tincture of gentian, and 4 of tincture of opium. In obstinate cases a morsel of bread and milk dusted liberally with carbonate of bismuth each day will help the cure. Should this fail to correct the trouble in a day or two the cause will probably lie in the general condition of the bird, and this must be looked into.

In cases of what we may call chronic diarrhoea (that is, where the bottom of the cage is continually wet, and in many cases evil smelling) long-continued treatment is required to obtain a cure. Egg food and greed food must be withheld, and in place give an occasional half-teaspoonful of maw feed; and, in addition, a teaspoonful of the following preparation daily: Take a slice of bread, say about one-quarter of an inch thick; toast it before the fire until both sides are thoroughly well browned and the inside perfectly dry; crush it up, not quite to a powder, but somewhere near the size of summer rape; add a small quantity of steel cut oats. Let the affected bird have as much of this as it will eat until looseness is checked.

In cases of "nesting diarrhoea" this remedy is also very useful; but here, if the birds are feeding young, we are bound to let them have the soft food and green food, and must give them this preparation in a separate vessel, a cure under such circumstances taking a rather longer period. A teaspoonful of limewater should also be added to each ounce of the drinking water. For general use throughout the year the above preparation is useful to give once a week, as a conditioning food.

Diet.—It goes without saying that the question of a bird's diet is one of the cardinal points which affect its health. It must be borne in mind that a bird in confinement has comparatively very little exercise, and that of the very mildest description; it is wholly excepted from all exhausting demands upon its energy; and it is always provided with a supply of food exceeding its immediate wants. The tendency is, therefore, always to overfeed, rather than the reverse. A rather plain diet, which should approach as nearly to the natural diet of the species as the exigencies of confinement will permit, should be adhered to in a general way, and the closer the bird is confined the less it should be indulged with dainties and rich, stimulating foods. During the spring and summer months, when birds are in high condition, and are not mated up for breeding, the diet should be of a spare description for a time, now and again, and a liberal supply of green vegetable food provided; or, in the case of birds which do not partake readily of green salads, either ripe sweet fruits, or a small crystal of sulphate of soda dissolved in the drinking water occasionally should be given.

Dysentery.—An acute inflammation of the mucous membrane of the large intestine, of which the prominent symptom is the droppings being copiously mingled with mucous and blood. There is little appetite for food, and frequently excessive thirst. A diet of bread and milk only, with 5 drops of pure liquid paraffin, the kind for internal use, which must be obtained from a chemist, dropped on it each day, with a little plain canary seed for seed-eaters, should be given whilst the symptoms last. A dose of from 1 to 5 drops, according to size of bird, of tincture of opium should be given in the beak each morning, and 5 drops of elixir of vitriol be added to each ounce of drinking water. Although the disease is most often met with in tropical weather, warmth is essential for the successful treatment of the patient during the acute stage. There is evidence of much pain and sensitiveness to cold, and severe griping pains are self-evident.

In more severe cases, if the above treatment does not give speedy relief the following alternative method may be tried: Give a diet of breadcrumbs scalded with milk for one or two days, and then add to the breadcrumbs an equal quantity of well-browned oatmeal, and add 15 drops of brandy to each tablespoonful of drinking water. In the earlier stage get a mixture of 2 drachms each of tincture of cayenne, and ipecacuanha wine; 1½ drachms of tincture of henbane; and 1 drachm of tincture of opium; and add 6 drops of this mixture to each tablespoonful of drinking water until the symptoms have abated.

Egg-Binding.—This distressing trouble can scarcely be termed a "disease" but as it is frequently due to some accident of weather it may well be included here. It is always a serious happening with a breeding hen, often spoiling all chances of successful breeding with her for the remainder of the season. The symptoms can scarcely be mistaken even by the novitiate. There is evidence of pain, and extreme weakness, and utter collapse follows rapidly. The hen may be found on the nest, or the floor of the cage, or occasionally may sit huddled up on the perch, from which she makes frequent excursions to the nest. She has apparently some difficulty in balancing herself on the perch; sits with eyes half-closed, feathers puffed out, and apparently not far removed from the one unfailing bourne. When these symptoms show themselves on the day when a hen was expected to lay an egg it is fairly safe to assume that she is suffering from this trouble. Do not, however, jump too hastily to conclusions and begin treating a hen for the trouble until it is palpably existent. So long as a hen keeps bright and active it is not wise to interfere with the natural course of things, even if eggs do not appear when expected.

The usual remedy of relaxing the parts by steaming is very useful, and is frequently all that is required. Procure a narrow jug, half-filled with hot water, a little olive oil which has been warmed, and a tiny camel-hair pencil, or a flight (wing) or tail feather. Some prefer these latter to the camel-hair brush, as being less liable to cause accident by breaking the egg. In the hands of inexperienced fanciers cases have been known where a sudden backward movement of the bird has caused the wooden, or quill, part of the brush to fracture the egg and end the life of the hen. Hold the bird for about three minutes with the vent over the neck of the jug, then dip the brush or feather into the oil, insert it gently into the vent, turning it around so as to well lubricate same. The moist steam and the oil usually bring about the desired results a few minutes after the hen is returned to cage, indeed, sometimes the egg will be dropped into the jug, unless one has taken the precaution to tie a piece of gauze or fine muslin loosely over it. Handle the hen very carefully; breakage of the egg inside her by undue pressure will probably kill her. The usual remedy of giving a drop of castor oil in the beak is positively harmful. What is required internally is a **stimulant, and not a purgative.** Inwardly, a few drops of equal parts of gin and water will be the best treatment. Egg-binding will rarely be met with if hens be given a plain, wholesome diet throughout the winter months, and allowed abundant space for vigorous exercise. From the end of moulting until mated up (about the first week in April) a little ginger and linseed should be given twice a week, say a teaspoonful to every four hens.

An old fancier, concerning egg-binding said: "It is a thing that I have not experienced for seven years. I have not had a single hen go egg-bound by giving them this this simple treatment: In the first place, about two or three weeks before I put my birds together, I give them egg food, mixing with one egg and the usual biscuit one teaspoonful of tasteless cod-liver oil, also a little niger thistle seed. When the hen begins to build her nest I put about six to eight drops of gin and glycerine in the drinking water every morning until the hen lays, which should be after three or four days. Mix the gin and glycerine in equal parts." This, of course, need only be followed out with the first nests, or in case of unfavorable weather during the early part of the season.

In all cases warmth is an important factor in combating the trouble, and in conjunction with the above remedies should suffice for all ordinary cases. But in very severe cases, should these remedies fail to bring relief, get a chemist to mix a little paste composed of extract of belladonna and glycerine—two parts of the former to three parts of the latter—and smear a little of this paste on the vent; give one drop of chlorodyne in the beak for a bird the size of a canary, and more or less in proportion; and repeat the steaming process. Then place the bird in a small cage and keep it in a quite warm place until the cause is disposed of.

General Debility is an exaggerated form of Debility (which see) showing a generally weak and unhealthy condition, frequently due to improper dieting, particularly among the soft-billed or insect-eating species, The only really useful aid to cure is to correct the diet, and provide one that is natural to the species, and of a generous character. A little bread and milk three times a week upon which 3 or 4 drops of cod-liver emulsion have been placed, and a course of chemical food, 10 drops in each tablespoonful of drinking water every second day for a few weeks, or a similar quantity of Byno-phosphates, or Fellows' Syrup, will materially assist Nature to throw off the complaint.

Hoarseness.—This is often a great trouble with singing birds, particularly Roller Canaries. Occasionally it may result from excessive vocal efforts, but is more generally caused by a cold draught, or an over-heated, vitiated atmosphere. If neglected, it may speedily result in total loss of voice, which will never recover its full purity of tone afterwards, so that no time should be lost in treating its first symptoms. If taken in hand as soon as the first sign of hoarseness is detected, a few drops of glycerine in the drinking water, and keeping the cage covered over closely to prevent the bird singing for a day or two, thus giving the vocal organs a rest, will often set matters right. But if this is not sufficient, the drinking water should be taken away and replaced by linseed tea, prepared by pouring a teacupful of boiling water over a teaspoonful of linseed, allowing it to stand until cold, then strain through muslin and add a teaspoonful of honey and as much chlorate of potash as will lie on a nickel. Stir until dissolved, and give to the bird in its drinking vessel instead of plain water two days in every three, until the hoarseness has quite disappeared. The diet should consist of plain canary seed; and a little bread and milk, with two drops of cod-liver oil emulsion on it and sprinkled with soft sugar, should be given each day until better. Complete the treatment by giving three drops of tincture of gentian and tincture of steel in the water for a day or two. See questions and answers.

Huskiness.—This is often due to exposure to a temporary cold draught, and singing birds, especially Rollers, are most liable to suffer from it. A morsel of bread and milk with two or three drops of cod-liver oil emulsion, according to the size of the bird, dropped on it, and finally sprinkled with soft sugar, is an excellent remedy, and if the causes are removed no other treatment should be necessary. If this does not bring about a speedy return to normal conditions, treat as advised under **Hoarseness.**

Indigestion.—When a bird is constantly picking over its food, eating little and wasting a good deal—seed-eaters cracking their seed and rejecting both kernel and husk—and after eating goes and sits on its perch, and tucks its head away in its feathers, if it is clearly free from cold or bronchial trouble, it is doubtless suffering from some dietic indiscretion. The diet should be looked into, and a nourishing one, approaching as nearly to the natural diet of the species as the exigencies of confinement will admit of, provide. A little bread and milk on which is dropped 4 or 5 drops of the pure liquid paraffin for a bird the size of a canary, will prove invaluable to nearly every species to help them over such a trouble, and a saline aperient, 6 drops of syrup of rhubarb and a crystal of sulphate of soda the size of a small pea, added to each ounce of drinking water for two or three days, and followed afterwards with 4 drops each and aromatic sulphuric acid, every second day of tincture of gentian, tincture of calumba, for a week, is the best treatment. See questions and answers.

Legs, Scaly.—This is a well-known disease of the poultry-yard, but although it is quite possible for it to attack small birds, it is not likely to give the bird-keeper much trouble unless it is transported from an infected poultry-yard by careless management. The disease is due to a microscopic mite which takes up its abode beneath the scales on the legs and feet, where it lives and breeds, giving rise to chalky excretions, which accumulate over and between the scales, and form rough-looking lumpy crusts. The disease is contagious, being spread from one to another bird by contact. The best treatment for small birds would be to wash the feet and legs quite clean with a warm solution of Jeyes', 1 in 80—equivalent to a teaspoonful of the fluid in half a pint of water. Then dry gently, and anoint well with sulphur ointment, in an ounce of which ten drops of Jeyes' has been well incorporated. Repeat every second day until well.

The scales on the legs and feet of all birds gradually become rough and enlarged with advancing age, and this is quite natural effect of age must not be mistaken for an unhealthy condition.

Lice.—When birds get a low condition of health and suffer from great weakness they are often troubled with these pests, which worry them considerably and increase their ill-health. These are not the well-known red mites, but grey-colored lice, which live constantly on the bird, and cause great irritation by gnawing the skin on which they subsist. The best method to exterminate them is to wash the bird as though preparing it for exhibition, adding some creolin—a teaspoonful to each pint of water—to the first two basins; or, better still, sulphuretted potash to the last rinsing water—about a teaspoonful to a pint. Repeat the process once or twice at intervals of four or five days. If one is not a very skillful washer, he should procure the aid of a fancier friend. The cage should also be well washed at the same time with insecticide.

Liver, Congestion of.—This is often brought about by overfeeding, or feeding too exclusively on a diet of egg food, or to an excessive use of stimulating articles of diet. A bird so affected is generally dull and listless, with loose plumage, though at times it becomes quite bright and lively for a short period. The appetite is variable; constipation may alternate with more or less diarrhoea, and in bad cases the droppings may be a yellowish color. The bird is also very susceptible to climatic changes. Taken in an early stage, syrup of buckthorn in doses of 10 drops in each ounce for the drinking water, repeated every second day until bowels move freely and regularly, is an excellent remedy. The diet must be given careful attention, and any necessary correction made in it, and a little fresh green salad should be added daily. In more advanced cases doses of 6 drops of dandelion juice (taraxacum) and a crystal of sulphate of soda the size of a split pea in each ounce of water should be given, and in cases where this fails to give the necessary relief the following may be tried: In each ounce of water dissolve a crystal of sulphate of soda the size of a small pea, a crystal of sulphate of iron half this size, and add 6 drops of dilute sulphuric acid, and give this every second day for a week at a time, missing an interval of a week between each course.

Metro-Peritonitis.—This is a very fatal disorder affecting breeding hens, from which they rarely, if ever, recover. It is an acute inflammation of the peritoneum generally set up by the rupture of an egg in the oviduct, and the escape of egg substance into the abdominal cavity. There is also in many cases rupture of the oviduct accompanying it. No treatment is of any avail. Prevention is the only remedy, and this may be done to some extent by keeping the stock hens in a good, hard and vigorous condition, to avert egg-binding troubles as far as possible. There is undoubtedly some risk of setting up this disorder when one attempts to relieve egg-binding by forcible manipulation, a course which we always caution the amateur to strictly avoid.

Mites—The chief mite which infests cage birds is the well-known red mite, which preys upon the blood of the birds. It will be found dealt with under the heading **Red Mite.** There is another minute grey mite which lives among the seed, particularly infesting rape and linseed. It gives the seed a clammy moist feel, and, when badly infested, a characteristic, unpleasant odor. Seed infested in this way is capable of setting up serious disease among birds fed upon it. Washing or sifting the seed will not render it wholesome, and the only course is to totally reject such samples.

Moult.—Though not, strictly speaking, a disease, the moulting period, owing to the strain it puts upon their systems, is a trying one for birds. At this time of the year they need special care and attention, and a good-sized cage or flight in which they may exercise their wings is very helpful. Let them bathe liberally on mild, fine days. If small cages only are used, draughts must be rigorously avoided. Damp is another fatal enemy. Do not subject birds to changes of temperature during the moult, or it may induce that dreaded complaint, "stuck in the moult"—i. e., the shedding of the feathers will be checked. For the latter the best remedy the writer has tried has been a vapor bath—that is, covering an open wire cage, with bird inside, with flannel and arranging it over a basin of almost boiling water for ten minutes or so. Afterwards put the covered cage near the fire, removing it gradually away again, to permit the bird a safe return to normal temperature. Feed all birds more liberally during the moult, allowing seed-eaters an ample supply of the richer seeds—maw, sunflower, linseed (in moderation), hemp, etc.—and their natural wild seeds and fruits, and soft-billed birds all the insect life that can be procured. Most of the seed-eaters also appreciate a few mealworms at this time of the year. A moderate supply of linseed during the latter part of the moult is very useful for adding a nice gloss, or finish, to the plumage, but it will be found that some canaries reject it. In this case it is best to give as a substitute a supply of chopped sunflower seeds, which are more appreciated and have practically the same effect.

Out of Condition.—This term is often applied to canaries in a weakened condition from being overshown. For its treatment, see below.

Debility and General Debility.—The term would be better applied to the disorder which often afflicts our native birds in the early summer months. It is a common occurrence for canary birds to become seriously indisposed during their natural breeding season. They sit all in a heap on the perch, or in a corner of the cage bottom, and only rouse themselves for a second or two to visit the seed or water, though they have no appetite for food. As these symptoms frequently follow a period of high spirits and condition, it is more probable that they are due chiefly, if not wholly, to the bird's enforced bachelorhood at this season; for it is invariably the males that are affected this way. The symptoms are very similar to those produced by inflammation of the bowels, therefore it is first necessary to satisfy oneself whether this is really the cause by gently catching the bird and blowing up the feathers of the abdomen. If there is no sign of the swollen and dark-red or reddish-purple appearance which accompanies inflammation, treat the bird by giving it a plain diet and a little non-stimulating green food, such as a spray of chickweed, watercress or, the tender flowering tips of groundsel, and add to each ounce of its drinking water for a few days as much Epsom salts as will cover a nickel, 10 drops of lemon juice, and 20 drops of whiskey. It is not wise to keep such birds in sight of hens of their own, or nearly allied, species, unless they are mated together, as this would only tend to exaggerate the complaint.

Sweating.—An unhealthy condition frequently occurring with hen canaries rearing young, and which also affects the young chicks, is known by this name. The hen becomes listless, frequently ceases to attend to her duties, or to feed the young, and the feathers on the breast assume a moist, more or less sodden, condition. This is often believed to be due to perspiration—or sweating—hence the term used to describe the condition. But it is in reality due to severe diarrhoea in the chicks— the watery evacuations thus saturating the hen's plumage as she sits on them. The affection is probably due in every case to infection by septic bacilli. The best way to combat it is to see that the cages, and all food and water vessels as well as the food and water itself, are absolutely clean, sweet, and fresh. In mixing the egg-food required for rearing the young use a third part of the bulk of well-browned stale household bread, as described under the heading Diarrhoea for cases of "nesting diarrhoea," and finally mix in a teaspoonful of arrowroot powder to a tablespoonful of the bulk of the egg food, and sprinkle with maw seed. In each ounce of the drinking water mix a teaspoonful of lime-water daily. Continue this treatment until the young have resumed their normal condition, and the hen is feeding freely again.

Wheeziness is a symptom of various disorders which is apt to be regarded as a disease in itself, though this is an erroneous supposition. It may be due to an over-fat condition, in which case a plain diet, with a liberal supply of green vegetable food or succulent fruit, and frequent saline aperients, until the bodily condition is reduced to reasonable proportions, will remove the wheeziness. If due to a slight cold a morsel of sponge-cake with a drop or two of cod-liver oil emulsion on it and slightly moistened with sherry for a few days will suffice to remove it. A piece of fat boiled bacon stuck in the wires for the bird to peck at when it chooses is also helpful. In serious cases keep a cube of the paste prescribed under the heading "Loss of Voice", stuck in the wires for a time. Should this also fail treat the bird as advised under the heading Asthma, and endeavor to discover the cause of the trouble. If not due to over-feeding, nor of digestive origin, it will probably be due to the incipient stage of asthma, which usually appears more pronounced at night, and a visit to the cage a few hours after the bird has retired to roost will prove useful in helping to elucidite the cause of its condition. A dust-laden atmosphere, or one that is heated by the fumes of burning lights, and irritating vapors or smoke are causes that may reasonably be suspected.

INFLAMMATION OF THE BOWELS

This is caused by having been fed too much rich, stimulating foods or fancy treats, or by sour or decayed food, foul water, and dirty seed and water containers.

Birds affected with this common malady will drink continuously of cold water, but refuse food, will sit huddled up on the perch like a ball of feathers breathing heavily and looking as in misery, leaving the perch only to drink for a long period which is the worst thing it could do, by all means remove all of the water, give the bird two or three drops of warm castor oil into the beak, place the bird in a cage alone and in a quiet warm place, heat is always beneficial to ailing birds, if the bird does not get busy and experience a bowel movement within an hour paint the vent lightly with warm turpentine, be sure not to allow this to penetrate the feathered parts of its body, paint the abdomen only and this lightly, if for several times permitting it to penetrate.

After the bowels have acted you may return the drinking water and put into it the amount or drops of any good tonic as is stated on the bottle as the tonics are all of about the same formulas, only some stronger than others. It should now be fed some arrow root biscuit or milk sop, (see index how to make milk sop), use real warm milk sprinkled with good small blue dutch maw or poppy seed, feed only this food for three days after which you can feed if one teaspoonful of mixed rape and canary seed and the milk-sop for three days after which time you can daily increase the seed food until you have reached the usual amount for its daily rations, do not feed any rich foods or green food for two weeks, after which time feed green food sparingly.

SOFT MOULT

This may be caused by the bird being kept in heated rooms, or hung too high on the walls or shelves, remember the hot air and the lightest air rise to the top about one-third of the height of the room is the best place for an ideal location to keep your bird, a burning gas stove is something that should not be found in the room where a canary-bird is kept. Often they are attacked by a parasite which bores into the quills of the feathers, causing them to drop. Special feeding should first be your program, no rich or fancy food, a mixture of seeds is advisable such as is found in numerous packs, but not the ground tonic foods, wash out the feeder daily and use extra precaution in feeding, again Milk-sop is good added to the mixed seed ration, give only boiled water (cooled) during this condition, sweet apple or green food fed lightly daily helps nature, plenty of washed grit or gravel at all times. If this care has failed to put your bird into condition then a dip or bath to combat the feather parasites is necessary, have the water rather hot, about 100 f. h., first cleanse the bird with lux, then rinse the bird in pure water all extra warm, then give it a good bath in water into which you may put some lysol or extract of quassia, then wrap the bird or roll it in a warmed dry bath towel, have towel extend an inch or more over the head of the bird, but be sure it remains open to afford air. Allow the wrapped bird to remain in a dry place, sunshine if possible for at least half an hour if in cool weather before or near a fire, (not gas). Now rub insect powder into the feathers of the bird and hang into its cage a small sack with short string hanging from bottom filled with sulphur. This drastic treatment will get the parasites and you will have a beautiful hand washed bird.

SORE FEET

Usually the result of dirty cages or filthy perches. Trim the claws if too long, bathe the feet in warm water, remove all dirt, clean the feet by rubbing with a soft cloth dipped in paraffin, when clean, rub in a little vaseline or milk weed cream.

BALDNESS

Baldness is caused by a number of reasons, mating two top-knots, and so on. By consulting the question and answer department you will learn a number of reasons, I shall however, deal here with what I think is the usual causes, that is INSUFFICIENT VARIATION IN THE FOOD. Always provide a change of foods, if you supply the usual staple food daily, they should have some green foods, winter or summer, milk-sop, (see index for recipe); rich mixture of seeds, nature foods. In the drinker, drop some good tonic according to the directions. Boiled carrot instead of water is most stimulating. Rub the bald spot with vaseline into which has been mixed some creosote, do this every other day for ten days, in the drinking water of two tablespoons of water add half a teaspoonful of the following (mixed by you in a small bottle), 1 oz. epsom salts, 1 oz. glauber salts, and one-half oz. common table salt, fill 8 oz. bottle with water that has been boiled.

INDIGESTION

When a bird is constantly picking over its food, eating little and wasting a good deal—seed-eaters cracking their seed and rejecting both kernel and husk—and after eating goes and sits on its perch, and tucks its head away in its feathers, if it is clearly free from cold or bronchial trouble, it is doubtless suffering from some digestive derangement, probably due to dietetic indiscretion. The diet should be looked into, and a nourishing one, approaching as nearly to the natural diet of the species as the exigencies of confinement will admit of, provided. A little bread and milk on which is dropped 4 or 5 drops of the pure liquid paraffin for a bird the size of a canary, will prove invaluable to nearly every species to help them over such a trouble, and a saline aperient, 6 drops of syrup of rhubarb and a crystal of sulphate of soda the size of a small pea, added to each ounce of drinking water for two or three days, and followed afterwards with 4 drops each of tincture of gentian of calumba, and aromatic sulphuric acid, every second day for a week, is the best treatment.

CONGESTION OF LIVER

This is often brought about by over-feeding or feeding too exclusively on a diet of egg-food, or to an excessive use of stimulating articles of diet. A bird so affected is generally dull and listless, with loose plumage, though at times it becomes quite bright and lively for a short period. The appetite is variable; constipation may alternate with more or less diarrhoea, and in bad cases the droppings may be of a yellowish color. The bird is also very susceptible to climatic changes. Taken in an early stage, syrup of buckthorn in doses of 10 drops in each ounce of the drinking water, repeated every second day until bowels move freely and regularly, is an excellent remedy. The diet must be given careful attention, and any necessary correction made in it, and a little fresh green salad should be added daily. In more advanced cases doses of 6 drops of dandelion juice (taraxacum) and a crystal of sulphate of soda the size of a split pea in each ounce of water should be given, and in cases where this fails to give the necessary relief the following may be tried. In each ounce of water dissolve a crystal of sulphate of soda the size of a small pea, a crystal of sulphate of iron half this size, and add 6 drops of dilute sulphuric acid, and give this every second day for a week at a time, missing an interval of a week between each course.

PREVENTION OF DISEASES

With ordinary care in cleanliness, freedom from drafts, and a well-regulated food supply canaries are subject to few ills. In fact, most troubles may be traced to some untoward circumstance in handling them. Their diseases are very little understood, and correct diagnosis is difficult. When birds become sick, care should first be taken in regulating the diet and general sanitary conditions. A sick bird must be removed at once to a separate cage, since its companions will continually peck and worry it. When numbers of canaries are kept it is best to remove ailing birds from the bird room. This precaution may prevent the spread of some contagious or infectious disease. It is always well to remove a sick bird to a warm place. Heat and protection from drafts work wonders with ailing canaries and often are sufficient alone to restore them to health. When medicine is necessary it is best to administer it in the drinking water. If this can not be done it may be given directly in the bill by means of a medicine dropper, .

FOODS · · · FORMULAS

Food is a subject that cannot be too thoroughly studied by bird lovers and bird owners, hence some repetitions.

The food requirements of Canaries are simple. The prime requisite is a supply of rape and Canary seed. People owning only a few birds usually buy package seed, mixed by dealers. Care should be taken in buying seeds. You must be sure it is fresh, clean and of a good quality, well matured. If your birds do not thrive upon the seed you are using, it is well to examine by cracking a few seeds; you are likely to find that empty husks alone were being fed.

In addition to this staple diet, lettuce, chickweed, or a bit of sweet apple may be fed twice a week. If diets of moist food are used, they must be strictly fresh, or bacterial diseases may result. In feeding moist food, special dishes are advisable.

There are small food receptacles sold at nearly all dealers, which can be placed between the wires of the cage, and which are handy and sanitary.

Soft food must not be too wet. Cuttle bone must be always available to the Canary. Maw seed is favored by the oldest breeders as a stimulant, maw or poppy is an opiate.

PORK

To satisfy the craving for animal food a small bit of salt raw pork, soak it in warm water over night to remove the surplus of salt. It should not be given to young birds.

Milk sop is another good food. To make it, take stale bread or biscuits, not rye or graham; stale dry bread is as good as toast. Over this pour fresh sweet milk, up to boiling point best but not necessary. You have a delightful food and a treat for your birds. Sprinkle with maw seed. Condensed milk can be used by diluting to strength of cow's milk, cream is too rich; dilute canned milk; pasteurized milk is fine. This sours in a few hours. Make it fresh; remove any surplus.

Carrots, ground with bread, raw or boiled, are a good food for Canaries. But care should be taken not to feed frosted carrots, as you will have a great loss of birds if you do. You can run the raw carrots through a meat mill and feed it in this manner, carefully washing the carrots first.

CONDITIONS, SEED, MIXTURE

Condition Mixture

In the list of seeds which can be used as suitable food for Canaries, there are at least twelve which can be used to advantage. Each of these have a different chemical analysis, and it is for that reason that they are valuable. A first class condition mixture can be made up of the following seeds. One part by measure of each of the following seeds. Hulled Oats, Hemp Seed, Flax Seed, Inga Seed, White Italian Millet Seed, Red Indian Millet Seed, and Teazle Seed. Now add half of one part of the following seeds. Sesame Seed, Gold-of Pleasure Seed and Best Blue Dutch Maw Seed. These should be well mixed together, and stored in the same way as the staple food. In feeding the condition mixture, the container should be well shaken before taking out the supply, for the small seeds get down to the bottom, and unless the bulk is well mixed, the birds will not get the benefit of the small seeds such as Maw and Sesame. Only a small amount should be given at one time for the mixture is stimulating, and will be found excellent for a conditioner before the breeding season.

Bird Grit And Cuttlefish Bone Necessary

Clean dry grit must always be before the bird. This is necessary for by its use the food is ground into digestible form in the crop of the bird. A Canary having no teeth, the grit is supplied as a natural substitute for the same. Cuttlefish Bone should be between the wires of the cage at all times. It aids the bird in keeping the mandible or beak trimmed, and as it is composed of a large percentage of lime, it is a bone forming food, and good for all birds to use, more especially those which are young and growing.

EGGS, HATCHING

Correct Time For Incubation

312 hours, or thirteen periods of 24 hours each is the correct time. Any variation will lie in the individuality of the hen in question. In practice we will find few birds that are exactly alike in this respect.

Some hens will be found to sit so close that they will seem to deny themselves the necessary amount of food, while other hens will be found to be the reverse. They will immediately leave the nest upon the entry into the room of their owner, and will not return to the nest until the owner leaves the room. The number of times that the hen will leave the nest, should they be frequent, will slightly delay the time of hatching. Under normal conditions, eggs which are set in the evening of a certain day, should all hatch out during the morning of the fourteenth day from the time of setting.

The Best Material For Shell Forming

Every year we hear of a large number of young birds being found dead in the shells and the reason has been that the young birds have been unable to liberate themselves owing to the strength of the shell. This trouble can be avoided by using the right material. Ground up oyster shell I consider to be too strong. Grit for the same reason should not be used. I have found that no trouble from this source will be experienced if the hen is supplied with powered '"Hen Egg Shells" a little silver sand, and a good piece of Cuttlefish Bone. No other material is required or advisable at this time.

The Diet For Hens During Incubation

The Fancier who persists in feeding egg-food to sitting hens is certainly looking for trouble. It must be remembered that for the entire incubation period the hen will take very little exercise. Stimulating food will clog the system, and due to sickness, the hen will lose interest in her work. Very often hens will be found to sit for several days quite closely, and then for no apparent reason quit the nest and will not return. It will be found that the food given is responsible for this condition. A sitting hen should be fed very plainly. Canary Seed and Rape Seed in equal parts should be the only food given. Every third day a small piece of bread and milk will be relished by the hen, and will serve the purpose of regulating the bowels, and keeping the system of the bird clean. Great care must be taken that when egg-food is given at the time of hatching, the amounts must be so regulated that the hen will have just what is necessary for the very small demands of her brood at this time. Over-feeding at the first few days after hatching is responsible for more losses than the majority imagine.

EGG BINDING

TINCTURE OF ERGOT FOR EGG BINDING

I have found the use of Ergot the most successful of all remedies that I have tried for egg-binding.

I put a drop of Ergot on the vent (wetting the parts quite freely with the Ergot), then I dip a teaspoon in hot water, retaining a drop of the water in the spoon. Then I tip the bottle of Ergot (wetting the cork) and then rinse what remains of the Ergot on the cork into the drop of hot water in the teaspoon (the water now being about luke-warm) and give this to the hen. Then I wrap her in a warm flannel cloth, keeping her real warm. Soon the egg is laid and the hen is all right again.

In severe cases the treatment may have to be repeated, but the remedy very seldom fails.

MILK FOR BIRDS

The remedial value of such a common and easily obtained article as milk is not recognized as it should be. With practically all kinds of birds it is, as with animals, both a food and a drink, and indispensible in such diseases as dysentery and inflammation of the bowels. When birds are exhausted from traveling long journeys, or rather low in condition, a drink of lukewarm milk acts as a splendid reviver and tonic. Bread and milk sprinkled with maw seed, is invaluable in helping birds over an illness.

(Egg-Food)

REMEMBER—

That egg-Essen will grow and rear your Birdlings. Place it in the cage as soon as they are hatched and the parent birds will feed it. Or better still, put some of it in the cage two or

three days prior to the hatching of the youngsters.

Egg-Essen is wonderful for birds in moult, ill or injured birds, singers that have lost their voice, or it may be given once a week as a relish, to your healthy birds.

Egg-Essen should be fed occasionally to the hens during the winter and early spring, if you expect to breed them, as it will help to prepare them for the mating and breeding season.

Egg-Essen must always be given in addition to the bird's regular supply of seed.

EGG-ESSEN

4 Eggs boiled thirty minutes—mashed to a fine paste.

2 Tablespoonsful of cracker-meal or crushed unsalted crackers.

1 Tablespoonful of Maw Seed. A dash of cayenne pepper.

3 to 6 drops of Sweet Oil. A pinch of sugar.

2 Tablespoonsful of Paprika.

1 Teaspoonful of German Summer Rape—crushed.

1 Teaspoonful of Hemp Seed—Crushed.

Mix all well together and make it fresh every day, or if you do not use it the first day it may be kept in the refrigerator and fed the following day.

The paprika in this mixture is used for producing a rich yellow color on the birds, and may or may not be added, as some people do not care for the artificial color. A richer color will be obtained by feeding the paprika in the Egg-Essen during the moulting period. However, the use of color food is entirely one's own personal choice.

ILLS, DISEASES

COLDS

Birds will sometimes appear dull and ruffled in plumage without any apparent cause. In these cases it will be found that they have in some way caught cold, for although many of our cage birds are perfectly hardy, yet caged life and protection from the weather enfeebles them somewhat, so that they quickly become chilled when placed in a draught or allowed to remain hanging outdoors too long in the early months of the year. I have found the best remedy for this ailment to be equal parts of whiskey, glycerine, and lemon juice put into a small bottle, and well shaken, and given as a dose twenty drops in the drinking vessel.

If a bird is one that will take soft food, a little milk sop given in a separate vessel will aid recovery.

Don't forget to look in the bottom of the cage every time you go into the bird room. It is a common occurence for a hen to lift a young one from the nest when she is leaving it, somehow sticking to her feathers or her claws, because she jumps off in a hurry. This may happen with young ones up to four or five days old, but seldom after that. A young one may apparently be dead, yet if it be put in the palm of the hand, and the hand closed and breathed into a few minutes, it will revive. Kind of artificial respiration. When life returns it can be put back into the nest and may do well.

TIME SAVED IS TIME GAINED

Don't forget to blow the seed husks from the seed box when a hen is setting. She comes off the nest and snatches a quiet respite like a man who is doing a Marathon race and is quick on the nest again. If the husks are not blown off regularly she has to forage amongst the chaff for a meal, and this takes up valuable time.

TROUBLING TROUBLE

Don't forget to sprinkle the nest with insect powder. Red mites are now troublesome, and ought to be kept in check. Run a small paint brush dipped in kerosene over the cage front where the perches fit. This is a favorite haunt for the mighty mite. A few precautions now will save you much worry and the birds much worrying in August when the moult is in full swing, while to neglect it is to borrow trouble—one of those things that have to be paid back with interest.

INQUISITIVENESS

If a hen has hatched, and you would like to have a peep in the nest to see how many she has, don't lift her off, as it were, by force. Give a little tempting bait, such as a morsel of lettuce or watercress. Put it where she can see it and walk out of the room. Stay out for two minutes then enter again and you will find her off. If you must look, that is a good device to get her off. But my advice is not to; most hens would rather be left alone, and do better.

MODEL MOTHERS

If you enter the room to do any work such as feeding, watering, or cleaning, and you see a hen that has young off the nest, walk straight out again and stay out for a few minutes. Some hens, however tame they may be in ordinary circumstances, are very nervous—or should I say jealous—when they are setting or have young, and if you catch them off the nest when you go in they will remain in that position, looking straight at you without moving an eyelid; as if you were some alien intruder. They will not budge until you get out, which means starved young if you remain in any length of time. These sort of hens are not usually good mothers.

CREEPY

Just at this time, if you will examine young ones after they have left their parents, you will find that many of them have those long gray lice on them. It seems a natural thing for anything young to be attacked in this way, but that isn't to say that they are not better without them. If you take the bird in your hand you will see them running in and out of the feathers. Hold the bird in your left hand and sprinkle insect powder on the feathers, gently working it in with your fingers. Do this at intervals of a few days and they will soon depart hence—the lice, I mean. A little patient exertion in this direction will be its own reward.

SHY FEEDERS

During the periodical cleaning operation, the work should be done expeditiously, because if you stay in the room too long, many hens will not feed the young. So if there is a lot to do, it is best to do it in halves. Work for a half hour, then go out for a smoke while the hen comes off to feed. Some hens are not quite so shy, but you have to adapt your work in the bird room to meet the whims of all your hens.

CRACKED HEMP

Hemp seed, cracked by rolling with an empty bottle or rolling-pin or put through the ordinary seed mill, must also be given when the youngsters are getting on. Do not crush it too much and make it a pulpy mass, as it very soon goes rancid if broken up too much. If the hen does not care for whatever green food you are using, try her with a change; give watercress one day, chickweed or groundsel another, and lettuce another day. Keep an eye on the young and you will soon see if their crops are full.

The choice of material for use with the eggs is varied; some fanciers use up all the household crusts, dried in the oven and then put through the egg mill. Others use a slice of bread which has been soaked and then squeezed dry, and still others prefer a biscuit, either plain or sweetened, and some prefer to use prepared foods such as are put on the market by the various food manufacturers. These latter foods certainly save a lot of trouble, as they are practically ready for mixing with the egg.

When the young are due to hatch, soaked rape seed must be added to the diet. This must be made by putting just the amount of seed you need in a cup and pouring boiling water over, allow to stand all night, feed dry next morning. Get the best rape seed you can procure, it is cheapest in the end and gives the best results.

Rape seed can be given in two ways—scalded and steeped. To scald rape, place a supply in a vessel and pour over it boiling water and allow to stand until cold. Steeped rape means just placing the seed in cold water and allowing it to soak. In both cases the seed should not be given to the birds until the water has been allowed to dry up by placing the seed upon a towel before giving it to the birds. This is a very good food but care must be exercised for it sours very quickly. So give only a little, and often.

UNCLEAN WATER

When we consider the quantity of water almost always right at hand, it is unbelievable that hundreds of birds are allowed to die for want of it, yet such is the case, and it is usually that when there is a little in the fountain, that it is considered enough, and this generally means trouble, as the bird may make up his mind to take a bath in it, or he may foul it, then he is compelled to be without, or drink poisoned water. It is impossible to give water too frequently, and this point should always be thought of and acted upon, but it is well in the coldest weather to take the chill off before giving the water to the bird.

DANGER
Draught

Draught is about the worst enemy of birds in captivity, and should be very carefully guarded against, even in the hottest weather, and a hanging cage should never be nearer than 18 inches to a window, and even then not in a position where the draught will strike it. Under this heading we may also include the changing of a bird from a very warm or hot room to a cool one, neither should a bird be left in a room at night, in which the temperature is likely to drop rapidly. It is very easy to give a little thought to these items, which mean so much in the life of a bird, when we consider the harm such changes mean to ourselves, then we can figure how much greater the danger to a mite of a bird.

BAD FEEDING
Improper Feeding

There are several meanings to this, such as Carelessness, Thoughtlessness, and worse yet, Supposed Kindness. In the first place, many birds are given tidbits of greens, which in themselves are very good when fresh, but how many people think to look into the cage and remove the food when stale? All green-foods should be removed as soon as the freshness has gone, as dried greens cause great trouble in the stomach. One great and very common trouble with lots of people is that when breeding Canaries, the egg food is left in the cage until it is stale and sour. This is a thing that I have seen times without number, and even if it does not kill the young birds outright, it gives them a very poor start in life, whereas everything should be done to give them a good start, and then at least 50% more young birds would mature. These items and lots of others can come under the heading Carelessness. Thoughtlessness is often responsible for a lot of suffering and deaths. For instance, I have seen Finches with no other seed than a mixture put up for Canaries, and the owners have wondered why the finches did not thrive and sing, and why they sat up in a corner all puffed up. Try and feed a dog on bananas and nuts and see if he will keep in perfect health and trim. When you buy a bird, find out the correct food for it, and feed it to him. Do not always take the word of the party who sells you the bird, as often he does not know as much as the man who is asking him. A reliable bird store insures you of facts, but when you are sure or reasonably so, that you know the correct diet, see that the bird gets it. Do not buy a large quantity of seeds at a time, unless it will be used up rapidly, as seeds dry out and not only become valueless as food, but cause various troubles, such as indigestion, etc. Never buy old package seeds. Goodness only knows how long they have been standing on the store shelves, and apart from this, in a great many cases they are put up merely as money makers, regardless of the requirements of the birds they are supposed to feed. Buy from any bird store that has their reputation behind the seed and sell enough to keep fresh seeds on hand.

It is a strange thing to say, but as many birds are killed by kindness (supposed) as

otherwise. Not long ago, I was talking to a lady who was most enthusiastic about her "Darling Baby," which it was explained was her **PARROT**. Her husband bought it from a friend a few weeks before, and it was talking and saying everything, "just like one of us," and its favorite food was home-made dough-nuts. When I was able to squeeze a word in, I told the lady forcibly that trouble was on its way, but she told me just as forcibly that I was mistaken, and that she positively refused to deprive the "Little Darling Baby" of his daily doughnut. A very short time after the personal interview I had with the lady, she wrote me asking what to do with "Baby" as all his feathers were falling out in patches, his head was covered with small sores, he vomited all he ate, and a number of other things were wrong with him, in fact only one thing was right as far as I could make out, and that was that he still breathed, although that was done in spasm. I answered that if she would stop the daily doughnut diet, and feed the bird properly, she would not only do the bird a great kindness, but would possibly restore its health. Am very pleased to say, (for Baby's sake) that he is once again a Darling, and is on the high road to health and comfort, but it is almost safe to say that before long "Baby's Mama" will give just a teeny weeny bit of doughnut again. That is the way Supposed Kindness works. I just state this case as one of thousands. There are lots of things which birds really enjoy, and which can be given occasionally with perfect safety, but unless you know just what, always remember that the staple food is best and safest in the long run, but must always be fresh and sweet.

Feeding Suggestions

So much of the success of Canary culture depends upon the food of the birds that a few notes on the various seeds will not be out of place. No matter what variety of Canary is kept, the seed used must be good and sound if the birds are to be maintained in good health. Cheapness in seeds is no saving; get the best it is possible to procure; see that it is thoroughly sweet and clean, sound and full.

Canary Seed comes first and foremost; this is the bread and butter of the Canary's existence, in fact it is the staple diet at all times. Spanish (when procurable) is the finest, being bold and bright, and it contains more feeding value than other varieties. This is the foundation stone, always keep a good supply on hand; some breeders give nothing else as a regular diet, others give a mixture about twice a week as a change.

I have frequently found that where a diet of canary seed only is in force, that being of a dry nature, the birds are often troubled with a loss of feathers in the neck and back of the head, and the skin of the bird feels dry and somewhat shriveled up. This may be traced to a lack of oiliness in the food, and when it occurs it is advisable to add a little linseed to the diet.

When the hens are feeding the young birds I find oatmeal or good Turkish or Spanish canary seed give good results, and when the youngsters are put on hard seed Turkish is much the best for them, as the husk or skin is thinner than Spanish, and is easier to crack; consequently there is less waste seed in the bottom of the cages. The Turkish seed is smaller and not so bright, but contains good feeding properties.

Hemp Seed is another useful stand-by, but it is very oily and fattening and must not be given too generously as a staple diet. Crushed hemp must be given when the hens are feeding the young as at that time it is of great importance. In crushing the seed, care must be taken to only crush a small quantity at a time as when the kernel is exposed to the air it soon turns sour and rancid.

This seed ought really to be only cracked, not crushed; and the best method is to put some in a thin muslin bag and crack it between two stones, or use an empty milk bottle as a rolling pin. This gives the best results, and takes up very little time. Hemp is very useful in the early stages of the breeding season in bringing the birds into condition, but use it in moderation at any time.

Rape Seed is also a useful food, but is somewhat of a purgative nature and requires careful use. In the breeding season it is invaluable for breeding the young, and is generally given soaked, that is, it is placed in water and allowed to stand overnight, is then strained to get as much of the moisture as possible taken away and is given in a separate vessel along with the egg-food. The breeders of Roller Canaries use it much more freely than any other seed, both soaked and as a regular diet in preference to canary seed; given in the bi-weekly mixture it makes a useful change.

Flax Linseed is very oily and is generally given fairly freely towards the end of the moult. It imparts an extra polish to the plumage; especially to varieties like the Cinnamons, Greens, etc. It is not given to any extent as a regular diet, but in cases where there is a tendency of loss of feathers and dryness of the skin, as already mentioned, then a little linseed added to the daily diet will have beneficial results.

Poppy or **Maw Seed** are very useful seeds given with the egg-food when feeding young, it is very beneficial, also when the birds are a bit off their feed it acts as a capital tonic. I always find it useful for show birds given the day before sending off, and also in their egg-food on return from a show. It is useful also as a stimulant in bringing the birds forward in the early part of the breeding season; in fact it is a grand conditioner at any time. It is invaluable in cases of looseness of the bowels, always keep it handy and feed regularly.

Millet Seed is very much in evidence in the packets and mixtures sold in the bird and seed shops, but has no specific feeding or tonic properties, and seems to be mostly used as a make-weight, although I have known many breeders who have had to use it freely, owing to the scarcity or high price of canary seed. The millet sprays are very useful in an aviary or where small foreign birds are kept, but

cannot be recommended as a staple diet for Canaries.

Thistle Inga, or niga, a black, long-shaped seed, is very useful in the early breeding season. It is stimulating, very oily, and has the credit of preventing egg-binding if given liberally to the hens during the early part of the year. It is useful at any time, given in moderation; it is especially good for the birds when they are being prepared for show; it makes them strong and vigorous and keeps them fit.

Other seeds, such as **gold of pleasure teazle,** and **dandelion,** are more in the nature of tit-bits to be given just now and again, or for British birds and Finches. Crushed oats and groats are sometimes used by Crest breeders or to help in the growth of other heavy-feathered varieties, but are very seldom used by breeders of the finer textured birds.

It is not advisable to accustom the birds to a regular "mixed" diet. Plain canary seed should be made the staple, with a separate dish or box of mired seeds as a change. Where a regular mixed diet is given there is generally a lot of waste seed, and this means wasted money.

Thistle or niga seed should be fed canaries especially Rollers, most all year round. "**Maw,** **Poppy,**" **Thistle** and **flax** are necessary. Canary and rape, some hemp and **lettuce seed.**

Other foods used during the breeding season are the egg and bread foods, but the Roller "cure all" is **bread** and **milk** with **poppy** or **maw.** If there are any ailing birds at all they are put on this diet. The bread is scalded and allowed to stand several hours; in fact, the longer it stands the better its recuperative properties. I have seen some as ripe as cheese with "whiskers" on, stuff that most people would throw out, but this porridge has a wonderful effect and will frequently pull round birds which would otherwise "go west."

This is not to be recommended as a regular diet, but given occasionally to healthy birds as a change from the ordinary egg and bread diet it induces them when ailing to partake more freely than if they had never tasted the mixture before.

These form an agreeable change from the daily seed diet, and have a beneficial effect on the birds; they can be given as tid-bits at any time, but are mostly appreciated during the breeding season. Care must be taken in their giving during the winter or early spring months, for if there is any frosted food put in at this time it is apt to set up inflammation of the bowels and probably cause death.

From January to March watercress or a piece of apple is the safest food. The watercress may be washed in lukewarm water over night, and this will remove any frost there might be; it may either be given stuck through the wires or chopped up in a mincer and mixed with the soft food; if given in the wires any remains must be cleared out of the cage at the close of the day, for if left in it becomes stale and injurious.

I have also found the tender green leaves of celery much enjoyed by the birds, also portions of the centers make a nice change; during the show season I used to give the birds a frequent supply of this, as I found it helped to keep them in good bloom and condition. During the spring months you can procure young leaves of dandelion, chickweed or groundsel. Dandelion flowers are also very much enjoyed, and are invaluable in bringing on backward birds at the commencement of the breeding season.

Another useful seeding weed is the much-written-about shepherd's purse. This is found by the wayside or on waste-ground and in gardens. The seed pods are triangular in shape and contain a small yellow-colored seed which is much enjoyed by all kinds of cage birds. I have given it liberally during moulting time, especially to dark-plumaged birds such as Greens and Cinnamons. I have also gathered large quantities and dried it to give during winter, but have never found the birds take so kindly towards it as when given in the freshly-gathered state.

A most useful wild seed is the **plantain,** or what is commonly called **"rats tail."** This can be given in the green or unripened state, but it is better when it has ripened. Birds of all kinds fairly revel in this, and when they have finished with it there is very little except the stalk left. When plantain seed is collected and allowed to dry it comes in very usefully in the autumn, and the birds enjoy it as a change.

Lettuce is another useful change of diet, and can be given at any time when procurable. A piece of boiled carrot put in the wires is another tit-bit, or it can be broken up with a fork, and a little portion mixed in the soft food; this also acts as a very good conditioner.

It will be seen that by careful attention the diet of Canaries can be frequently changed, and by the judicious use of wild seeds in season the food bill can be considerably reduced without in any way curtailing the quantity of food.

In several places "Hard Boiled Egg," is mentioned as food. In all these instances and in fact on any occasion where egg food is given, the egg should actually be in boiling water, for at least twenty minutes. Many bird fanciers recommend giving the yolk only, but I always fed the whole egg, so the reader can please himself what he does in this score.

New arrivals should always be isolated for a few days and kept in a well ventilated and well disinfected room until it is absolutely certain that they are perfectly healthy and free from disease. Even then it is hard to guarantee that they do not have any fault such as feather pulling in which case they should never be allowed in the sight of other birds. When transferring them to the bird room, it is advisable to keep them in a separate cage for a time in full sight of the birds they are to be mixed with so that they can get well acquainted before being introduced into the same cage. As a rule two days is sufficient for this. I have known aviary birds to get very jealous of new comers and to injure them severely, but I never knew this to happen when the birds were allowed to become acquainted first.

There should always be a few Hospital cages on hand for sick patients. These should be much smaller than the ordinary cages and the best kind are very simply made. Take a box and put a wire front on, leaving of course, space for a tray or false bottom and arrange the feed and water cups on the outside. This gives a clear space on the inside without any projections for the bird to injure itself against. This makes a cage with an all wood back, ends, top, and bottom which absolutely excludes all drafts and also subdues the light and the bird can find a nice quiet comfortable corner.

Whenever medicine is to be given, glass or earthenware vessels should always be used. Never use metal in any shape or form and even enamel ware should be shunned as there may be a crack in it, which bares the metal to the action of the various drugs.

Oil stoves should be strictly barred from the bird room, as the fumes they give off are very injurious and a friend of mine lost a whole collection of very valuable canaries through his oil stove smoking during his absence.

A German method of rearing was used by a then well-known successful Roller breeder, and was kept by him as a close secret until his death. This "Secret Mixture" was composed as follows: ½ yolk and all the white of one egg; 100 grammes, 4½ oz. bread; finely crushed rape, linseed and maw seed; 3 drops of cod liver oil per teaspoonful of the mixture. We mention it for what it is worth to those who care to give it a trial.

It is not advisable to accustom the birds to a regular "mixed" diet. Plain Canary should be made the staple, with a separate dish or box of mixed seeds as a change. Where a regular mixed diet is given there is generally a lot of waste seed, and this means wasted money.

Other foods used during the breeding season are the egg and bread foods or cakes mentioned in the articles on feeding. Or bread and milk. Milk sop is a very fine sweet milk and white bread and poppy seed. If you have any ailing birds at all, try them on this diet. The bread is scalded and allowed to stand several hours; in fact, the longer it stands the better its recuperative properties. We have seen it as ripe as limburger cheese with "whiskers" on, stuff that most people would throw out, but this porridge has a wonderful effect and will frequently pull round birds which would otherwise "go west."

This is not to be recommended as a regular diet, but given occasionally to healthy birds as a change from the ordinary egg and bread diet, it induces them when ailing to partake more freely than if they had never tasted the mixture before. A pinch of maw seed sprinkled over the milk food is an additional benefit, and if the birds are very run down a few drops of emulsion of cod liver oil may be added to the porridge.

GREEN FOOD AND SEEDING PLANTS

These form an agreeable change from the daily seed diet, and have a beneficial effect on the birds; they can be given as tit-bits at any time, but are mostly appreciated during the breeding season. Care must be taken in their giving during the winter or early spring months, for if there is any frosted food put in at this time it is apt to cause inflammation of the bowels and perhaps death.

From January to March watercress or a piece of apple is the safest food. The watercress may be washed in lukewarm water over night, and this removes any frost there might be; it may either be stuck through the wires or chopped up in a mincer and mixed with the soft food; if given in the wires any remains must be cleared out of the cage at the close of the day, for if left in it becomes stale and injurious. Sprouted rape and Canary seed sprouts cut up in the egg food is splendid.

OTHER USEFUL FOOD SUGGESTIONS

To one hard-boiled egg (30 minutes) add some more bread crumbs than you have mashed egg, and one teaspoonful of powdered milk (baby food). To each bird give one teaspoonful a day, three times a week. A few drops of gentian (procurable at any drug store) or Syrup of Buckthorn in the drinking water is a good tonic. 4 drops to one oz. of water; if sick, 10 drops.

A slice of breakfast bacon or a meat skin hung in the cage secured by a hairpin is a splendid lubricator and conditioner, also liver knob, a piece of hard boiled liver, grated up with scraped carrot, makes a much relished food and is very beneficial as a conditioner and a change. The liver must be boiled hard.

Charcoal, finely ground, is also a splendid tonic or food with which to supply your birds, also grits and ground cuttle bone and shell. Keep this before them all the time.

Grit or gravel is essential to all birds, not the fine sand but a rather rough grit. Grit in the gizzard is called the bird's teeth. See that they have some clean grit and sand at all times.

CHEMICAL FOODS, Etc.

MEDICINES

Chemical Food is the compound syrup of phosphate and contains the phosphate of iron, lime, potash, and soda, equal parts. It is an excellent tonic and contains the necessary material for enriching the blood and forming bone. For young stock in particular, whether children, birds, or puppies, it thoroughly merits the popularity which it enjoys. The formula has been modified somewhat, and the syrup as now sold is considered to be an improvement on the original. Get the best quality. When required for birds, one teaspoonful mixed with two ounces of water should be given three or four times a week for one day each time. To obtain the best effect from this remedy give in distilled water or water that has been well boiled and allowed to stand until cold again. It is best to buy it in small quantities, as it deteriorates somewhat in keeping.

Cod Liver Oil Emulsion needs no description. It is a concentrated form of food rather than a medicinal drug. Its use is to build up and strengthen weakly and ailing birds. The emulsified form being more tasteless and easily assimilated by a debilitated system should always be employed. Birds usually take it quite readily if mixed in a little soft food or dropped on a morsel of bread and milk. Two drops daily in cases of serious illness when the patient is in a low condition, or a similar quantity every second or third day in other cases, are suitable doses for a canary.

Epsom Salts.—A very useful and safe general purgative, especially serviceable for reducing excessive fatness. As much as will cover a six pence in an ounce of water is a suitable general dose.

Eucalyptus Oil.—This is an essential oil distilled from the Blue Gum tree of Australia. It possesses good antiseptic properties and is very efficacious in colds, coughs, and the early stages of bronchitis. It should be given in combination with a stimulant, and a little emulsifying agent such as glycerine to hold it suspended in the water. One drop in each tablespoonful of water, well shaken together, is the best dose.

Lemon Juice.—The juice of a lemon in combination with honey is very useful in minor and throat troubles in singing birds. If given in a sufficient early stage it will often prevent total loss of voice. Five drops in a tablespoonful of water is plenty to give.

Lime Water possesses feeble antiacid and astringent properties, and has been recommended for diarrhoea. It may be used in place of drinking water, either alone or mixed with an equal quantity of ordinary water.

Magnesia.—As a cooling and antacid aperient, fluid magnesia is a very safe and reliable remedy for many minor troubles if given in time. Its use in cases of loss of feathers, attended with a scurfy and unhealthy condition of the skin, is often fraught with exceptionally beneficial results. Twelve drops in a tablespoonful of water for one day is a suitable dose. The dose may be repeated if necessary every second or third day as long as the droppings do not assume a watery condition.

Milk.—The remedial value of milk is not recognized as it should be. With practically all kinds of birds it is both a food and a drink, and indispensable in such diseases as dysentery and inflammation of the bowels. When birds are exhausted from traveling long journeys, or are rather low in condition, a drink of lukewarm milk acts as a splendid reviver and tonic. Bread and milk sprinkled with maw seed, is invaluable in helping birds over an illness.

Potash, Permanganate of, dissolved in water forms a useful deodorant, which has the great advantage of being free from disagreeable smell. When made of such strength that the color resembles that of port wine, it is suitable for rinsing cages, loose sand trays, etc., after scrubbing, and as a general disinfectant.

A little of this solution added to the drinking water in just sufficient quantity to very slightly tint the same acts as a valuable preservative. It is free from danger and does not appear to be objectionable to birds. Water so treated keeps sweet longer than ordinary tap water.

Pure Paraffin, Liquid.—A very useful and efficacious remedy for birds suffering from intestinal irritation and congestion, or in a low debilitated condition through digestive derangements. Only the purified preparation of paraffin sold by all chemists for human use must be used. Four or 5 drops daily on a morsel of bread and milk for birds the size of a canary may be given and continued for a week or two if necessary.

Quassia, Infusion of, is used in the bird room for destroying red mite. One ounce of the chips should be mixed with a pint of boiling water poured over it and stirred occasionally for an hour, when the clear liquid may be poured off, and is ready for use. Boiling is not necessary, as the wood readily yields its active principle. As in the case of infusion of gentian, convenient concentrated infusion is sold by chemists. Quassia preparations, although capable of destroying small insect life, are not poisonous in the ordinary sense. The infusion may be used as a tonic in the same way as infusion of gentian.

Soda, Sulphate of.—Also known as Glauber Salts. May be bought in a white powder, but its more usual form is that of small crystals. It is a very valuable saline purgative. Its action is somewhat milder than that of Epsom salts, and it also possesses a stimulating action on the liver. It has very little taste, and birds take it quite readily. As much of the powder as will cover a sixpence, or a crystal the size of a small pea, should be dissolved in one ounce of water.

Stimulants.—When these are needed to help a bird over a crisis or serious illness, a few drops of brandy, whiskey, or sherry in the order named are the best. Half a teaspoonful in an ounce of water is sufficient. If more is added, the object in view is defeated by deterring the bird drinking as freely as it would with a weaker solution.

Sweet Spirits of Nitre.—A well-known popular remedy of the early stages of a cold. Given immediately in case of a severe cold or sudden chill in combination with squills and ipecacuanha wine, it is most effective in breaking up the cold and cutting it short. Five drops in an ounce of water is the correct dose, and the bird should be kept moderately warm for a few days.

Zinc Lotion.—Useful for bathing inflamed and watery eyes. Five grains of sulphate of zinc dissolved in an ounce of rosewater, and 20 drops of laudanum added, makes a very good formula. It is poisonous, but in this strength not dangerously so; still, caution should be exercised.

Zinc Ointment is a cleansing and healing ointment, of good antiseptic properties, in which the active principle consists of oxide of zinc. For wounds and abrasions of all kinds it is useful, and it is especially efficacious in cases of ulcers, or discharging sores and festering sore feet.

LIQUID MEASUREMENTS

(Not scientifically exact, but in every case near enough for all practical purposes.)

1 drop is equal to 1 minim.
60 drops are equal to 1 drachm.
60 drops are equal to 1 teaspoonful.
1 teaspoonful equals 1 fluid drachm.
1 tablespoonful equals ½ fluid ounce.
2 tablespoonfuls equal 1 fluid ounce.
1 wineglassful equals 2 fluid ounces.
20 fluid ounces equal 1 pint.

1 teaspoonful (as much as it will easily hold, but not heaped) of small crystals or powder of average gravity will weigh about 1 drachm.

1 tablespoonful, under similar conditions equals 1 ounce.

As much as will stand on a 5c piece of any powder or very small crystals of average gravity will weigh about 5 grains.

As much as will stand on a 25c piece, under similar conditions, will weigh about 10 grains.

A pinch: As much as can be conveniently picked up from a bulk between the tips of the thumb and forefinger. With small seeds, and similar articles, it will equal about one-third of a teaspoonful.

FOR GAUGING THE STRENGTH OF SOLUTIONS FOR LOTIONS, AND FOR DISINFECTING AND FOMENTING PURPOSES

(Not scientifically exact, but in all cases near enough for all practical purposes.)

1 drachm of solid in 1 fluid ounce of water equals a 10 per cent. solution. 1 ounce of solid in ½ pint of water equals a 10 per cent. solution. ¼ lb. of solid in 1 quart of water equals a 10 per cent. solution. 1 lb. of solid in 1 gallon of water equals a 10 per cent. solution.

8 or 9 drops of a 10 per cent. solution contain 1 grain of the solid.

1 fluid drachm, or 1 teaspoonful, of liquid added to 1 fluid ounce, or 2 tablespoonfuls of water makes a 10 per cent solution.

1 fluid ounce added to ½ pint water makes a 1—10 per cent solution.

1 tablespoonful fluid added to ½ pint water equals a 1—20 solution.

1 fluid ounce added to 1 pint water equals a 1—20 solution.

1 fluid ounce added to 1 quart water equals a 1—40 solution.

1 pint fluid added to 5 gallons water equals a 1—40 solution.

(1—40 is very good strength for general use.)

1 tablespoonful fluid added to 1¼ pints water equals a 1—50 solution.

1 teacupful fluid added to 1 gallon water equals a 1—50 solution.

¼ pint fluid added to 3 gallons water equals a 1—50 solution.

Other strengths may be readily calculated from the above.

Should the treatment of the owner of a sick bird fail to bring about the necessary relief, it is most probable, assuming the case is not beyond relief, that the diagnosis has been wrong, or, perhaps, the exciting causes have not been removed.

A SUCCESSFUL BREEDER'S BIRD ROOM

PRACTICAL BREEDING TIME
HELPFUL HINTS

That the proper mating time coincides with the awakening of nature in the spring is well-known to most canary breeders. But some, particularly the younger fanciers, are apt to start mating in January or February. They have a feeling of pride if they can go to some other breeder and tell him that they have already mated birds, have eggs and possibly even youngsters.

But, dear breeder, this feeling of self-satisfaction is not warranted. Your youngsters, bred in these last winter months, are at a disadvantage. They are handicapped because the young males start to sing too early in the season. They need an efficient song leader, who is hard to find because the older males are at this time in the moulting period, while the young males have just finished moulting. Having no one to properly teach them at this critical time their song is full of false notes, sharp whistles and other noises which are anything but music. At exhibitions these youngsters might be classified as second prize birds but are generally lucky to get in the third prize class.

These birds also mature earlier in the following year for breeding purposes, so that the fancier is tempted to repeat his mistakes of the previous year and again start the breeding time in January and February. Thus one failure to have them properly trained by example is added to another. Nature indicates the correct mating time. When things start to get green, the end of March or at the beginning of April,

when you no longer need to heat your breeding room, then begin with the mating. So long as you need to heat your breeding quarters during the day, there is danger of the eggs becoming chilled at night or in the morning when the hen leaves them for feeding purposes. This chilling is very likely to kill the germ in the eggs. All your expectations are apt to end in disappointment. Many become disgruntled and conclude that as they have no luck, they will give it up, leave the club, etc.

So, discouraged fancier, listen to the advice of your old, experienced club members and do not begin mating until the proper season. Many articles have appeared in trade magazines on the subject of wintering the hens in cool, or rather cold, quarters. I have tried this method of keeping the hens during the winter in cold quarters and can say from experience that I have had great success, both as to percentage of birds raised and also from the point of their quality as songsters. If you keep your hens from fall on in an unheated room with good mixed feed and some rape seed, you will have a big advantage during breeding time over those fanciers who keep them in heated rooms. A bird, with proper food, can thrive at a temperature of 10 to 14 degrees. If it is sick it will not survive and this is of advantage to the fancier, as a hen lacking in constitution and health is only a liability. It cannot furnish vigorous progeny. Thus wintering them in a cold room acts as a sieve to eliminate inferior animals. Only healthy parents can produce healthy offspring, youngsters that you can be proud of.

The Care of Canary Birds
GENERAL ADVICE

A canary changed from a small cage to a larger one may act strange and timid, but will soon become accustomed to the new quarters and exhibit pleasure in its more spacious and comfortable surroundings.

Always feed a canary in the morning. Give it fresh seed and drinking water, not too cold. During hot weather give it fresh water at least twice a day.

Permit frequent baths in water not too cold. If the bath water is too warm, however, the canary may refuse to bathe. If he refuses to bathe in water of the same temperature as his drinking water there is little that can be done about it, a small piece of lettuce in the bath water often gets them started to bathe. Do not force the canary to bathe, he will keep his feathers clean by preening them. Prevent chilling, both before or after the bath, by keeping the cage in a place where drafts will not strike the bird at any time.

Birds placed in a draft will catch cold as they are easily chilled. An overheated room is also injurious.

A uniform temperature of from 65 to 70 degrees Fahrenheit is best to keep the bird in good condition.

Overheated or impure air and uneven temperature will cause birds to shed feathers out of season. Consequently the cage should not be near a radiator or stove. Canaries can endure much below zero temperature if no draught. Keep the cage and perches clean.

Give the canary the best quality of seed. Fresh clean canary and summer rape seed is an ideal mixture.

Do not feed millet seed to a canary, unless very little in a mixed diet for pepping up. Its use is confined to fancy aviary finches, and song birds.

Inferior bird seed containing millet is often used as a filler, it is so much cheaper than canary and rape seed and is often the cause of lost song.

Canaries relish certain fruits and vegetables such as sweet apples, pears, bananas, pineapples, lettuce, and some of the other greens.

Cage birds, especially, need exercise to keep in health and song. Canary vitamin highball suspended in the cage for this purpose in order to furnish a readily available food supply should the seed cup be forgotten. The vitamin highball contains yeast and cod liver oil, which serve as a tonic and give the canary more pep and energy.

Cuttlebone is absolutely essential to a canary's welfare. It aids digestion, sharpens the bill, and supplies the necessary lime in the diet.

Use bird gravel on the cage pan.

Follow the above advice and you should have no trouble in deriving the maximum pleasure from a healthy, happy, songful canary.

Always give the bird the best and cleanest seeds. Do not keep seeds in an airtight container, they must have ventilation.

Canaries are subject to colds and hoarseness which can often be avoided. Do not place the cage in a direct draft or where subject to sudden changes in temperature. Ice cold drinking water, or cold and forced baths are other causes.

The symptoms are sneezing and coughing. This prevents normal breathing and the bird makes strenuous efforts to relieve itself of the phlegm in its nose and throat.

Without delay place the bird in a warm and sunny room. Cleanse the nostrils with a solution of warm water and witch hazel by dipping a feather in the solution and applying it to the nostrils.

When the phlegm has dissolved apply just a little plain white vaseline in each nostril.

During this condition feed a little poppy seed (maw) mixed in with the other seed. Give the bird some egg-food and every other day a small portion of stale wheat bread moistened in boiled milk and sprinkled with Poppy seed.

Loss of Voice.—This is the result of exposure to drafts of cold air and sudden changes of temperature, or, by singing too much and overstraining the voice. See Question and Answer section in back of this book.

BIRD ROOM VENTILATION

Birds themselves give forth a surprising amount of heat, their temperature is 110, their heart beat 400, therefore you may understand the reason. Ventilation is the thing, cold never kills canaries, but draughts are generally fatal, beware of any window, they are all draughty, have some glass or permanent wind shield, keep the window open in summer time and in winter time during the day time for a while to change the air in the room, unless you have a perpetual ventilation. Canaries can stand well below zero weather, (this I know personally, in many instances in Chicago, in Louisville, Ky. even in San Antonio, Texas, I have had below zero weather in my bird room, but no draught, no one had healthier birds, I had to cover my room singer at night to make it cease singing). Bathing is essential especially during the moulting period, a small piece of lettuce placed in the bath will often induce a slow bather to get started by his getting his head wet from the lettuce in his bath tub.

The companionship of a singing canary, or of raising a few nests, or of keeping some of the beautiful finches or love birds have brought great comfort and relaxation, and even joy to many a sick person or a shut-in and have made the hours pass quickly, it has even been credited with having soothed the anguish of pain. The singing of a bird companion brings happiness, cheerfulness and amusement and comfort to the home. Many an humble home in a crowded tenement house on the narrow back streets of our cities have been made happier, brighter by the jolly singing canary.

93

HOW TO DISTINGUISH SEX IN CANARIES

It is difficult for the beginner to separate the males from the females, when all are in a large flight-cage together. Sometimes you may notice a bird twittering at two months old, and by standing near the cage with a mouth full of water, watch your chance to get him apart from the others, and squirt the water from your mouth on him, which will enable you to catch him from the flight, marking him from the others. Or you may use a small spray, successfully.

Experienced breeders are able to distinguish sex by holding the bird in the hand and feeling the abdomen gently, beginners should make such tests with mature birds only.

When birds are fully grown it is usually easier to distinguish sex by examining the vent—blowing the feathers away from the vent, you will notice that the vent of the female is smaller and in a straight line with the body, while the vent of the male is more pronounced, more prominently developed.

Notice also that the note of the male is short and sharp—the shape of the head longer with a flat skull, and he is more energetic in his movements than the female, whose call is much longer and more decided—has a rounding skull crown, more inclined to a round head. These points are well to notice, because we often find a singing female.

GETTING HENS READY FOR BREEDING

I strongly protest against breeding too early, first you cannot successfully take too many nests from a bird, in the winter or early season the nights are longer, days shorter and the baby birds are forced to go too long without food, unless electric lights are used and they will not grow and mature as well. Should your hens become too forward, a crystal of soda in the water will often help to cool them off, I have had to put them on plain canary seed for a time, with milk sop, (bread and milk) about twice a week, the greatest aid is to keep the sexes out of sight of each other when getting too forward.

SLOW TO GET INTO BREEDING
CONDITION

There has probably been something wrong in the past winter or the birds are not in normal health. The first thing to do is to give them a mild saline aperient, not too salty and barely warm, give six or eight drops in the beak with a medicine dropper for two days, then give a tonic composed of equal parts tincture of gentian, cofumba and dilute sulphuric acid, five drops of the above to each tablespoon of water in the birds water container, be sure to mix, give the above every other day until four or five treatments, then begin to feed gradually richer foods and alternate with them, rarely ever will this treatment fail to bring a healthy hen of breeding qualities into condition, an old hen, or one that has been over bred the year previous is not worth fooling with.

COLOR FEEDING

It is possible for any owner of a canary to color-feed their yellow or buff birds by taking some pains to gather some Nasturtiums or Marigold blooms, if you are breeding color-fed show specimens they should be fed color food from seven or eight weeks of age. The surest and safest and certainly the easiest way is to purchase any of the good orange color foods on the market and feed the color food sparingly but at least twice daily, three times daily is much better. To feed the color food but once a day has a tendency to cause a spotted coloring. Don't forget GREEN FOOD DAILY is as important during the color-feeding as at any time, and I believe somewhat more important. Feed green food daily, sparingly of course, green food works on the liver and this benefits an even smooth coloring. The blood assimilates the color-food. During this period it is well to alternate in your regular diet, change the bird's daily staple food and do not over-feed, of course, and feed sparingly to avoid having the bird throw out some seeds looking for the seed of its choice, show bench color feeders of the old school cover the cage in order to have an even color and exquisite bloom. Any thin calico cloth will do. In color-feeding a number of birds I have used a certain kind of sheet material to pull along a wire, an even light benefits even color-feeding.

SUNSHINE FOR CANARIES

Many people think the Canary originated from a bird of the tropics and that it should be kept in a hot or warm climate or temperature, THIS IS NOT THE CASE. Canaries thrive best in moderate temperatures, they stand extreme cold weather well, but sudden changes are not the best as it is not the best for any living thing; avoid sudden change of extreme temperatures and by all means AVOID THE GLARING SUN. Many place their bird out on a porch or sunroom where it will remain in the glaring sun for hours, this in many cases wrecks its constitution, I have known it to result fatally, in many instances the loss of song is the result and a year's moping around. They do like sunshine a wee bit for a short duration, but it is best not to have direct sunshine, being near rays of sunshine is inspiring to the bird. Make possible some shade when cage is in the sun.

The Canary Islands are on about the same latitude as South Georgia, Florida and South Texas, and it is a well known fact that these places at times for a short duration do have some pretty cold spells. I have had to break ice an inch thick in San Antonio, Texas, for my birds to drink I did not put in hot or warm water which is the best thing to do. I was however, experimenting.

BIRD POISONS SELF IN CAGE
Beware of Chipped Enamel or Paint on
Your Cage.

The enamel is a pyroxylin lacquer. The upper or wire portion of many cages is constructed of copper plated wire, covered with a thin coating of pyroxylin lacquer, many cages are dip painted.

CARE OF YOUR CAGE

When the cage becomes soiled, make a tepid soap suds, and wash it with a very soft cloth, do not use washing powders as it will destroy the lacquer, drying it with an equally soft cloth, or place the cage where it can dry in the air. Never use any cleaning powder and never scrape the cage. After being polished by the manufacturer, brass cages are covered with a hard lacquer, or sometimes enamel paint, and the use of a scouring soap would take the lacquer or paint off. Little bits of verdigris would then be liable to form on the brass, and these are poisonous; also the cage will become dull and lose its brightness.

In view of these facts we think it probable that a bird's death can be due to poisoning, attributed to its having pecked at a spot where the lacquer or paint was chipped off, and thus obtained some of this poisonous verdigris. Verdigris is a basic copper carbonate which forms on copper when exposed to damp air.

BIRD PUFFED—A BALL OF FEATHERS

Should you notice, in the flight-cage where you are keeping your females, one all puffed, perhaps squatting on the perch or the floor, picking around or trying to sleep and showing very plainly that it is not well, it would be best to remove the bird and give it special treatment.

It is probably suffering from a cold or from constipation. First give a laxative (epsom salts in the drinking water—and repeat on the third day) then some warm milk over some stale white bread with some poppy-seed sprinkled over it (which is often spoken of as "milksop").

Usually this simple diet will bring the bird back to normal condition. But be sure to take away all green foods, and all rich foods during this treatment.

This special food diet is one reason that you should remove the sick bird—for there is no reason to inflict the treatment on those not needing it, and then too, they might have some trouble which would be contagious.

Choose for breeding the very best healthy, active females, (for weaklings only bring grief and failure). Get your breeders into condition before you mate them. Consult the columns "Questions and Answers" where you will find many answers to your problems.

SUNSHINE FOR CANARIES

We have inquiries from many beginners as to the advisability of breeding canaries in a basement or an attic, where it is not possible to have the direct rays of the sun, and feel that a few lines on this subject may be of interest.

Light, plenty of light is most essential in raising canaries, but this light is often supplied by electric lights.

Natural light, and some sunlight are very good, of course, but the direct sun-ray is not best. The prepared Cod-liver Oil foods are very good and supply the vitamin D (near sun-ray).

Birds may be properly raised in any dry, well ventilated place which is free from draft.

Ventilation is necessary. A damp, musty place will bring nothing but grief. Keep the quarters clean, dry, well ventilated and free from draft, and you will have no difficulties because of the absence of direct sunlight.

Fresh water, grit, cuttlefish-bone, with good foods and you will have no worries, for the electric lights will give all the lighting necessary for breeding purposes and the rearing of the young. Adopt a method of dimming the lights toward night time, rather than to suddenly turn off the lights, which might leave a mother-bird off the nest.

ALWAYS

A Scotchman found it necessary to notify his wife that he might not be home that evening, in which case he told her:

"I'll ring you at 6 o'clock. When you hear the bell you'll know it's me. Don't answer it and I'll get my nickel back."

THE LINNET

(Linota cannabina)

THE LINNET is well known all over England, Ireland, Scotland, and Wales for its singing abilities, and is, in the opinion of many, next to the Nightingale for its song. They are easily kept, and very cheap, too, considering their wonderful song. The best time for buying a Linnet, or for catching a number of Linnets, is from the later end of September onwards, as at that time the majority of them are over the moult.

The Linnet, being one of the most adaptable to cage life of all our British seed-eating birds, is keenly sought after by fanciers for show purposes, and for Mule and Hybrid breeding, as well as by those who like it for its song.

This bird is one of the most useful for Mule and Hybrid breeding. Numerous crosses have been obtained by it. As a father, he is generally a good feeder, and looks well after his young. He is almost the first bird chosen by a novice for crossing, and many a full-fledged fancier has become such by his initial success with his Linnet-Canary Mules.

The Linnet has a range which extends throughout Europe, nests mostly in bushes common to the several countries throughout its range. Subsisting mostly on seeds and congregate into large flocks during the migration season. When under a year old, its chief color is of a light greyish brown. They are then called Grey Linnets. After the second moult, the male finch shows a crimson hue on the forehead with crimson blush on the breast and brownish hue on the sides, lower breast and flanks but of a richer hue than in its first year. It is then called a Brown Linnet.

When the third moult has taken place the forehead and breast become a bright carmine, it is then called a Rose Linnet.

These colorations only appear in its wild state, for after moulting in captivity the beautiful crimson never returns although the brown becomes much richer and its song increases in melody. Yet the throat which is greyish is finely penciled and the outer web of the primaries show a distinctive white margin. It is graceful in movements and proves very satisfactory as a pet, filling the room with melody and cheer. In size it compares somewhat to a small sized Canary.

There are few birds of better disposition and none comparable to it for not seeking trouble with other inmates of the cage, seeking no trouble, getting into no trouble, but will not tolerate interference from any bird.

As to food, they are fond of good rape, canary and seeding grasses, also soaked teasel as a tid bit. They will over feed and become too fat to fly. This condition will prove fatal to them causing liver troubles then lack of song, so watch carefully not to over supply with food. If out of condition, crack some sunflower seeds and feed up on same until in condition again. Cuttle bone must not be kept from them as the salt it contains is very beneficial to their system.

BENEFITS OF HAND WASHING

First of all I will explain why a cold water bath does not wash the feathers of the birds, but only gives the birds a beneficial effect, which can only be considered in the light of a tonic, and not as a cleanser.

In canaries, as in most birds, nature has supplied them with a source from which a supply of oil can be obtained, and the birds will be noticed to make use of this oil at the time that they are preening their feathers.

At the extreme end of the back, and at the point from which the tail feathers radiate, will be found a small white sack, which very much resembles a white pimple. If this sack is gently pressed a small amount of oil will exude. The birds make use of this oil when preening the feathers, and they will be noticed to reach around to the oil sac, and then run the feathers through the beak, one feather after the other. In this way the feathers gradually become coated with a film of oil. The underflue and very small feathers being nourished as they are from the blood stream of the bird, are supplied with the oil in this way.

In the average house, no matter how well kept, there is always a certain amount of dust. This dust will adhere to the feathers of the birds, and in time the same will be just as thick with dust as they are with the oil mentioned. We all know that oil and water will not mix, and it is for this reason that cold water will not remove the oil and the dirt. We must use an agent which

96

will cut the oil and at the same time remove the dust. The only agent to use is soap.

Many fanciers use the best brand of castile soap, for the reason that it does not contain soda, which is supposed to prevent the feathers from drying out as silky as they should. A soap which is very good for the reason that it contains a very slight amount of carbolic, is the brand known as Lifebuoy Carbolic Soap. Never add any form of disinfectant, for if this is done, the bird will be poisoned, owing to the very absorbant nature of the skin of the birds.

Handwashing is safe and without doubt it has a very beneficial effect upon the birds, as it opens up the pores and cleanses the skin as well as the feathers, and seems just as essential to our birds as a bath is to ourselves.

To those Fanciers who have never seen a bird washed, I will say that the principal things to consider are speed and carefulness to follow the necessary details, and I would advise that for the first experiment, a cheap, common hen bird be used, and when this has been washed and the Fancier gained a certain amount of confidence he may wash more valuable birds.

First with a small pair of bent scissors, clip the beak and claws if required. Now place the legs of the bird between the second and third fingers of the left hand, and close the fingers, so that any attempt to escape will be prevented, owing to the claws not passing between the fingers. The water should be about 75 or 80 degrees, you may test it by dipping your elbow into it.

Another very nice way to dry the birds is to put the cage over an electric toaster, which will give off just the heat required.

Be sure and clip the claws of your birds if they seem to be too long, also the tips of their beaks. It is a delicate operation, but is easily done with a pair of manicure scissors. Excelsior in the flight cages keeps the bird's feet clean and can be turned over like a carpet after a few weeks use. Paper is not dangerous, but by far less valuable than sawdust, sand or excelsior which is much the best of all. It is most necessary that you clean your breeding cage and nest with kerosene; with some pine tar in it will prevent mites.

With two cages side by side with opening for male to go from cage to cage, yet the hens usually, in nine out of ten cases, remain in their own home and do not trouble the other hen, that is if you keep opening closed until they become settled and start to housekeeping. These hen breeders are very easy to make. Secure from your fruit merchant an apple box, the ordinary box apples are packed and shipped in, cut an opening in each end, one to hang the outside nest over, so the hen can come in and build, the other end in top of back end of box or cage, this permits the male to visit each hen at will. Remove the bottom, get a piece of tin, cut it to be two inches wider than the box; this two inches you use to catch the loose seeds, etc., in front of cage, also have the front of the tin bottom or slip (as it should be a loose slip that can be removed quickly and easily) turned up one inch, and at each end of the slip bottom have turned up one-half an inch, and make one inch longer than the box to make removing easy. With this you can remove the bottom to clean and replace an extra

one you have already cleaned and in a few minutes you have a clean cage, the cage or box has no bottom and rests on the tin sliding tray bottom until removed; then it sets on the shelf until you replace the tray. Most anyone can make this cage. You can buy the bottom for 75c; the fronts and the outside nests for 35c, the box 10c, hence you have a cheap nest and as good as any. Each week paint the cage from outside with kerosene, (Coal Oil), and moth balls. This keeps mites down. This kind of a cage can be kept easily from mites.

Many people prefer to breed in an aviary. Whether it is on the indoors or out, my experience has been the most satisfactory way for profit or pleasure the individual breeding is best. Better birds are assured by scientifically breeding and using closed bands always, the better your birds the larger your profits. Breeding two, three or four hens to one cock in a large cage is colony breeding. It is not best to have two hens in one ordinary breeding cage. Separate cages for the hen with opening for male to travel is the best plan. By all means do try to get the best out of your birds by cage breeding and not lawn aviary breeding.

Linnets when caged for the first few weeks are somewhat wild, so place the cage where they can always see what is going on. With the top of cage covered, this will prove effective in steadying them much sooner than otherwise. Don't forget to give them some seeding plant in stalks when the seeds are ripe. Contrary to most advice, do not feed them hemp seed. It is too fattening and in most cases proves fatal.

Linnets live to a good old age and under proper supervision will breed with female Canaries readily, producing offspring of wonderful song. October is the best month to purchase these finches, as at that time the importations consist mostly of current year young, which have become fully feathered and have just started into song.

Do not be over anxious to steady them, have patience with them and you will never regret the time spent in making a pet of this singer of singers in the Finch family.

THE LINNET WHEN BREEDING

The Linnet appears to breed twice in the year, the first eggs being laid in April. I have seen nests with eggs as late as the end of August. The eggs are from four to six in number, and are of a French grey ground color, with light reddish-brown or pale purplish-red. The nest is usually formed of fine twigs and more or less tinged with green and speckled fibres outside, and is mixed with moss and grass stalks, being lined with hair, or vegetable down. It is generally built in any low bush, such as blackberry, gorse, hazel and hawthorn bushes.

When breeding, the cock has a very red breast, the hen being of a very light brown with heavy dark markings. I have found that the cock helps the hen to sit, and in one nest I was watching he did so as many as five times a day. The young Linnets are dark brown in color when first hatched, but when they are feathered and are ready to leave the nest, their plumage is a light brown all over.

THE SONG OF THE LINNET

As songsters, few birds, perhaps, are more variable than Linnets; they have a very considerable compass and sing in a continuous manner, though some, of course, can only repeat two or three unconnected notes, which may be of the harshest tone. The song of caged-up Linnets is much improved in the second year, and reaches its best in the third.

My reason for listing the Linnet here with the most popular breeds of Canaries has been prompted from information I have gathered during some visits among fanciers in a number of States in the U. S. who have stated their birds were part Linnet. This is impossible as the young from a Linnet and a Canary will not produce themselves hence they are Hybrids. Only the males are of value as a pet. To those laboring under this impression permit me to dispell any ideas that you have part Linnets if they are breeders, Linnets have been used for Hybrid breeding for many years and the crosses make good singers for those who prefer the song of the wild birds, or the loud sharp shrill song, and are not partial to the soft sweet melodious song of the Roller. The Linnet is easily tamed when caught in the wild state, and breeds readily in captivity. Some birds of dark green plumage we know have been sold as Linnets. This was entirely a misrepresentation as in appearance the Linnet is not as attractive as any of the present day Canaries that have been so artistically perfected.

THE NOTES OF THE BIRD

It is very difficult to explain the song of the bird on paper, but this is how an expert has done for a bird paper.

I wish it to be understood that I am perfectly well aware that in different parts of the country, fanciers have different names for their notes and ways of singing; the Linnet is a mocking bird; the song consists of the following notes: Chattering, chowing, reeing, peeing, whinnying and scraping.

All Linnets sing two or three of these notes, and also turn them. Some are longer, some are deeper, and some will get more turns together than others. The lightest note is tittering, taken from the Tit-lark, tit-tit-titrun and turned heavier or deeper whinny titter and jungle titter. There are various ways of chattering, running chatter, rolling chatter, cater chatter, stammering chatter, chattering, ree and locking chatter. Reeing is a kind of tremulous note, and consists of the following: Fine reeing, rollingree, trumpet reeing (very seldom heard) hollow reeing, curling ree, and blubbering ree.

Next comes peeing, from the Bullfinch, pee pee, fear fear, pi pi, po po. Here are also the various ways of peeing. Plain peeing, whistling pee, feeing pee, piping pee, bell peeing, and pooing pee. Whinnying is a nice note, and very hard to sing. It is taken from the Cuckoo, Nightingale, Waterhen, Snipe, and Blackbird. The names of the different ways are filly whinnying, Blackbird whinny, huffing whinny, and laughing whinny—he—he, ha ha, ho—ho—all right from the stomach.

Scraping is taken from Corncakes, Skylarks, Siskins, Rooks and Ducks wiff wiff, wyke wyke, car car, cow cow, quack quack. Here are the different ways of scraping: Sharp, broad, kind, cowing, marking, draker, and quacking scrape. The next is chowing, the worst of the classical notes.

This note is taken from several kinds of birds, and has various forms of expression—chict chict, chey chey, chi chi, chow chow, the last being the best.

The Linnet has yet some more classical notes, but not so often sung as some of the above mentioned notes. First we come to bell pether, taken from the Canary indoors, Cuckoo pether, Woodlark woodle, and Nightingale pugging.

Allow me to advise in closing. Do not try to imitate these notes unless away from all human listeners, otherwise your neighbors will be justified in your banishment to the mountain tops.

*   *   *

TIMELY TIPS

A double breeding cage is twice as va'uable as a single one, because it is twice the size.

*   *   *

It gives more room for the pair. There is more chance of healthy young and more chances of fertile eggs.

*   *   *

The double cage is essential to the success of the single mating system, which means one male to one hen.

The one male to one hen method is the most natural, and if followed on right lines it is the most successful method of breeding canaries.

*   *   *

In double breeders all you have to do when the hen commences to sit is push the slide in the cage, instead of catching the male and transferring him to another cage.

*   *   *

Many a hen refuses to sit unless the male is within sight, and you cannot easily have him within sight when single breeders are used.

DON'TS

Don't allow your canary's cage to stand where it will be subject to drafts, near window or door.

Don't place the bird too near a radiator or any other heating device.

Don't keep bird in a room where the temperature will vary too much at night. A constant temperature of about 76 degrees is the best.

Don't keep the bird in kitchen while cooking.

Don't set the cage higher than six (6) feet from the floor, or in a low-ceilinged room, even less.

Don't keep your bird in a wooden cage as this type cage easily becomes infested with mites.

Don't expect your bird to digest its food unless you have a clean supply of Gravel.

MULES—HYBRIDS

An Excellent Specimen Cock, Goldfinch, Canary Hybrid—Mule.

For pleasure, pastime and study in the art of breeding birds there is nothing to equal the fascination of breeding Hybrids or Mules. It is somewhat illogical, but neverthless true, while there is neither difference or distinction between the breeding of Hybrids and Mules, however many bird lovers, even breeders often refer to this or them as though there were a difference or a distinction.

To the average breeder or fancier, Mules are the progeny, resulting from the crossing of canaries with some native or foreign finch, while they presume Hybrids are the progeny from mating to different breeds of finches. The fact is that both are Mules, and both are Hybrids, according to the dictionary signifies they are not given credit of being able to breed, or re-produce themselves, however in rare cases mules in animal and bird life have been known to be fertile and have reared young. This however, is very rare and should not be considered here.

MATING FOR MULES

In breeding mules and hybrids, a brief explanation as to what is a mule, and what is a hybrid. As a matter of fact all crosses between wild birds and canaries, and between two wild birds are hybrids, but wherever one may travel, we find both terms are used by fanciers, and, briefly, here is the explanation: An old rule is any young bird bred from a male finch and a

female canary is always called a mule by old fanciers. Any cross between two wild birds is termed a hybrid, viz., a bird produced from a male gold-finch and a female canary is a gold-finch mule, one from a linnet and canary a linnet mule and so on, while a cross between a Greenfinch and Bullfinch would be a Greenfinch and Bullfinch Hybrid. However actually there is no distinction nor difference.

What type of canary do we require to get mules from? Well, any kind of healthy canary will do if we only want songsters and don't wish to show the offspring, thus we require good singers, as a matter of fact while we all admire the song of a robust singing mule we must give song the secondary consideration, as our mule must be a fine, large, grand colored bird, and to produce such a bird any old canary will not do. The best females for producing good big males are undoubtedly Norwich and Yorkshire type, personally I prefer the Norwich female as her offspring are large, nice cobby birds, but some wonderful birds have been produced from Yorkshires. Whichever type you decide on get nice large tight feathered birds with good bold heads, as particularly with Goldfinch canary and Siskin canary mules a good big head is a wonderful asset on the show bench, so get busy and get hold of one or two good females. What kind of mule should we strive for? I think I can say, without fear of contradiction, that the Goldfinch mule is the most popular, with a fight for second place between the Linnet Mule and the

99

Siskin Mule. Suppose we take the Goldfinch first. Our Goldfinch must be large, with a large square cut blaze, the blaze, of course, is the deep red on the face and throat, this red should be pure in color, and, in a male bird, should extend behind the eye and should come well down the throat where it should be square cut, a rounded blaze never looks so well as the square one, the breast should be well tanned, that is, it should have as much rich dark brown feathers on it as possible. We don't like white breasted Goldies.

SUDDENLY CHILLED BIRDS

Birds suffering from chill or cold often recover from illness, brought on by chilling or changes in the weather, following the use of sun dried white bread, ground equal parts red pepper and honey for birds.

Another treatment that I have found that has been of any value to me in treating birds ill from the results of chilling or draft is the extremely simple one of putting a Mazda light where the bird can get close to it; best if the bird can get under it, close enough to touch it, the sick bird will back up to the lamp almost against it, when the lamp is almost hot enough to singe the feathers, spread its wings and feathers.

The breeding of mules and hybrids is a very elusive but fascinating branch of aviculture.

A mule is a cross between a finch and the domesticated canary, a hybrid, a cross between two wild finches.

This is one branch of the bird fancy that is never over-crowded. It is seldom you see large stocks of either mules or hybrids for sale at any of our dealers; in fact, there are thousands of fanciers in this country that have never seen either mule or hybrid. In fact, I have known a variegated canary to be called a mule by persons that had never seen any other kind of a canary but a clear bird. Another fallacy that has been aired over and over again by different parties at different times is that they had possessed a mule that had bred with a canary. When investigated it proved to be a variegated canary, as all mules and hybrids are sterile.

In the breeding of mules it is not a very difficult matter to breed Linnet, Greenfinch and Goldfinch mules, but it is a little more difficult to breed Bullfinch, Chaffinch and Yellow Buntings.

I am now writing of the European finches, as it is necessary to obtain a special permit before we are allowed to trap and cage our American finches, so mules from American finches are out of the question. Now we have two varieties of mules—light and dark. The light mule is what we all strive for, and to obtain this we must have clear blood on the canary side to counteract the dark blood on the finch side. To obtain this we try to breed to a strain of canaries that have been bred clear for several generations; these are known as sib bred canaries and always have pink eyes. These hens bred to finches do throw clear or variegated mules at times, but, even so, you cannot always expect them.

To the beginner I would recommend a good clear Norwich hen, sib bred if possible, mated to a Greenfinch male, for I find the Greenfinch to be the easiest of the finches to breed in captivity, and that is the reason I give it first choice.

One of the prettiest mules I ever saw was bred from a Cinnamon hen canary and a Greenfinch mule. It was bronze in color and I don't believe it was ever beaten on the show bench.

My next choice of a finch is the Brown Linnet. This bird I believe is kept by more fanciers than any other finch. I know if it settles down to cage life it is a very free breeder with the canary. The mules from this cross are in great demand for singers, especially if bred to a roller hen canary.

The next is the Goldfinch; this bird, being much prettier than the last two, is given first choice by a lot of mule breeders, but he is not so reliable to fertilize eggs nor is he reliable with eggs; some are safe enough, but the majority will break the eggs at the first opportunity. Now this bird must be taken out of the cage each night and replaced in the morning after the egg has been removed or you must have a false nest; that is, two nests, one a little above the other, the bottom one containing bran or other soft material, the top one having a small hole in the center just large enough to let the egg pass through onto the bran below. Mr. Goldfinch is usually perched on the rim of the nest waiting for his breakfast, but the moment his wife moves, he is too late, for the egg disappears into the nest below.

Now we come to the Bullfinch mule. This was claimed to be impossible for a number of years until one was found by accident bred by an old lady. In this case she had a singing canary, and, being a lover of birds, a friend gave her a female Bullfinch, which she put with her canary to keep him company. How long they were kept together I cannot say, but in the spring the Bullfinch laid several eggs to the cage bottom, so she put in a canary nest pan, with the result that she raised several mules that season. Since then thousands of Bullfinch mules have been bred, but always with the Bullfinch hen and male canary.

The Chaffinch and Yellow Bunting mules are very rare; only two Chaffinch mules have ever been seen on the show bench, one during the past season and one several years ago. The Yellow Bunting or Yellow Hammer, as it is sometimes called, was seen during the last season for the first time, although I myself bred one in 1910, but lost it by an accident when it was six weeks old.

The reason that there are so few of these varieties is the feeding of the young. The Chaffinch and the Buntings both use a lot of insects in the rearing of a family, so it is only reasonable that the young mules will also need insects, and it is very difficult indeed to get a canary to feed on live insects. The only method is to mix the insect food with the egg food. By doing this it is possible to rear the above mentioned variety.

Some fanciers have a great deal of trouble in getting the finch and canary to mate correctly so as to get fertile eggs. There is no trouble in getting the canary into breeding condition, but it needs a little more care in getting the finch into breeding condition. Your finch ought to be singing freely, if not he will be a doubtful breeder. Should you have clear eggs in the first nest, try this tip: I always put a singing canary in a wire cage and hang it on the front of the breeding cage containing the muling pair, and when Mr. Canary sings his love song and the female answers by wanting to mate the finch will take the opportunity nine times out of ten and fertilize the eggs for him.

In the breeding of hybrids each pair must be kept in a large cage together all winter, and in the spring a suitable shrub or bush should be placed in one corner and in the center of it a wild bird nest should be placed; this will encourage them to start nesting operations. The following varieties have been often bred—the first named bird is the male of the parents, the last named the female: Linnet-Bullfinch, Greenfinch, Bullfinch, Goldfinch-Bullfinch, Twite-Bullfinch, Redpoll-Bullfinch, Siskin Bullfinch, Linnet-Greenfinch, Linnet-Goldfinch, Redpoll-Linnet, Redpoll-Siskin, Redpoll-Goldfinch, Goldfinch-Greenfinch, Bramblefinch-Chaffinch. Of course some of the crosses have been bred both ways, so there is no hard and fast rule in any of the crosses, with the exception of the Bullfinch, where the female must always be used.

The diet for a cock goldfinch and hen canary when paired up would be three parts canary seed, two parts teazle, one part German rape, one part niger, one part linseed and one part hemp.

Now this is a little different to the seed mixture given to canaries, but no one need fear that it will affect the hen canary.

The quantities are so small that the finch will get the bulk of them, and they are necessary to keep him in good condition.

The hen canary will take good care that she gets the bulk of the little egg food you give them daily, or every other day, while paired up, until she has laid.

Don't forget a little fresh green food daily, or, better still, dandelion seed heads if procurable.

Seed only should be given the hen while she is incubating the eggs, until the day before they are due to hatch, when a little egg food should be given and continued daily.

In fact, they should be fed just the same as when rearing young canaries, with this difference: give the green food a little more freely when rearing mules.

When the young can feed themselves let their diet be similar to that for young canaries, not forgetting a little crushed hemp the first week or ten days, say a heaped teaspoonful between four youngsters daily.

A little seedy chickweed, rape seed, stalks of plantain, or shepherd's purse, should also be given.

They are partial to these succulent seeds, which are good for them and should be given whenever procurable.

The same routine is applicable to breeding linnet canary mules, with just a slight variation in the seed diet.

When the cock linnet and hen canary are paired up drop the niger seed out of the above seed mixture and add two parts German rape instead of one to the rest of the mixture.

Green food and wild seed heads as recommended for the goldfinch and canary, bearing in mind that two of the favorite wild seeds of the linnet are dandelion and shepherd's purse, followed by knapweed.

One or other of these seed heads should be given daily if at all within your power to do so, as they assist quickly to bring the linnet into breeding condition.

Such condition is easily recognized by his incessant song, carrying it at times into almost screeching runs, as if he could not get it out quickly enough.

When in full breeding condition his beak becomes a rich—as if polished—bluish-lead color.

In selecting the linnet, let him be as large as possible and of good color; the rich, nutty-brown shade.

The richer this brown is on the breast and flanks, the better will be the color of the mules.

FORGET IT.

By Mrs. Bartsch.

If you see a real fellow ahead of a crowd,
A leader of men marching fearless and proud
And you know of a tale whose mere telling
    aloud,
Would cause his proud head to in anguish be
    bowed,
It's a very good plan to forget it.

If you know of a skeleton hidden away,
In a closet, and guarded, and kept from the
    day
In the dark; and whose showing whose sudden
    display,
Would cause grief and sorrow and lifelong dismay,
It's a very good plan to forget it.

If you know of a thing that would darken the
    joy
Of a man or a woman, a girl or a boy,
That would wipe out a smile or the least bit
    annoy
A fellow, or cause any gladness to cloy
It's a very good plan to forget it.

Hand Washing

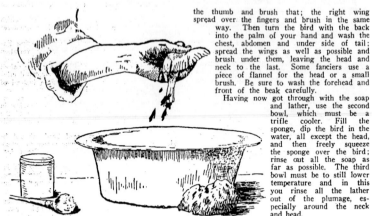

The thumb and brush that; the right wing spread over the fingers and brush in the same way. Then turn the bird with the back into the palm of your hand and wash the chest, abdomen and under side of tail; spread the wings as well as possible and brush under them, leaving the head and neck to the last. Some fanciers use a piece of flannel for the head or a small brush. Be sure to wash the forehead and front of the beak carefully.

Having now got through with the soap and lather, use the second bowl, which must be a trifle cooler. Fill the sponge, dip the bird in the water, all except the head, and then freely squeeze the sponge over the bird; rinse out all the soap as far as possible. The third bowl must be to still lower temperature and in this you rinse all the lather out of the plumage, especially around the neck and head.

The greatest anxiety of the amateur at the commencement of his show career is the hand-washing process. This is quite simple after the first two or three attempts, but the best thing to do if possible is to see some of the old hands put them through it.

For a successful wash there are several things you want, and some you don't want. Things wanted are a bright fire, three bowls of hot water, a kettle with more water ready, a good soft shaving brush, some soap in a mug of hot water, some linen or soft cotton rags, an old bath towel to wrap the birds in for drying purposes, a silk handkerchief for finishing off, and an empty cage or a drying cage in which to transfer the birds when dried.

The things you don't want: Your wife and family, if any, or your best girl, if single, hanging around you exclaiming "Poor little thing, what a shame, you're going to kill it!" It is surprising how much better you can get on without them. A well washed bird is a pitiful sight until dry, seems most dead but it comes out O. K.

GETTING ON WITH THE WASHING

Having got the things you want, and got rid of those you don't want, get your birds ready. The water must not be too hot, but just comfortable. Get the bird in your left hand, head between the first finger and thumb and the tail towards the wrist. First soak the bird's plumage either by dipping it in the water (keeping the head out, of course,) or by squeezing the sponge over it. Next take the shaving brush, work up a good creamy lather with the soap, and commence on the back of the bird, brushing down to the tail (always brush the same way as the feathers lie); use plenty of lather on the back and tail. Then spread the left wing over the fleshy part of

Having given the bird a good sousing in this third water, take the sponge, squeeze it as dry as possible, and take as much of the moisture out of the feathers as you can. Have your linen or cotton cloths (old bath towel will do) warmed beforehand in front of the fire, and take the bird and roll it up in one of these, leaving the head just inside the roll; don't roll up too tightly nor yet too slack. Have a drying board or box in front of the fire and place the bird on this.

Bird in the Cloth, Showing the Position of the Head.

Then take bird number 2, and go through the process again, having added a little more warm water from the kettle. By the time number 2 is through the wash No. 1 will be ready for another dry warm cloth, and if you have more birds to wash they can be done while Nos. 1 and 2 are drying.

When the first birds are in a semi-dry state, unroll them and mop up as much of the moisture as you can with the cloth they are wrapped in, and then place them in the drying cage.

A piece of flannel should be spread on the drying cage.

The birds will quickly shake themselves and soon get on the perches and begin to preen themselves. Put in a thin covering over the front, but do not put the drying cage too near the fire, for if the birds dry too quickly the feathers will be harsh. Let them dry slowly,

Rolling the Bird in Cloth.   Drying

and when they are nearly dry take them out and rub down with a silk handkerchief, and put each one back into a cage and cover up for the night. Put in a little egg-food with maw seed sprinkled over the top.

It takes two or three days for the birds' feathers to fine down again, and it is best to keep the cage covered at night, or all day if in a room where there is any work going on. A spray bath the day after washing does them good, and assists in fining down. The birds should have egg-food with maw-seed and a little Ko-vita or cod-liver oil emulsion mixed with it.

HAND FEEDING

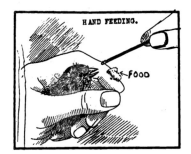

HAND FEEDING.

It is simple enough to rear young birds by hand. Full information is given in this book elsewhere. This, however, is not a pleasant service and requires feeding every two hours. Often feeding for a few days saves the bird's life as the mother may again start to feed its baby. It is best to use a foster parent if the male will not feed, unless very young.

Time and Manner of Banding Young Birds

Closed leg bands or rings on a Canary are certainly an asset for the owner. The year hatched is very plainly stamped on the band, thereby giving the age of the bird. The bird's age has long been a mystery. There is no definite time to ring your birds but usually five to eight days of age. There is a difference in the size of closed rings. The smaller rings must be placed on at from five to eight days old. This is not hazardous, and is often done. The placing of rings on your birds is a simple process and requires no experience whatever. Very seldom is there any ill effects from ringing your birds. Take the chick in your left hand with tips of thumb and fingers free to hold the leg and foot. Some sprinkle with talcum powder; some use vaseline; many use nothing, some wrap thread around toes and run thread through the band. In any event have leg clean and dry when placed back in the nest. Now place the hind toe back against the shank of the leg, and the three front toes straight out and close together. Now place the three front toes through the ring and pass the ring out over the foot back, screwing or turning as you slip band on, and pass the hind toe which is against the leg; when the ring passes the end of the toe it returns to its normal position and the ring cannot slip off. Now make a record of the ring number and nest and parents.

* * * *

"'Tis sweet to be awakened by the Lark,
Or lull'd by falling waters;
Sweet the hum of bees, the voice of girls,
the song of birds,
The lisp of children, on their earliest
words!"

—Milton

HAND FEEDING BABY CANARIES

If you have a real love for birds, plus time and patience, you may save many baby birds by watching closely to see that the mothers are feeding as much and as often as they should.

If, after feeding four or five babies for a week or ten days, you notice the mother acting restless, getting off the nest too often, and calling to her mate, then watch out, for the babies are being neglected, and even if saved, will be undernourished and not the strong, healthy birds you desire, and sometimes, if you do not supply extra food, they will slowly, but surely starve to death.

Now is your time to try hand feeding, giving each one a small amount, each and every hour of the day. Our friend, Virginia Miller is very successful in hand feeding, and she writes that you need never lose a single baby from starvation if you follow these directions:

It is best to use egg biscuit or any nestling food that contains no ground up seeds of any kind. Feed the food as dry as you can. It's much easier to get the food into the little beaks if pretty wet, but not so good for the babies, as it is apt to cause diarrhea. You may add a few (and just a few) small grains of grit to the food and a little cuttlebone.

Never put cold food down the beaks. Mix it fresh two or three times a day and either keep it in a warm place, or warm it up just before feeding. Always put the food through a fine sieve after it is moistened with water, so as to be sure there are no hard lumps of any kind in it. Rape, greens or spinach should be fed once or twice a day and should be crushed through a sieve; or masticate it yourself before feeding. A good way is to mix a little of the greens with the nestling food that is fed during the morning. A little strained boiled carrot mixed in the nestling food is also good. If droppings get too loose, cut out greens and carrot for a day and moisten nestling food with raspberry leaf tea and feed it a little drier. Masticating the food yourself before feeding it is a good method, for then the food is warm and you need not put any grit in it.

Babies should be fed every hour or so. It is far better to feed often and not so much at a t me. Remember a mother bird can only feed at a time as much as her own little crop will hold. Three good swallows of food at a time are enough for morning feedings. As the day advances, feed a little heavier and toward evening have the babies pretty well filled up. They can be fed late in the evening, but I usually feed from early dawn until dark and follow the mother bird's way of feeding as closely as possible. Where babies are thin and weak from lack of food, then one or two extra feedings before you retire will help a lot, but don't get out of a warm bed at night to feed them and run the chance of taking a nice cold yourself.

Some Fanciers use a toothpick, some match ends. I use an ordinary manicure orange stick for hand feeding. It doesn't make any difference what you use, as long as you get food down the bird without smearing him up until he can't see out of his eyes. The little beaks are very soft and delicate, so be very gentle and careful not to bend or break the lower mandible.

Where a mother bird deserts her six or seven day old babies, it's very difficult to raise them by hand. To take up the feeding of two weeks old babies and putting them on the perch is no trick at all after you have had a little experience. They are partly feathered out at two weeks and it's not so difficult to keep them warm, but they must be kept warm, even after they have crawled out of the nest.

Let me state here, where babies refuse to open their beaks for food, put them down in a box and cover with dark cloth. In a few minutes talk to them softly (sometimes they will answer you by little peeps) then quietly uncover them and have food ready to put in their beaks. You may have to repeat this a couple of times if the birds have never been hand fed and are two weeks old or older. In rare cases, I have had to force feed for half a day, using bread and milk, as that is about all you can get down them when you have to open the beak, but great care must be used in doing that, in order not to bend or break the beak.

I have found the ordinary pasteboard shoebox answers very well for holding one or two nests. The nests can be placed in berry boxes first and then put into the shoebox. I keep the nests covered day and night with pieces of white woolen sweater, and at night put lid on shoebox in which several holes have been cut for air. The shoebox is then wrapped up well in two or three thicknesses of an old woolen blanket or sweaters. I have kept baby birds nice and warm this way when room temperature dropped to 45 degrees at night. Do not be afraid of smothering them and be sure to wrap them up well. Some fanciers have written about nice little brooders they have made which seem to work all right, but I have always had fear of brooders getting too warm and preferred trusting to the old woolen blanket method. Always use loosely woven woolen material like blankets or sweaters and not cotton ones.

104

NATURE'S SYMPHONY ORCHESTRA

BEAUTY, COLOR AND ART PERSONIFIED.

No. 1 —The Ribbon Finch.
No. 2 —Brazilian Crested Cardinal.
No. 3 —Pekin Nightingale—Jap Robin.
No. 4 —Society Finch.
No. 5 —Diamond Sparrow.
No. 6 —Zebra Finch.
No. 7 —Cinder Finch.
No. 8 —Red Headed Parrot Finch.
No. 9 —Indigo Finch.
No. 10—Strawberry Finch.
No. 11—Cordon Blue.

No. 12—Masked Grass Finch.
No. 13—Butterfly Finch.
No. 14—Spice Finch.
No. 15—Saffron Finch.
No. 16—Magpie Finch.
No. 17—Star Finch.
No. 18—African Finch.
No. 19—Australian Fire Finch.
No. 20—Orange Cheek Waxbill.
No. 21—Green Avadavat.
No. 22—Silver Bill.
No. 23—White Java Rice Bird.
No. 24—Grey Java Sparrow, or Rice Bird.

No. 25—Sugar Bird.
No. 26—Black Hooded Nun.
No. 27—Fire Finch.
No. 28—Green Avadavats.
No. 29—Paradise Wyday.
No. 30—Pintail Wydah.
No. 31—Napolian Weaver.
No. 32—Peach Faced Lovebird.
No. 33—Cocketiel.
No. 34—Parrakeet.
No. 35—Fisher Lovebird.
No. 36—Madagascar Lovebird.

FINCHES

BEAUTY AND SONG IN ALL ITS GLORY

The Goldfinch

There are two varieties of Goldfinches, but they differ very greatly in almost every respect, in fact as far as I know, the only way they are alike is that they both have feathers.

The American Goldfinch is more commonly known as the Lemon or Yellow bird, and is fairly common throughout this Country, and in most parts is protected by law, and is fairly well known, and very seldom used as a cage bird, therefore we need not go into details, but will try and cover the European Goldfinch, which is one of the best cage birds obtainable.

These birds are in very great demand in England for several reasons. They are very brightly colored, are excellent songsters, and make most wonderful cross with canaries, the male Goldfinches being used for this purpose. They are also very common in shows, where quite a rivalry exists, but this only tends to make the owners of the birds treat their pets with greater kindness and consideration. It is easily possible to write a whole book on these delightful birds, but we will condense our remarks to the consideration of the chief characteristics and points of our feathered friend "Goldie."

In England, these birds are also known as Seven Colored Linnets, Red Linnets, and many other names, such as Pear Tree, Pea Throat, etc., but the majority of these names are merely local names given in the various districts in which they abound. The males are very nice singers, and far better adapted to cage life than the females, as they do not seem to bother about mating season as do the females, which often pine away and die in mating season, especially if caught just before that time. These birds should

not be trapped during the time they can obtain the greens or seeds they live on when in the wild state, as it is then far harder to get them accustomed to cage life and dried seeds, but if they are caught or trapped when frost or snow is around, and the weeds are dead, they readily settle down to domestication, and rapidly become most attractive house pets. The sexes are exceedingly hard to distinguish, and only a person with wide experience can make a fairly sure pick, and even then it is next to impossible to guarantee a surety. As a general rule, the male has a long snaky head, more slender than the female, and the head takes an even taper from the top of the skull to the tip of the beak. He has a bright shiny eye, a perky cheeky way of hopping around or perching, and brighter colors. It is far easier to pick them out of a bunch, as then the differences are more noticeable, but even under these conditions, it is quite easy to be mistaken. I have heard lots of fanciers say that they could tell them in a minute, but I have also known the same fanciers to be fooled badly. The only sure way is to buy a bird that is singing, and although it may cost a little more at that time, it pays in the long run. It is very seldom that dealers will guarantee the sex, but they will often give a guarantee that the bird is a male, so that if it turns out a female, the purchaser has the privilege of exchanging it.

These birds are of a domineering nature, especially around the seed tray in an aviary, but their bite is not nearly as bad as their bark would suggest, so that after a time the other inmates of an aviary get to know this, and do not pay any attention to the bullying demeanor of Goldie. He seldom resorts to force, and I have seen them take complete possession of the seed tray, and keep as many as two or three hundred other birds away, but only for a short time, as the other birds soon got to realize that Goldie was just a supreme bluff, and they would settle down to eat, while he jumped around with wings out-stretched, beak open, and yelling his wild war cry. The colors are wonderfully blended, and it is hard to describe them, but the following description will serve to give a good idea of the beauty of these birds. The tail is black, the back brown, the front of the head is bright red, of a very glossy appearance, and this is known as the blaze. Throat and cheeks are white, and the wings have a bright golden stripe on the feathers, and are otherwise black with white tips. This is a fair description, but the birds must be seen and carefully examined before their full beauty can be appreciated.

Goldfinches are very easily tamed, and quickly learn to do many amusing and clever and interesting tricks, such as pulling up their food in small buckets, turning somersaults, waving flags, etc,

Lots of seeds are put up in packets for them, but these I never used, aways making a mixture which I tried and found excellent in every respect. It is as follows : ¼ lb. Sicily Canary Seed, ¼ lb. Rape Seed,¼ lb. Millet Seed, (small), ¼ lb. Lettuce Seed, ¼ lb. Thistle Seed ⅛ lb. Maw Seed, ⅛ lb. Linseed, and ¼ lb. Wild Grass Seed. Your bird store now will mix the above for you.

They are also very fond of fresh greens and sweet apple, also insects of every description, and as they are quite inexpensive, and very frequently in the markets, they should be far more popular as pets than they are at present.

The Bullfinch

Throughout the whole of Europe, this is one of the most popular of the Cage Birds, and it is rapidly becoming a favorite in this country, although it is far from having reached the popularity it deserves, as it is in every way a wonderful pet. The colors are really beautiful, although somewhat quiet, the male being bluish grey above; the crown, tail and wings are deep silky black, white underneath, with the exception of the breast, which is rich red. The female is similar in color, with the exception of the breast, which is chocolate brown. The natural song or call is of a low plaintive description, but both male and female have the wonderful gift of imitating and will readily learn to pipe a whole tune through without the slightest mistake or waiver, and they seem to take as great a delight in doing this, as one does hearing them do it. In the wild state they are great fruit and berry eaters, rarely touching anything else to eat unless compelled to, with the exception of insects, but their favorites are blackberries and as long as they can get these they seldom bother about anything else. They have an abundance of good food all year round, as they start out in the spring with Chickweed, Dandelions, and such wild weeds as come their way, even to the tender bark of the willows. In the fall are all the berries and the "Ash-keys." These hang in bunches on the trees, the seed being at the butt end, and they last during the hardiest part of the winter, at which time there are also the private berries. Nature has provided very well for the requirements of "Bullie" as regards food, and the only likelihood of trouble, would be with water freezing up, as Bullfinches are very great and frequent drinkers. They build nice comfortable nests of little twigs, lined with fine grasses and if at all possible to procure horsehair, that is cleverly mixed in. Usually the nest is about five feet from the ground, and five or six eggs are laid, of a pale blue ground color, speckled and spotted with purple. The young birds hatch out in about fourteen days and are starting to fly about two weeks afterwards. The mother is a very close sitter, and during this time Mr. Bullfinch is remarkably pugnacious, and woe betide any feathered intruder at that time, as it means severe punishment if not death, to any bird that tries the Peeping Tom tricks. Whenever possible, Bullfinches mate for life, and cases are actually known, where birds have been marked, and it has been found that the same pair has been mated up for several seasons, and at all times the male proves a most loving and faithful husband. The best time to obtain a Bullfinch for training is just about the time it is ready to fly, as it will then only be necessary to hand-feed it for a very short time before it will start to pick for itself, without any trouble, but very few can be obtained that way in this country, therefore it is necessary to buy them from the dealers, and take a chance on obtaining the kind you want.

A trained bird is always very much higher in price, some of them bringing as high as $200.00 each, whereas an untrained bird can usually be purchased at anything from $4.00 to $8.00. Even if an untrained bird is purchased, it is exceedingly easy to tame and train it, even if it is too old to learn a tune. Care must be taken in feeding these birds, as they are great gluttons, and will always pick and choose the seeds they are most fond of, which are invariably the most fattening, such as Hemp, Sunflower, etc. Hemp Seed is a good medium when training the bird, which is usually done in the following manner : When a Bullfinch first arrives in a new home, he should be transferred to his cage very carefully and slowly, and no sudden movements or noises allowed close to him. Give him a name, and call him by it as often as possible. After a day or so, approach the cage slowly, frequently mentioning his name in a low voice. Have a Hemp Seed on the end of the finger, and put same between the wire of his cage, at the end of the perch he uses mostly. Be very still, but keep calling his name softly, and try and imitate his call or whistle. Bye and bye he will venture towards your finger, very slowly and reluctantly at first, but gradually he will become bolder and bolder and finally snatch the seed and hop away to eat it, but after a few times he will take the seed and stand still. From then on, it is easy to gain his complete confidence, and once gained, it is very easy to retain it, and you will find him just as anxious to please and be a close friend as you are.

It is almost impossible to teach an old bird to pipe a tune all the way through, but if one is whistled repeatedly in the bird room, "Bullie" will most likely pick it up, at least a bar or so of it, and once he has learned, he never forgets.

The stock seed mixture I always fed with excellent results is as follows: Sicily Canary Seed, 4 ozs.; Linseed, 1 oz.; German Rape Seed, 2 ozs.; Sunflower Seed, 1 oz.; Thistle Seed, 2 ozs.; Lettuce Seed, 2 ozs.; Yellow Millet Seed, 2 ozs.; Maw Seed, 1 oz.; Wild Grass Seed, 1 oz. This is a first class mixture, but berries and fruits must be given in abundance, and above all, LOTS of clean water.

Male Bullfinches have been crossed with female canaries, but it is too disappointing a chance to take to be worth the trouble, and if Hybrid breeding is sought, it is best to use a female Bullfinch with a male of any of the following: Goldfinch, Greenfinch, Linnet, Canary.

The Zebra Finch

This fascinating little Australian bird is not at all difficult to breed if care and attention is given.

The Zebra Finch (Toe niapygia Castanotis). This interesting and amusing little foreigner is a native of Australia, spending most of his time on the ground, feeding upon wild grass seeds, which are abundant there. All ornithologists agree that they are usually seen in small flocks of from twenty-five to fifty, until the breeding season approaches, when they pair off and only the male and female are seen together.

After the nest has been built, which is usually in a thick bush or vine, there is seldom more than one bird in evidence.

Judge Griffith, who lived many years in Australia, informed me that the birds seemed to select a certain amount of territory when breeding, and woe betide any intruder.

This reminds one a good deal of the American Blue Birds, who are so common in our orchards, yet seldom trespass upon each other's chosen ground without a battle.

In a wild state the nest is said to be flask-shape, containing from four to seven eggs, and in some cases even nine, but in captivity they seldom build their own nest, excepting in an outdoor aviary, and in all cases that have come under my observation the nest has always been spherical with the entrance hole in front.

For some reason the Zebra Finch seems to have a fondness for those wooden canary shipping cages that one sees in the bird shops, as a breeding place in captivity, although lacking this he will use a box or anything else that appeals to him. In one instance, I had a pair make a nest and raise a brood in an overturned flower pot in a green house. They also seem to appreciate an empty cocoanut shell and cocoanut husks are also favorite meeting places.

But no matter where or how they decide to nest, the result is usually the same, both birds carrying straws and hay and whatever they can pick up until they have built a round nest, inside the receptacle with only a small opening in the front. In many cases this opening is so tiny the birds have difficulty in squeezing through and have to repair the entrance after every exit and entrance.

Indeed, it is very rarely that the opening is large enough to give one a good view of the inside even with the aid of a strong flashlight.

Naturally more people will want to attempt breeding in cages than in bird rooms or outside aviaries, and for that reason I am going to give some hints on that subject first.

The larger the cage the better, but one that is three feet long, two feet high and at least sixteen inches deep will do nicely for two pairs. The kind with the wooden tops and backs are preferable.

Of course, those all-metal are still better but are rather expensive.

Do not attempt breeding in an ordinary canary breeding cage as nine times out of ten it will be a failure.

At least three nesting boxes or husks should be installed against the rear wall and near the top (and four would be better).

If you will go to your local dealer he will probably sell you some Hartz Mountain Canary cages for a few cents and they really are the most satisfactory for cage breeding.

Remove the food receptacle, also a couple of wooden bars at one end, then scald thoroughly for a few minutes to remove all danger of insects and disease, and after they are dry fasten to rear of cage with opening either to front or side, but the opening to the front seems preferred by most birds.

Be sure to fasten them in such a manner that they are easily removed and yet cannot be jarred loose by the constant entrance of the birds.

The bottom of the cage should have plenty of bird gravel, and food receptacles should be either arranged on the outside convenient to the perches or on the inside in such a way that the droppings of the birds cannot fall into them. Bathing water should be supplied at least once a day at all times.

If the food containers are on the outside, care should be taken when replenishing them that the birds do not escape through the openings. These little mites are like lightning on the wing and it is a most difficult task to capture them in a room without injury.

Never throw anything at them or use a hat. Put a little food out and wait until dark, noting where the bird settles for its night's rest and you will have no trouble in capturing the truant and will also have the satisfaction of knowing he has not been injured in any way.

The use of nets, hats and waste baskets and other such things cannot be too strongly condemned. There is only one chance in many you won't injure the bird, to say nothing of the fright you give him.

Have patience until dark but be sure of one thing and that is: that you have no cat lurking around, no matter how tame and how little attention it pays to the birds when caged. They cannot resist pouncing upon a bird with nothing between them. I don't blame the cat. It's inborn.

Now that I think we have one cage arranged for a successful season, what about the birds?

The sex in the Zebra cannot be mistaken and no dealer would think of selling two males or two females for a pair, unless he was himself ignorant of the distinction and in that case he has no excuse for being in the business.

After the birds have been procured, put them into your cage and observe them for a few days. If they are in good health, they will show it after the first day or two, by their lively actions and constant visits to the food trays. If out of condition, they will sit around with their heads under their wings and while making some attempt to feed usually only scatter the seed around as if they were looking for something they cannot find, which probably is true as undoubtedly wild birds are subject to illness but instinctively know where to find the remedy; and lacking this remedy in captivity they soon pass away.

We will take it for granted your newly arrived birds are in good condition. Now is the time to introduce a little nesting material.

For Zebras, I find the best is grass stems, such as you can pick in your back yard or the kind that bananas come packed in. Some of them like wheat straw. In spring and summer wild grass cut and put in the cage furnishes both food and nesting material.

String or twine should never be given as they will only become entangled in it and either lose a leg or maybe hang themselves.

Pure white cotton should be supplied for lining the nest, but a very little at a time. Better nesting material in small quantities and often for best results.

In cage breeding the birds will sometimes pay little or no attention to the nesting material for a few days yet be constantly visiting the breeding box.

If, when the breeding boxes are first put in a little soft hay or straw is put into them it sometimes helps them make up their minds.

After they have finally decided which nest suits them best it is only a question of time before the eggs are laid. In some cases the hen will lay within a day or two after selecting her nest and even before it is completed. Again, some hens are very fussy about their house-keeping and sometimes the first egg is not laid until nearly a week after the nest has been completed.

However, after the first egg has been laid there is usually no more delay and things proceed smoothly.

As a rule, Zebra Finches are not subject to eggbinding and I can remember of only one or two cases in many years of breeding. Incubation lasts about twelve days.

Usually the hen does most of the incubating, the male very seldom relieving her, but most always sharing the nest with her at night.

Sometimes though, the little lady will not even allow him to do this and he has to sleep outside.

After the young are hatched, both parents take turns in feeding them and usually prove wonderful parents; and I can truthfully say that up to and including the third brood in one season they seldom lose a nestling, and if they do, it is usually through a cause with which they had nothing to do.

It stands to reason that after raising three broods the birds are tired and should be given a rest.

There seems to be no particular time of the year for breeding them; in cages or inside bird rooms, providing the temperature doesn't go below 50 degrees. They breed as readily in December as in May or August.

In outside aviaries they usually breed from May to September in this locality, but in some of our southern states I have been informed they breed the year around.

In California I've seen them rearing young in outside aviaries that had shelters attached all through the rainy season, which lasts from November to February, and lost very few birds.

I have generally found it a good plan to give them some soft food just before and after the young are born. Egg food that is used by canary breeders is the most satisfactory but I have also tried prepared mocking bird food and found it very good, and it has the added qualification that it does not have to be prepared fresh every day. Some Zebras are also fond of dried ants' eggs when they have young. However, the staple food is canary and millet, both white and yellow.

I would not advise giving bread and milk as some canary breeders do. It seems to cause the bowels in the nestlings to become very loose.

The time for the young birds to leave the roosts seems to vary considerably. I've had them out in fourteen days and again they would take as long as twenty-two days. While I've made many efforts to find the cause of this discrepancy, so far I only arrived at the conclusion it must have something to do with the season and the kind of food given. Close observation has shown that birds that leave the nest late are just as hardy as those that leave earlier.

The young look very much like the hen bird excepting that they have black bills and are always clamoring to be fed. This duty seems to be mostly the cock's, as the hen immediately starts looking for a new home, but she does not neglect her babies.

And right here I want to say while I've heard it stated upon good authority that the Zebra Finch will lay and build on top of her nest again time after time, such has never been my experience. In all the birds that have been bred by myself and friends that I have visited, there has been no case of this kind recorded. It is true they will sometimes desert the eggs and even the young and allow them to starve, but where this occurs, I think there will always be found a good cause.

And never in any instance that I can recall has the hen used her old nest the second time. In a few cases where more than one pair were kept in a cage and the nesting places were all in use or did not suit them, they made an attempt to construct a new home. This was usually a failure, though, unless some branches were in the cage, giving them a good fork for a foundation.

In outdoor aviaries where there are plenty of growing plants or even only dead branches they will sometimes build a really wonderful nest. One I remember seeing in a friend's aviary that was at least ten inches in diameter and must have weighed at least two pounds.

Many out of the ordinary things have happened to most bird lovers that are well worth recording.

A few years ago a pair of Zebras in a small bird room had four young and both parents gave them every attention. On the sixth day after hatching the hen bird hung herself on a piece of twine. (This did not occur in my bird-room.) For two days the male fed and cared for the babies as if nothing had happened. On the third day a Nutmeg Finch was seen to come out of the nest. The natural conclusion was that she had finished the young Zebras.

But she continued to visit the nest and you could hear the young clamoring so it was pretty certain her visits were not destructive. The male Zebra paid no attention to her whatever. Twelve days later four young Zebras left the nest in perfect condition and were cared for by the Nutmeg Finch until able to feed themselves.

Here is another rather out of the ordinary incident—about four months ago a pair of Zebras had four young (their third effort that year). After the birds had left the nest the old birds refused to feed them for some reason and two soon died from starvation (as it is impossible to hand feed young Zebras, owing to the peculiar position they assume when taking food).

The other two were very weak and were expected to pass out any moment. But on the contrary they are living today. For some unaccountable reason a male Cordon Bleu, who had just lost his mate took charge of them and today they are as two fine cocks as one would want to see.

Some years ago a friend of mine had an indoor aviary with an outside flight. This was usually closed in November and not opened again until spring. This year he closed the flight as usual when he thought the birds were all in the bird room.

But it seems that a pair of Zebras had started a nest in the flight outside and refused to come in. They were not discovered until a couple of days later (but fortunately did not lack for food.)

As they already had eggs and did not seem to want to desert them, they were left alone and fed and watered every day.

On October 26, four young birds left the nest in perfect condition. The temperature had ranged around 30 degrees all the time.

It only remains to answer a few of the questions I have been asked that the above does not cover.

Where there is room it is always advisable to breed all birds in cages as large as possible; bird rooms are better still where the climate is favorable in outdoor aviaries.

Bathing water should be given every day, regardless as to whether they are nesting or not.

Young birds show their sex when ten to twelve weeks old.

Young stock can be bred at eight or ten months, but for best results wait until one year old. Some have been bred at six months but will produce weaklings.

Very seldom are more than four birds hatched, regardless of how many eggs are laid.

Young birds should be marked with bands of some kind to prevent inbreeding, which is bad for future generations. It tends for weak stock and very often disease.

No weak bird or bird in poor condition should be placed with others and positively no attempt made to breed from such specimens, as it only means disappointment.

Zebra Finches will do well with most of the Grass Finches and can be safely kept in the same inclosure with Shell Parrakeets or so-called Love Birds.

No birds can stand draft and Zebras are no exception. When exposed to a draft there is usually no cure and in most cases you will be chief mourner at a funeral.

Take no chances and avoid drafts as you do many things you personally don't like yourself.

Lady Gould Finch

All birds like sunlight and require a certain amount to keep them in the best of health and condition, but don't place the cage where the sun beats down on it all day long. Just stand in that position where you would hang the cage and think how you would feel.

If you thought you could be comfortable all day in that location the birds will be the same.

Above are shown several kinds of nesting receptacles favored by Finches, see other articles in this book for complete information.

ADDITIONAL FINCHES

Saint Helena Waxbills. This is a very common variety, and they are also known as the Red Bellied Waxbill, and Pheasant Finch. They are birds whose full beauty is not noticed at the first glance, but the more they are studied, the more beautiful they are found to be. The body color is grey, shading to lighter underneath, with a reddish tint observable, which collects to a crimson patch at the bottom of the stomach. There are fine grey bars running transversely, which give the plumage a beautiful silky appearance.

Orange Cheeks. No collection of Waxbills can be considered complete unless some of these little beauties are included. They are not so vividly or brightly adorned as some of the others, but the very neatness of the plumage instantly draws attention to it, and to the delicate coloring, which might otherwise pass by unnoticed. Another good point with these birds is that they are not nearly as delicate in health as some of the other varieties. The adult males have dark grey heads, back of a reddish brown, tail is blackish with crimson at the top. Underneath is darkish grey, toning down to light grey. The beak is crimson, and the cheeks are orange, from which they get their name. They are most pleasing little pets, and well worthy of a foremost place in any collection.

These beautiful birds are an American family of the Buntings, and are closely related to the Snow Birds and several others. They are about the size and shape of canaries, and the males are of a most beautiful blue color, which seems to vary in density as they fly in and out of the sunshine and shadows. The females are not as brilliant, being more of a brownish-grey color, but are very beautiful. The males change to grey in the winter and back again to blue in the early spring, just in time for the breeding season. They have been crossed with canaries, but the result is very disappointing, as the beautiful colors are much broken and smudged, and the song is far from being a prize winner. The Indigos are very fond of bathing, and are quite proud of their plumage, spending a lot of time preening each feather to insure its perfect appearance, so they should be given every encouragement in this by being provided with a suitable both of clean soft water, and plenty of space so that the plumage need not become ruffled as they fly around.

They require a seed diet of a mixture of Sicily Canary Seed, Rape Seed, Thistle Seed and Lettuce Seed, and should also be plentifully supplied with fresh crisp greens, but these should be removed if they become the least bit stale.

LADY GOULD

These are always known as the most beautiful birds, which are so easily kept. They are natives of Australia, and there are three varieties, namely, Red-Head, Black-Head and Yellow-Head, but as the latter is exceedingly rare, we will deal only with the first two mentioned. They do not have any song, which does not matter in the least, as we would not want our attention taken from their beauty by any singing, however sweet it might be. Their one fault is that the new arrivals are very delicate, but after the first house moult, they are quite as hardy as the majority of cage birds, but far more beautiful. Against the lack of song complaint, we can place everything else necessary to make them PERFECT pets, as they have the most marvelous display of wonderful coloring, perfect shape, good tempers, and the disposition which ensures perfect happiness, not only for themselves, but also for their cage mates. If at all possible to obtain a pair or so that have been house moulted, it is far better to do so, even if the cost is more, as this almost insures good, hardy birds. It seems almost ridiculous to attempt to give a word picture of these beauties, but the following description will help to give an idea of their gorgeous coloring: The head, cheeks and face are carmine. Chin and throat are deep velvety black, with an edging of blue. The neck, back and upper wings are bright green and deep gold, while the flight feathers are grey and green. The upper tail is blue, the rest of it black with the tips of a lighter shade. The breast is purple, the abdomen is deep yellow, and the beak and legs are pink. It is hard to imagine anything like a true picture of these birds, as the description could be better given by saying, "Cut off the end of the rainbow and shape it into a bird," and the only trouble with that would be to know where to put the colors. The females are duller colored than the males, but this only serves to show to better advantage the real beauty of the males.

The three varieties mentioned are of the same body coloring, and the only difference is in the heads, which are colored as the individual name implies.

As before mentioned, these birds are very delicate until after the first moult, but when once they are acclimated, they are very little more trouble than any other birds, and the most important thing to remember is to keep them comfortably warm, and entirely free from draughts. The flight should be as large as possible, as space is a great thing in the lives of Gouldians, and the roof should be peaked, so that the birds can get out of sight as much as possible, as they are of a very retiring nature, and they always make for the highest point possible when disturbed, and this is just the same in wild life as in captivity. They like plenty of nesting places and these should always be provided, in the shape of small boxes, cocoanut shells, etc. A shallow bath should always be provided with clean, soft water, also plenty given for drinking purposes.

If you should have a pair of these birds mated, it is necessary to watch very closely for signs of egg binding, as the female is more subject to this trouble than almost any other bird, and must immediately be treated for same, but with more careful handling than the average bird.

The seed mixture for them is very simple being equal portions of Sicily Canary Seed and Millet Seed, but they must be perfectly clean and free from dust, and as fresh and plump as possible. Gouldians are also very fond of fresh crisp greens, also flowering grasses and ripe fruits and occasionally stale bread and scalded milk. Needless to say, grit and cuttle bone are absolutely essential, as with all other birds. Upon the arrival of a shipment of these birds, great care should be taken not to suddenly startle them, or disturb them more than absolutely necessary, and fresh water and grit supplied, but only in very small quantities. Give them a few hours rest in a quiet room, and this will probably give them a first-class start in their lives in the new home.

Cut-Throat Finches. These birds are also known as Cut-Throat Sparrows, and are very popular pets, as they richly deserve to be. They derive their name from the fact that they have a deep Crimson band around the throat, reaching from ear to ear. The rest of the plumage is of a brownish grey, marked with white, which gives it a very pretty appearance. This variety comes from Western and Central Africa, and there is another variety from South Africa which have the whole head and throat red, and this is called the Red Headed Finch, although it is merely another form of the Cut-Throat Finch. The latter variety that is, the Red-Headed, is far more uncommon than the Cut-Throat, therefore is more expensive, but it makes a very attractive addition in an aviary. The Cut-Throat readily breed in captivity, and are very hardy, so should be well represented in every collection. The young birds do not need any special attention, as the parents are very attentive of their offspring.

Diamond Sparrows. These beautiful little birds are also known as Diamond Finches, and Diamond Birds, and they are indeed lovely little gems. They are natives of Australia, and are very common around the gum tree forests, where they can be seen in great numbers. They usually build in hollow logs, but sometimes several pairs will form a company and build a tunnel in the hard ground, often in the bank of a stream, at a good height above the water level, and the tunnel is always built sloping upwards from the water. All the birds work together, some digging, while others remove the refuse. If they can find any deserted nests of Swallows or Sand Martins, they confiscate these, altering them a little to suit their peculiar needs. Although they are very small birds, they have remarkably loud calls, which seem altogether out of proportion to their size. The colors are really wonderful being silver grey on the head and back. The wings and tail are dark grey, and the breast and body are chestnut, decorated with white markings of a diamond shape, from which they get their name. A dark black band crosses the chest, and the root of the tail and end of the back are bright crimson. One of the most pleasing traits of these little gems, is their extreme tameness, and they put all their confidence in mankind, so remember this and act accordingly, as I consider it a hideous crime to betray such confidence when it is given in such a free and unsuspecting manner. They very soon learn to know who is who around

them, and if kept for any length of time in a particular cage and room, it is quite safe to release them and tie the cage door open. They will soon clean any room of flies and any other insects, and will return to their cage without any trouble, immediately jumping out again at the sight of a fly, especially if it happens to be near a window.

Cinder Finches. These are rather delicate birds until after the first house moult, although if carefully looked after until that period, and kept warm and entirely free from draughts, they very seldom die from it, but will live several years, and they are indeed very beautiful birds, and more than worth the little extra trouble needed to pull them through the first house moult. When in good health they are ready breeders and the young birds when raised are always far more hardy and very little trouble, so that it is well worth trying to get a good healthy pair, and raise a family or two, which are far superior to the imported birds. It is of course natural that a few pairs may be lost before a strong pair gets established, but they will repay any losses, as the young can be readily sold if necessary. They have crimson beaks, the tail and lower part of the body is purplish, while the rest of the coloring is lavender. Even from this short description, no stretch of imagination is necessary to picture what a wonderful sight a few pairs of these birds are in a collection, in fact it is hard to procure any birds which call for such deserved admiration as these.

Silverbeaks. These quaint little birds are also known as Silverbills and Quaker Birds. They can quite safely be put with any other birds, as they are noted for their agreeable and amiable dispositions, which more than compensates for their rather plain but unusual plumage. They vary in color from dark fawn to white, and their beaks or bills are silver or silver grey, from which they obtain their name. They are quite hardy little pets, and readily breed in captivity, and the young are very easily raised and reared. They are exceedingly affectionate, and the males have pleasing little songs, which are usually delivered accompanied by a dance, which makes it doubly attractive. They are quite inexpensive, which, in addition to all their other good traits, put them in great demand, but they very richly deserve even greater popularity than they now enjoy.

Magpie Finches. These little birds are also known as Bronze Wanakins, but the latter name is very seldom used. They make attractive little pets, as they are extremely playful and good tempered and their coloring is quite different from the majority of the Fancy Finches. They are mostly of a velvety black, with a tinge of purple on the head, wings and back, and white on the breast. They are fairly hardy, and when once they have moulted in captivity, they very readily settle down to housekeeping. They are of the most pleasing disposition, seeming to do their utmost, and even going out of their way to be sociable and friendly with their cage mates.

Fire Finches. These are fairly common birds, but their chief fault is that they are very rarely in perfect condition of plumage, as they are of a rather delicate nature, and must be kept at an evenly warm temperature to be at their best. They are natives of Central Africa, and wherever they are kept in captivity, they should be kept warm enough to remind them constantly of "Home Sweet Home," then they do not seem to mind the cage life, and will live for several years in good health. The males are of a deep red plumage mostly, but have a dark greenish-brown tint in the tail and back, and on some of the older birds, there are white spots on the sides. The females are of a brownish cast, with red at the tail roots. They have coral red beaks, and a yellow ring around the eyes. They have a habit of building nests which they do not use, and although they frequently do go to housekeeping, they do not always raise the young birds, as they are of an indifferent disposition. The above description covers the most commonly known of the Fire Finches, but there are several other varieties known in the markets at different times, but great care should be taken when purchasing, as some of them are extremely delicate. The best seed mixture for a collection of these little pets is 1 lb. small Millet Seed, ¼ lb. Sicily Canary Seed, ¼ lb. small Rape Seed, ⅛ lb. Maw Seed, 7/16 lb. Lettuce Seed. Give plenty of fresh crisp greens, such as Water Cress or Lettuce, also Sweet Apple, and vary a little with plenty of insects. These birds are great lovers of sunshine, so should be placed in as much warm sunshine as possible, but a cover should be arranged so that they may get in a little shade if need be. When at all convenient, or if it can in any way be arranged, build a large aviary with both indoor and outdoor apartments, and have the outside planted with various evergreens and thick undergrowth. Introduce as many pairs of these Fancy Finches as possible and you will have an attraction never to be forgotten, and the initial cost is unmentionable compared with the great pleasure derived therefrom. Whenever possible, purchase house moulted birds, as they are much stronger and far hardier, and amply repay the extra cost in the long run.

Cordon Bleu. These birds are also known as Crimson-Eared Waxbills, but which ever name is given to them, their beauty cannot be denied as they are among the most showy of the fancy Finches, but are not by any means as strong or hardy as some of the others, but they have a very happy song which is delivered with great sprightliness. The coloring is as follows: Back is pale grey. The face, throat and chest down are a lovely shade of sky blue, and the males have extra adornment in the way of crimson cheek patches. By far the majority of these birds which arrive in this Country die very soon after, but of course some of them pull through, and if they are pulled through a moult here, it is a safe bet that they will be O. K. for cage life, so I always advise a novice not to buy any of these birds unless he can be reasonably sure that they are house moulted in this Country.

Chestnut Finches. These little beauties are also knowns as Nutmeg Finches or Spice Finches, and although not as handsome as some of the others, they are, to say the least of it, very curiously and uncommonly marked birds, being of a rich chocolate brown, closely marked underneath with small white crescents, which give them a very curious appearance. They have a peculiar call or song, not by any means sweet, but it cannot be truthfully called objectionable. They are quite hardy, and as a rule inexpensive. Altogether they have many appealing qualities, and a pair or so should be included in every collection.

STRAWBERRY

These little gems are very popular favorites. The Strawberry Finch is the smallest of the Finch Family, their native habitat, the Malay Peninsula to Southern China. They breed readily in captivity when they are properly and comfortably quartered.

Strawberry Finch

They readily adapt themselves to cage life, but must be kept in a Finch cage, as they easily escape between the wires of the ordinary canary cages.

There are two varieties, the Red and the Green, but the latter is seldom seen as it is not so common as the Red, which I will describe.

Male. In breeding season, the plumage is far more gorgeous than at other times, and it is a wonderful sight to see them darting around in an outdoor aviary, in which green trees, etc., are planted. The upper part of the head and back are of a copper color, cheeks, throat and upper end of tail vary from fiery red to scarlet the breast practically the same but spotted with white, and the wings and back are thickly dotted with white. The beak is coral red and it has pinkish legs.

Female. Upper parts are brown, the wings are darker with white spots. Cheeks are pale brown, throat and breast yellowish, with brown shading, beak and legs as in the male.

Sugar Birds

When I first ordered Sugar Birds, I quite expected to see some lovely birds, but when I received the shipment, I looked at them, then rubbed my eyes, and looked again. To call them lovely, is like calling water moist. There are the Yellow Winged, the Black Headed and the Blue. Some of the Sugar Birds are not so gorgeous, but the majority are Blue, Purple, Green, Yellow, Chestnut and Scarlet and of the most brilliant lustre and every move they make shows more colors. They somewhat remind me of over-grown Humming Birds. They feed on banana, boiled egg, and almost any soft fruit and I often rolled a piece of banana in cracker meal, which was greatly relished. These birds should be hung where they will not often be disturbed, especially until they are perfectly tame and are used to the people around them. They are rather delicate until after the first house moult at which time very great care must be taken or they will certainly die as they are excessively weak at this period.

Green and Red Avadavats are natives of India, but the Red are very different, and are more expensive, although I consider them cheap at any price. It is really impossible to give a description which does them justice, however the nearest I can give is as follows:

Male. Upper surface rich olive green, lower back and upper tail yellowish green, tail almost black, throat and chin light, breast and under yellow, sides clear white with black bars. Crimson beak and pinkish legs.

Female. Almost the same as the male, but if you can imagine what the male would look like if faded or dirty, then that is a description of the female. It is hard to state the sex if only a single bird is examined, but if a collection of them is looked at, it is easy to pick out the sexes.

The Green varieties are not such ready breeders as the Red, although given plenty of room and congenial surroundings and necessary materials, they will often go to nest.

The first few weeks after importation are critical and more birds are lost than are saved, but the survivors are hardy little gems, fully as vivacious as the Red.

Both varieties will live together comfortably and agreeably if lots of room space is provided, but if cramped or crowded they are liable to pluck one another bald, and they will not allow the feathers to grow again. In a case like this, it is necessary to isolate the bald heads, and enlarge the cage. When the bald heads have recovered their plumage, they can be returned to their play mates, but in a LARGER cage than before.

If in an outdoor flight, Cellar Window Wire of one-half mesh should be used, and bushes of Box, Privet or Fir planted, with lettuce, chickweed, etc., as undergrowth.

There should always be an indoor shelter where they can fly for warmth and rest and it is advisable to put feed and water inside as well as outside.

There are several things to remember when stocking these little beauties, one being that the purchaser should be fully prepared for any losses and another and more important point is to limit the stock, do not crowd them, in fact far better results can be obtained with lots of room and a few birds than vice versa.

Food. If kept in an outdoor aviary these birds are better able to help themselves, as they catch and eat practically every insect that enters the flight and then only the seed and water is to be provided. The staple seed diet is a mixture of one-fourth part canary and three-fourths part small millet, with an occasional pinch of grass, lettuce or Maw seed, in turn.

Seeding grass should be given green, also lettuce, chickweed and ripe apple, pear, banana or orange.

If kept in an indoor cage, insect life must be provided, such as spiders, small caterpillars, flies, etc., and clean grit and cuttlefish bone must be constantly in the cage.

Never introduce newly purchased stock into the cage, but keep them separate for 10 days or 2 weeks, until absolutely sure that they are entirely free from disease.

Nuns

These are very pleasing little birds, and make a decidedly pretty showing in an aviary, although as individual cage birds, they are not as appealing as many of the small birds, as their song is far from sweet, although it is not exactly offensive or disagreeable, still it is peculiar, and is better described as a call than a song. They are very quick on the wing, and exceedingly lively, seldom resting for many seconds at a time. They are very lovable little birds, and when several pairs are together, they are usually to be found in a cluster, and if on a perch, they try and crowd so closely that the end birds are invariably pushed off, but they immediately jump on the backs of the others and will wriggle themselves like a wedge until they are in between the others, regardless of whether they are mates or not. They live just like one happy family, each one helping the other, and there is never any sign of jealousy on the part of any of them. There are several varieties of Nuns, but they all get along quite comfortably and peaceably in either large cage or aviary, and no collection is complete without a few pairs of them. The most commonly known are **THE BLACK HEADED & WHITE HEADED,** but these very often go under other names such as Black Capped, White Capped and so on, so it is advisable if buying by mail, to be sure what birds are being purchased, before sending the money, as it is quite a task sometimes to get the birds exchanged after they have once been shipped, and it is very disappointing to order what is supposed to be the required stock, and find upon arrival of them, that they are not at all the birds desired, and this very frequently happens unless care be taken when purchasing from price lists.

In the Black Headed Nuns, the body is of a very rich Chestnut Brown, and the head, neck and upper part of the breast are deep velvety black. The White Headed Nuns have a body color of a softer Chestnut than the Black Headed, and the head is of a Silver Grey, delicately shaded at the shoulders.

The feeding is quite simple, as all they need is a mixture of Small Millet Seed, with a sprinkling of Sicily Canary Seed and Maw Seed, and occasionally a little of the larger Millet Seed, but this should be watched, so that in case they do not eat it, it can be stopped. They should also be supplied with plenty of greens, as they are very fond of these, and the supply can be regulated by the condition of the bowels.

These little birds must be kept in a special Finch cage, as the wires of the ordinary canary cage are too far apart, and they would escape between them, or probably get injured trying to, and this condition is greatly aggravated if the wires are made of brass, therefore it is far better to make sure by either buying a Finch cage, or making one using cellar window wire, of a half inch mesh.

These birds cannot by any stretch of imagination be called free breeders, but if any results in this line are to be obtained, it will be necessary to have the birds in a very large cage or an aviary, and the chances are far better when they are in an aviary, but they must be supplied with Rustic Cedar Bird Houses, or hollowed out cocoanut shells, with a small hole cut in one end. To prepare the latter, it is best to cut the cocoanut through the middle with a saw, extract the nut, then glue the two half shells together with a good waterproof glue, and securely wire them, taking great care to have the ends of wire safely tucked away, so that the birds cannot injure themselves as they fly around. Soft dried grasses and moss must be provided for nesting, but even with all these preparations, it is not safe to say that they will go to nest, and even if they do, they are so easily disturbed, that the chances of raising young ones are very remote, and it is a very disappointing proposition to try and figure on raising any families of Nuns.

Nonpariels

These are exceedingly beautiful birds, and are natives of this Country, and they have an attractive agreeable song, which is quite unusual in the highly colored birds, so this makes them doubly attractive, and very desirable as pets, if they can by any means be obtained, but I believe they are now protected by law, so in that case they will not be found in the markets. I have known them to be shipped in from Mexico, as natives of that Country. In South Texas they are plentiful. I had many wild in my yard at San Antonio, but that is sailing too close to the wind for my liking, and I would rather be without the birds than risk the law. The coloring of these beautiful birds is indeed striking to the eye, as they have violet heads and necks, and a greenish back. The wings are green, and the rest of the plumage is mostly red, and the way the colors are blended beggars description, and it can readily be imagined that they are truly beautiful. They are about the size of a small canary, and the feeding

is about the same as for a canary, but they are far better adapted to life in an Aviary than a cage, so if at all possible, this should be their quarters. They are great bathers, and should at all times have free access to fresh clean water. I was successful in pairing a nonpariel with a canary hen and a beautiful Hybrid was the result.

Troupials

It has been said that these birds belong to the Orioles, but the truth is that the Orioles belong to the Troupials, or Hang Nests of the family Icteridoe. The Purple Troupial is the most gorgeous of the family but is very seldom seen in private collections and is even less frequently in the markets, but if at all procurable at least one should be obtained. The sexes are very similar in plumage, but the colors of the female are more subdued. The colors are black intermingled with green, purple, blue, violet and bronze.

The Common Troupial is a beautiful bird of deep orange and black and is about the size of the American Robin. It is quite a good mimic and readily picks up tunes and soon gets to know its owner's whistle, which it readily answers. When it gets well acquainted with its owner, it can safely be allowed out of the cage and will sit quite contentedly on his shoulders for a long time. It requires quite a large cage, arranged for length more than height or width, as it is quite active when in the cage.

Troupials are all soft billed birds and the staple food should be of Mocking Bird Food, but they are also particularly fond of a slice of orange which makes a nice variation in the usual routine of their diet.

In comparison, a cock will be found to have a bolder and more jaunty manner than a hen, the eye is fuller and bolder; and in clear lightly-marked birds the throat just at the base of the under mandible will generally be of a brighter tone of yellow. The "tweet" of the cock has also a bolder and more defiant ring, and when he sings the throat swells out and pulsates or palpitates very plainly. Some hens will "sing" very tolerably, but in their case the song is disconnected, and there is rarely much trace of the pulsation of the throat, which is such a feature of the song of the cock. In the hen the "song" is really a more or less sustained twitter. To the young beginner all differences are very subtle, and he need not feel discouraged if he fails for a time to recognize them in a given bird. A keener insight will grow up after learning to distinguish them by comparing two or more birds together at one time.

Brazilian Cardinal

These are very handsome birds in their way, and always command attention on account of their stocky build and general liveliness. Both male and female are practically of the same color and it is very hard to distinguish the sexes. The back is dark grey, gradually shading down the body to white. The wings and tail are dark, and the head, crest and front part of chest are red. The crest can be raised and depressed at will, but it is erected more often than not. They have strong powerful voices, of a distinct whistle type and are perfectly free with it at all times, regardless of weather conditions, and I have known a bird to sit out in my Aviary in the hottest of summer weather and sing away and the same bird would sit out on the same perch in the middle of winter and sing away with just as lively and happy a song.

They cease singing only when in a strange place or if sick or moulting, otherwise they are among the happiest of cage birds, but at times they seem to take a dislike to some other bird, and they will not rest satisfied until the subject of their displeasure is either removed or dead.

I had a large Aviary of mixed birds, always between seventy-five and one hundred specimens, from the smallest Waxbills to Cockatiels. Included in this collection was one Brazilian Cardinal, known as "Rufus," and he was about as lively as any bird in the whole lot. I just loved to watch him constantly on the go, hopping and jumping around, first here then there, always singing away as though his life depended upon it. He was exceedingly tame and even the smallest finch would chase him from the seed tray at times, but he would just hop away, never seeming to resent the puny attacks of the tiny mites, but always presenting a perfect picture of "Dignity and Impudence." This went along for quite a few months, then I was presented with another fine Cardinal which I named "RED." After a few days isolation, which every new arrival had, and finding Red seemingly in perfect health, I introduced him into the aviary. For a time, all went well, then one day Red burst forth into melody, and the voice was far too large and strong for the size of his body. Never in all my experience did I hear so large a voice for the size of the body, and it was quite evident that none of the birds had either, because for a short time, the majority of them flew around in terror. Rufus was one of the few that was not disturbed, and for a short time he glared at Red, then without the slightest warning, he swooped down on Red, and before I could interfere, Red was transported to the feathery Heaven, wherever that may be. Whether Rufus was just jealous, or whether he took a sudden and violent dislike to Red and his voluminous voice, I shall of course, never know. Rufus was never the same after. His temper was not altogether bad but he was always boss of the aviary, especially the seed tray, and finally I had to part with him on that account, although I greatly regretted doing so, but I might say that if ever I can collect another aviary, I shall not be satisfied until I have another Rufus. In captivity they feed on Pada, Canary Seed, and a small quantity of Hemp and Sunflower Seed with Sweet Apple and Banana, and sometimes they greatly relish a small piece of raw carrot. They are particularly fond of spiders, so these should be fed as often as possible, also as many other insects as possible, such as grasshoppers and crickets.

Jap Robin

(PEKIN NIGHTINGALE)

These beautiful and gorgeous birds have almost as many names as feathers, being also known as Pekin Nightingales, Pekin Robins, Japanese Nightingales, and many other names. Their scientific name is Lithroix lutea, and they are natives of India. They have almost every desirable point pet birds should have and about their only really bad point is their extreme fondness for nice new laid eggs. They rapidly make friends with any and all the birds they may be boarding with, but if any of these friends should happen to lay eggs in the aviary and "Jappy" can get to them it is a perfectly safe bet that no young birds will be born from those eggs. That is their only fault as far as I know and their redeeming features are so many that they can readily be forgiven for that back-sliding. They have almost all the colors possible to get on them and these colors are blended so wonderfully that "Jappy" is a real work of art. The back is olive green changing to yellow on the crown and forehead. The outer edge of the tail feather is black and the inner parts brown. The wings are yellow red, and blue black. The chin and throat are dark yellow running to the breast which is orange. The under parts are yellowish dwindling to white, while the bill and feet are very bright red. This is rather a poor description but will serve to show what beauties they really are. The female is somewhat duller than that of the male. They have been known to breed in captivity but this is more of an exception than a general thing so do not expect much from them in that line and then if they do decide to favor you by raising a family it will be a far greater pleasure. In a natural state they are very retiring and love to hide deep in bushes, but in captivity they will very soon learn to recognize their master's voice, especially if he takes a tasty morsel along and gives it to them each time he goes for an interview. If kept in an open cage they seem to ask for admiration as they appear to know that they are really beautiful, and to give them their due, we cannot blame them for their apparent conceit. They come and look up into a visitor's face as much as to say, "Well, I know I'm beautiful, what have you brought for me?" Then if you have a nice Caterpillar or Meal Worm to hand them, they are your friends for life, but be sure and take a similar treat the next time you pay them a visit. They are extremely active and sing heartily just as much if not more when they are flying or hopping around as when they are still, but the latter is very seldom. Live food is a great part of the diet of these birds and variety must be studied also. Soft foods with Mocking Bird Food as a basis should be given and plenty of ripe fruits, preferably a little over ripe, also a little millet seed can be kept in the cage separately. These birds vary much regarding their song, some of them being far superior to others, but even if they only chirp, what is that compared with their many other attractions? "Jappy" is indeed a most wonderful and engaging little pet.

African Finches

Under this heading will be included a selection of the wee little gems often called African Finches, although in some of the cases, that is a misnomer. I know quite a number of fanciers who have a collection of these birds, of different varieties, and they always refer to the collection as "My African Finches." However, by whatever name one wishes to call them, they are still the same wonderfully colored, animated little beauties, and they are very well known for their sweetness of temper, and the amiable way they live together, each and every one trying to make the most of life, and I have very frequently seen a bird of one variety that had lost its mate, settled comfortably on a perch between a pair of another variety entirely. Another fact that appeals to most fanciers is that the majority of these birds breed readily in confinement, especially if they are kept at a steady warm temperature, and given suitable nesting places and materials. Most writers and fanciers strongly recommend cleaned out cocoanut husks for nesting boxes, and I always supplied a quantity of these, but found that the birds preferred the Rustic Cedar Bird Houses which I had made to suit my fancy, and they must have suited the fancy of my pets too, as they took to those in preference to the Cocoanut Husks, and seemed to be more comfortably settled for housekeeping, as they immediately started in to raise families.

The cage must be a special Finch cage, as the wires of a canary are too wide apart, and some of these birds are so small that they can escape between the wires of an ordinary cage. Others can get so far in between that they cannot get either in or out, with the result that many birds are injured in this way. I always preferred to use square mesh cellar window wire, using a mesh of two or three squares to the inch.

"Build for yourself a strong box,
  Fashion each part with care;
When it's strong as your heart can make it,
  Put all your troubles there.
Hide all your sorrows in it,
  So the world will never dream half—
Build for yourself a strong box
  Then sit on the lid and laugh!"

THE AVIARY

Site for Aviary.—As regards the construction of a garden aviary, it is not my intention to say much, for aviaries vary according to the taste and purse of the designer and builder; but a few general directions will not be amiss. Always select a wall (or build one, if necessary) for a background. Lawn-aviaries open to the air all round are pretty to look at, but unsafe for birds, which are exposed in them to every blast that blows; and as the wind from some quarters is very bitter and searching, it is as well not to subject birds to its influence. The aviary should be erected against a wall that faces either south, south-west, or even south-east; but an exposure due east, or one into which north enters, must be avoided. If no other exposure is available, the fancier had better forego the delight of an outdoor aviary and keep his birds indoors.

Food in Outdoor Aviary.—The feeding of canaries out of doors should be about the same as that recommended for such of these birds as are kept in the house; but more green stuff may be allowed, and almost anything will do, with the precaution that no stale vegetable matter be left on the floor of the aviary, which must be kept clean. If the flight part of the aviary is turfed, the birds will want little else in the way of green food, but some rape-seed may be advantageously sown in a border against the wall, and covered with a wire to keep the birds off it until it is sufficiently grown for their use.

Canaries are very fond of Canary Grass—that is, Canary Seed sown and allowed to grow to a height of a few inches—and it is good for them.

FINCHES SUITABLE FOR AN AVIARY

If you wish something beautiful, interesting and inspiring equip an aviary, with any, or all of the following finches. They can be kept together in harmony.

Zebras, Fire Tails, Cordon Bleus, Indigo, Lady Gould, Javas, Cherry, Saffron, Double Banded, Nutmeg, Mannikins, Silver Bills, Orange Cheeked Waxbills, Pheasant, Grey Waxbills, Avadavat, Weavers, Diamond, Red Eared, Grass, Silver Bills, Ribbon Steel, Parrot Nonpareil, Whydahs, and others. I cannot imagine anything more beautiful and interesting, I have never at one time had all of these finches together in an aviary, however, I have seen all of them associated in groups, and to have such a display would make any heart rejoice. The above collection gives forth a great array of colors which will delight the eye of an artist. Very little is required to keep them healthy and happy, plenty of flying space, plenty of sand, green food, dandelion, groundsel, shepherds purse, plantain, watercress, chickweed, lettuce, fresh water (twice daily in hot weather), occasionally some dried or dead flies, the usual finch mixture seed sold by all pet shops or mixed as given elsewhere in this book. Cuttlefish bone always before them, steeped seed is a splendid treat for them once a week, place the seed in a cup, or vessel, cover the seed with hot water, allow this to stand over night, pour off the water in the morning, put seed on a dry towel and roll around to take up the surplus water. As this food sours quickly it should be fed sparingly and best if given twice on the same day, sour food of any kind is very bad, often fatal. The above finches are for a good size aviary, there being the two sizes of birds, for a small collection, the Fire Finch, Avadavats, Lavender Finch, Waxbills, Pheasant Finch, Redtail Finch and Cordon Bleus. These are of about the same size, if one were prepared to do a real job by selecting the first mentioned list and adjoining a collection of the Whydahs, Ribbon Finch, Turquoisine Parrakeets and Love Birds such as Pennants, Crimson Wings, Kings, Alexandrinos, Indian, Port Lincoln, Green Leeks and many other love birds and cockatoos.

Nothing would attract more attention nor give greater pleasure and satisfaction. Just try a nice outside aviary, it can be made comfortable without artificial heat, and will pay good dividends.

Shrubs.—Unless the aviary is a very large one, and not too many birds are kept in it, there will not be much use in attempting to grow plants, or even trees, within it, for the birds will soon pick them to pieces, not so much to eat as for sheer mischief, or maybe occupation. The better plan is to introduce plants in pots or small tubs, which can be removed when the plants have been disfigured, and be replaced by others.

I have found ivy, euonymus, and the different kinds of elder (the common, golden, silver, and parsley-leaved) resist their attacks better than anything else. Lilac and laburnum are both poisonous, especially the latter, and must on no account be allowed in an aviary.

Covered House and Open Flight.—It may be stated in a general way that every outdoor aviary should consist of two parts, namely, a covered-in house for the birds to roost in and for their food (which last should be hung from the roof by a single wire, so as to keep mice from getting at it), and an open part, or flight. It is this latter part that the aviarist should try to embellish with shrubs. One enthusiast we know even attempts to grow flowers in his, and has, to a certain extent succeeded with some of the hardy annuals and biennials, such as marigolds and wallflowers; but the birds are bad gardeners, and have a mind to taste everything that grows, or tries to grow, about them.

BEGIN WITH THE BEST

The foregoing advice is equally applicable either to those who wish to breed for pleasure or for profit, only with this difference—those who can afford to put more cash down at once, and only breed for their own hobby, should get their stock birds from a breeder or dealer who has the best, so as to start from a good foundation.

(Continued from Page 31.)

undersized canary hen may also be used to mate with the Siskin and produce a hybrid of which you will be very proud.

It will be best to shut off the Siskin during the night for he will probably peck at the eggs in the nest since he is inclined to be very meddlesome.

Watch the baby hybrid, too for he is apt to follow his father's example and eat more than he should. Follow the general instructions and you will have a real thrill from your experience.

The Lancashire hen is also often used in this cross with good results. Better try your luck.

Another suggestion is to try your hand at cross breeding in order to produce more brilliant colors in your stock. The natural orange-red is quite a new creation in this country and may be produced by introducing a Redhooded Siskin male to a deep yellow female. It is much better to have a male Siskin mated to a female canary than a female Siskin to a male canary for the reason that the female Siskin is not easily persuaded to nest and rear the young. The Redhooded Siskin is, indeed, a beautiful bird with its red and black plumage, the head and throat being a rich, velvety black and the breast and lower part of the body a brilliant red color. The back has both red and black feathers, the wings are black with a red stripe and band running through the middle of each feather. Can you imagine anything more strikingly beautiful?

Crossing the Siskin with a female canary has become very popular because we have recently learned that the offspring is fertile and will reproduce.

Here are some facts which you must know and be prepared in advance to expect—the **first** generation of **females** will be **sterile**, therefore they must be discarded. However, the **males** will be fertile and may be used for breeding and you will keep the ones which have the most brilliant plumage.

The second year the son should be mated to his mother and the other young males may be mated to canaries of deep yellow color. Always keep the strongest and best from such matings for future breeding. The third year you may mate father and daughter, as well as mother and son. You are now just beginning a study and a hobby which will bring untold satisfaction.

Parrot and Parrot-Like Birds

PARRAKEETS

(Love Birds)

BUDGERIGARS

Under this heading we may as well collect all of the above, as their habits and keeping are so similar, and very often they are misnamed for each other. There are several varieties of each of them, in fact there are quite a few varieties that are not known to private cage life, but we will take them under the headings as they come.

Paroquets or Parrakeets vary in size from that of a sparrow to the size of a small parrot. Their name means "Small Parrot" and some of them are exactly like miniature parrots. The Australian Paroquet, which is by far the most common, has been described under a separate heading, so we will pass them by now. The Multicolored and the Blossom Headed Paroquets are amongst the most common known to cage life, although the whole family consists of at least thirty varieties. Another very well known specimen is the Bee Bee, although this is more often classed as a Love Bird. The Ring Necked Paroquet is also fairly common, and is very moderately priced, and as far as I am concerned this is about the only recommendation I can give it, as I do not know of any particularly appealing qualities.

This beautiful bird has quite a few names in addition to the heading. It is also known as Shell Paroquet, Love Bird, Australian Grass Love Bird, Budgerigar Undulated Grass Love Bird and others, but whichever name it is known under, it is always a popular favorite, as it has so many favorable points and very, very few (if any) unfavorable. The wild bird is a na-

tive of Australia, from where vast numbers are shipped, but the supply does not seem to diminish at all, as they are ready breeders, even in captivity. The majority of the birds which reach this Country, however, are bred in Russia, but they are easily picked from the wild birds, as the colors are less brilliant. There are several varieties to be obtained now, such as Green, Yellow, Blue, Olive, and others, but the original and native bird is the Green, so I will endeavor to give, as near as possible, the colorings of them. The crown is light yellow, back of the head and part of the wings, deeper yellow, also a patch on each cheek. The shoulders are green, chin and throat, rich yellow, and a bright blue line runs between the cheeks and throat, and a few black spots at the back of the throat. The under-parts are of the most brilliant green, while the back is rich emerald green. The wings are variegated with green, grey, yellow and black. The tail is about six inches long and the two middle feathers are rich blue, while the outer tail feathers are yellow. If you can imagine this combination, you can partly figure the gorgeous display of a number of these birds.

As mentioned before, they are easily bred in captivity, but need a very large cage, unless an Outdoor Aviary can be supplied, and it is in the latter that best results can be obtained, and the most pleasing display made, and always get along better where a number of pairs are kept together. They should be supplied with Rustic Bird Houses for nesting, and at least 3 or 4 more houses than pairs of birds, and it is advisable to only keep one variety in one Aviary, as the different varieties are more liable to cross in.

I always found long fibrous Moss very acceptable to them for nesting material, and always kept a liberal supply within their reach.

They usually lay a clutch of two eggs and the old birds take turns at sitting. A little over a week after the young birds are born, two more eggs are laid, and by the time the first two young are able to get out of the nesting box, there are two more young birds in the nest, and this continues through the breeding season until four or five nests of young have been raised.

They are remarkably easy to raise, and are hardy and usually healthy. They will do equally well outside in winter as in summer, if given an indoor shelter where they can roost comfortably at night and in the very worst weather.

The sex distinction is very slight except at breeding season, when the male has a bright blue cere (around the nostrils) and the female a ruddy brown. At other times the coloring is very similar, but a practiced eye can usually pick them out. Only the brightest colored birds should be kept for breeding, and they should be in first class health and condition.

Larger and vigorous birds, with close and smooth feathers should always be picked, as much better results can be obtained than when poor conditioned or weaklings are used.

The feeding of these birds is very simple, their chief food being Canary Seed, White Millet and Padda. In breeding season a little Rolled Oats (uncooked) should be given daily and for greens, flowering grass, apple and lettuce can be given.

They very rarely bathe in the usual way, but love to roll and gambol in moist or wet grass, so if kept in a cage, a sod should be frequently dampened and given, and the joy they display upon receiving same, amply repays the wee trouble it takes to provide this pleasure for them. They are remarkably adaptable to learning tricks of various kinds and some of them show wonderful skill in performing really intricate little acts. Some years ago, I had the pleasure of meeting a man who had a troupe of about thirty of these beautiful birds all trained to do various tricks both as individuals and in troupes. He had a Fire Brigade, Police Force and several other bodies all represented by these wonderful little birds, and the way the feathered performers went through their various acts and tricks is almost unbelievable. The Professor, as he was termed, was most emphatic in asking the audience not to clap their hands, as sudden noises caused confusion in his troupe, which would mean the loss of some of them, as the performance was given in the open air on a large table covered with green felt. Needless to say, I attended every performance given, as they were of great interest to me, in addition to an education, but I remember very clearly that one day a small boy suddenly clapped his hands, and one of the birds took fright and flew. There are people in this Country who train these and other birds, and sell them for show purposes, as well as pets, but in the majority of cases, this business is merely a money-making proposition.

I have quoted these instances to show how readily these birds learn to do tricks. In addition to this, their beautiful plumage and winning ways, their hardiness, and the many other excellent qualities, make them well deserve a place among the favorites. If kept in a cage in one room for about two weeks, they get quite familiar with their surroundings and the people around them, and then the cage doors should be fastened open, and the birds allowed the freedom of the room, and they will very soon learn to come to the call of a whistle, or by names, and they show great affection towards their keeper. In addition to this, they have the pleasing habit of always going to their "HOME" to eat and sleep, and they keep good hours, which is probably more than their keepers could say.

A whole book could easily be written on these pets, and even then something left out, as there are so many wonderfully interesting things which can be said about them, but space here is limited, so my advice to the reader is certainly to get a pair or more of these wonderful little pets. They live very comfortably in an assorted Aviary, as they are not at all of a quarrelsome nature.

These birds have only been bred in captivity for about 50 years. There is a wonderful opportunity for a budding aviculturist to create a variety for himself. It is just a case of blending colors as an artist would. The first question a person will ask, and usually after the ejaculation "Oh how pretty!", is, "Do they sing?" My answer is, "yes," but not like the song of the Roller. The song of the canary is more or less artificial, and should we neglect its training, what would result? It would in time revert back to the song of the common songster. Budgerigar breeding is only in its infancy, and there are on record cases where the owner could not tell the difference between a "Budgie" and a Goldfinch when singing, as the two birds were kept in the same aviary, and the Budgerigar in this way acquired the song of the Finch. Again we have several cases on record of "Budgies" talking, so is it not possible for some enthusiast to create a strain of birds that would talk? As I have said before, the breeding of these birds is comparatively new, and we do not know what they really can do. The next question is, how to tell the sexes. This is an easy matter when both birds are in breeding condition. The CERE at the base of the upper mandible (or beak) in the males is always dark blue, and in females it is always brown, but when out of breeding condition it may turn a light blue, but never dark blue as in the case of the male.

BREEDING SHELL PARRAKEETS

The Parrakeet can stand as much or more cold than a canary. Some advise not letting them raise during winter weather, but my experience has been that it is best to let them nest whenever they desire reardless of the time of year. I had a few females to go to nesting in January and it was surely cold weather, 15 to 20 degrees below zero and I had them in an indoor aviary in a spare room without heat of any kind. They hatched and raised every bird just as well as if it had been July.

The Budgerigar is a real little acrobat climbing with beak and claw here and there, hanging head downward. You will find him an amusing little clown and they always seem cheerful and happy keeping up a lively chattering with their fellow parrakeets. This bird is often called Love Bird but that is an incorrect title.

The Budgerigars require a different nest to a canary, note the skeleton view of the Budgerigar nest box, shows approximate style and dimensions. These dimensions may be varied. Note how the bottom of the box is hollow out concave to prevent the eggs from rolling apart. You can make these nests, or purchase them from your dealer.

The illustration shows economical Budgerigar cage, one side should be left open as illustrated and wired over with door frame built in, be sure to have the open side FACING THE SOUTH. Place some sand on floor.

You should arrange your nests as illustrated, because Budgerigars (or Love Birds) do much better if you have half dozen pairs, as they thrive best with associates.

Egg binding seems to bother them a lot but can be overcome. See Question and Answer Dept.

HOW TO FEED

Now we come to the feeding. The staple diet should be good plain Canary Seed. White Italian Millet and Red Indian Millet. They are very fond of Hulled Oats. Spray Millet, that is to say, growing millet seed before it has been thrashed. Green food in the varieties of Dandelion, Chickweed, and growing grasses when in season are very much relished by both old and young stock. On no account must green food be given if it is covered with frost. While on the subject of feeding, I might say that I give my birds when feeding young, egg food the same as is given canaries. Once a week both summer and winter I give "Glauber salts" in the drinking water. Just sufficient to make the water taste saline. Do not mix it too strong or the birds will refuse to drink it. As much as will cover a nickel for the ordinary cage drinker will be found about the right amount. This I find keeps them in perfect health. Do not forget a liberal supply of Cuttlefish Bone and lots of good gritty sand. In the spring of the year I usually get some old sand, lime and mortar from an old building that is being dismantled. This I find that they greatly enjoy.

THE AVIARY AND NESTS

If cage breeding is the intention, I would suggest that the cage be as large as possible, say 3 to 4 feet long, 2 feet high, and 18 inches from front to back. A cage of this size would accommodate two pairs. Now we must put in four nests, so that there is the opportunity of selection, and which will prevent quarrelling in case both hens take a fancy to the one nest, and which would most likely result if only two nests were used. There are various kinds of nest boxes, and almost any kind of a closed box will do, so long as it has a concave bottom, for these birds use no nesting material whatever, and therefore the need of the hollow bottom to keep the eggs from rolling about is very necessary. A box is made as follows : One piece of wood 1¼ inches thick and 6 inches in diameter. This I hollow out in the center about half of one inch deep and about 3 inches across, thus leaving a ledge of 1½ inches on the outside. I next take a piece of 3-ply wood ⅛ inch thick and 9 inches long. The reason for using the three ply being that if the grain of the wood is in the right direction it will bend quite easily. This piece of wood I steam in hot water until it becomes quite pliable. Next I nail it around the bottom putting a few nails or staples into the splice to make it rigid. I next take 2 pieces of ½ inch lumber. One piece 5½ inches in diameter, and the other 6½. I nail these together to form a lid, the smaller piece fitting inside the box, and the larger piece resting on the three ply. Now I cut a hole 1½ inches in diameter, and about 2 inches from the top. I nail a perch under the hole. I have made dozens of different types of nests for Budgerigars, but the description of the one I have given here, you will find that the birds like the best. Any Fancier with a garden aviary could put in an old rotting stump of a tree, which would of course supply the birds with a natural nesting place, and also give endless amusement to the owner, in watching their work in burrowing into the old stump like so many rats. The big disadvantage to such an arrangement would be the impossibility of looking into the nests for inspection.

SELECTION OF STOCK

If you have decided to try your hand in the breeding of these interesting little birds, I would recommend you to go to a reliable bird store and leave it entirely to them to supply you with birds which are aviary bred. I might say that it is not so easy as one would imagine, unless you do start with aviary bred stock. Two Fanciers I know had several pairs for years, one five and the other six years, and in that time never produced a single young bird until they got aviary bred stock. You should be willing to pay a fair price remembering that the stock that you will get will be the very foundation of your future work along this line. With the right stock and good management I can say that success will be yours.

In the selection of the stock, always start with big, strong, healthy birds. Pick out the slim birds as these have a tendency to obesity, and get lazy and sluggish and which means poor breeders. Preference should be given to birds with good color and with markings that are clear and distinct, also see that the throat spots which usually number four or six are of good size and color. These are known as the necklace and must be about ⅛-in. in diameter. Of no account accept poor, small, weakly birds, which are usually very poor in color and in markings. It pays to start with the best stock it is possible to buy, for by doing so you will breed birds that you will be proud of. On the other hand weakly, poor specimens are always an eyesore to yourself and to those Fanciers who come to visit you.

After we have selected the stock, we must put them through a period of conditioning, just as we would do with our Canaries. All of the females are placed into one large cage or flight, and the male birds are put into another. Give them a staple diet of equal parts good Canary Seed and Millet Seed. The Millet can be either white or yellow, or a little of each can be used to advantage. As soon as the frosts have passed and it is possible to give green food, a little should be given each day. Dandelion, Chickweed, Lettuce, Cabbage and flowering grasses when possible. During the winter months be very careful that any green food given is entirely free from frost. The Budgerigar does not show a preference for apple or other fruits as a rule, but when other green-food is not obtainable, these fruits can be tried. Twice or three times each week give a little egg food just the same as you would give to a Canary.

I make mine out of Cod Liver Oil Food with hard boiled egg added. Boil the egg for ten minutes, and when cold mince fine and add an equal amount of the Cod Liver Oil Food. A small teaspoonful of sugar and occasionally the sugar can be omitted and a little salt added in its place. Moisten the food with a few drops of hot water, just enough to make it crumbly moist, for if it is made sloppy the birds will refuse to eat it. Now after a few weeks of this treatment your birds will be in splendid condition for breeding, and the males and females will be calling to one another. Now at the beginning of April we will decide to mate them up. If your stock is all of one color, we can put them all into the breeding cage or the aviary as the case may be, and allow them to choose their own mates. In the case of a mixed variety such as Yellow-Green-Olives, Blues, etc., it would not do to let them choose their own mates, as they would in all probability cross mates, and this of course would entirely spoil the colors, but if we keep each color separate then we can expect the colors which we are most anxious to produce. To accomplish this end each pair must first be mated up in a separate cage, and the pairs must be together not less than one month before being liberated into the aviary. Before the end of the month they will be frequently noticed billing and feeding one another, and these indications will show that the birds are paired together. They can then be liberated into the aviary. It will be noted in the above fact that a wide difference exists between the Budgerigar and the Canary. A male canary will mate with a number of hens when liberated into an aviary, but with the Budgerigar this is not the case. These birds show a remarkable characteristic in the affection they show towards one another. It is very seldom that a pair which have been mated in a cage, will, when liberated into the aviary, leave one another. If it is found that they do change, then of course they would have to be taken out of the aviary, but the number of times that such a change will be likely, can almost be considered as a negligible quantity.

All pairs should be placed in the separate cages at the same time. Not one pair today and the next pair in a few days after. This also applies to the liberation of the birds into the aviary. Always put them into the aviary all at the same time. The reason for this being that if the early pairs in the aviary have settled down and started to nest, those pairs which are placed in later will no doubt interfere with their work, and this will sometimes result in the loss of both eggs and later young birds.

Now another important point. On no account must a spare female be allowed in the aviary. There must be an exact equal number of birds of both sex. There must also be just twice the number of nests placed in the aviary as there are number of pairs to breed from. A little later when the birds have settled down and have made their selection of a nest, you can then remove all of the spare nests. This will tend towards each of the hens keeping the same location for her nest all though the season. If you have say six pairs, then put in first of all twelve nests. If two hens should choose the same nest, they will fight like bulldogs, and many a time will fall to the ground still fighting. Even if one should eventually get that particular nest, these two hens will fight more or less all through the season. I had one hen this last season which broke five nests of eggs. Twice this occured but eventually I found the culprit, and then I lost no time in removing her, but not until almost fifty eggs had been lost. Often you will find them go into nests of other hens and kill the young. The culprit this time is easily found, as she

neglects to clean the blood from her face. My advice in a case of this kind would be to destroy such a bird, for when such a habit is formed they will continue with it upon any occasion that they can do the same. My advice is never have a spare hen in the aviary if you wish to avoid troubles of this kind. There are of course always cases which prove the exception to the rule, for I have a friend who keeps several spare hens in his aviary. Two hens will lay in the same nest and will incubate and raise the young birds between them.

I have also had occasion to note another case of one male breeding with two hens in an aviary, and without loss of any kind throughout the entire season, but this I might say is very unusual. This is the first case of this kind on record to my knowledge.

I might say that these particular birds were flying in a very large aviary and this no doubt accounted for the good luck for good luck it certainly was. Now when a hen makes up her mind to go to nest, she is not long in getting down to real business She will start to incubate on the laying of the first egg, and she will lay another egg every OTHER day afterwards. The incubation period differs from the Canary, being six days longer. Incubation taking twenty days it therefore takes eleven days to lay six eggs. This means there are eleven days difference in age between the oldest and the youngest birds in the nests. Still these birds very seldom lose any young. In the last season I have not lost 2 per cent which I consider to be very good results. When the young are hatched they are entirely naked, then the body will become covered with a grey down. At two weeks old they start to feather, taking another two weeks before a full coat of feathers are grown. By this time they are able to leave the nests for they are between four and five weeks old.

I read an article published recently which stated that they leave the nest and feed themselves, and when only three weeks old. This is not correct for I know from experience that this variety of parrakeet is not feathered at that time, for when they do leave the nests at five weeks old their tail feathers are then only half grown. I find that they can usually feed themselves upon the first day after leaving the nests, and if some soaked seed is provided for them. If you wish to have one or more of these birds "Finger Tamed" and for pets in the home, I will describe my method of accomplishing this result. Take the selected bird the first day that it leaves the nest. Cover one wing with soap so that the bird cannot fly, and for a few hours put the bird into a very small cage. Take them out one at a time and give them their first lesson. Hold the bird loosely in one hand, and put the fore finger of the other hand just in front of the bird, so that it will creep out of your hand and on to your finger. It will perhaps try to fly a few times, but repeating this until it will stay on your finger. This must be done at least once each day. They are a most desirable pet for the home, and when finger tame will become very affectionate to their owner. Quickly recognizing the person who feeds them, and showing affection to a degree not shown by any other domesticated bird in any other variety.

EGG-BINDING AND FITS

In the Spring of the year, one is liable to have trouble, unless you have been feeding correctly all winter. I had many troubles in the early day of breeding, but now everything goes like clockwork, and which I put down to nothing else but careful management and correct wintering. The most general causes of trouble are Egg-Binding and Fits. Egg-Binding is caused by insufficient cuttlefish bone and gravel, and it is with this in mind that I advised a supply of sand and lime mortar. Do not put your birds up too early. You cannot afford to take chances with your first pair, as it might mean losing the whole season. Wait until April, and you will have lots of time for two nests before the end of August or September. Now in the case of egg-binding, you will usually find the female on the bottom of the cage or aviary, all huddled up. Treat the bird as follows: Take her out of the cage or aviary as the case may be. Take care that she does not bite, for an egg-bound budgerigar can sure bite.

Take her in your left hand, holding the tail between your finger and thumb, and the head with your little fingers. Take a long feather, and dip it into a little warm olive oil, and anoint the vent. Then put her into a small box or cage, and keep her warm. If this treatment does not relieve her, and she seems far gone, then get a jug of warm water, and not too hot. Put over the top a cloth. Make a little hollow in it. Rest the back of your hand in it. If the temperature feels all right, then place your bird in a position across the top of the jug. Gently press both sides, and she will feel you helping her. She will strain and very often relieve herself of the egg. After this she ought to be kept by herself for a few days.

FITS

Fits are caused by the birds not having sufficient green-food and exercise, during the winter months and thus getting over fat and sluggish. When they do have one, it usually leaves them paralyzed in one or both legs. This I found happens to birds from a warmer climate, losing all of my hens in the first and second season, but the next season, with the next consignment from England I seemed to get hardier birds, although I lost a few through eating the leaves of a cedar tree that was growing in the aviary at that time. I lost no time in tearing it out, but it proved to me, that they needed greenfood, and now that they get it the result is no egg-binding and no fits for the last three years.

REARING YOUNG

Two nests are enough for a season, if you desire strong healthy birds, as it takes about two months to lay and incubate the eggs and to rear the young, but often you will find them laying eggs in the nest long before all the young have left it. When they do the eggs get foul with droppings and must be taken out and cleaned, or they will never hatch. To do this take a bowl of warm water, and soak the eggs in it, for a minute or so, then wipe with a soft cloth, which removes the dirt quite easily. At this time the nest must be inspected for Red Mites. I have not found them troublesome, but they do occasionally get into individual nests and if allowed to remain, will suck the life's blood from the next nest of young, but this all true bird lovers would not allow. Insect powder is very good, but I use a liquid sold by all chemists for killing flies, moths, beetles, etc. This I spray in and around all crevices. It is not necessary to wait until the Mites are on the scene, for prevention is better than cure. Now I find that after the birds have had and reared three nests of young, the young do not have the same size and stamina as have their earlier brothers and sisters, and they also lose color. This last year I have been experimenting with a few pairs to get knowledge first hand. I let a few pairs go to nest for the fourth and fifth time, and I found that the young birds never feathered as they should do. With No. 1 in the fifth nest, two of the young never feathered at all, they were naked. In the other nest they had all body feathers but no tail feathers when leaving the nest, but I might say, the flight and tail feathers did grow until they were about half the usual length, then they seemed to rot and break off, leaving the quill in the flesh which makes it impossible for any more to grow until they moult. You will therefore see the folly of over-breeding. The feeding may have a lot to do with it, as in the fall of the year, they do not get the green food, flowering grasses, etc., as they do in the summer, and the hours of feeding get shorter with the coming of the longer nights, which means that the young must go longer without food.

DISEASES

These birds are entirely different to canaries in regard to disease. They very seldom have any ailments, if they do it is of short duration, but I can assure you, my readers, if you heed to my instructions in previous article, and see that the water is always pure, and once each week put Glauber Salts in the water, I see no reason why you cannot have the same results that I have, but be sure that when giving salts or drugs of any kind, to always use a glass drinker, not metal.

STANDARD FOR BUDGERIGARS

Condition is essential. Type: Straight from the nape of neck to tip of tail and gracefully tapered from the same point. Back and breast, rounded and free from hollowness. The bird should be perfectly balanced and convey the impression of being well proportioned. Head—round, eyes bold and set well away from top of skull. Wings—About two-thirds total length of bird, well braced and not crossed at the tips. Tail—to be straight and tight, with two long feathers. Position—Standing on perch at an angle of 30 degrees from the vertical, looking fearless. Mask—Well defined, with cheek patches large. Spots clear, large and symmetrical. Markings—wavy markings on cheeks, head, neck, back and wings to stand out clearly. Color—clear and level in shade. (A description of various colors could follow.)

As I mentioned before, we have at the present time a large number of different varieties of color, so a few words on these will not be out of place. Following the **Green** we have the **Yellow.** This variety has been bred now for a number of years, and are fairly common. They are yellow all over, but with very faint markings on the back, as on the green variety, but it should be the ambition of every breeder to breed them pure yellow without any marking whatever. They cost a little more than the greens. Now we come to the more rare varieties which are all man's creation. In the blues we have two varieties a **Sky Blue** and **Cobalt Blue,** in the whites **Mauve Gray** and **Very Rare Black.** There is now quite a number of these blues upon the market from time to time, but they are rather expensive. They were bred in the first place some forty years ago by an aviculturist in Belgium, but they appeared to die out, and the next were seen in 1911 and since then have gradually progressed, especially in France where I think all credit is due for bringing them up to the present standard. There are quite a number of fanciers in England that have bred them directly from Greens in recent years. It is a gradual process of selecting the palest color bred each year, breeding out the yellow blood and thus they eventually become blue and white instead of green and yellow. It is possible at the present time to get green birds bred from or directly related to blues. They are known as "Blue Bred Greens." In the case of the Cobalts they are known as "Blue Bred Olives" and in these the blue can be distinctly seen. Next we have the Olive Green. These are marked like the Greens, only the yellow in the face is a little richer color, and the Olive Green replaces the light green in the body color. Then we have Mauve and Violet. These colors are sports from the blues. We have also the French Grey and White. All these latter varieties are very scarce at the present time. I might say it takes several years to create a color so do not be disappointed if you do not succeed in breeding the desired color at the first time of trying, but make up your mind what color you will adopt, and stay with it until you get it. That is where we get the thrill. The pleasure is when we have achieved our object.

Here are a few questions that are asked from time to time:

Do they sing?
Yes, a little, but not like a canary.
Do they talk?
Yes, if taken when young and trained.
Do they screech?
No.
Do they drink?
Yes, but in the wild state they live hundreds of miles from water, and the only method they have of drinking, is by sipping the dew from the grasses in the early morning.
Do they need grit?
Yes it must always be before them, so that they can masticate their seed.
Do they need Cuttlefish Bone?
Yes.
Can you keep an odd male or female in the aviary when breeding?
One odd male is all right, but never a female, for she will cause endless trouble with the other nests, throwing out eggs and young.
What kind of nesting material do they use?
None, they lay their eggs on the bare wood.
What kind of a nest plan do they use?
Any kind of a closed box, about six inches square and with a concave bottom.
Do you take out the eggs as you do in the case of the canary, and put them back on the third day?
No. Do not touch the eggs, as she starts to sit with the laying of the first egg.
How many eggs do they lay?
From four to ten, usually six. In the wild state they lay two, and as soon as they are hatched the hen will lay again, and which results in a steady stream of young birds leaving the nest all through the season. The young birds incubate the eggs during the day and the hen stays on only at night.
Do they require egg-food when rearing young?
Yes.
Do they need bread and milk (milk sop)?
No, only when sick, but it must have a little seed mixture with it, and all other seed taken away.
Do they eat green-food?
Yes, but it must be free from frost.

Raising Budgies

A VERY LARGE MAJORITY of people who start raising budgies have gotten the idea from owning a pet. You like the bird and want to try to raise them so you can give some to friends, or sell a few to pay for their feed. If your pet is a cock you will seek a hen. Then you will get a nest box and expect the miracle to happen—eggs and chicks. And, you may be successful, I have known people who have had chicks from one single pair of birds.

This, however, is only the beginning, because soon you will want all the colors of normal birds and will buy different colors. As you do this, you buy more cages, more nest boxes, etc. At first, the single pair were probably kept in a corner in the kitchen or utility room. When more pairs were added you had to look for more room—perhaps a spare bedroom, attic or basement would do for the time. Then as time went on and you expanded into rare birds, you needed flights, an outdoor aviary, more cages, more nest boxes, and by this time there were more headaches. Because, from letters received, I learn many people have had a hard time with their birds. This, I will say, however, comes before the outdoor aviary stage—it usually occurs in the spare bedroom, attic or basement. What are the headaches I speak of? Clear eggs is one, chicks dying in the shell, hens pecking the young, cocks and hens scattering and breaking eggs in the nest box—trouble all over the place! And, how well I can sympathize with all of you!

Every time you add a new bird to your aviary, you may expect some trouble, unless you introduce it slowly. In the first place, you are inviting trouble if you do not isolate the bird at least a week to thirty days. You should make certain the bird is in good health. Feel the breast bone to make certain it has meat on it and not all bone. You want to be sure the bird can fly as this is its only protection in a flight cage. You want to be sure it is eating good. Check the vent to be sure it does not have diarrhoea. You should watch your new bird for a week or so and after you are positive there is nothing wrong with it, spray it good and then move bird, cage and all into your bird room and leave it there for several days. This way the new bird can talk to the other birds and get acquainted before it is put in with them. When you finally do put it in the flight, the other birds may not even pay any attention to it. On the other hand, if you bring in a strange bird and plop it right into the flight, several other birds may start picking on it as soon as it lights on the perch.

Now can you imagine what would happen if you had only a few breeders and you brought home some new birds? Suppose your old hen had a clutch of eggs coming along as well as can be expected. You set up a strange pair of birds right beside the old pair you have. This new hen isn't setting yet—she is about the cage looking her prettiest for her cock. Do you think your old hen is going to remain on her eggs while her cock is hanging on the wire trying to talk to the new hen? Well, don't be too sure. This old hen is going to poke her nose out of her nest box and is going to see this new hen next door. If her cock is strutting his stuff trying to attract attention next door, this old hen is apt to leave her eggs and come out to prove to her cock she is as attractive as the new upstart next door. Of course, the cock may be on the ball and shove her right back into the nest box and try to make her set on the eggs. But, if mama hen is uncertain, she will fight him and in the long run you will lose the clutch of eggs. This sounds fantastic, but we who have raised our birds in the house and have spent hours watching them, know this can happen. Unless some one tells you new breeders of this possibility, you may go on buying new birds and wonder why you can't raise any chicks.

The more you can leave your birds alone, the better off you will be. Don't move them about from one side of the room to the other. It is all right to move them cleaning as quickly as possible and get them back in their spot. But, be sure you do put them back the same—don't turn the cage around, or change perches, or put the food in a different place. Keep everything going as smoothly as possible.

Another thing, don't do any remodeling in your bird room, or in a room nearby while your hens are setting on eggs. Birds are very sensitive to paint odors. They don't like pounding, or scraping and the sound of things moving. Loud strange noises should be avoided. Don't let strangers come in with children who may pound on the cages, or poke fingers in at the birds. Just leave them alone!

As mentioned above, there is the proper way of introducing new birds to your bird room by isolation and keeping the bird in a separate cage when first brought in. You may remodel your bird room when all your hens are through hatching. Wait a few weeks, or a few months, if necessary. You can go ahead and make your nest boxes, and get everything all ready to do the job. You will find it to your advantage to wait until the chicks are old enough so the frightened hen will not hurt them. I don't know what makes them act as they do—perhaps it is like mother nature trying to take care of her young—if she thinks they are in danger, perhaps she thinks they are better off not to be—so destroys them. Whatever it is, guard against it. Always remember, leave your birds alone. See that there are no loud noises or interruptions and they will do all right for you.

Aviary, Cage and Pen Breeding

THREE METHODS OF RAISING BUDGERIGARS are in common use today: aviary, cage, and pen breeding. There are advantages, and disadvantages, to each system. The novice breeder will have to decide which method best meets his desires and financial means.

Aviary breeding is undoubtedly the simplest, and calls for the least effort on the part of the breeder. For these reasons it is still of interest to those who desire a flight of bright-colored birds in their yard, and to those who are interested in the mass production of pet stock. Breeders who are interested in the production of exhibition birds, or top quality pet stock, will find, however, that its disadvantages far outweigh its advantages.

For a simple garden aviary, construct a flight ten to twelve feet long, six to eight feet high, and six to eight feet wide. The rear of this flight should adjoin a small shelter building for the birds. Construction may be as simple or as ornate as may be desired. In England, and many other countries, well designed garden aviaries housing budgerigars, canaries and various species of wild birds, form an attractive addition to many country and city estates.

An aviary such as I have described will nicely handle several pairs of budgerigars and their progeny. And when equipped with large seed hoppers, and running water, the task of caring for the birds is reduced to a minimum; a few minutes each day to supply fresh greens; a half hour each week to refill the seed hopper, and clean out the flight. Furnish the birds with an adequate number of nest boxes in the spring (three for each two pair) and by fall the flight will be filled with a colorful array of young birds.

Unfortunately, aviary breeding is not as ideal as the above picture makes it seem! In spite of the best precautions that can be taken, un-controlled in-breeding produces degeneration of size and quality in a few years' time. And when several types, and colors, of Budgerigars are involved there is a gradual reversion to the normal light green type.

Many plans have been suggested as means of avoiding these difficulties, but none have proven successful. Breeders of pet stock who use the aviary system (and few of them do) replenish their breeding stock with control bred birds, and devote each flight to the production of budgerigars of one type color only. While it is unnecessary to devote a garden aviary to only one color, or type, of budgerigar, owners of this type of aviary should follow the mass production pet breeder's policy of periodically replacing his breeding stock with control bred birds.

Pen breeding is, simply stated, aviary breeding on a one pair basis. Each breeding pair is furnished with an individual flight from six to eight feet long, of similar height and any convenient width; usually on the order of two and one half to three feet. Each flight connects with a breeding pen inside the shelter building. These are the same width as the individual flights and about three feet deep. In height they may extend from floor to ceiling, or storage cupboards may be placed below the pens.

Pen breeding is without doubt the ideal system. It provides the breeding pairs with a maximum of exercise, fresh air and sunshine; all essential for the successful production of vigorous, healthy progeny. Most fanciers find the original cost of this system to be prohibitive, and for this reason adopt the simpler, and yet practical, method of cage breeding.

Under the cage breeding system, large flights are provided for the young birds, and for the males and females when they are not in the breeding cages. These flights should be as convenient, and if the flights for cocks and hens can be out of sight and hearing of each other, so much the better. And the more time your birds spend in the flights, and less in the breeding cages, the better off you will be.

Breeding cages for budgerigars should be large; the larger the better! The minimum size recommended by the American Budgerigar Society is three feet long, by eighteen inches high, and of any convenient depth. These are simple open front box affairs, fitted with a shallow droppings tray or drawer, a sub-floor of quarter inch hardware cloth resting on cleats above the droppings tray, and a wire front either of home-made or commercial construction. Seed hoppers and grit pots may be placed inside. The water fountain is usually of the sanitary type, with the container on the outside of the cage and a small drinking cup extending inside; these are held in place by the tension of the wire front. Another method is to fit the cage with a narrow front board just above the tray. Open seed and water containers may then be located on the inside of small doors fitted into the front board.

Cages such as I have described may be tiered up in a neat and orderly fashion, and provide the basis for an attractive bird room. For the comfort of the birds, and ease in care, the bottom row should not be located too close to the floor, nor the top row too close to the ceiling. For the production of pet stock, four cages high with the bottom cage located a foot above the floor is ideal. Three cages high is just right for the production of exhibition stock; then the space above the breeding cages may be used for training cages.

Unlike canaries, budgerigars won't use an open nest pan. Nest boxes must be provided. Many styles of nest boxes have been developed, and all have their advocates. The simplest, however, and the one that seems to be in most common use, is of the simple vertical pattern. It consists of a wooden box about five inches square, and eight inches high inside. The top is hinged to give access to the interior, or one side slides into place in grooves. An entrance hole, about one and one half inches in diameter, is located near the top of the box on one side. Beneath the entrance hole another small hole is drilled. A projecting perch is inserted in this hole and fastened to the opposite side of the box.

As Budgies do not build a nest, all nest boxes should be fitted with a removable concave nest board. This is simply a board five inches square, with a hollowed-out place about four inches in diameter, and a half inch deep, located in its center. Place nestboard and a handful of cedar sawdust, or fine cedar shavings in the nest box and it is ready to hang up in your aviary, or breeding cage.

With the breeding cages, and nest boxes, completed, most beginners will immediately ask, "When can I mate my birds?" They will, unwittingly, have asked what is undoubtedly one of the most controversial questions among Budgie raisers. The answers he would receive would range all the way from, "The normal nesting time of wild birds in your area," to "Any time of the year." One experienced, and keenly observant British Fancier recently expressed the opinion that "Budgerigars come into breeding condition every four months." Clearly there must be a reason for this apparent confusion, so let us see if we can trace it to its source.

Our modern Budgerigar is, at best, a semi-domesticated species. Its wild counterpart is a native of Australia, which as you know is located in the Southern Hemisphere. As a result the seasons are just the reverse of those within which we are acquainted. So, too, are the nesting seasons of birds. Therefore any wild bird which is transplanted from the Southern Hemisphere to the Northern Hemisphere is beset by two conflicting influences; the inherited tendency to breed during our Fall and Winter months; and the influence of our Spring and Summer weather.

Some species of birds imported from South America, Africa and Australia never become adapted to our seasons, and will breed only during the fall and winter months; others are more affected by the seasons and soon lose their tendency to breed during those same months. The Budgerigar seems to be equally affected by both influences, and these influences seem to have been further modified by man until it will now breed at any time of the year it may be in breeding condition.

That to me seems to be the key point with Budgerigars; BREEDING CONDITION! And, breeding condition is determined by care given the birds THROUGHOUT the year, not just at breeding time; the conditioning of birds is a year round job! Many a beginner's first year success is due to the fact that his newly purchased birds had been properly conditioned by an experienced breeder; and, the second year failures because of improper care on the part of the beginner.

Breeding condition is indicated in several ways. The ceres become deeper colored; bluer in the cock, browner in the hen. But don't mate your birds until they are mature, (at least one year old,) even if they do come into apparent breeding condition prior to then. Needless to say, the birds should be healthy, fit as a fiddle and tight of feather. They should also show as great an interest in members of the opposite sex as a "Country swain out courten his gal." When the flights for cocks and hens are separated only by a wire partition, they will feed each other through the wires. They will also engage in mating flights; the male and female flying side by side, from one end of the flights to the other repeatedly.

When the birds are in that condition, they are ready to mate. But, if the flights are located as described above, they may be unwilling to accept the mate of YOUR choice. It is better to have the flights separated, and thus avoid that difficulty. The birds should show an active interest in each other as soon as placed in the breeding cages. Don't be alarmed, or separate the birds, unless you feel sure that the life of one is at stake.

Three days after you have mated the birds, place the nest box in the breeding cage; not before. Placing the nest box in the cage too soon may result in a percentage of infertile eggs. Leave the birds alone as much as possible and you should soon see your first egg, and an egg every other day from then on till the clutch is laid. That is the way they hatch starting with the 18th to 20th day. Keep the beaks and feet of the young birds clean, and in a month's time your first hatched birds will be on the perches.

Budgie Breeding Time

THE BREEDING SEASON is here again and Ma and Pa Budgie are ready to begin the task of rearing youngsters, after having had a good rest and plenty of flight during the summer months and having been fed soft food for a few weeks prior to their being placed in the breeding cages.

These things are essentials in preparing your birds for the tough job of raising two clutches of youngsters. The wise breeder allows his birds only two and also limits the number of young per nest to not over five; four being even more desired. Now the question arises. Should I destroy these surplus eggs? The answer is, no. One should always provide a few extra pairs to be used as foster parents. Usually these are birds which do not measure up to show quality or are not the desired color. They do excel as good parents. A few reliable foster pairs are worth plenty to the successful breeder.

Also in watching the feeding habits of birds, one finds a variation, and once one recognizes that a pair is not taking good care of their young they should be put under good feeders as it is vital that your birds get the best possible feeding in the first few weeks of their life. Growth of feather and size give one a pretty good idea whether parents are performing well. If the young are growing rapidly and have plenty of down on the body you can rest assured the parents are doing a conscientious job and all will be well. Giving the parents an aid by feeding soft foods is sure to pay dividends. In preparing mated pairs we give them the soft food a few weeks prior to putting them to work. Soaked seed and oiled seed are also excellent.

After the young begin to leave the nest we watch them and as soon as we see they do not need further assistance in feeding we remove them to a primary flight which is 4 feet long and 2 feet high; the depth being 20 inches. This gives the young a chance to learn the art of flying and gauging distance. Usually this cage can accomodate about fifteen to twenty-five young. We allow them a few weeks in the smaller flights and then introduce them into a larger flight which is 8 feet in length and 6 feet in height; the depth being 2 feet.

They are allowed in this flight to develop. After they go into their adult moult we grade them and place them into the combination outdoor and indoor flights. It is now that they are allowed to mingle with the older birds as one finds that the older birds tend to be domineering and often will keep young birds off perches and away from feeding stations. It is now we also segregate the sexes. This eliminates lost time at a later date as the pairs seem more ready to work.

In closing, remember your preparations for the breeding season start with the end of the season before. Most people just place the birds in the flight and cut down special feeding. Birds need special care for a period after the nesting season also during the moulting period. To you newer breeders, do not get impatient if results aren't forthcoming as rapidly as you wish. You must give your birds a chance to acclimate themselves and get used to you. When they get darn good and ready and at their convenience they will go to work.

⊕

J. M. Braunstein,

with finger-tame

Budgerigar.

⊕

Flighted Budgerigars.

Concave nest bottom showing six eggs and three newly hatched baby budgerigars.

Basic Color Varieties

ONE OF THE GREATEST ATTRACTIONS of the beautiful Budgerigar is its numerous varieties, and brilliant colored types. In no other bird are so many vivid combinations of color available. Truly, it is the living rainbow of the Cage-Bird fancy. Yet, each of the various varieties, in all its colored types, are easily reproduced, once one knows the "Tricks of the Trade."

And that is what I will cover in this new series of articles, on everyone's favorite bird. In doing so, I must touch lightly on the subject of genetics, but I'll do this as gently as possible.

GREEN, BLUE, YELLOW and WHITE

The four colors listed, green, blue, yellow and white are the four basic colors found in all varieties of Budgerigars. Therefore, what is learned concerning the methods of breeding Normal variety Budgerigars in these colors is equally applicable to all other varieties.

Color in Budgerigars is produced by the presence or absence of but two coloring agents. The first is eumelanin, a dark pigment present in the axial cells of the feathers; it is responsible for the blue and black colors in the Normal Budgerigar. The second, yellow lipochrome, is present in the feather sheath overlying the axial cells, roughly speaking it might be termed a ground color since it extends to all feathers. And on a similar basis white, which is the absence of melanin and lipochrome, may be termed a ground color.

We therefore have in the Budgerigar two ground colors, white and yellow, similar to the canary. And, if a recent Australian mutation (change in inheritable characteristics) is successfully developed, we may soon add orange and possibly RED to the series of Budgerigar ground colors.

Variegation (eumelanin distribution) may be displayed by birds of any ground color. When present on a white ground we have blue, and when present on a yellow ground we have green. Variegation color does not extend to the mask (face) and on the wings and back of head appears as a black lacing, and striation, respectively. The difference in color between wing markings and body is due NOT to a difference in the pigment involved but due to a difference in the physical characteristics of the feathers involved.

Since eumelanin distribution does not extend to the face, green Budgerigars have a yellow mask; and blue Budgerigars a white mask. Upon this is displayed the typical cheek flashes and chain of six dark spots. These are completely absent in a good yellow, and but faintly visible in a white.

All varieties and types of Budgerigars have been created from the wild type light green by mutations and/or by selective breeding. One mutation resulted in the suppression of melanin formation with the result that clear yellow birds appeared. Another mutation resulted in the suppression of lipochrome formation with the result that blue Budgerigars appeared. And, when both mutations are combined in one bird by selective breeding we have the white Budgerigar.

Mate a pure green to a pure green and all progeny will be green. Also, if you mate a pure green to a pure blue, or a pure yellow, all progeny will be green. They carry, however, in hidden form, the ability to when suitably mated produce some progeny of the color to which their green parents were mated. Such birds are said to be split to the hidden factor; green split blue, and green split yellow. And this is usually abbreviated; green/blue, and green/yellow.

The previous paragraph is understandable when one considers that all factors are grouped in pairs. And that each parent transmits one member of each pair, to each progeny. The green Budgerigar carries two wild type genes (factors) for melanin formation (blue) and two for lipochrome formation (yellow). The blue Budgerigar carries two wild type genes for melanin formation, and two mutant genes for absence of yellow lipochrome.

The progeny from such a pair will each receive a factor for melanin production from each parent, a factor for lipochrome production from the green parent, and a mutant factor for absence of lipochrome (actually a nonactive gene for the production of lipochrome) from the blue parent. Since the progeny carry active factors for both lipochrome and melanin production they will be green. And since they carry a factor for absence of lipochrome they are said to be split blue, and are capable when suitably mated, of producing birds of that color.

The green to yellow mating is quite similar. The yellow mate carries two factors for absence of melanin formation; the progeny one such factor and since they inherit active factors for the production of both melanin and lipochrome they must be green in color, but in their case they are split to yellow instead of blue.

Also, if we mate a pure breeding green to a pure breeding white, all progeny will be green. They inherit one factor for lipochrome formation, and one factor for melanin formation from the green parent and must therefore be green. And, as they inherit one factor for absence of lipochrome formation, and one factor for absence of melanin formation, from the white parent, they are split to both blue and yellow; green, blue and yellow. These birds, when properly mated, are therefore capable of producing a percentage of blue and yellow progeny. In addition, since they carry factors, for the absence of both blue and yellow, they are capable of producing a small percentage of whites when suitably mated.

For this reason, greens split to blue and yellow are known as green split white; green/white. The point for the practical breeder to remember is that a green/white, when suitably mated, is capable of producing not only green progeny but a percentage of blue, yellow and white progeny as well.

To summarize what has been said, a pure breeding green mated to any other pure breeding color, produces only green progeny. These however are split to the second color and carry in hidden form the ability to reproduce these colors in a percentage of their progeny when suitably mated.

We therefore have four types of greens, each identical insofar as their physical appearance and color is concerned, but capable of quite different breeding results. To differentiate between those physical characteristics and colors which may be seen, and those split characteristics which may NOT be seen, special terms have been adopted.

Feather Plucking Budgerigars

Many breeders ask this question, "I've a hen Budgie who plucks her chicks. Can I cure her and what shall I do with the plucked chicks?" Fortunately this state of affairs is very rare, but it is troublesome especially if the hen is a valuable bird and one from which it is most desirable to obtain some stock. I have had experience of this condition and while I cannot cure the hen of this nasty habit, and can only suggest the cause, I have been able to save the young birds from being plucked. Also I've a method of dealing with those which have been plucked so that the majority do grow their feathers and look none the worse for this misadventure.

The Hen

The cause is not definitely known and I suspect it is mainly a question of budgerigar mentality plus feminine temperament. I find that if after plucking the chicks are removed from the nest box, death may occur through her refusal to feed them. I have even taken plucked chicks and placed them in a small open box in the corner of the breeding cage in the hope that the male would feed them. The male bird did try, but his mate fought him off and then proceeded to try to scalp the young birds. The feather plucking usually commences just after the heads are full feathered and at first is confined to an area which extends from the crown to the nape of the neck. It is obvious that the hen wants the chicks out of the nest box be-

cause she is anxious to lay more eggs which she does after the chicks have been removed. Giving a larger nest box does not affect the condition. She wants the nest box to herself and means to have it. Such a hen is useless as a mother but she may be valuable as a layer and in my experience plucking hens are good sitters.

Plucked chicks

Just as soon as you find a chick has been plucked remove it and all other chicks have been removed parents, after banding. I make it a practice to put up a pair of foster parents as soon as any other pair is put up for breeding. The foster parents eggs are always taken away and they are given other eggs, even if only one or two. I limit my hens to four eggs per nest. This gives the young in that nest a better chance of being properly fed.

Before putting the plucked chicks in another nest, just smear the plucked flesh with olive oil, or even cod liver oil and usually, if the flesh is not raw and bleeding, the feathers will grow normally.

In some cases where the flesh is raw and the feather cells are damaged, the feathers will never regrow—but such a bird although unsightly can be bred from and, in my experience, the condition does not appear to be hereditary. In some instances, it will be found that a hard scab-like growth will appear on the plucked portion. This will prevent the feathers growing, but do not attempt to remove it, not even by bathing with warm water. If you do, you will not only cause the bird a lot of pain but it will usually grow again. You can, however, try painting it with olive oil in the hope that it will soften and drop off. I had one chick which responded to this treatment but the feathers never regrew.

Prevention of Damage

Prevention is better than cure and once you know a hen plucks her young, you would be foolish to let her continue. You must prepare for her attack by having foster parents ready to receive her young.

I band the majority of my young budgies on about the sixth or seventh day and just as soon as this is done, I remove them from their plucking parent. If you do this you can let her incubate as many eggs as she will lay in two nests—but don't treat her as a mere breeding machine. If you follow my practice you won't cure the hen but you will save the young, and if she is a valuable breeder then the extra trouble is well worth while.

From your side also comes the news that during cold weather the temperature in a Budgerigar Breeding Room is maintained at a minimum of 65 degrees. This is much too hot. Forty degrees is ample. Remember, the seasonal changes in temperature have a definite bearing on the sex-urge cycle in bird life and if temperatures of 65 degrees are maintained it may affect the condition of the budgies. They will go soft. Their feathering will not be as good as it should be. Just remember that nature has provided the budgie with an insulating system which enables it to surround its body with a blanket of blood when it sleeps or rests. Also that the three essentials apart from food are fresh air, natural light and protection from damp and draughts. A stuffy overheated bird room is a menace to well being.

My birds get artificial heat only when I find their water pots a solid block of ice and then only sufficient to keep the water from freezing and I've never lost a single bird through cold.

Don't neglect your birds, but don't hothouse them like a rare orchid or tropical flower. Let them have all the exercise you can possibly give them.

Feeding Your Budgerigars

In comparison to Canaries, the feeding of Budgerigars is simplicity itself. And yet, simple as it is, the unwary and inexperienced may make mistakes which will disrupt their entire breeding season; or even endanger the health of their birds. I'll point out these mistakes, some of which I made myself, as I go along.

The standard seed mixture for Budgies is four parts canary seed to six parts white millet. Yellow millet may be used if white is unavailable, but red millet should be avoided at all costs. Buy only the best recleaned, well-filled seed. Good seed should NOT smell mouldy, should be free of dust, plump and bright in color; it should be alive and have a high germination test. This you can determine for yourself in a rag-doll tester. Once you have located a supply house which consistently furnishes good clean plump seed with a high germination rate—stick with that supplier!

Purchase only that quantity of seed which your birds will consume in a reasonable length of time; then store it properly. A cloth sack, or a well ventilated wooden bin, is an ideal storage container. It should be stored where it is not subject to either undue dampness or excessive heat. Don't place the seed under the kitchen sink, in a frosty room, or near the furnace. And above all things see that your seed is stored in such a manner that it is not subject to the inroads of mice. A few unnoticed mice droppings in their seed will not only upset your birds, but may be the cause of serious illness.

Oat groats (hulled oats) are used as a supplement to the regular seed mixture during the winter months, and while the birds are feeding young, by most breeders. Great care must be used when feeding oats. They are highly beneficial when adult stock are in cool quarters,

and in the formation of "pap" for their young. But if fed in excess while birds are in warm quarters, or small flights, the result will be fat birds, and birds that fail to breed when paired up.

Most Budgies prefer oat groats to the regular seed mixture, to such an extent that they will peck over and waste a pound of seed to get a

dozen oat groats—if they are mixed in with the regular seed mixture. For this reason feed them in a separate container; then you will be able to control the amount consumed by your birds. The usual practice is hoppers for the regular mixture, and open dishes for the groats.

Whenever open seed dishes are used, loose husks must be blown off from the top of the good seed, at least once each day; otherwise your birds may starve with plenty of seed in front of them.

During cold weather, and while the parents are rearing young, your seed mixture should be fortified with the sunshine vitamin found in Cod Liver Oil. Use only the best grade of non-emulsified oil. Most of the emulsified oils are emulsified by the addition of chicken eggs and are therefore a possible source of infection for your birds. Breeders who quarter their birds where they receive very little sunshine at any time, should feed fortified seed the year around.

The usual proportion is from one-half to one teaspoon of cod liver oil to each pound of the regular seed mixture; the amount needed depends upon the temperature of the bird room, the amount of direct sunshine received by your birds, and the quality of the green food they receive daily. You may add the oil to the oat groats and feed separately; add the treated oat groats to the regular seed mixture; or add the oil directly to the regular mixture. While there is less waste of oil when it is added directly to the oat groats, I consider the third method to be superior to the others. In any case mix the oil in thoroughly, so that it is well distributed throughout the seed, and let the treated seed stand at least forty-eight hours before giving it to the birds.

Budgies also need the fertility (wheat germ) oil prior to, and during, the breeding season. About three months prior to the regular breeding season, add wheat germ oil to your regular seed mixture in the proportion of one part to each eight parts of cod liver oil. To obtain even distribution of this oil, add it to the cod liver oil, shake well, and then add this mixture to your seeds in the usual proportion.

Care should be taken to obtain the right type of Wheat Germ oil. There are two methods of producing this oil. One type is an effective fertility aid; the other has little or no effect. Unfortunately the type cannot be ascertained from the label. For this reason obtain your wheat germ oil from a dealer who specializes in bird supplies, and you will be reasonably certain of obtaining the right type.

Certain precautions are necessary in the use of fortified seed. The oils must be fresh, as they lose their potency with age. Also, do not suddenly switch from non-fortified to fortified seed at the start of the breeding season. Such a sudden change in diet can easily throw your birds into a heavy moult, and out of breeding condition. In addition wheat germ oil, to be effective, must be used consistently for several months prior to the breeding season.

Some people believe that Budgerigars do not require water. This belief is quite in error. Budgies must have pure, fresh water daily, and the water supply must be protected from possible contamination. This can be done either by locating the water container above the perches, or by using a sheltered type aviary fountain. Two sets of water containers should be used; one set being cleaned while the other is in use.

As a health measure, one day each week, three drops of Lugol's Solution should be added to each quart of drinking water. This is an essential precaution throughout the Goiter Belt, and is advisable elsewhere. Seeds and green foods raised on deficient soils may be lacking in the vital element supplied by Lugol's Solution; iodine. This solution may be obtained at any drug store, and the cost is insignificant compared to its value.

Budgies need both grit and lime. The grit serves as your birds' teeth, and the lime is essential for egg production and healthy well-boned progeny. The usual mixture consists of equal proportions of smooth river sand and crushed oyster shell. (This grit should be slightly coarser than that used for canaries.) Pulverized and sterilized egg shells may be substituted for part of the crushed oyster shell. To this mixture may be added small quantities of fine charcoal, table salt and trace minerals.

JAVA SPARROW

These beautiful birds have the enviable reputation of being the best groomed of all the cage birds, and they richly deserve it, because their plumage is so wonderfully smooth, that from a distance it appears to be painted on them, so closely do the feathers lie. There are two varieties, the Grey and the White. The Grey is quite common, and has a slate colored body, pure

white cheeks, while the face and throat are black, and the back pink. The White Javas are pure white with the exception of the beak, which is a beautiful waxlike pink, and they present a most beautiful appearance in a mixed aviary, resembling a piece of statuary. These birds are remarkably easy to attend to, as they require only a mixture of Canary Seed and Padda or unhulled Rice, with an occasional Sunflower Seed, and a little fresh green food or sweet apple. They very readily breed in captivity, in either cage or aviary and appreciate a half cocoanut shell for a nesting box. They cannot be really called songsters, although some of them have quite a nice song, but this is more the exception than the rule. They are very hardy, and seldom suffer from ill health and are extremely easy to keep. In addition to these good points, they are very reasonable in price, quite frequently in the markets, so ought to be even more popular than they already are, and no one could ever regret purchasing a few pairs of these beautiful birds. The white variety usually cost at least twice as much as the Grey, as they are quite rare, seldom being in the markets, and usually the demand is far greater than the supply, as they are not natural, being bred by the Japanese, whereas the Greys are trapped wild birds from Java and parts of Asia, where they are regarded as pests on account of the damage they do in the rice fields. They settle down to cage life almost as soon as they are introduced to it, and very quickly get attached to their keepers, and are quick at picking up tricks, especially when they are caught young.

PARROTS, LORIES, LOVE BIRDS

PARROTS

I am inclined to believe the Parrot when adopted into a home becomes the most interesting pet, they possess rare intelligence, learn to know their masters and their habits. The double yellow head from Mexico is a delightful companion, if taken when very young from the nest and raised by hand. A trapped or bronco parrot seldom talks. The best method of teaching a parrot is to hide from view of the parrot and repeat often, slowly, in the same tone of voice the words you wish the parrot to learn, four or five words at a time is sufficient, two or three is better, they whistle, sing and are very entertaining.

Many owners of Parrots kill their birds with kindness. Their sincere love for their pets prompts them through their ignorance to give them table scraps, meat, cakes and pastry which upsets their digestive organs and overheats their blood and causes them to pluck their feathers and sit around listlessly. Parrots thrive on bread and milk as an occasional food with the usual special mixture of seeds and plenty of grit, gravel, fresh water daily. Once a week the water cup should be washed out and scalded with soda water. Don't forget to feed them green food such as cabbage, lettuce, dandelion, plantain, watercress, carrots, onions, turnips, celery; in the way of fruits feed apples, oranges, pears, bananas, grapes, raspberries, blackberries, but of course use judgment, not too much at a time, certainly not more than one at a time. They like green foods and fruits as treats only; their general diet should be the seeds as given herewith or sold at all Pet Shops. Members of the Parrot family are the Cockatoos, and Macaws which seldom make good talkers.

Feeding a parrot properly is very necessary for the health of the parrot, they enjoy a long life if properly fed and their blood not made too rich by unnatural foods. Their most relished food is a mixture of fresh plump sunflower seed 4 parts, 1 part raw peanuts, 1 part hemp seed. They are fond of fresh fruits such as sweet apple, bananas, grapes; raw vegetables, carrots, turnips and cabbage. Do not feed acid fruits, such as oranges, grapefruit, etc., never feed a parrot cake or sweet food, whole wheat bread fed two or three times a week is good. It is best not to change from the foods mentioned as this is sufficient food for the life of a parrot. Water always fresh, changed often in hot weather as the parrot will soak its food and wash its mouth in the water.

THE GOUT: While canaries seldom are troubled with the Gout, Parrots and Parrakeets are subject to it when over-fed as above stated, in this case they become feverish and drowsy, do not eat much but drink a great deal of water, the feet and legs are swollen and inflamed; treatment, paint the parts affected with tincture of iodine and put a good size pinch of Epsom salts in their drinking water daily to keep their bowels open.

The best food for parrots is a mixture of sunflower, unhulled rice, hemp seed, raw peanuts, "Pinyonens or pine nuts" and pumpkin seed.

Occasionally feed sweet apple or banana sparingly.

Crackers, hard shelled corn, and other nuts are also beneficial and relished.

Mexican peppers fed two or three times a week help to keep parrots in good health.

Many parrots like stale bread or crackers soaked in coffee or boiled milk for breakfast. Either is good, and coffee may be given with or without cream and sugar as the parrot may desire.

Frequently feed buttered toast, boiled rice, boiled or baked potato and boiled corn on the cob.

Except for seed and water, do not leave any soft food in the cage after the parrot is through eating as the food may turn sour and prove very injurious.

Always provide the parrot with fresh cool water (not iced) but take the water away if the parrot shows any signs of diarrhea.

In such cases immediately use diarrhea powders, obtainable at any pet shop.

A little more attention must be given a young parrot until it is a year old.

Young parrots should be fed crackers or stale wheat bread soaked in hot water every morning adding a little sugar. Half milk (boiled) and half water may be given instead and is more nourishing, but the parrot may not care for it. Let the parrot have the above soft food mixture while food is real warm but not too hot.

In the evening give the parrot a little more of the cracker food in warm water. Corn meal mush or any other breakfast cereal may be given occasionally if they like it.

Keep a supply of the mixed seeds in the cage at all times so that the bird will become accustomed to eating hard seeds. Fruits should be fed sparingly to young parrots, but peanuts and other nuts are good for them.

135

Young parrots may have water to drink but care must be taken to give only boiled water which has been allowed to cool.

Be sure that the parrot is fed soft food during the first few months until he shows signs of wanting dry food such as seed. Then instructions for older parrots should be followed.

Parrot Diseases.—When parrots have colds they are usually accompanied by sore eyes and sore throat. They should be given any good parrot tonic and kept in a dark or semi-dark room. Honey and borax given with a medicine dropper will help to relieve the sore throat. A saturated solution of boric acid in warm water should be used to bathe the eyes and a one percent solution of argyrol dropped into the eyes. The mexican peppers should also be given.

Diarrhea is often accompanied by nausea and vomiting. Diarrhea powders should be given immediately. Six drops each of lemon juice and olive oil should also be given with a medicine dropper to relieve the nausea.

When lumps form on the head or eyes they should be painted with a tincture of iodine.

NYASSALAND LOVE BIRDS

LORIES OR PAROQUETS are much of the same order as the parrots, but are smaller and lighter in build. There are several varieties, and they can almost safely be called the most brilliant of the small parrot tribe. Some are very adaptable to home keeping and become exceedingly tame, and when tame they make most gorgeous pets; as the colors are very striking and beautifully blended. **THE KING LORY**, the **BLUE MOUNTAIN LORY** and **SWAINSON'S LORIQUET** are perhaps the most popular, but of these, Blue Mountain Lory is about the most common, and this is a wonderfully colored bird, about the size of a small pigeon, with a beautiful plumage of blue, scarlet, purple and golden yellow, so it can be left

to the imagination as to the beauty of these birds. They are natives of Australia, where they are quite frequently found in immense numbers. In the wild state, they live chiefly on honey and ripe fruits.

The family includes the Nyassaland, Peach Faced, Madagascar, Black Cheeked, Masked, Abyssinian, and Fisher's Love Birds. Their eggs hatch in 18 to 24 days, depending on the breed.

Several of the varieties mentioned will breed in captivity, so nesting boxes should be provided, as soon as the birds have comfortably established themselves in a home.

They are very fond of fruits such as bananas, apples, figs, etc., and a little honey given in the comb is very good for them and also appreciated, and it helps to keep away colds and sore throats.

They are very susceptible to cold and draughts, and must be carefully guarded against them. Never give them drinking water unless it has been boiled and cooled off, but a drink of scalded milk is good for them occasionally, also a little coffee if they will drink it.

BREEDING LOVE BIRDS

It is about as simple to raise Love Birds of the foregoing species as it is to raise Parrakeets. Their nest boxes must be larger and they should be supplied with coarse straw, grass, "and such like" for nest building. They build a rather heavy nest and it is not advisable to try to see their eggs. From 18 to 24 days the eggs hatch, depending upon the species. The Lovebirds can be crossed and often will do so if it is convenient. A plain diet is advisable in breeding time: sunflower, hemp, canary seed and millet. Plenty of grit, fresh water, cuttlefish bone, egg-shells or old lime mortar for making egg shells is advisable.

QUESTION AND ANSWER DEPARTMENT

BABIES DYING

Question—Asks reason for loss of young birds between one and three weeks old.

Answer—From your letter I would judge that the trouble lies principally in the feeding of the hens while caring for their broods. A large number of losses each year result not from the quality of the egg-food used, but due to the hens being overfed when their young are from one to six days old. After sitting for 13 days, and being fed during that time on a plain seed diet, most hens will partake of too much egg-food if the amount given is not regulated. The result is biliousness and an entire lack of interest in the needs of the young birds. Try giving the hens just a quarter of a teaspoonful of egg-food made from the yolk only of a well boiled fresh egg, to which you mix the same bulk of home made bread crumbs. Do not give more until all previously given has been used. Watch the hen at her work and that will give you a good idea of how the young birds are being taken care of. Slightly increase the amount from day to day, and give each day in addition to the egg-food, just a morsel of bread which has been steeped in warm milk. This will help carry off the effect of overstimulation, keeping the blood of the hen cool and the bowels clear. At four days give just a little green-food in between the regular feedings. At six days add half a teaspoonful of GOOD cracked Hemp Seed. The white and yolk of the egg can both be used after the young birds are past three days old.

EGGS DRIED UP

Question—Asks the reason that a number of Canary Eggs dry up during the period of incubation.

Answer—To correctly answer this question it will be necessary for me to know if the eggs upon examination have shown the body of a dead young bird, partly dried up in the shell, or if the eggs are infertile and with the contents dried as mentioned.

The use of poor material for the making of the shell will often cause eggs to be laid which are too thin in the shell formation, and result in the shell being cracked by the hen in frequently leaving and going back to the nest from feeding. Another cause of eggs being so damaged will be found in the claws of the hens being long and sharp, thus perforating the shell of the eggs with one or more very small holes. Immediately the outer shell and inside skin of the egg is punctured, from that time on incubation is stopped, and successful hatching cannot take place. Try clipping the claws of all hens before pairing them. Use powdered fowl's

egg shells, a little fine silver sand, and a piece of cuttlefish bone as the only material for shell making. Make sure the hens are not disturbed while sitting, and the eggs chilled in this way. Do not give the bath from the first day of incubation until the tenth day.

Question—Asks the reason for birds moulting continuously.

Answer—The diet mentioned in your letter is good. I would suggest stopping at this season, apple, lettuce and the nesting food (if a patent food) and substitute in their places, flowering Chickweed, and a little freshly made egg-food. The rest of the diet can be continued as you have mentioned. See that the birds are kept free of draughts, and for the present box cages would be the most suitable. Make quite sure that there are no Red Mites in the cages. When giving the bread and milk add three drops of Cod Liver Oil, and mix well into the food. A good tonic effect will result by giving twenty drops of "a Good Chemical Food" in the drinking water every other day for a week. I would not advise you to attempt breeding the birds in their present condition for the chances of success during the partial moult will be very small.

Question—Asks for cause and treatment for a complaint resulting in the loss of 20 birds.

Answer—From the complete description of the symptoms mentioned in your letter, no doubt was "Diphtheria." I would suggest that the trouble has been brought into your bird room by the introduction of one or more birds newly bought, or by the use of one or more cages which have been used in another room, and which were not disinfected and thoroughly cleaned before you commenced to use them. **Diphtheria is an extremely infectious disorder** and very prompt action is necessary if any of the birds are to be saved. Unless the first bird affected is of special value the wisest plan is to destroy the bird and the cage in which it has been kept. The treatment is as follows. Early symptoms show as though the bird was affected with a severe cold. It soon begins to refuse food, and is dull and languid. The head and parts around the eyes appear swollen. The bird frequently makes a clicking sneeze in its endeavor to expel matter from its nostrils. If caught and the beak opened the mucous membrane of the mouth and throat and also the tongue will be found swollen and inflamed, with more or less ulceration according to the stage which the disease has reached.

For treatment first strictly isolate the bird. Remove all seed. Give a diet of bread and milk adding a little sugar or honey to the warm milk before steeping the bread. The mouth and throat should be washed out several times a day with a small feather or camel's hair brush using a lotion. One drachm of Sulphate of Copper in two ounces of distilled water. This should be kept up until all ulceration has disappeared. Also make a mixture of 20 drops of Liquid Fluid and one drachm of Spirits of Wine mixed into one ounce of Cinnamon Water. Add 20 drops of this mixture to each ounce of drinking water daily until the bird is quite well. Keep in a comfortable temperature, and allow the bird to remain quiet and free from excitement.

STERILITY, EGGS DON'T HATCH

Question—Asks for the reason of sterility in a two year old male bird, and what can be done to correct the defect.

Answer—Unless the trouble is the result of inherited weakness the bird can be quickly brought into breeding condition. First allow the bird to have unlimited exercise. Give each day a quarter of a teaspoonful of rich egg-food and a complete root of Dandelion. Wash off the soil from the root, and split open with a knife, exposing the inside pith of the root. Give a bath early in the morning and add a half teaspoonful of table salt to the water. If the bird is thin a half teaspoonful of good fresh cracked Hemp Seed will help to improve his condition. Do not mate the bird until it is in steady song, and shows signs of breeding condition when placed near a cage containing other birds. Allow the bird to be in a position where he can hear the call of one or more hen birds.

BREEDING A TUTOR

Question—Asks if it is correct to use a Tutor for breeding.

Answer—Under certain conditions it is possible to use a Tutor for breeding, but it is advisable not to do so if the bird is in his first year. It is a wiser plan to keep the bird in perfect song, and later use the bird for stock purposes after he has trained a number of young birds, and when two or three of these birds so trained can be given the work of training in the season to follow. It is not fair to place a Tutor into the breeding room where he will be exposed to the song of every male bird in the room, and then expect his song to be as good as it was. If you can arrange to mate the Tutor in a room out of hearing of the other stock, little risk will result in mating the bird for not more than two nests. Place him in the breeding cage with the hen each evening, and remove him from the cage about nine o'clock in the morning. Keeping this up until the hen has laid her third egg, when he can be removed entirely and taken back to the contest cage in a room separated from the other stock. Be careful not to over stimulate the bird as this will tend to high or faulty song.

NON-FEEDING HENS

Question—Asks what food could be used with hens that will not eat egg-food given to them, at the time when they have young birds in the nests.

Answer—Quite often cases will be found where some hens will not use egg food made in the usual way. Some hens will feed entire-ly upon seed and green food, if other soft food to their liking is not available. Try this recipe which I think will help you over the difficulty. Cut two thick slices of stale white bread. Place into a dish of cold water and allow to stand overnight. Pour off the water, and squeeze from the bread as much water as possible. Place the bread into the inside pan of a double steamer. Pour in a good half cup of sweet milk, and a teaspoonful of sugar. Now add two fresh eggs, and mix all well together. Bring the water in the steamer to a boil, and with the lid on the pan allow the water to boil for not less than 25 minutes. Pour the food into a dish, and allow to grow cold. It should then be so thick it can be cut with a knife. Feed to the hens in the same way as egg-food, and place a pinch of good Maw Seed at the side of the food given. This custard I know to be a first-class food and suitable in every way. I have used it all the way through a complete breeding season, and have proven its worth with hens that will not use egg-food in any other form.

WEANING AGE
SEXING

Question—Asks at what age should young birds be taken from the parents. Is it possible to determine the sex of young birds at one month old.

Answer—The age that a nest of young birds can be taken away from the parents will all depend upon how the young birds have been fed from the first day onward. The young birds from a hen which is what might be termed an indifferent feeder will be far slower in getting around and making a showing of doing for themselves. A strong healthy nest of birds should commence to stand in the nest at 15 or 16 days old. They will leave the nest in the daytime at 18 or 19 days, and leave the nest entirely at 20 to 21 days. When this takes place the nest should be removed from the cage. After the young birds are five days older, they should be able to pick food themselves, and at this time it will be safe to place them on the reverse side of the partition in the breeding cage, or in the nursery cage. The hen can then be mated again, and while busy in the building of the nest for the second round, the hen will still find time to give any of the backward birds an occasional feed. Often the male bird will assist in this work. When it is found that all of the young can feed themselves without help from either parent, they can be safely removed to the flight cage.

It is possible to determine the sex of the young birds at one month old, but it takes considerable experience to do so. Even with the most expert Fanciers occasional mistakes will be made, but not more than one in every ten or more birds. The principal points of difference between the males and females are briefly as follows: The males are uually slightly larger than the hens. The color is richer, especially round the head and throat. The head is slightly larger in the male. The eye is larger and bolder in the male than the female. The call of the male is louder and with a more musical note than the female. These points coupled with frequent handling of the birds will bring to any fancier the ability to quickly determine the sex of each young bird, when they can later be placed in the aviaries according to the sex. Young Rollers will make quite a showing towards singing at from five to seven or eight weeks old, but this test should not be depended upon, only in conjunction with the other points as mentioned. Young hens will often be mistaken for singers if the song itself is the only guide to be used.

ASTHMA AND DIARRHOEA

Question—Asks for treatment and cure for Asthma and Lime Diarrhoea.

Answer—Asthma is caused by a neglected cold. Keeping the cage in a drafty position, or hanging in a room where the air is not pure, such as a kitchen in which gas is used for cooking or heating. Before a cure can be secured, it is necessary to remove the cause. For the present, keep the bird in a warm room, and where a free circulation of air is possible. Give each day a small cube of stale white bread steeped in warm milk, and add a sprinkle of Maw Seed. Have the following mixture made up. One ounce each of Glycerine, Ipecacuanha Wine and Oxymeal of Squills. Mix well together and give a half teaspoonful of the mixture to each two tablespoonsful of drinking water for three days together, then every other day until an improvement is noted. Keep the bird free from draughts. Do not give a bath until cold has gone, and cover the cage at night.

Lime Diarrhoea is caused by unsuitable or stale food—Musty or infested seed. First give the bird an aperient to remove any irritating matter from the intestinal tract. Two drops of salad oil direct into the beak, or ten drops of syrup of buckthorn in each tablespoonful of water. All water used should be first boiled. The next day remove all seed from the cage. Discontinue feeding egg-food. Fruit, or green food of any kind. The first day give a small piece of well toasted stale bread ground up coarse, and dust this over with as much "Carbonate of Bismuth" as will cover a ten cent piece. Mix well. Second day give a small cube of stale white bread, which has been steeped in warm milk. Pour off surplus milk, and mix in as much "Powdered Arrowroot" as will cover a dime. Alternate from day to day for eight days. If the excreta is then normal, you can give a little Canary Seed. Later a little Rape can be given. Each week give teaspoonful of Lime Water in the drinker for one day, mixed with other water to fill the drinker. Do not give the bath often until the bird is quite well again. Half a teaspoonful of Best Maw Seed (Poppy) can be given occasionally during the treatment.

VENT SWOLLEN BLISTERS

Question—Question concerns a bird with swelling at the vent and later small yellow spots developing around the same.

Answer—The cause of the trouble was undoubtedly an abscess, and owing to the same not breaking other points of infection have been brought about. I think the bird could have been saved if taken in time. These painful swellings are not very common among small birds. The treatment was to have bathed the parts with warm water until the abscess came to a head, when it should have been opened

with a sharp sterilized needle, and the pus removed. After bathing again the swelling should be painted with diluted solution of iodine, and the painting repeated after two or three days. Always take the precaution of isolating new birds until you are sure that they are in perfect health.

PICKING BAND

Question—Question concerning a bird always picking at the closed ring on the leg.

Answer—You have got nothing to worry about, for the picking of the ring is nothing more than a sign of breeding condition. At this time of the year it is quite a common thing for birds to not only pick at the ring, but to place food between the ring and the leg, just as they would do if feeding young. You will find that as soon as the bird in question is mated, it will stop playing with the ring. In any event the bird will not hurt itself you can be sure of that. I take it of course that the ring is quite loose, and that the leg is not sore or swollen, for you would have mentioned that point in your letter. Possibly you are feeding the bird too well, and if kept in a warm room, that would account for the forward condition. If you are not going to mate the bird for some time, you could reduce the condition by giving an aperient. A small crystal of sulphate of soda about the size of a large Hemp Seed placed in the drinker will answer the purpose. As much "Glauber Salts" as will cover a dime can be substituted. Give this every third day until the birds are paired up.

MITES
INDIGESTION

Question—Questions asked for best remedy to destroy Red-Mites. Cure for Indigestion.

Answer—To rid a cage of Red-Mites nothing you will ever find can beat a mixture of Coal Oil, Turpentine, Gasoline. Equal parts of each mixed together. Place in a bottle, and cut up a small block of Camphor. Put this into the bottle and shake well until the camphor is dissolved. Cork well and use as required. With a small brush paint all joints and seams of the cage, and allow to stand for one hour. Then wash off with hot water and dry. There will be no mites left I can assure you. For the bird a good handwash is the best and most effective remedy. You can add two tablespoonfuls of "Quassia Bark" solution to the bath, and this will help considerably.

The symptoms of Indigestion can be noted by birds picking over their food, husking their seed, but rejecting both husk and kernel, sleeping quite a little during the day time, and losing flesh and condition. Put the bird onto bread and milk, and every other day for one week give 4 drops of liquid paraffine mixed in the same. This is an invaluable cure for this trouble. Give an aperient of 6 drops of "Syrup of Rhubarb" added to each ounce of drinking water. Give this for three consecutive days then stop for a week and repeat again. Feed a little seed as soon as an improvement is noted, and watch the seed supply to see if the bird is using and not just husking the seed. Follow up the treatment with a tonic of equal parts of Tincture of Gentian, Tincture of Calumba and Aromatic Sulphuric Acid. Add four drops to the ordinary cage drinker of water and give every second day for ten days.

STERILITY

Question—Asks reason and treatment for a male bird which although mated to several hens has failed to fertilize any of the eggs laid.

Answer—I have gone carefully through the details given in your letter and am forced to the conclusion that the male bird in question is one which you would be well advised to leave out of your breeding stock. The age of the bird (three years) should not be the cause of infertile eggs, for many cases are on record proving that a male can be used up to seven, eight and nine years. The way that you feed your birds, while quite varied is still a good and suitable diet, and should keep even backward birds in breeding condition. In your breeding operations you have proven the fault of the male in the fact that you have raised nests from the hens when they have been mated to other singers. From the remarks made in your letter, I take it that your personal obesrvations during the mating period, leave no doubt in your mind other than the fault lies with the male bird. If the male is in tight feather and full song at the time of pairing with the hen, then there is nothing more that you can do to remedy the situation. It is just a case of sterility, and this can be brought about by the male coming from closely related parents, or the bird possessing a constitutional or physical defect. My advice would be to dispose of the bird as a singer, and to a purchaser whom you know does not require the bird for breeding.

WHEEZES

Question—Asks for cause and treatment for a bird which wheezes so that he can be heard across a room.

Answer—The trouble with this bird is Asthma, no doubt brought about from a neglected cold, or the keeping of the bird in an unsuitable room, or the cage in a poor location in the same. As to whether a complete cure can be affected will depend upon how long the bird has been in its present condition. A severe cold can be checked and cured if taken in hand as soon as noticed, but if neglected until the bird shows symptoms of difficulty in breathing, then such cases will require considerable time and treatment to effect a complete cure. First of all make quite sure that the position of the cage is one which will not permit of the bird being in a draught. Hanging the cage close to an open window, is just about the most unsuitable position that could be selected. Keeping the bird in a room with a varying temperature, or in which gas is used for lighting or cooking purposes will soon result in trouble. Give the bird a large roomy cage, and place it where it can get plenty of light, but at the same time be free from a draught. A free circulation of fresh air is essential, but the cage should be so placed that it will not be in the direct line by which the fresh air will enter the room. Discontinue

all patent foods. Let the seed diet be only the best grades of Canary and Rape mixed in equal proportions. Give a half teaspoonful of egg-food twice each week, and on alternate days give a small cube of stale white bread, steeped in warm milk, and to which has been added just a sprinkle of white sugar. If the bird is thin, and in a run down condition, place three drops of Cod Liver Oil on the bread and milk, mixing in the oil so that the bird will get the benefit of the same. Have the following mixture made up at the drug store. Equal parts of Glycerine, Oxymel of Squills, Ipecacuanha Wine and Chlorodyne. When these are mixed together, then add eight grains of Iodine of Potassium to the mixture. Shake the bottle each time upon using and put 15 drops of the mixture into the drinking water every other day for two weeks. Then discontinue for a week, and resume the next week. Follow this course until a cure has been effected.

PICKS CLAWS

Question—Asks for reason and cure for a singer which continuously picks at his claws.

Answer—Seeing that there is no swelling or soreness, the cause of the continuous picking is nothing more nor less than an idiosyncrasy or habit developed by the bird, and the only thing that you can do, would be to try to divert the attention of the bird along another line. During the period of conditioning, and just prior to the breeding stock being paired up, it is a very common thing to find the male birds picking at the ring and claws in the way that you have mentioned. I have seen males at this place placing food in between the claws and between the ring and the leg, just as they would do if feeding a nest of young birds. Just as soon as the pairs are mated the practice will stop from that time. You can be quite sure that no matter how much the bird picks at his claws, he will not hurt himself or cause any soreness as a result of the picking. Try fastening to the side of the cage a small piece of thin hemp rope which has been tested out at the end. Also keep a good sized piece of Cuttlefish bone between the wires of the cage, so that the bird can pick at it at any time. Bathe the feet of the bird in a strong solution of Quassia Bark, which will in no way harm the bird, but being exceedingly bitter will have a tendency to stop the practice of picking as you have mentioned. You could also try placing another bird in the same cage as the singer for a time, and at the end of which you will most likely find that the picking has been stopped.

HOW MANY NESTS
25 BIRDS 1 TRIO

Question—Asks three questions. (1) How many years can you successfully mate a healthy male bird, and how many nests during the year. (2) Is twenty-four healthy young birds from two hens and one male a good average for one season. (3) I have raised a young bird from six days old by handfeeding. Is that unusual?

Answer—The number of years that a male bird will successfully breed will be governed to a great extent by the constitutional fitness of the bird, and the way that it has been managed during the period of its development and until it reaches the age of maturity. Then again the methods used in the breeding have a bearing upon the matter. I have known cases where one male bird has fertilized all eggs laid by five hens by the aviary breeding system. This of course would not be possible when following the system known as cage breeding. In the first season I would not advise you to mate a young male to more than three hens. In my own rooms two hens only are allowed each male. You will find that when a singer is not overworked in the first season, and if the bird is strong and healthy, he will successfully breed up to six years, and in many cases longer. The management, diet and the stamina of the bird will determine the exact time.

(2) Twenty four young birds from two hens is decidedly excellent results. Not many Fanciers who are keeping a number of pairs can show such results. If all pairs mated were to produce 12 young birds each season, then there would undoubtedly soon be a large surplus of birds upon the market. A fair average is six young birds for each hen mated. Eight young per pair would be very good but twelve young birds or in other words three nests of four young birds each from each hen I consider to be extremely good, and far better than is produced in the average stud.

(3) To hand raise a young bird from six days old is by no means unusual. There are unfortunately too many Fanciers who are willing to assume the work that rightly belongs to the hen. At such an age it is almost impossible for a person to even imitate the food that under other circumstances would be given to the young birds by the hen herself. The food when eaten by the hen passes to the crop, and while there is ground up and pre-digested before fed to the young birds. At such an age the young birds are not able to assimilate the necessary nutriment from food given in any other way, and for that reason I never advise hand-feeding. Occasionally a hen will go back to nest before she has completed raising her previous nest of young birds to the stage where they can take care of themselves. At such a time hand-feeding will often help to prevent a loss, but with young birds at say six days, should the hen show signs of neglecting her brood, then I think that better results can be obtained by changing the diet of the hen, so that she will improve in the work of feeding more to the youngsters. To undertake to hand-feed a nest of young birds from six days old, is to say the least a very tiresome process. Of course the principal object is to raise the young birds, and anything that the Fancier does to make this possible is quite permissible but as I have stated I do not recommend the practice.

BREEDERS MOULTING

Question—Asks (1) Please advise the best way to take care of parent birds during the moulting season. (2) What brand of mixed seed do you recommend.

Answer—The correct management of your breeding stock during the present moulting season, will have quite a bearing upon the results that you will get from the birds when mated up in the spring. It can be safely said that many of the poor results often complained of, can be traced to wrong or careless management during this important time. Immediately after a busy breeding season, all stock birds will be in a sense run down, and it is necessary to improve this condition before moulting actually begins.

The first important consideration is exercise. If space will permit, you should provide an aviary for the males and another for the hens. The larger the better. If you have not an aviary available, then the use of a spare room will answer the purpose well. The birds should not be crowded but given plenty of room to fly and exercise. A little egg-food per bird should be given at least once each week, and two days later a liberal supply of bread and milk can be given. The seed diet should be best grade Canary and Roller Rape mixed in equal parts. Plenty of clean dry grit. Keep a large piece of Cuttlefish Bone constantly before the birds. A bath given early in the morning and on fine days is a good conditioner. In mature stock the first feathers to moult are the primary feathers in the wings and tail, and as soon as these are found you will know the moult has started. A good quick moult is necessary, and when a bird does not moult quickly, it is an indication that the bird in question is not in the best of condition, and therefore not able to cast the old feathers, and at the same time supply the nourishment necessary to promote the growth of the new ones. If the front of the aviary is kept partly shaded most of the day, it will help greatly in promoting the growth of the new feathers. Once each week place a cupful of best Flax Seed in a pitcher. Pour boiling water over the seed and allow it to stand overnight. Then fill the drinkers with the liquid. This will cool the blood, clean the system of the bird and bring a sheen and gloss to the new feathers. Flax Seed is a most useful and valuable seed especially during moulting time. (2) I do not recommend the purchase of mixed seed, but rather advise each Fancier to purchase the best quality in each variety, from your dealer, and then mix them in the proportions to produce the best results. It will be found in the average package of ready mixed seed, that there are a number of seeds such as Red and White Millet, and in a proportion that results in considerable waste. Each seed has a different chemical analysis, so it is important to obtain a well balanced mixture. The following will be found to give satisfactory results as a conditioner. One part by measure of Hemp, Flax, Inga, White Italian Millet, Red Indian Millet, Hulled Oats. Add half of one part of the following: Best Blue Dutch Maw Seed, Gold-of-Pleasure and Sesame Seed. Mix well together each time used, so that the small seed such as Maw (Poppy) will be well distributed throughout the bulk. Feed a teaspoonful per bird twice each week, then reduce to once each week as the moult is finishing. Six drops of Tincture of Iron added to the small wire cage drinker, will help as a tonic.

PARRAKEETS, CANARY FLIGHT CAGE CINNAMONS

Question—Asks eight questions as follows: (1) Can parrakeets be bred in captivity. (2) If so what kind can the best results be obtained from. (3) What is the method of breeding. (4) Please give any information you can about parrakeets and their care. (5) What is the smallest sized flight cage for Canaries that can be used for good results. (6) What breed are the most cinnamon colored birds found in. (7) Are they found in all breeds. (8) In judging cinnamons how should the coloring and marking if any be for the highest scores.

Answer—Parrakeets can be bred in captivity and with good success, see article on another page in this book. The determining factors being the variety fancied, and the methods used in their care and general management. There are of course a very large number of varieties in the parrakeet family, and about the most popular is the bird known as the "Budgerigar" or as called by many the "Love-Bird." In appearance they resemble a miniature parrot. They can be found in Solid Green, Yellow and Yellow-Blue color. The body being a little larger than a big Norwich bird, with long tail feathers which are about equal in length to the body. While it is possible to breed these birds in large cages, the best results will be obtained in a fairly large aviary. They are first mated in cages, and when kept in pairs in cages for some time they are then liberated into the aviary.

These birds differ from Canaries in the fact that in the aviary each pair will remain together for the entire season's work, and in breeding are not polygamous as in the case of the canary. (4) Answered in question 3. (5) If you will refer to other parts of this book you will find suggestions, a three compartment breeding cage, which by withdrawing the sliding partitions can quickly be turned into good flight cages. These are the type of flight cages I would advise you to make. A flight cage is nothing more nor less than a large well made box, without a lid or cover. The box is turned upon its side, and wire fronts fitted into the front. Without partitions this type of cage can only be used for one purpose, namely to hold a number of birds during the moulting time. With little additional trouble or expense this cage can be made to serve a double purpose, for by fitting in the sliding partitions it can be used as a triple or four compartment breeding cage. To give good results a flight cage should not be less than five feet long, for a cage of this size will afford the birds plenty of room for exercising the wings, and that is really the purpose that such a cage is made for. (6) Cinnamon color is found in all breeds of canaries, and has been brought to a high state of perfection in the breeds which are shown as type birds. The reason of course being that in all of the larger shows special classes are provided for Cinnamons, thus giving the necessary encouragement to certain Fanciers to breed to the Cinnamon standard. The breeds in which Cinnamon blood predominate are the Yorkshire, Norwich and the Border Fancy and in the order named. (7) Answered in question 6. (8) In the judging of Cinnamons the first and chief consideration is the purity, depth and tone of the cinnamon col-

orings. These should be clear, bright, and quite free from any green tinge, or smutty or smoky lines, and this color should run as level as possible over the entire body of the bird. Black stripes on the back, or light tinges under the throat or the underparts of the bird all detract from its merit as a true Cinnamon. The judging standard is as follows: Color, 35 points, Feather, 15, Good Wing carriage and compactness of tail feathers 10, Shape and Type 20, Size 10, Health and Cleanliness 10. Total 100 points.

GREEN FOOD

Question—Asks, please tell me what is Watercress, Chickweed and Dandelion. Where do they grow, and how am I to know them.

Answer—I can understand this question being asked in regard to Watercress, but I thought that everybody would know the two last named plants. Dandelion can be found in every field and pasture. It is one of the first plants to show up in the early Spring. The bright yellow flower is similar to a small marigold bloom. After the full bloom of the flower and the plant goes to seed, the flowering head turns to a round fluffy ball and consisting of a large number of very fine stems. At the end of each will be found a seed, and when the head breaks up these seeds are carried for a considerable distance in the wind, and thus the seeds are sown to produce other plants. One single bloom only is attached to each flower stem. Dandelion is credited with exceptional medical properties. The Italians gather the leaves of the plant early in the Spring and use them in just the same way as we would use lettuce leaves in a salad. Tincture of Dandelion is used extensively in medical prescriptions. The seed of the plant is sold at $1.00 per pound. Any fancier can secure a good supply of the seed by gathering a large number of the flowering heads when they are seeding. Place these in a linen sack and hang up the sack for a week so that the heads will dry and the seeds fall off. To remove the seed from the heads, beat the sack with a rod, and then sift the seed. You will find this seed invaluable as a Spring conditioner or as a "Pick-me-up" or a bird in a run down condition.

Chickweed is another very common plant. It causes considerable work for the "Gardener" for it seems to thrive best in beds that are cultivated. The leaves are small and oval, branching off in pairs from the main stem. When the buds appear they form at the end of a stem just the same as the leaves. The buds are about the size of a small Hemp Seed. The flower is exceedingly small and white in color. It is made up of eight little petals. The birds are exceptionally fond of this plant, and as the leaves and stem are tender they are much more suited to the feeding of very young stock. Watercress is cultivated extensively in England and used as a salad. The same are a dark brown color and round. This plant grows in still streams but close to the bank, so that the roots are always under water. It has a peppery flavor. In using Watercress one should be careful that the supply has come from a clean location and has not been grown in stagnant or polluted water.

Your best plan is to have a fancier in your city identify these plants for you.

TWISTED BEAK

Question—Asks what should be done for a young bird which has a bill twisted to one side. Could this have been caused by eating too much Hemp Seed.

Answer—Nothing in the way of treatment will be of any avail. While it is always best to crack Hemp Seed before feeding to young birds, still I feel sure that this has nothing to do with the case. It is one of those physical deformities which will show up from time to time. The mandible of a young bird is quite tender and flexible, but when they arrive at the age at which they can husk seed, then the mandible is hard and set just like bone. You should make quite sure of the breeding of the pair from which you have produced the bird. If all other youngsters from them are up to standard, you have no need to worry on this score, but if any other young birds show a physical weakness it would indicate a relationship that is too close in the mated pair. In that case I would rearrange matters mating the male to another hen, and the hen or mother of the bird in question to a male bird not related to herself.

HARTZ AND ROLLER DIFFERENCE

Question—What is the difference between a Roller and a Hartz Mountain Canary as far as type is concerned. How did the difference originate?

Answer—The trade term "Hartz Mountain" means nothing in reality. It was first used to designate a certain location from which large numbers of birds were yearly exported. Many of these birds and the progeny (from year to year) from them are being bred upon this Continent, so they have lost their identity as far as original location is concerned. The name Hartz Mountain is now given to birds which have a song that could not be correctly called roller song. As far as type is concerned there is practically no difference between the birds known as "Hartz Mountain Canaries" and the birds that we know to be Rollers. In color many of the former are clear yellow and buffs or lightly variegated birds. In the best strains of Rollers the predominating color is green.

NAKED BABY

Question—Asks what can be done for a young bird which is ready to leave the nest, but which has no signs of fluff or feathers on its back or breast. The head, wings and tail feathers are all right. This bird is the only one in the nest.

Answer—I am afraid that you have not yet learned just how quickly a hen can strip a young bird of feathers once they commence to do so. This is more likely to take place when only one bird is in the nest, but often a hen will strip a nest of four or five young birds in a few hours. When young birds reach the age of 15 or 18 days, the hen will often be noticed picking at them as though to urge them to leave the nest. At this time she will be coming into breeding condition and her interest is centered more in laying the second or third round of eggs. I am sure that before you read this reply you will have taken the young birds from the breeding cage, and you will find that the missing feathers will quickly be replaced.

COLORS DESCRIBED

Question—Asks, will you please give an explanation of how the different colors in our birds should be described. What is the difference between a variegated and a mottled bird. Is the latter term a correct one to use?

Answer—The question of color is a very minor detail in regard to Rollers. A correct description should be given upon the registration papers, but that is the only place that the same would be required. In showing birds in all of the different breeds (except Rollers) the birds are not entered with any idea of competition as regards song. It is simply a question of picking the best bird in type, color, size and condition of the particular breed that it represents. This being the case the birds are entered in classes designated by colors. They are named as follows:

(1) Clear yellow or clear buff, meaning a bird either yellow or buff totally and not showing one feather of any other color.

(2) Self green or cinnamon, meaning a bird which is either solid green or solid cinnamon in color and without a single feather of any other color.

(3) Foul green or cinnamon, meaning a bird with a ground color of green or cinnamon, but which is broken or "Fouled" by two or three feathers of any other color, usually yellow or buff.

(4) Heavily variegated, meaning a bird with a ground color of yellow or buff, but which is not represented by more than 50% of the feathers, or in other words a bird heavily variegated with another color than the ground color.

(5) Medium variegated, meaning a bird either yellow or buff and variegated with green feathers to an equal proportion.

(6) Lightly variegated, meaning a bird of a fixed ground color, but which is lightly variegated with feathers of another color.

(7) Ticked, meaning a bird with 95% of the feathers of one color, and which is only broken by a small patch of feathers of any other color. A tick should not be larger than a ten cent piece, and the position of the same upon the body of the bird has no bearing as regards classes.

There are still three classes which are provided for birds which are evenly marked. They are known as two point, four point and six pointed birds. A two pointed bird will have two circles of green, one around each eye, or green feathers on both sides, or green feathers at each side of the tail. A four pointed bird will beat a two pointed bird, and a six pointed bird will beat a four pointed bird, condition and type being equal.

The word "Mottled" is quite wrongly used in describing the color of a bird. For a bird to be mottled the ground color would have to be broken by innumerable little dots of VARIOUS COLORS and I have yet to see the first bird marked in that way. The word is used to imply a bird which is variegated, but the correct definition should be (yellow, heavily green variegated) or (Yellow, lightly green variegated) yellow meaning the ground color, and heavily, medium or lightly showing the amount of the green variegation.

CONTINUOUS MOULTING

Question—Asks for reason and cure for a hen, which moulted ten months ago, and continues to cast feathers.

Answer—You will find that the trouble arises from one of the following reasons, and you can determine which of the three reasons is responsible by your own personal observations: FIRST—Keeping the bird in a room that is not suitable. Possibly a kitchen in which the temperature fluctuates and where gas fumes prevail. Keeping the cage close to a window, and thus allowing the bird to get into draughts and contract a cold. SECOND—Moulting will result from the cage containing Red Mites, or the bird being infested with Grey Lice. THIRD—The possibility of the bird in question coming from a closely related pair, and thus being a weak specimen, the bird has not been able or had the strength to come back into condition after the moult at the proper time. If you find that reason No. 1 is the cause of the trouble, then before you can expect a cure, you must remove the cause. Keep the bird in a position quite free from draughts of fluctuating temperatures, but one in which a free circulation of fresh air is possible.

No. 2. If Red Mites are the cause, then you can free the bird of them by repeatedly changing it from one cage to another, doing so always in the morning. Each time that the change is made, be sure to give the used cage a thorough cleaning, using the solution mentioned previously, and then washing the cage with boiling water. Place one large tablespoonful of Quassia Bark solution into the bath each time that it is given. The bird should be fed well in order to increase flesh, and to regain condition.

No. 3. If you find that the trouble is from inherited weakness then there is not much that can be done. I would give the bird plenty of room for exercising. Feed on a good liberal diet, and try to get the bird into the best possible condition before the fall, when under ordinary circumstances the bird should moult again. If that period is not safely passed, then it is not likely that the bird will be of much use to you as a breeder. It is hardly necessary for me to say that you should not consider mating such a bird, while in its present condition.

LAYS ALTERNATELY—WON'T SET

Question—Asks for reason that a hen will skip days in laying, and will not attempt to sit after all eggs have been laid.

Answer—From what you have told me in your letter, I do not think that there is anything seriously wrong with this hen. The fact that days are passed in between the laying of the eggs, and that the bird carries her feathers loosely while laying, are indications of poor breeding condition. It is not likely that should you have fertile eggs from this bird, that she would incubate them, or successfully raise her young.

If the bird is of special value, then I would place her into a large flight for at least two weeks. Feed on a good stimulating diet, and see if the exercise and care will not bring about some improvement in condition. If this should not be the case, then I would not attempt to mate the bird again this year, but rather take good care of the bird, in an attempt to make up for the loss in the future breeding seasons.

AGE BIRDS MOULT

Question—Asks for the reason that a number of birds have lost feathers from around the beak, eyes, and on the back of the head, and to give her into a cure for the same. No. 2—State the age at which young birds should commence moulting.

Answer—The fact that you are experiencing this year a recurrence of the same trouble, would indicate that the cause of the loss of feathers is really a skin infection, and which is being transmitted from one bird to another, principally through birds being transferred to cages in which one or more of the infected birds have been kept. This fact is proven by the details of treatment which you have given in your letter. The use of the Sulphur and Chlorate of Potash would, under ordinary circumstances, have effected a cure for you. It will be a rather difficult matter for you to effect a cure at the present, for it would mean considerable interference with the bird while in the breeding cages, and also the giving of medicine, which would also incline to spoil the results of your work at this time. The cause is known as "Fungoid Skin" which forms from the growth of a fungus, and which produces a scurvy encrustation on the surface of the skin, and loss of plumage on the parts affected. The principal point of infection, or I would say the transmission of the infection, will be found upon the wire fronts of the breeding cages. You will notice how often a bird will rub the beak and head feathers against the wire front. When cleaning your cages, you should go over all wires carefully with a cloth moistened with a strong disinfectant, and which will go a long way to prevent any further spread of the trouble. You should get the young birds away from the parent stock, the cages which have been used by birds so affected. Just as soon as the breeding operations are over, then I would treat every bird affected as follows: Obtain a small box of sulphus ointment, and mix into the same 25 drops of feather tonic. Take the bird to be treated in your hand, and with the tip of the finger, lightly smear a little of the ointment all over the top of the head, being careful to keep it away from the eyes of the bird. Allow three days to pass and repeat the process, and after three treatments in this way, all germ life in the growth mentioned should be destroyed. In the fall the birds will moult as nature intended, when of course they will get back their full growth of feathers. You can then by careful management prevent a recurrence of the trouble. It is likely that the trouble might have been brought into your bird room, by a bird newly purchased, and which has come from a stud infected with the trouble.

No. 2—You have nothing to worry about in connection with the young birds. The moulting that is taking place at the present time, is quite as it should be. Young birds from the first nests will moult when two months old. The moult at this time is only partial, and it is referred to as the "Baby Moult." All secondary feathers are moulted, but the primary feathers (Large feathers in the wings and tail) are not moulted until the season to follow. A young bird in its first season is therefore called an UNFLIGHTED bird, and when this bird has passed through the second moult (at which time all feathers, both primary and secondary are moulted) the bird is then referred to as a FLIGHTED bird, and which means that the bird in question has passed through its second moult, and the large feathers in the wings or FLIGHTS have been moulted.

RAISED MOSTLY FEMALES

Question—Asks for the reason that out of nineteen young birds, only six males are found.

Answer—The answer to this question will most likely be found in the possibility of losses in the early part of the breeding season. In practice you will find that with few exceptions, the first nest of the season will be found to produce more males than females. The second nest is usually equal in the percentage of males and females, while in the last nest the tendency is more towards females than males. When the work of the season is considered, the percentage is usually very close to 50 per cent of each sex. Any variation from this will always be found to be a higher percentage of male birds.

There is no doubt that the physical condition of the stock has a bearing upon the matter, and it is a common belief amongst a large number of Fanciers, that to pair an adult male in first class condition, to a young hen, will produce a preponderance of males in the young bred from them, while the mating of an adult hen, to a young male will produce the reverse results. When breeding stock along pedigreed lines, it is not always convenient to have one side of the stock mature, or birds over one year old. Pairs are usually selected from results obtained in the previous season. However I do think that it is a wise plan to have males selected from the first nest, in order that they will be well developed and in good physical condition at the time of breeding.

YOUNG DYING

Question—Asks for cause and treatment of an infection, which is resulting in the loss of all young birds, and also a number of the breeding pairs.

Answer—From the details given in your letter, there is no doubt in my mind, that the number of imported birds you recently purchased are in the main responsible for all of your trouble. The symptoms mentioned point directly to "Septic Fever" and if this is the cause, then I am sorry to have to say, that your prospects for this season do not look at all good. The first thing to do is to put into effect the strictest kind of isolation for all birds affected. You must arrange to divide your stock birds in-

to at least three classes, and get as much space between each class as is possible. Breeding operations should be stopped, for it will only magnify the trouble by continuing further. I would fit up a room temporarily for class No. 1. Take a number of your best cages. Give them a complete and thorough disinfecting and cleaning, and when dry, place them in the room. On the bottom of the cages, scatter some coarse sawdust, and first of all dampen this with a diluted solution of "Coro-Noleum" or carbolic. Place into these cages all of the birds which to you seem to be in perfect health and condition. Class No. 2, which should be kept in another room, and quite separate from the first, will consist of birds that do not seem to be in good tight feather and condition. Class No. 3 will consist of birds which are now affected with the trouble. With those that are very sick, and if you have not the room to completely segregate them from other stock, it would be better to follow this course with a few birds, rather than to have the trouble go through your entire stock. All cages should be kept perfectly clean, and the trays should be changed daily. The excreta from infected birds only serving to spread the infection. Use the moistened sawdust on the bottom of all cages. Keep the rooms a little on the warm side, but do not prevent a free circulation of fresh air all the time. Add 25 drops of milk of magnesia to each drinker, and use only water which has been boiled and allowed to get cold. Increase the amount of Canary Seed in the staple seed mixture. Discontinue feeding green-food of any kind. Give each day a small cube of stale white bread (per bird) and first of all steep the bread in a dish of warm milk, to which has been added a little sugar. If the birds are losing flesh, then add three drops of Cod Liver Oil Emulsion to the bread, and mix in well so that the birds will get the benefit of the oil.

LAYING OFF AND ON

Question—Asks for treatment for a hen not laying regularly, and which is affected with Lime Diarrhoea.

Answer—With a bird in the condition you have described, it is not at all likely that you will get good breeding results. I would place the hen into a large flight cage or aviary, and treat as follows:

First give an aperient to remove the cause of the diarrhoea. This can be two drops of salad oil, given directly into the beak with a medicine dropper. Ten drops of syrup of buckthorn added to the water in the drinker will give the same results. All water used during the treatment should first be boiled, and allowed to stand until cold. Discontinue feeding Egg-food, Green-food. Fruit and all extras, and for the present do not give the usual seed supply. The first day give a small piece of well toasted white bread. Grind this up coarsely and dust over it as much "Carbonate of Bismuth" as will cover a ten cent piece. The second day give a small cube of stale white bread, which has been steeped in warm milk, pour off the surplus milk, and mix with the bread as much powdered Arrowroot as will cover a dime. Alternate with this food for six days, when you will find that the cause of the trouble will be entirely removed. You can then get the bird back to the normal diet. Stale or musty seed is one of the principal sources of this trouble, so you should examine the seed supply, and make sure that it is sound and fresh. When the hen is over the trouble, and shows signs of breeding condition, you should mate the bird.

GOOD MOTHER STOP FEEDING

Question—Asks for reason that a hen will not feed her second nest of young birds.

Answer—Your letter does not contain sufficient detail to enable me to give you a really helpful answer to your question. You have not stated if this hen raised her first nest, nor have you told me just how you are keeping and feeding the birds. I would suggest that this particular bird is exceptionally nervous, and that you have the breeding cage in a room which does not permit of the privacy necessary for the bird to work as she should. If you have the cage in a living room, try moving the cage to a position where the birds will not be disturbed.

CHILLS

Question—Asks for cause of "Shaking Spells" resulting in the loss of several mature birds.

Answer—A serious chill accompanying the shaking spells as you describe is often the initial symptom of Acute Bronchitis or Pneumonia. This can be brought about by allowing a bird to bathe too freely, or late in the day. Also by removing the bird from its regular position, to take a bath in a room with a lower temperature than the one to which it is accustomed. This, I think, is possibly the cause of your trouble. The bath should only be given on fine days, and then early in the morning. If you experience the same trouble again, as soon as it is noticed, move the bird to a warmer position. A small teaspoonful of good whiskey in the ordinary drinker will give immediate relief. A good mixture for the same trouble can be made up from the following: Oxymel of Squills, Glycerine, Ipecacuanha Wine and Sweet Spirits of Nitre. Mix equal parts of these, and give five drops in each tablespoonful of water in the drinker. Add to the diet a small cube of bread and milk, and keeping the bird free from draughts will soon effect a cure.

ALL DIE

Question—Asks if I can account for 100 per cent mortality in young birds this season. Birds die from three days to three weeks old. They all have a peculiar crook in their necks after death. The bill being tightly closed, and the body appears to be much shrivelled up.

Answer—This trouble has been brought about by the nests being infested with Red Mites. It is possible that before you read this reply, the cause of the trouble will have become apparent to you. The nest should be watched carefully, for owing to the warmth created during the time of incubation, should any Red Mites be in the nest, the rate at which they will multiply is astounding. When a nest is badly infested, the young birds become a prey to the mites. Sleep is out of the question. The blood of the young birds is sapped, and instead of daily progress, they actually become smaller as time goes along. You will note that the skin under the lower half of the beak is tight, with the appearance of being drawn in cords. In clear birds the skin appears white instead of the healthy pink color under normal conditions. If you are using the box type of nest, then I would advise you to try the porcelain nest pan, which hangs on the back of the breeding cage. Put in a brown felt lining, and thickly coat this with mite powder and this will form the base for the nesting material used by the hen in forming the nest to her own liking. If you will take one of the breeding cages, use a solution of gasoline, coal oil and turpentine mixed in equal parts, and to which you will add a small block of camphor, go over all seams and crevices with this solution, applying the same with a small brush, you will see the cause of the trouble.

BABIES DIE WEEK OLD

Question—Asks for reason of a big number of losses in young birds all dying at one week old.

Answer—I am sorry that you have not given me the full details of how you are feeding the birds. To say that you feed hard boiled eggs, grit, crackers and bird seed does not give me much to work on. There is no question but one or more items in the diet are the cause of the trouble, and if you will send me full details I will try to help you further, I would in the meantime advise you to purchase the "Fresh Eggs" from another source, as there may be something in the feeding of the poultry from which the eggs are obtained which might be responsible for the losses. Discontinue the use of the crackers, and use "Home Made Bread Crumbs," and when mixing add a little sugar and a sprinkle of salt. If you are using any green food, make quite sure that it comes from a source that you know to be free from any infection or contamination. Examine the seed supply closely, and if you can find a trace of "Mice" having been in the seed, then reject the bulk that you are using, and purchase a supply that you know to be good and clean. I would further suggest that you read the reply given to questions elsewhere in this department, and put one or two pairs of your birds on the same diet. If you have better success it will at least prove that the feeding is the cause of the trouble.

BAD MOULT

Question—Asks for treatment for a male which moulted quickly, and has failed to come back into condition and song.

Answer—I have read your letter carefully, and it seems to me that your bird is slowly improving, and would have passed over the moult safely, if you had used a better system of feeding. I strongly advise you to discontinue the use of the food you mention, and try the following:

Place the bird into a box cage and in a position quite free from draughts or fluctuating temperatures. Feed as a staple, best Spanish canary seed and good Roller rape mixed in equal parts. Give three times each day a small cube of stale white bread, which has been steeped in hot milk, and to which a pinch of sugar has been added. Pour off the surplus milk, and add three drops of cod liver oil to the bread. Mix this in so that the bird will get full benefit from the food. On the days that the bread and milk is not given, you can substitute a half teaspoonful of egg food made fresh, or a little separate allowance of a first class condition seed mixture. Do not give the bath only once each week until a change is noticed. I am quite sure that with proper care, the bird will be back in condition and song in the near future. Add six drops of "Tincture of Iron" to the drinking water, and give this every other day for four doses, and after that once each week until the bird is well.

ST. ANDRESBURG ROLLERS

Question—Why is the St. Andresburg Roller never mentioned in the Encyclopedia? Is it not superior to any other bird? Just what is the Seifert Roller? Do you think the Water Organ is as good a trainer for young birds as a good Tutor should be?

Answer—(1) The name "St. Andresburg" does not signify the name of a breed or strain, but rather the location from which a certain class of birds have come, this being a district to which the hobby of raising canaries has long been associated. This name is applied principally to the store variety of roller, and for which no special claim of quality is made. (2) Rather than being superior, the birds known as St. Andresburg Rollers are considered to be very much inferior to our present day strains; no doubt in this fact, you will find the reason why the bird in question is not featured in the Encyclopedia. (3) The Seifert Roller is a distinct strain which was originated and brought to a state of perfection by the founder of the strain. Heinrich Seifert of Germany. Twenty years ago this strain was widely known and birds of the best quality in great demand. While the strain has always been admitted as limited in the range of rolls and tours delivered, still it was credited with rare purity in those rolls which today are considered as basic parts of the Roller song. The name Seifert Roller, I feel sure is now applied to many thousands

of birds which in reality do not possess any of the original blood of the strain, and for this reason the term "Seifert Roller" is only too often wrongly applied. (4) The water organ is not and never will be of the same value for tutoring young birds as a proficient Tutor himself. There are several types of water organs in use and some of far more value than others. The best types will be useful at a time when the Tutor has passed into a moult, but if the services of a really high class trainer can be used, then the final results will be much more satisfactory than any water organ that can be purchased.

MILK FOOD AND EGGS—TWO GREENS

Question—(1) I have bought two green birds as a pair for breeding, and have read that if I mate two green birds together, I will get "Grey Birds." Can I force the person who sold them to me to take one or both birds back on the grounds that the stock has been misrepresented. (2) Will you explain the tour Bell Glucke more fully? (3) Is it possible to mate half brother and sister together? (4) Minneapolis Fancier claims that males bred in the third nest of the season are always the best singers. Is this correct? (5) Another Fancier advises egg food but no bread and milk. Do you think that these two foods should be used together to obtain the best results?

Answer—(1) I am afraid that if I am going to answer your first question correctly I must say that your request would be unreasonable. If a Fancier has sold you two solid green birds, that have been produced from greens, and has told you that your pair will produce greens, then I believe you will find the statement to be correct. I have one line of breeding in my stud which for seven years has not produced one single marked or variegated bird; all have been solid green. Green is the original and foundation color of the Roller. I am therefore at a loss to know where the "Grey Birds" come from that you claim might result from mating two green birds together. I would advise you to pair the birds together and should you get any other color but greens or heavily variegated birds, then I would like to hear from you again.

(2). Bell Glucke is a tour which has been the cause of lots of "heart burnings" in the fancy at different times, because of the diversion of opinion as to its correct rendering. The real pronunciation when the tour is sung right has a ground tone U with an I accompanying, thus: Glui-Glui-Glui which gives it a double effect. The tour can be quickly distinguished from Double Glucke for in the latter there is no "I" as in Bell Glucke immediately after the deep glucke sound, one hears as it were a faint echo an octave higher, it should therefore be correctly explained as Glucke Bell for it rises or ricochets very rapidly from the Glucke to the Bell. The beak of the bird should be closed, but show a slight movement at each intonation of the bell.

Bell Glucke is the cheapest of the Glucke Tours and according to the standard, 3 points are awarded for correct rendering, and it is therefore NOT a tour which a Fancier should strive to cultivate. It is also possible with Bell Glucke for deterioration to take place on either the ground or the accompanying portion of the tour, which as a good deep portion of the tour, which as a good deep Glucke rising to a sharp bell, or worse still, a flat Glucke rising to sharp Bell. This tour in different strains varies widely from slow to fast, and no doubt this fact has been the reason for so many different opinions in regard to it.

(3) Half brother and sister can be mated together only under certain conditions. The Fancier considering the mating, must know for sure that there is no relationship between one parent and the other two birds. A male can be paired to two unrelated hens, and the progeny from each hen can be paired together. The different and unrelated males can be paired to one hen. One for the first nest, and the other male for the second nest. Young birds from the first and second nests can be paired together, only when you know for sure that while the two males are of the same strain, there does not exist any relationship between them.

(4) I do not believe the statement to be correct. Young males from the first nests at a given time, say the end of December, will be more mature and in better song than the males from the third nests. The breeding of course is the same, and as perfection of song can only be secured by good training (with the right breeding behind it) I fail to see how birds from the third nest can possibly be better than those from the first.

(5) I once heard a "Real Old-Time Fancier" say that Bread and Milk during the breeding season was worth $1.00 per ounce, and my experience has proven this to be the case. A little bread and milk given with egg-food will help to carry off any inclination to "Surfeit" from the use of egg-food only, on the part of the hen or the young birds. I have known many cases in which hens would show such a preference for this food, that well made egg-food would be refused if bread and milk was also given. Personally I prefer this food to green-food, and I consider it far safer to use. I do advise its use in conjunction with egg-food during the entire breeding season.

HOW OLD WHEN BEGIN TO SING

Question—How old should a canary bird be before it will commence to sing?

Answer—The time will be found to vary according to the breed. A well bred young Roller can be seen making a good start at six weeks old. Two or three weeks later this bird will pass into its first or baby moult, and usually while moulting does not show the same vigor, due of course to the effect of the moult. Birds of the other breeds will seldom be found to make any attempt to sing before passing through the moult. A young Roller hatched in April, May or early June, should be well developed in song by the last week of November, and be in full song by the third week of December.

CONDITION BREEDER

Question—How can a five year old male be brought into condition for breeding? First nest of eggs proved infertile.

Answer—Due to the age of the bird, special care will be necessary, but there is no reason why you should not be able to get fertile eggs from a bird of that age. Read the answer to question on "Bad Moult" and condition the bird in the same way. Separate the pair until you have the male in full song, and showing every sign of wishing to mate, as soon as his cage is placed in view of the hen.

MATING YELLOW BIRDS

Question—Give reason why two Yellow birds should not be mated together.

Answer—As the Roller is a breed which is bred for song, the question of color becomes a very minor consideration, for the birds are paired more with a view of first class song production, rather than type of color. The result of mating two Clear Yellow birds will be that the progeny from them will be reduced in size, and the feathers softened, which in turn will take away the tight and trim appearance which is so much desired. I take it that your object in wishing to pair two yellows together is to intensify the color. If this is the case, you can get just as good results by pairing a Yellow to a Buff-Green marked bird, and at the same time you will keep up the size and stamina of your stock.

YOUNG ALL DIE

Question—Asks for the reason of so many losses in young birds.

Answer—I do not think that there is anything in what you have said regarding a disease in birds so young. If this should be the case, it must certainly be transmitted to the young from the hen herself. I think that your trouble lies in your system of feeding. For the next hatch, discontinue the use of soaked rape, green food and apple. Give the hatching hen from the first to the fourth day, just a small half teaspoonful of fresh egg-food and at the same time give a small cube of stale white bread which has been steeped in sweetened hot milk. Allow to go cold before feeding, and put just a pinch of best blue Dutch maw seed at the side of the food in the egg drawer. At four days give half a teaspoonful of BEST QUALITY cracked hemp seed. The Hemp can be given in the morning feed, and in the afternoon give a few sprays of budding or flowering chick-weed.

Hand-feeding should not be attempted with birds so young. Its use will occasionally save a nest at from fourteen to twenty days old, and when the hen, due to breeding condition, is inclined to neglect her brood. Give your birds as much privacy as possible, and do not interfere with the hen and her young more than is absolutely necessary. By changing the food and following this rule, I think that you will get better results.

DIE EIGHT WEEKS OLD
WHEN TO PLACE MALE IN CAGE

Question—(1) Why do so many people lose their birds at from 7 to 8 weeks old? (2) How much should a baby bird eat at the time the hen stops feeding, and starts the second nest? (3) How can I tell when to place the male in the breeding cage for the second nest, so that all eggs will be fertile? (4) Would it be of any benefit to feed cod liver oil to young birds with a medicine dropper?

Answer—(1) If a Fancier loses young healthy birds at 7 or 8 weeks old, he has only himself to blame for the loss. The desire to get young birds off soft food and on to hard seed is the most common cause. Young birds at 7 or 8 weeks are just starting into the first moult, and that is the time when stimulating food is mostly required. They have not only to be able to keep themselves in good flesh, but also supply the nutriment necessary for the new growth of feathers. To withhold soft food from the young stock at this time will result in weakly stock later on.

(2) You should not attempt to regulate the amount of food that young birds will use at this time, so long as it is of the best quality and freshly made, you need not worry should they appear to use more than you think necessary. Give them all that they want, and keep this up until they are fully developed.

(3) You should figure upon getting the male bird back into the breeding cage as soon as the young birds have left the nest for two or three days. If you are using the double breeding cage, you can place them on the other side of the wired partition, and then place the male in the other half of the cage with the hen. If you are using single breeders, then

you should get the young birds into a "Nursery Cage" and get the pair mated again. Remember if a delay should take place, and the hens wish to nest, the eggs will be laid no matter whether the male is in the cage or not.

(4) To feed cod liver oil directly into the beak with a medicine dropper would not be a wise course to follow. The food would be too strong for the young birds to properly assimilate it. If the young birds have been well fed in the nest and are making good progress, then this food should not be required. You could use a little while the birds were in the aviary, but only by mixing it into the soft food.

If you think that your birds are backward and are not thriving as they should, then a few drops of the oil mixed into bread and milk will help to build them up.

BUILDS NEST—NO EGGS

Question—Asks for reason that a hen will build a good nest but does not lay.

Answer—The trouble will be either one of the following causes. The hen might be one hatched very late last year, and not mature enough to breed at this time. The second reason would be that the hen is "Sterile" and this condition can be brought about from inherited or physical weakness. If you are not able to determine these questions from what you know of the bird and the stock that it has come from, then I am afraid that there is little that you can do further, so long as you are sure that the bird is healthy and has been conditioned. I believe the best plan would be to place the hen into a flight cage, and try her again later in the season, and when you can see from her condition that there are indications that the bird wants to mate.

SIX HENS ONE MALE
FLIGHT CAGE TUTOR

Question—(1) Of six hens used, three have mated and laid their eggs, and the other three have not laid. Why should they not do the same as the other three? (2) Should young males and hens be kept together in the flight cages until training time? (3) Would it be possible to keep breeding stock, both male and female, in the same flight cages from September to January? (4) What is the size of the standard contest cage? (5) How many times each day should a tutor be allowed to sing and for what length periods? (6) Is it too much of a strain on a male bird to put him into the cages of four different hens each morning for ten minutes each? Is it a wise course to follow?

Answer—(1) It is more than likely that the three hens are later hatched than the others, and they will come into breeding condition at the proper time. No doubt before you read this answer, you will have noted an improvement and they will be nesting now. (2) Young males and females can be kept together as you have mentioned, but if you have the space convenient, it would be wiser to keep them separate. Never overcrowd the flights for it will result in feather plucking, and once this starts much damages will result. (3) Breeding stock can be wintered in the same flight, but I would figure on separating both sexes before January, especially if the birds are in heated rooms. (4) The size of the English Standard Contest Cage is as follows: Height, (outside measurements) 10 inches. Width (side to side) 11 inches. Depth (front to back) 5½ inches. Thickness of wood, one quarter inch. Turnrail, 1½ inches deep. Wire front, 9⅞ inches wide, 7¼ inches high. There are 19 wires in the front, each spaced one half inch apart. Note.—If you are thinking of getting some cages made, your best plan is to purchase a new standard cage, and use this for a sample. Contest cages must be identical in every detail, even to the color of the enamel, which is back on the outside and "Ultra Marine Blue" inside. (5) The tutor should be opened up at least three times each day. When not being used for training, the song should be restricted as much as possible. This can be done by giving a bath in the morning, and while doing so the bird could be run into a breeding or flight cage. Each period should not be less than one hour, but should the bird begin to sing too freely, then the doors of the shutter cage should be partly closed and the light subdued. When the bird is opened up for light and exercise, the giving of a little special food will have the tendency to keep the bird from singing. During training time, he can be allowed to sing freely during each lesson, and then kept quiet when the lessons are over. Care must be taken in the feeding of a Tutor while the breeding season is on, for too much stimulating food will result in louder tone, and possibly an inclination towards faulty singing. Never keep the tutor in a position where it will be possible for him to hear the song of males in the breeding room, or the call of any of the hens. (6) I would not advise you to follow the method you suggest in the mating of your male birds. If you are forced to use one male with four hens, I would mate two hens in the same cage, and with a nest in either end. When both hens have laid their eggs, one of the hens can be transferred into another cage, with the same nest and in the same position in the second cage. If you wish to have all four hens set at the same time, then place the male with the first two hens for the morning, and with the other two during the afternoon. To follow the plan you mention, I am sure would result in a number of eggs being infertile. To be successful with

the system you mention, each of the five birds would have to be in very forward condition, and even with such favorable conditions, it would be necessary for your personal observations to be used as a guide.

DIARRHOEA

Question—Asks for cause and treatment for a number of birds which seem quite well but are troubled with a form of Diarrhoea, which subsides and then comes back worse than before.

Answer—It is more likely that you are giving one item in the diet that is causing this trouble. It may be green food that is frosted. Stale musty seed, or some kind of special food that contains harmful ingredients. Seeing that all birds are affected, I am sure you will have little trouble in deciding which item is causing the trouble. First of all check over your seed supply. See that it is fresh, clean and sweet. Now for the present stop giving any kind of green food. Take a thick piece of white bread, and toast this until quite brown. When quite dry, crush the toast into crumbs about the size of Rape Seed. Add to the crumbs a third of the bulk of Best Hulled Oats, and to each teaspoonful mix in as much powdered Arrowroot as will cover a ten cent piece. Give this to the birds in an egg-drawer. For three days together add to each drinker as much "Powdered Chalk" as will cover a ten cent piece. You should shake the drinker as often as possible, for the chaff settles to the bottom. When you see an improvement, you can discontinue the chalk, and every second day add a small teaspoonful of lime water to the drinker. This you will find will quickly stop the trouble, and it remains with you to see that it does not commence again by using only fresh clean seed and food.

Do not think of mating your stock while in the present condition, for it would no doubt result in "Nesting Diarrhoea" with the hens, and no doubt mean some losses for you. Rather delay breeding operations until the birds are quite well.

DEFORMED FOOT

Question—Asks for treatment for a young bird with a deformed foot. The back claw growing up between two of the front claws making it necessary for the bird to stand upon the joint.

Answer—This is a very common trouble in young birds and is known as a slipped claw. It is the result of a crowded nest, and possibly from the hen sitting too close during the time when the birds were quite young. If taken in time the cure can be made quickly and it will remain permanent. Take a thin rubber band. Cut the same and starting in the center of the band, make a number of turns loosely around both the leg and the hind claw and at the same time pulling up the hind claw backwards until it almost touches the leg of the bird. Be sure not to bind the turns of the rubber too tightly, or else circulation will be stopped, and the result will be permanent injury to the bird. Another method is to take a thin strip of adhesive plaster. Cut this about one eighth of one inch wide, and three quarters of one inch long. Warm it so it will stick firmly. Hold the hind claw close to the leg, and make at least three complete turns loosely around both the leg and claw. You will find that with the hind claw held back in its proper position, the bird will commence to stand on the perch correctly. You can allow the rubber or plaster to remain upon the leg for at least six weeks, and upon its removal, the claw will remain in its proper position.

INFERTILE EGGS

Question—Asks for possible reason for every egg from six hens all proving infertile in the first mating of the season. Birds were apparently in good condition and the males in song when the birds were put into the breeding cages.

Answer—This is just another case of mating birds out of season. It does not follow that because the males are in steady song that they are in breeding condition. They should always be in song only when actually in the moult. The natural breeding season is the late Spring of the year. Take an object lesson from the birds outside, and you will not find any of them carrying nesting material, or going about in pairs, the same as you will see in a month or more from now. My advice to you would be to separate all pairs for a time. Read up the previous articles on conditioning for breeding. Feed the birds on a good stimulating diet. Examine the hens and see if the vent shows the signs as mentioned in the article. Give each bird just a little "Tid-bit" every day. Alternating with Dandelion (Root and a few leaves). A little strong egg-food. Bread and milk with a pinch of good Maw Seed added. Also a little supply per bird of a good condition mixture. You have not mentioned the temperature of the room that the birds are kept in. If this is 60 degrees or over, then you will be able to pair the birds again in the course of say two weeks. After you put the two birds in each cage, remain in the room for one hour or so, and allow your personal observations to guide

you as to whether they are improved in condition sufficiently to make sure that the next round of eggs will be fertile. A bad start sometimes means a good finish, so stay with the work. Better luck next time. I would advise that you discontinue using the patent food that you mention. The name is new to me, and without seeing a sample of the food I would not feel inclined to say anything about it.

PLUCKS HIS FEATHERS

Question—Asks for reason and cure for a singer that continually pulls out feathers on one side of its body, and eats the quills.

Answer—This is simply a habit and unfortunately one to which many birds are addicted. If you will examine the quill of a feather, and pull the same between your finger nails, you will find that a small amount of oil will leave the end of the quill. It is the common supposition that once a bird tastes this oil it will become a regular feather plucker. Some think that it is because the bird is not given a supply of animal fat. The only remedy lies in providing a counter attraction for the bird. You could try placing a small piece of fresh lamb suet between the wires of the cage. Sometimes a small piece of hemp cord, teased out at the end will take the attention of the bird away from plucking its own feathers. I would feel inclined to put the bird into a flight cage with two or three other birds, and in this way it will be kept busy avoiding quarrels with others in the same cage. I would not advise you to place anything on the feathers in an attempt to stop the practice. When this is done the cure sometimes proves worse than the disease, and a loss results. If the bird is young it is quite possible when it is placed in the flight after the breeding season, that the habit will be stopped. Make quite sure that the bird is not troubled with mites. If it plucks at the feathers at the butts of the wings and under the same, it is almost sure that red-mites are troubling the bird.

BALD—DID NOT MOULT

Question—Asks for treatment for a male bird eight years old which did not moult in the fall, and which has gone quite bald. Also treatment for a young male, a son of the old bird that is showing the same trouble.

Answer—From the details given in your letter, I do not think that the fact that the old bird did not moult in the right season, has anything to do with the loss of feathers on the head at this time. Quite often you will find cases in which birds that are getting old will miss a full moult at the proper time. This is termed "Stuck in the moult" and should such a bird be allowed to miss the moult entirely, it always follows that the bird will go out of condition in the spring of the year following. You can quite easily force a bird into moulting, by changing it from a warm room to a cold one, do this alternate days, and you will soon find that the bird will commence moulting in the natural way. Just as soon as the feathers are coming out regularly, then the change from one room to the other should be discontinued, and the bird kept in an even temperature, and fed well to aid it to cast the feathers quickly.

I am inclined to think in the case of your birds, that the head trouble comes from an infection, especially if you have been changing the two birds from one cage to another, so that they would one week occupy the cage that the other bird had the week before. Try the following treatment. Mix together equal parts of "Flowers of Sulphur" and pure lard. Just make sufficient to last for a few days. Obtain a small bottle of good feather tonic and add just two drops to the small amount of ointment. With the end of the finger just smear a little of the ointment upon the bare patch. Do this every third day for three applications. Add to the ordinary glass cage drinker as much Chlorate of Potash as you can lift on the handle end of a small teaspoon. Shake the drinker to mix well. Keep the birds in an even temperature and cover the cage at night with a white cloth. Examine the cloth in the morning to make quite sure that Red-Mites are not troubling the birds. If any are found add a large tablespoonful of solution made by infusing a small amount of Quassia Bark. Thoroughly clean the cages and change as often as you can, so that the mites will be removed from the cages. Discontinue feeding the Cabbage, Celery and Lettuce to the old bird, and substitute for the same a small cube of bread and milk. Sprinkle the same with a pinch of best Blue Dutch Maw Seed.

STERILE FIGHTING HEN

Question—Asks if it is possible for a hen bird to be barren or sterile, and thus prevented from laying fertile eggs. This bird laid three nests of eggs last year and all proved infertile. Two males were tried. Hen is mean tempered and continuously fights with any male bird placed in her cage.

Answer—Yes it is quite possible and often the case. Some hens do not lay fertile eggs as the result of a physical deformity. I am inclined to think that the hen has been mated before the proper time, and that would account for the display of temper. I would allow this bird plenty of room for flying, and would feed her well. Give a little "extra" every other day,

alternating with bread and milk. Egg-food, and an allowance of good condition mixture. Do not plan to mate the bird until about the middle of April. Keep her in a cage where she will be able to hear the song of a male bird. Give a few small tender leaves of Dandelion, and occasionally the root of the plant also. When you can see from the condition of the bird that she is quite eager to go to nest, then place her in the half of a double breeder, with a male bird in the reverse half. Place a wire partition between the two birds so that they can see one another, and in this way they will become paired. When you remove the partition you will find that very little quarreling will take place. After the hen has laid her eggs, and has incubated them to the time that they can be tested, if you find they are infertile then I would not mate the bird again. You can make use of the bird as a Foster Mother by giving her the good eggs of another hen, which you can then mate up again after a week's rest. In this way the hen will at least work for you in the raising of some of the young birds.

AVIARY BREEDING

Question—Asks how many birds should be placed in an aviary 12 feet square and 8 feet high. No. 2, would Northern Balsam Pines placed in the aviary be suitable for nesting places.

Answer—In your aviary you have 144 square feet, and allowing one square foot per bird, your aviary will comfortably accommodate 144 birds. Now this number means a total and includes both Young and Old birds. On the other hand if it is your intention to remove the young birds from the aviary as soon as they are getting around and doing for themselves, you will of course be able to place a larger number of stock birds in the aviary. In aviary breeding you must always allow for a greater percentage of losses. Seven or eight young birds per hen will be good results, and taking it for granted that the young birds are to remain in the aviary, then five strong healthy males can be placed in the aviary along with fifteen vigorous hens. If you remove the young birds as raised, then you can increase the number of stock birds to twenty hens and seven males. You might find it necessary to remove one or two of the males until a few of the hens have gone to nest. You must be prepared for considerable quarrelling until the hens get settled down and commence to lay their eggs.

No. 2—I am not prepared to say whether Northern Balsam Pines placed in the aviary would make suitable nesting places. I have never used them. I have known several cases where a number of birds have been poisoned through eating the leaves of certain small trees placed in aviaries. Cedar boughs are greatly favored by some varieties of Finches, while the same material is poisonous to others. However I would advise you to play safe by trying the branches to be used in the cage with one bird for a while. I would advise nesting boxes placed in positions as widely separated as possible. It will give you a better chance to watch the progress of the young birds, which of course would be quite out of the question should the nests be placed in branches of small trees fastened to the sides of the aviary.

BALD-WHEEZY

Question—Asks what to do for a number of birds which are going bald and losing their feathers. No. 2—What to do for a bird which is wheezy but is still singing.

Answer—Read answer elsewhere in this department. No. 2—The wheeziness is the result of a neglected cold, possibly contracted by the bird through the cage being placed in a draughty position in the room in which it is kept. Possibly close to an open window, or through the cage being left out on the veranda until late in the evening. The time required to effect a cure will depend upon the length of time that the bird has been so affected. First of all remove the possible cause. Keep the cage in a room with an even temperature as near as possible to 65 degrees, and avoid a room in which gas is used either for heating or cooking. Take the bird in your hand, and with the first finger feel the breast bone. If it is run down a noticeably sharp edge will be felt. The reason for this being that if the bird is in poor flesh, it must be put on a stimulating and fattening diet, so that it will have the stamina to help it to ward off the effects of the trouble. Give every day a small cube of stale white bread steeped in warm milk, and to which add two drops of Cod Liver Oil and two drops of pure honey. Work this into the bread so that the bird will get the full benefit of the food. Get this mixture made up: Equal parts of Oxymel of Squills, Glycerine, Ipecacuanha Wine and Sweet Spirits of Nitre. Mix well together and add ten drops to each large tablespoonful of water, every other day for ten days. When you note a big improvement, this can be discontinued and substitute the following: Make a paste by mixing on a hot plate a teaspoonful of pure honey. The same amount of Cod Liver Oil Emulsion, and as much Chlorate of Potash as will cover a quarter, and a similar quantity of powdered Grains of Paradise. Mix thoroughly and while doing so add sufficient finely powdered Arrowroot biscuit to bring the mass to the consistency of soft cheese. When cold, it will set quite a little harder. Cut into small cubes and keep one of the cubes between the wire of the cage, allowing the bird to pick at it, at any time. You will find this much superior to any bird treatment you can get. Cover the cage at nights, and do not give the bath often, and when given it should be very shallow to prevent the bird getting more cold. Give bath early in the morning, so that the bird will be thoroughly dry before going to roost for the night.

LAY EGGS—DIDN'T SET

Question—No. 1—What would cause a hen hatched May 26th and mated January 27th to lay on February 3, 4, 5 and 6, skip to the 12th and then to lay again on the 13, 14, 15, 16 and 17th. Did not sit steady from the 3rd to the 17th but after laying the 9th egg would sit O. K. No. 2—How long before a hen lays do you think is required for the male bird to be in the cage to make sure that all eggs will be fertile? Is two or three days before the eggs are laid time enough, especially if you know they have mated?

Answer—The number of eggs laid and the short intervals between the laying of the two nests of eggs prove three points: First, the hen must have been in very forward condition, and no doubt brought about by artificial heat in the breeding room, and stimulating food. Secondly, the hen is a strong, healthy bird. Thirdly, she comes from a line of breeding which is to say the least, prolific.

If you have ever examined the ovasac taken from the body of a fowl, you will have noticed how the eggs are formed and attached to this organ, very much like a cluster of grapes, with the largest yolk at the lower extremity and diminishing in size towards the reverse end. Fertilization must take place while the yolks are still attached to the ovasac, for immediately they become detached, the inside skin and outside shell commence to form, and at which stage fertilization is not possible.

If you had the male bird in the breeding cage with this hen for at least four days before the laying of the first egg, then it is more than likely that all eggs will be fertile. The circumstances are rather unusual, and the only thing that could be done would be to transfer the last eggs laid to another nest. It is just a case of the bird being in forward condition, and the eggs ripening more rapidly than is usual. It is not at all likely that this will occur again with this hen for the rest of the breeding season.

No. 2—The question is partly answered in question No. 1. From my own observations I think that if the male bird is not placed in the breeding cage at least four days before the first egg is laid, then that egg is almost sure to prove infertile. It has been definitely proven that the male bird can be taken from the cage after laying of the second egg, and all of the eggs laid to complete the clutch, say the 3rd, 4th and 5th will be fertile. This proves that fertilization takes place while the eggs are still attached to the ovasac and before they become detached from the same. I would be interested in knowing how you made out with this nest of nine eggs, for it is hardly possible for a bird to properly cover nine eggs without accidentally breaking a number of them, and should they hatch successfully, that number of young birds would certainly keep one hen very busy trying to raise them.

COLOR FEEDING ROLLERS

Question—Asks do you advise color feeding for young Rollers and if so, please give the particulars of same.

Answer—With most types of exhibition breeds, color feeding becomes almost a necessity, but in the case of the Roller it is not required or advisable. To make a success of color feeding, the young birds must have the food from the first start of the moult, and until the same is entirely completed. When young Rollers are placed in the training racks they are hardly at the end of the moult, and I would not consider it advisable to feed color foods to them, while in the close confines of the training cage. Then again color food can only be given mixed with weak egg-food, and if this food was continued daily with young Rollers, they would quickly get into a fatty condition. You can, however, greatly improve their color by substituting for the regular supply of green-food, a supply of African Marigold blooms or the flowers of the Nasturtium plant. In the latter the deep red variety is the best. Both of these plants have a strong coloring agent in the blooms, and when fed liberally to the birds they will have a much deeper color. In the case of selling such a bird be sure to state that the bird or birds have been color fed, otherwise you may hear more about the question of their color after the second moult, when, of course, they will moult out to their natural color, unless again supplied with color food of one kind or another.

INCREASE ROLLER SONG

Question—Asks what can be done to make a low singing Roller louder in song.

Answer—This is quite an unusual question. I have often been asked how to prevent young birds from singing high and consequently faulty, but I do not recall ever being asked the question above. Well, it is the easiest thing in the world to spoil the song of a Roller. Just keep the bird in an open cage all day, and in a sunny, bright position. Feed liberally and allow the bird to sing at will. Allow the bird to hear others with the volume of song that you like, and in a very short time the low

singer will compare quite favorably with the rest. The quality of a Roller is classed according to the depth, tone and variety of his song, and without depth no bird can be classed as a really good Roller.

MATED—WON'T LAY

Question—Asks the probable cause of the loss of two hens and also the young birds in the nest of each, and after they had reached the seventh day. No. 2—What to do for a pair of birds which have been in the same cage all winter, but do not show any signs of wanting to mate or nest.

Answer—There is hardly any doubt that the cause of the losses can be traced to one of the items in the diet given to the birds. Seeing that the hens mated, layed, hatched and raised their birds up to the seventh day, there is no reason why they should not have progressed as well until the young birds were raised. If you added any item to the diet at say from the fourth to the seventh day, then I would suspect that to be the cause. Stale musty hemp seed, green food gathered from a location that was not free of impurities, or growing close to stagnant water, etc. Seed that had become contaminated by mice. These are three of the possible causes.

No. 2—You are not following the proper system of management in keeping your pairs together all through the winter. You should cage the birds separately. Give the hens a large, roomy cage, or a small aviary, so that they will get plenty of room for flying and exercise. The singers should be caged alone.

NAKED

Question—Asks what can be done for a hen which is only half feathered. Carries the same loosely. The body is dark colored and feels hot like a fever. Eats well but does not seem to improve. The bird was bred from February to September last year. Not moulted this year.

Answer—The effect of the strenuous breeding season last year has left its mark, and I doubt that you will find this bird of any service this season. It is simply a case of the bird being completely run down and out of condition. The fact that it has not moulted is sufficient in itself for you to forget about matting this bird for the coming season. Give the bird plenty of room for flying, and in a room with a temperature not lower than 65 degrees. Feed on a stimulating diet. Give plenty of bread and milk, which will keep the bowels regular and the system clean. When the bird has been built up and is stronger, you can reduce the diet so as not to bring the bird into breeding condition in the warmth of the summer. If you do not mate this hen and she

goes up to August or September before moulting, then it is more than likely that she would
make a good stock bird for the next season.

MATED—WON'T LAY

Question—Asks for treatment for a pair of
birds which are out of condition, and have
been for a year or more. Mated last year but
with no result. Sits puffed out in the morning,
and in the afternoon will tighten the feathers
and the male will sing. Cannot see anything
wrong, both birds well but cannot be brought
into breeding condition.

Answer—I have read your letter carefully,
but without a full explanation as to how you
have been feeding the birds, and which you
do not mention, I am not able to give you a
very helpful answer. Unless both birds are constitutionally weak, there does not appear to
be very much wrong, only as you say a lack
of breeding condition. I think that you will
have been able to improve matters before now,
by following the advice given to other questions of a similar nature in this department.
It is hardly necessary for me to say that you
would simply be wasting time to pair the
birds in the present condition, and even if
you do not mate them until as late as the end
of May, still it will pay you to keep them
apart until you have them in the required condition. Treat them as follows: If the birds
are together, then cage them separately. Put
the hen into a large flight or aviary. The
male in a good roomy cage. Examine your
seed supply and be quite sure that it is good
fresh sound seed. If in doubt obtain a fresh
supply and from another source. Feed Canary
and Roller Rape in equal parts as the staple.
Give an extra each day and to both birds.
Bread and milk with three drops of Cod Liver
Oil for the first day. Second day a teaspoonful of good condition mixture, in which should
be a liberal proportion of Best Maw Seed,
and a few cracked Hemp Seeds. Third day a
little strong egg-food, made from equal parts
of hard boiled eggs mixed with Arrowroot
biscuit. See that the birds are kept in a room
with an even temperature. Give plenty of clean
dry grit, and a piece of Cuttlefish Bone should
be between the wires of the cage at all times.
If the male bird is not in full song, then do
not give the bath often until you note an improvement. It may be that the birds are suffering from a slight cold, not severe enough
to give any indications. As soon as you can
obtain a supply, and which must be quite free
from frost, give both the root and a few tender leaves of Dandelion. Dig up the plant,
wash off the soil from the root, split open the
root with a table knife, and fasten the same
between the wires of the cage, so that the
birds can get the inside of the roots. This is
both a good tonic and conditioner. Nothing
better for this season of the year.

TWISTING FEATHERS

Question—What is the reason and cure for
a bird which spends most of its time twisting
feathers upon its back. Not pulling the feathers out, but just wetting them and twisting
them constantly, (2) Is it possible that this
practice could have been acquired through the
bird being kept close to a cage containing a
parrot. (3) Is this practice contagious?

Answer—The picking of the feathers as
mentioned is nothing more than a habit, and
possibly contracted by the bird when quite
young. While not common, still many cases
will be noted that are identical to the one you
mention. The only treatment lies in trying to
provide the bird with something that will prove
a counter attraction, and which for a time will
take his attention from the habit. I would
place the bird into a flight cage, and along
with other birds. His time then would be taken
up in exercise, and keeping out of the way of
others that may be a little quarrelsome. You
could try fastening a play bell and string to
the wires of the cage, and at which the bird
can pull, just as you would provide hens with
nesting material. I would not advise painting
the feathers with anything that might prove
harmful to the bird. If you decided upon this
course, I would use a strong solution of Quassia
Bark, and which as you will know has an extremely bitter taste, but which would be quite
harmless to the bird.
(2) I do not think that it is likely that the
habit has been acquired from the cage being
placed close to one containing a parrot. The
habit is due as much to a nervous and highly
strung condition, more than anything else.
(3) No this trouble would not be contagious,
nor do I think that it would be transmitted to
young birds which might be produced from the
bird. There is no reason why such a bird
should not prove a good stock bird.

LOSING FEATHERS

Question—What is the cause and treatment
for a number of birds which are losing feathers from around the beak and the head. Birds
eat and sing well, but are affected in the way
mentioned.

Answer—The answer to this question was
given in the Journal. The trouble is a skin
complaint, and it is more than likely that it
is spreading from one bird, and will get around
the entire stud unless you take immediate steps
to stop it from doing so. The complaint is
known as "Fungoid Skin", and if you will examine one of the birds, you will find that on

the bare patches there is a number of small encrustations, and from which the skin is peeling in small flakes. These small flakes carry the germ of infection. You are no doubt transferring birds from one cage to another, and as the birds are constantly passing their heads through the wires especially at the seed and water cups, these small encrustations are thus communicated to other birds. The treatment lies in first of all isolating all birds affected. I would place them all into a large flight cage, and place them for the time being in a room apart from the rest. Daily cleaning must be the rule, so have two cages, so that one can be thoroughly cleaned while the other is in use. When cleaning use a strong solution of disinfectant, and with a cloth moistened in the same, go over all fittings in the cage as often as convenient. The tray of the cage should contain coarse saw-dust, and this should be dampened with a disinfectant. Keep the temperature of the room about 65 degrees. Get a small tin of pure Sulphur Ointment. Mix thoroughly into the same 20 drops of feather tonic (disinfectant). Take each bird in your hand, and with the end of your finger dipped into the ointment, rub in a good application on the head of each bird. This will remove the encrustations mentioned, and at the same time will kill the germs contained in them. Two or three applications may be necessary, and they should be spaced at least one week apart. I would then advise that each bird be "Hand-Washed" using Lifebuoy Carbolic Soap. After this treatment you will find that the birds will be cured. Give the birds every second day a small cube of stale white bread steeped in warm milk, and after pouring off the surplus milk, add a small pinch of "Flowers of Sulphur" which must be well mixed in the food. Do not give a bath for some time, and until a cure has been effected.

Discontinue giving the sulphur after four feeds, and if the birds are not in good flesh, then substitute with a little egg-food, alternating with a teaspoonful of condition mixture.

AVIARY BREEDING

Question—Is an aviary 54 inches long, 54 inches high and 24 inches wide suitable to breed three males and six hens in? (2) Should the birds be placed in now, or kept separate until the start of the breeding season?

Answer—The size of the cage is suitable for the number of birds which you intend to breed in it, but it is not large enough if you intend to allow the young birds so produced to remain in this flight. I would suggest that you limit the number of males to two for the six hens, and you will find that this will reduce the quarrelling at the start of the breeding season. You should have the hens in the cage now, and keep the male birds caged separately for the present, but you could place the cages containing the male birds close to the flight containing the hens. Do not put the males into the aviary until the days are longer and the weather warmer, and signs of Spring are evident. Make arrangements so that you can remove from the aviary all young birds from each nest when they have reached the stage where they can feed well and do for themselves.

PICKING-LOSING FEATHERS

Question—What is the cause and cure for one male and two hens which are losing feathers and constantly picking, especially under the wings?

Answer—You will find the cause and treatment exactly the same as given to question above. Your letter confirms the cause of the trouble for you say, I CAUGHT THEM ABOUT A WEEK AGO AND FOUND THAT THEY THROW OFF FROM THEIR FEATHERS LITTLE SHINY PARTICLES LIKE DANDRUFF. You will note that I have mentioned this feature in answering question above. Treat your birds in the same way and you will get results. Needless to say you should not consider breeding with the birds until they have been cured. The male bird is apparently coming into breeding condition. Possibly you are feeding a little too stimulating and keeping the bird in a room a little on the warm side.

(3) Examine the body of the bird, and if he is in good flesh, then add a pinch of "Glauber Salts" to the drinking water. Just as much as will cover a ten cent piece, and dissolve the same in a spoonful of hot water before adding to the drinker. Just sufficient to make the water taste saline is all that is required. This will reduce the forward condition of the male, and will help in the treatment for the trouble that you wrote about.

WHEEZING
COAL OIL CAGES

Question—(1) Is it likely to prove injurious to the birds if I paint my breeding cages with kerosene oil twice each month, and without removing the birds from the cages while doing so. (2) Suggest a preventative (not a cure) for Red-Mites. (3) Cause and cure for a two year old hen, which while at times is active, spends most of the time sitting on the perch with feathers puffed out like a ball. Good appetite and very fat. (4) Cause and cure for a young hen which makes a noise very similar to the whining of a young puppy both day and night, and which appears to have difficulty in breathing.

Answer—(1) I do not approve of the use of Kerosene Oil being painted on the breeding cages, and while the birds are in the same. First the strong smell of the oil would fill the room, and if all cages were treated at the same time, this would not clear away for two or three days. The second objection being the possibility of the oil coming in contact with the birds if used freely. Red Mites can be successfully combated for the entire breeding season, and to such an extent, that not a single mite will be seen in the full season, but it requires considerable work to obtain this desired result. The Rule for the entire period must be scrupulous cleanliness to obtain this result. There should always be provided four or five breeding cages in excess of the number which will actually be in use, and these cages must be held in readiness for changing at convenient times. Trays should be cleaned three times per week during the period of mating and laying, and from the day that the hen commences to sit, the trays need only be changed twice during that time. The reason being to avoid disturbing the hen more than is absolutely necessary. Just as soon as the hatch has taken place, and the young birds are raised to the time that they can leave the nest, then both the hen and young birds should be transferred to a clean cage, and the used cage taken from the room without delay. The used cages should be dismantled, and every seam and crevice thoroughly painted with a solution made from a mixture of equal parts of Gasoline, Kerosene, Turpentine. Mix these together in a large bottle, and to each half gallon add two small blocks of Camphor, which is cut up into fine pieces. The contents of the bottle well shaken until all the camphor is thoroughly dissolved. After painting allow the cage to stand for one hour, and then wash out with hot soapy water, to which has been added a strong disinfectant. The cage should then be dried and allowed to stand for several days to remove the strong smell. It can then be used in the changing of the next nest of birds to require a clean cage. If this rule is followed throughout the season, and the racks washed down before the clean cage is placed in position, then I feel sure that Red-Mites will not get the upper hand. As a rule the leaving of dirty cages, and old used nest pans and material upon the racks are the direct causes for Red-Mites becoming a pest in the season. I can assure you that when cages are cleaned as stated above, there will not be any red-mites left to worry the birds. (3) In the case of the old hen there does not appear to be anything radically wrong with the bird, and it looks like a case of laziness due to the fatty condition. The first thing to do would be to place the bird into a large flight cage or aviary, and if these are not available, then allow the bird to fly in a small empty room if possible. Feed upon a very plain diet, and for the present stop giving any extras. Every third day for four doses, give as much "Glauber Salts" in the ordinary glass drinker, as would cover a dime, and which will make the water

taste saline. In addition give a small cube of bread and milk daily. In one week you will note a reduction in the fatty condition, and the bird will improve from that time. It would be useless to consider breeding from this bird until her condition improves, for it is sure that failure would result, and the possible loss of the hen from egg-binding.

(4) The young hen is suffering from a severe cold, and the length of time that she has been making the noise that you mention, will determine how quickly a cure can be effected. If the cold is of long standing, then it may have resulted in Asthma, and which is hard to cure. Treat the bird as follows: Give a fairly roomy cage, and keep the bird in a room a little on the warm side, temperature not less than 60 degrees. Take the bird in your hand, and with the first finger feel the breast bone. If the bird is in poor flesh, the bone will have a noticeably sharp edge. If the condition of the bird is normal, then the bone should be covered with a thin layer of fat, so that the sharp edge cannot be felt. The reason for making this examination will determine whether the bird is under-nourished or not, and the diet regulated accordingly.

Give every day a small cube of bread and milk, and mix in two drops of Cod Liver Oil Emulsion. Keep this up until the wheeziness stops. Add to the drinking water 15 drops of Juice. You will find that this mixture will give instant relief. If the case is of long standing it will be harder to effect a cure, so have this mixture made up. Glycerine, Ipecacuanha Wine and Sweet Spirits of Nitre. Add 5 drops to each tablespoonful of drinking water. If you find the bird will not use this freely, remove the drinker from the cage for one hour, then shake the contents well, and the bird will drink as soon as it is replaced. Remove again, and keep this up so that you will know that the bird is using the mixture given. Keep the cage in a position quite free from draughts, but a free circulation of fresh air should be in the room. Cover the cage at night, and until you can see that the bird has been cured.

DIARRHOEA AVIARY BREEDING

Question—(1) What will cure "White Diarrhoea." If I breed from birds with this trouble would it be likely to affect the young birds bred from them? (2) Wishes advice regarding breeding birds in an aviary 6 feet high, 6 feet long and 3 feet wide.

Answer—(1) The color of the natural excreta of a healthy Canary is black, with white patches at either end, and which is the natural elimination of Uric Acid from the system of the bird. When the excreta is as you say green and white, and watery, then it proves that the bowels of the bird or birds are in a disordered and unhealthy condition. Before a cure can be expected, you must first remove the exciting cause of the trouble. You must carefully examine the diet, both as regards the quality of the seed used, and the extras which are given to the birds. Unsound or mouldy seed will cause this trouble, and other causes are leaving stale green food in the cage, failing to thoroughly clean the drinking cups, etc.

Follow this treatment and you will soon have your birds in a healthy condition. First day gather together all birds which are now affected, and place them in a part of the room apart from the healthy birds. Keep the cages quite clean by changing the trays daily. Dissolve a quantity of "Glauber Salts" in hot water, allow to go cold, and add one teaspoonful to each tablespoonful of cold water. This will clean out the system. Now remove all seed entirely from the birds to be treated. Feed only bread and milk, giving a small cube per bird, and adding to the same as much powdered Arrowroot as will cover a dime. The next day take a piece of white bread and toast it quite brown. When cold grind up to crumbs about the size of Rape Seed. Into these crumbs mix in the same amount per bird of Powdered Bismuth as the Arrowroot given.

The salts must not be given only on the first day, and in the drinking water each day add a small pinch of Powdered Chalk. Do not give any seed at all during this treatment. Alternate with these two foods each day, adding the chalk to the drinker daily, and this should be shaken frequently so that the bird will get the benefit. The chalk quickly settles to the bottom of the drinker if not shaken often. At the end of the six days you will note a decided improvement. Now you can start with a little seed, giving a few grains of Canary Seed first, and later adding the Rape. If you find that either of the varieties of seed bring back a recurrence of the trouble, then you will know that the seed is bad. Better make sure of the quality before you start to use it again. (2) I would not consider mating these birds in the present condition, for it would only mean poor results. Delay for a time and get them cured, and your chances of success will be that much greater. The trouble would not be transmitted to the young only by infection, but you should not consider mating unhealthy birds in the first place.

The Aviary that you mention will accomodate 18 birds for breeding. The proportion I would recommend to be 4 good strong males to say 12 hens. You will have to plan upon removing the young birds from the aviary as soon as each nest can properly feed themselves, or else the aviary will quickly become overcrowded. You can remove the possibility of the young birds from falling out of the nests by placing the nest upon a board, and upon which the young birds would fall if accidentally brought over the edge of the nest. As soon as they reach the size when this accident would not be possible, then the board could be removed. In addition you must have a perch placed close to the nest, and which the hen will use in leaving and returning from feeding.

SPASMS OR FITS

Question—What is the cause and treatment for a bird which takes spasms every two or three days, falling to the bottom of the cage, with the head drawn back and the feet drawn towards the body. After a few hours the bird will be quite all right and singing.

Answer—This is a case of Fits. Both apoplectic and epileptic fits are met with in canaries, and in 99 cases out of every 100 are the result of mating birds which are very closely related. In apoplectic cases death quickly results and often before treatment can be given, and unless the bird is of particular value, birds subject to them should be destroyed if they should survive an attack. In epileptic cases the subjects are usually anaemic weaklings, and a permanent cure is rarely effected.

When taken with an epileptic fit the bird will fall from the perch, struggle violently for a minute or so, and then sit in a dazed condition for some time, until it gradually recovers its usual brightness and gets up on the perch and appears to be as well as before the attack. Birds so affected should under no condition be used in the breeding room, for that would mean transmitting the affliction to the young birds produced. If treatment is considered advisable in such cases, the first thing to do when a fit takes place is to quickly dip the head of the bird into cold water, and upon withdrawing the head of the bird from the water, hold the bird until it is over the seizure. A recurrence of the trouble may be avoided by following these directions.

Give the bird room to exercise. Always keep in a room fairly warm, but with fresh air. Feed liberally. Keep bowels regulated by frequent use of bread and milk. Give in rotation every third day. First, eight grains of Bromide of Potassium well mixed into the drinking water for one day. Plain water for the next two days and then give 10 drops of Parrish's Chemical Food in the drinker for one day. Plain water for the next two days and then six drops of Tincture of Iron added to the water for one day. By following this treatment and feeding the bird in a good liberal diet it is possible that the bird will get over the trouble, and be strong enough to withstand any possible recurrence. If after the treatment the bird still takes these fits, I would not keep the bird, but destroy it.

CHOKES

Question—What is the reason and treatment of a young bird which is singing well at four months old, but seems to have spells in which it appears to be choking. What can be done to prevent this.

Answer—I regret that you have not given me sufficient details to allow me to figure the cause of the trouble. You have failed to mention, if the bird when troubled in the way you mention, disgorges the food back into the beak from the crop. If this is one of the symptoms, then it is a case of Indigestion, and the cause is unsuitable food for a bird so young. You might try this treatment, First give a small cube of stale white bread steeped in warm milk. Pour off the surplus milk, and add four drops of "Pure Liquid Paraffin." Mix this in well so that the bird will get the benefit of the oil. Give this every other day for three doses. In the drinking water add 6 drops of Syrup of Rhubarb for an aperient. Give this on the days that the bread and milk is not given. If the symptoms do not recur, stop this treatment after one week, and for a tonic follow up with a mixture of Tincture of Gentian, Tincture of Calumba and Aromatic Sulphuric Acid. Mixed in equal parts and give six drops every day for one week. Now miss a week, and then place a small piece of Sulphate of Soda (about the size of a small pea) in the drinking cup, and leave this in the drinker when changing the water for one week. I am sure that this will cure the case if I have taken the right meaning from your letter. It may be that the bird is suffering from a severe cold, but the fact that he is singing well would prevent me from thinking that a cold was the cause of the trouble.

WHEN STOP FEEDING EGG-FOOD

Question—At what age should egg-food be stopped from the diet of young birds?

Answer—This question has been repeatedly dealt with in the Encyclopedia, and too much stress cannot be given to it, for it seems that quite a large number of losses are taking place, owing to the belief that young birds should be placed upon dry seed as soon as possible. Nothing of the kind. A young bird cannot be expected to husk and use the amount of dry seed that is required, and even if it could it is not able when so young to properly assimilate the food. From the time of taking the young birds from the parents, they should have a little egg-food twice each day, and given fresh each time. After they have been feeding themselves for one week, then you can stop egg-food at the afternoon feeding, and in its place give

bread and milk. You will not find it necessary to use any form of green-food if you follow this plan. Keep this up right up to the time that the young birds have passed into the moult, and you can of course decrease the strength of the egg-food towards this period, by mixing in a larger proportion of biscuit. When the young birds are showing the small new feathers breaking through upon the neck and head, that is the time to consider reducing the quantity of soft food, and getting them into the training racks. You can then start to reduce the quantity of Canary Seed given, but make quite sure of the quality of the Rape Seed, which will now become their principal diet. By following this plan, and giving the birds plenty of room for flying during their early life, you will not have any losses to record in your stud books.

PLUCKS HER BABIES

Question—Why will a roller hen feed her nest of young birds well up to ten days, and then commence to pluck the young birds and neglect to feed them.

Answer—You have answered the question in your letter to me. You have said that at ten days this hen started to call the singer, and from that time not only neglected her birds, but started to pluck them. The hen was coming back into breeding condition, and wanted to go to the nest for the second time. The course that you should have followed was to have placed the singer in the reverse half of the cage, with the wire partition between the two, and to have given the hen a treatment which would have reduced the breeding fever. This should be as much "Glauber Salts" as would cover a ten cent piece. Place this amount in an ordinary drinker, and see that it is properly dissolved. You can also improve conditions by slightly reducing the stimulating nature of the food used, and by adding a little bread and milk, and also some "Chickweed" each day. It is quite possible with the change of diet, and the singer being in view of the hen, that she would again take up the care of her young. If you found that this did not result, then you should allow the singer to run with the hen. No doubt he would assist the hen with the work, and after they had been together in the breeding cage for a few days, you would have to place another nest in the reverse half of the cage. This precaution would be advisable in the event that the hen commenced to lay sooner that you expected. You would find that in most cases that the male would continue feeding the first nest of young birds, and at the time when the hen was commencing to sit on the eggs laid in the second nest. I am sorry you lost the nest, but better luck next time.

SNEEZES, WON'T SING

Question—What is the cause and treatment of a bird which has gone completely off song. Sneezes quite violently, and is very hoarse. Otherwise appears well and eats good.

Answer—The cause of the trouble is a severe cold, which has become deep seated, and which should have had treatment just as soon as it was first noticed. The cold no doubt has been contracted by the cage being kept close to an open window, or the bird being kept in a room with an unsuitable and changing temperature. First remove the cage to a comfortable position. Away from any chance of a draught, but still where the bird will get plenty of light. Keep the temperature as near as possible even and take the precaution of covering the cage every night with a woollen and dark colored cloth. Keep the staple seed diet before the bird, but each day give a small cube of bread and milk, and work in three drops of honey and two drops of Cod Liver Oil. This will quickly relieve the labored breathing. Instead of giving ordinary water for drinking, give the following—Take a teaspoonful of Flax Seed, pour over it half a cup of boiling water. Allow to stand until cold. Now fill the drinker with the liquid, and add five drops of pure glycerine. Shake up well to thoroughly mix. Give this every other day for a week. If the bird is thin and run down, then a little egg-food can be given occasionally, and when you have the symptoms of the cold removed, you can add a little condition seed mixture to the diet.

RINGS PULLED OFF

Question—What can be done to stop a hen from trying to pull the ring off young birds while in the nests. The hen in question having damaged the leg of a bird, and thrown another out of the nest while trying to remove the ring.

Answer—This trouble will quite often be experienced. As soon as the new bright rings are placed upon the young birds, the attention of the hen will be attracted to them, while cleaning the nest. Some fanciers hold each ring in the flame of a match, which will blacken the metal and in this way remove the brightness, so that the hen will not be attracted by them. I do not favor this course as the figures are also blackened. You can get the best results by covering each of the rings with a small piece of "Valve Rubber" as used in the valve of the tire of a bicycle. This can be bought from any "Cycle repair store." You will find that the tubing mentioned is just a nice fit for the ring, and is green in color. Place the ring on the stem of a match. Slide the rubber tubing over the ring, then withdraw both ring and rubber off the stem of the match, and trim the rubber with a sharp pair of nail scissors. This will leave the bright surface of the ring covered with a layer of green rubber. You will not then have any further trouble in the way you have mentioned. When the young birds are being taken from the breeding cage, the rubber can be taken off the ring. This is not necessary, for if the rubber should be left, it will later become impoverished and will break off, long before it will be necessary for ring numbers to be examined.

STARVING YOUNG

Question—What is the reason that breeding pairs will refuse to feed their young after the 2nd and 3rd week. What would cause birds to kill their young in this way. How should they be fed at this time, and how many times per day should fresh food be given. Whether or not they should have water.

Answer—It seems to me that your troubles arise from your system or management, more than from any faults in the birds themselves. I have taken it from your letter that you have been breeding from straight pairs, and that the male birds have been left in the breeding cages with the hens during the time of incubation and hatching. When this system is followed the hens will come back into breeding condition really earlier than is convenient, and just about the time you mention. When their young are from two to three weeks old. If you keep the same birds in the coming season, you should try removing the male birds when the hens have gone to nest with a full clutch of eggs. Let the hen do her own work of incubating and feeding, and I am sure you will get better results. If you have not a second hen to mate with the singer when removed from the cage of the first hen, then keep in a stock cage and in another room away from the breeding hen, and he can be kept in condition for the second nest. The birds have not killed their young, for that is very seldom done. They have simply refused to feed them and the birds have died of neglect. In your work in the next season follow the system as you will find given in the pages of this book, and I think you will get better results. You should not breed from any hens for four times in the one season. Three nests are plenty from mature birds over one year old. For hens in the first season's breeding, you should not mate them for more than two good nests. Fresh food should be given to feeding hens not less than three times each day. Early morning, noon and late afternoon. The food given should be varied according to the individuality of the birds. Some hens show a preference for certain foods, which you will notice by the amount that they will use. Always give a feeding hen plenty of the food that she will use. She in turn will feed plenty of it to her young birds. Fresh water should never be denied the birds at any time, and this applies to both old and young birds.

MATING YEARS
24 BIRDS ONE TRIO

Question—(1) How many years can you successfully mate a healthy male bird, and how many nests during the year. (2) Is twenty-four healthy young birds from two hens and one male a good average for one season. (3) I have raised a young bird from six days old by hand-feeding. Is that unusual?

Answers—(1) The number of years that a male bird will successfully breed will be governed to a great extent by the constitutional fitness of the bird, and the way that it has been managed during the period of its development and until it reaches the age of maturity. Then again the methods used in the breeding have a bearing upon the matter. I have known cases where one male bird has fertilized all eggs laid by five hens by the aviary breeding system. This of course would not be possible when following the system known as cage breeding. In the first season I would not advise you to mate a young male to more than three hens. In my own rooms two hens only are allowed to each male. You will find that when a singer is not overworked in the first season, and if the bird is strong and healthy, he will successfully breed up to six years, and in many cases longer. The management, diet and the stamina of the bird will determine the exact time.

(2) Twenty four young birds from two hens is decidedly excellent results. Not many Fanciers who are keeping a number of pairs can show such results. If all pairs mated were to produce 12 young birds each season, then there would undoubtedly soon be a large surplus of birds upon the market. A fair average is six young birds for each hen mated. Eight young per pair would be very good, but twelve young birds or in other words three nests of four young birds each from each hen I consider to be extreme good, and far better than is produced in the average stud.

(3) To hand raise a young bird from six days old is by no means unusual. There are unfortunately too many Fanciers who are willing to assume the work that rightly belongs to the hen. At such an age it is almost impossible for a person to even imitate the food that under other circumstances would be given to the young birds by the hen herself. The food when eaten by the hen passes to the crop, and while there is ground up and pre-digested before fed to the young birds. At such an age the young birds are not able to assimilate the necessary nutriment from food given in any other way, and for that reason I never advise hand-feeding. Occasionally a hen will go back to nest before she has completed raising her previous nest of young birds to the stage where they can take care of themselves. At such a time hand-feeding will often help

to prevent a loss, but with young birds at say six days, should the hen show signs of neglecting her brood, then I think that better results can be obtained by changing the diet of the hen, so that she will improve in the work of feeding more to the youngsters. To undertake to hand-feed a nest of young birds from six days old, is to say the least a very tiresome process. Of course the principal object is to raise the young birds, and anything that the Fancier does to make this possible is quite permissible but as I have stated I do not recommend the practice.

CARE WHEN MOULTING

Question—(1) Please advise the best way to take care of parent birds during the moulting season. (2) What brand of mixed seed do you recommend.

Answer—The correct management of your breeding stock during the present moulting season, will have quite a bearing upon the results that you will get from the birds when mated up in the spring. It can be safely said that many of the poor results often complained of, can be traced to wrong or careless management during this important time. Immediately after a busy breeding season, all stock birds will be in a sense run down, and it is necessary to improve this condition before moulting actually begins.

The first important consideration is exercise. If space will permit, you should provide an aviary for the males and another for the hens. The larger the better. If you have not an aviary available, then the use of a spare room will answer the purpose well. The birds should not be crowded but given plenty of room to fly and exercise. A little egg-food per bird should be given at least once each week, and two days later a liberal supply of bread and milk can be given. The seed diet should be best grade Canary and Roller Rape mixed in equal parts. Plenty of clean dry grit. A large piece of Cuttlefish Bone constantly before the birds. A bath given early in the morning and on fine days is a good conditioner. In mature stock the first feathers to moult are the primary feathers in the wings and tail, and as soon as these are found you will know the moult has started. A good quick moult is necessary, and when a bird does not moult quickly, it is an indication that the bird in question is not in the best condition, and therefore not able to cast the old feathers, and at the same time supply the nourishment necessary to promote the growth of the new ones. If the front of the aviary is kept partly shaded most of the day, it will help greatly in promoting the growth of the new feathers. Once each week place a cupful of best Flax Seed in a pitcher. Pour boiling water over the seed and allow it to stand overnight. Then fill the drinkers with the liquid. This will cool the blood, clean the system of the bird and bring a sheen and gloss to the new feathers, Flax Seed is a most useful and valuable seed especially during moulting time. (2) I recommend the purchase of mixed seed, but advise each Fancier to purchase the best quality in each variety, and then mix them in the proportions. Each seed has a different chemical analysis, so it is important to obtain a well balanced mixture. The following will be found to give satisfactory results as a conditioner. One part by measure of Hemp, Flax, Inga, White Italian Millet, Red Indian Millet, Hulled Oats. Add half of one part of the following: Best Blue Dutch Maw Seed, Gold-of-Pleasure and Sesame Seed. Mix well together each time used, so that the small seed such as Maw will be well distributed throughout the bulk. Feed a teaspoonful per bird twice each week, then reduce to once each week as the moult is finishing. Six drops of Tincture of Iron added to the small wire cage drinker, will help as a tonic.

PINK EYES
RAT TAILS

Question—(1) Explain what would be the cause of a young bird having pink eyes. Is it the result of inbreeding. (2) Give the botanical name of the enclosed sample of seed. We call it "Rat's Tails" here. Is it good for the bird, etc.

Answer—(1) Inbreeding has nothing whatever to do with the matter. Your young bird is the progeny from a mating carrying a percentage of "Cinnamon Breeding". All cinnamon colored canaries have pink eyes and this characteristic will show up in birds of other colors coming from mating in which a percentage of cinnamon breeding is present. It may be in both of the parent birds, or in either one of them. (2) The right name for the plant that you have sent in is PLANTAIN. "Rats Tails" is the name used for this plant in most locations. It is a real valuable food for our birds and one which they greatly enjoy. I have never known of a case in which its use has given anything but good results. When gathering the plant always take the precaution to see that it has been grown in a clean location and not close to stagnant water. Gather the biggest seeding heads. You will note that the largest seeds are at the bottom of the stem, and when the seeding head is fully ripened the seeds will be changing from a green to a reddish color. Make sure that the pods are not gathered close to a dusty road. The plant can be found in any field or pasture. If you gather a good supply you can tie a bundle of the seeding heads together. Place these into a paper or linen sack. Hang up the same in a clean dry place and you can use the seeds during the winter months when other green food is not available. Give

your young birds all that they will use. It will be good for them. Fasten a number of the pods to the front of the aviary and let them pick out the seeds for themselves. (3) Roller Rape and Canary seed can be sown in flat shallow boxes and the sprouting plants from them fed to the birds at any time of the year.

STRAWBERRY FINCHES

Question—Will Strawberry Finches breed in captivity and if so, what kind of nesting material should be given to them?

Answer—Strawberry Finches can be bred in captivity, and under ideal conditions they are very prolific. They will not do as well in cages as in a fairly large aviary, which is by far the best way to produce them. For a nest the Strawberry Finch requires a "Cocoanut Husk." These should have a hole about 1½ inches in diameter cut into the pointed end of the husk. They should be hung up in places where good light is possible, and the husk should be covered with small boughs or branches of young trees.

Question—At what age should young birds be taken from the parents. It is possible to determine the sex of young birds at one month old.

Answer—The age that a nest of young birds can be taken away from the parents will all depend upon how the young birds have been fed from the first day onward. The young birds from a hen which is what might be termed an indifferent feeder will be far slower in getting around and making a showing of doing for themselves. A strong healthy nest of birds should commence to stand in the nest at 15 or 16 days old. They will leave the nest in the daytime at 18 or 19 days, and leave the nest entirely at 20 or 21 days. When this takes place the nest should be removed from the cage. After the young birds are five days older, they should be able to pick food themselves, and at this time it will be safe to place them on the reverse side of the partition in the breeding cage, or in the nursery cage. The hen can then be mated again, and while busy in the building of the nest for the second round, the hen will still find time to give any of the backward birds an occasional feed. Often the male bird will assist in this work. When it is found that all of the young can feed themselves without help from either parent, they can be safely removed to the flight cage.

It is possible to determine the sex of the young birds at one month old, but it takes considerable experience to do so. Even with the most expert Fanciers occasional mistakes will be made, but not more than one in every ten or more birds. The principal points of difference between the males and females are briefly as follows: The males are usually slightly larger than the hens. The color is richer, especially round the head and throat. The head is slightly larger in the male. The eye is larger and bolder in the male than the female. The call of the male is louder and with a more musical note than the female. These points coupled with frequent handling of the birds will bring to any fancier the ability to quickly determine the sex of each young bird, when they can later be placed in the aviaries according to the sex. Young Rollers will make quite a showing towards singing at from five to seven or eight weeks old, but this test should not be depended upon, only in conjunction with the other points as mentioned. Young hens will often be mistaken for singers if the song itself is the only guide to be used.

MOULT CONTINUOUSLY

Question—What is the reason for birds moulting continuously?

Answer—I would suggest stopping at this season, apple, lettuce and the nesting food (mixed seed) and substitute in their places, flowering Chickweed, and a little freshly made egg-food. The rest of the diet can be continued. See that the birds are kept free of draughts, and for the present box cages would be the most suitable. Make quite sure that there are no Red Mites in the cages. When giving the bread and milk every second day, add three drops of Cod Liver Oil, and mix well into the food. A good tonic effect will result by giving twenty drops of "Chemical Food" formula in this book, in the drinking water every other day for a week. I would not advise you to attempt breeding the birds in their present condition for the chances of success during the partial moult will be very small.

AGE OF BREEDING

Question—At what age will a hen bird have passed the stage of successful breeding?

Answer—A direct answer cannot be given to this question, for there are at least two details which determine the question. (1) The health, stamina and vigor of the hen in question. (2) The care and general management that the bird has been given from the first breeding season. Before the best average breeding results can be expected it is essentially necessary for the operator to select only the biggest and strongest hens for the work. When these selections have been made in the fall, the best attention possible should be given to the birds. Plenty of room for exercise is important. A good wholesome, but plain diet must be supplied, and care taken to see that the birds are not subject to extreme temperatures. Commencing early in the year a period of conditioning should be followed, but no attempt should be made to force the birds by

stimulating feeding into too early breeding condition. Hen birds which are neglected during the winter months, will seldom do well when the breeding season comes along. In speaking of the second detail, I have noted many cases in which the owners of good hens have completely spoiled their birds by working them too hard in the first season. A young hen in her first season should not be called upon to raise more than two good nests. With many the temptation to mate a good breeding and feeding hen for the third and sometimes the fourth nest is allowed to override the better judgment of the owner.

It is quite permissible to mate a hen for the third nest, but this should not be attempted until the bird is fully matured. Young hens which have done well with two nests in the first year, will often come back and produce twice the results in the second and subsequent seasons, but a young hen which has been worked out in the first season invariably proves a failure in the second year. Good healthy hens are at their best in the second season, and will continue to breed with slightly reduced results from that time onward. Four years can be considered a fair average for hens used in each of the years, but many cases are on record where hens have bred and raised their young in the fifth, sixth and even the seventh years.

NUMBER NESTS FROM A MALE
NUMBER HENS ONE MALE
CRESTED ROLLERS

Question—(1) Is it advisable to use more than one hen with each male. (2) Are four nests in one season too much to expect from one male. (3) Concerning the use of Red-Mites exterminator in the bath, etc. (4) Are there any crested birds among pure bred rollers?

Answer—(1) In breeding Rollers the answer to this question is YES. You will find in breeding straight pairs that while the males will often remain quiet and gentle with the hen during the period of laying and for the first few days of incubation, they will when left in the breeding cage begin to interfere with the work. They will sing to the hen, pluck her feathers and try to induce her to leave the nest. Some males will go to the nest when the hen leaves to feed, and will not let her return when she wishes to do so. You will find that 90 percent of the healthy hens will get along much better, if allowed to do their own work of incubating and feeding the young birds, without assistance from the male. From experience I am sure that the male is better employed mated to second hen, rather than to be left in the breeding cage with one hen for the entire season. Nature has provided in the male bird the characteristic which permits of pairing with several hens in the same season, and it is due to this fact that they will be found to interfere in the way mentioned.

Many Fanciers follow the system of mating one male to three hens, but I do not favor the plan unless the system is aviary breeding. In the latter case four hens or even more can be successfully paired to each male. For cage breeding you will find that when three hens are matched to each male, the services of the male will be required with more than one hen at the same time, and this is the real objection to the system. I favor double breeding by matching not more than two hens to each male. Only one hen is placed in the double breeder, and as soon as this hen has laid her full complement of eggs, and has been sitting for two days, the singer is removed from her cage, and mated to the same type. The center partition in the cage is only used when the time comes that the first nest of young birds are able to leave the nest, when they are placed in one half of the double breeder, with the wired partition in place, thus separating the young birds from the parent birds. The parents will continue to feed the young through the wires of the partition, and the hen at the same time will build her second nest, and commence to lay as in the first case.

(2) Six good nests can be taken from one male in the same season, and without any detriment to the bird. From a young hen you should not expect more than two good nests in the first year, and three nests when the bird is two years old.

(3) It is a mistake to dust the body of the birds with any kind of "Insect Powder." The majority of the powders sold for that purpose will not injury "Poultry" when used in this way, but the skin of the canary is far too tender, and the use of the powder will result in irritation. I would not think of using any fluid exterminator by adding the same to the water for the bath, unless I knew exactly what the fluid was, and if any of the ingredients used in its making would prove injurious should a bird drink from the water given for the bath, any good bird wash is o. k. "Quassia Bark Solution" is not injurious in any way. The bark can be obtained from any Florist's Store. It is used extensively in the making of spraying fluid for plants. The bark should never be boiled in the water to be used in the bath for the birds. Place one heaping tablespoonful of the bark into a basin, pour over the bark one pint of boiling water. Allow to stand overnight. Then pour the liquid through a piece of muslin or cheese cloth. Put the liquid into a bottle, and when giving a bath, add one tablespoonful of the solution to the ordinary small glass bath. This will remove any Red-Mites that may be on the body or in the feathers of the birds.

(4) There is a strain of Rollers which have feathers upon the head in the shape of a crest, but as the birds are bred for song, no attempt is made to intensify the size or feathers of the crest. These birds are very often referred to as "Topknots", and many specimens of this variety will be found in the cheaper class of imported German Rollers.

MATING YELLOWS

Question—Why shouldn't two Yellow birds be mated together?

Answer—As the Roller is a breed which is bred for song, the question of color becomes a very minor consideration, for the birds are paired more with a view of first class song production, rather than type or color. The result of mating two Clear Yellow birds will be that the progeny from them will be reduced in size, and the feathers softened, which in turn will take away the tight and trim appearance which is so much desired. I take it that your object in wishing to pair two yellows together is to intensify the color. If this is the case, you can get just as good results by pairing a Yellow to a Buff-Green marked bird, and at the same time you will keep up the size and stamina of your stock.

PEPPER IN FOOD—COD LIVER OIL

Question—(1) Is cayenne pepper mixed in egg-food beneficial for young birds in the nest? (2) Are you in favor of using Cod Liver Oil food for birds feeding young? If so, what quantity would be right when mixed with one egg? Does it cause looseness of the bowels? (3) What con be done to bring a first class stock male back into song and condition after a heavy breeding season?

Answer—(1) I do not recommend the use of any kind of pepper in egg-food for young birds. I consider the food too strong and injurious for birds so young. There are several makes of patent foods which are known as nesting foods. Some are claimed to have Cod Liver Oil as a base. Some Fanciers use this food exclusively during the breeding season, and claim average results. Personally I prefer to use freshly made egg-food, until the young birds are in the aviaries. After that time and during the moult I believe that several brands of Cod Liver Oil foods are very useful additions to the diet. At this age the birds will take considerable exercise, and in so doing are able to assimilate the food, and derive benefit from its use. I think you would be well advised to stay with the recipes that are given in this book.

There is a form of diarrhoea which affects the birds during the breeding season and which is known as "Nesting Diarrhoea" and which is brought about from no other purpose than the use of unsatisfactory items in the diet at this time. (3) I note in your question that this bird has just completed his moult. It is quite natural for him to be off song at this time. When a bird has been through a hard breeding season, their vitality at the moulting period is lower than it should be, and for that reason the moult is slow. I do not think you have anything to worry about. Give the bird a good roomy cage. Plenty of exercise is essential. Give a tepid bath on warm days, and do so early in the morning. In addition to his regular staple seed diet, i. e. Canary Seed and Rape, give every other day half a teaspoonful of a good condition mixture: one part each of Hemp-Flax-Millet-Inga and Hulled Oats, half of one part of best Blue Maw Seed, Gold of Pleasure and Teazle. Mix these well together so as to make sure that the bird will get a little of each kind of seed. On the days that you do not give the mixture, alternate with a small cube of bread and milk one day, and a little freshly made egg-food the next. Make sure that the bird has a good supply of clean grit, and a piece of cuttlefish bone. Every second day for ten days add six drops of Tincture of Iron to the ordinary sized cage drinking cup.

PULLING FEATHERS

Question—(1) What is a good remedy to stop young birds from pulling feathers out of one another? (2) Is there a remedy for old birds breaking their tail feathers?

Answer—"Feather plucking" is usually started by too many young birds being placed in one flight cage. As the young birds develop, they will be found to become quite quarrelsome, and to spend considerable time in flying after one another. It is usually after such a quarrel, and in the settling of the dispute, that one or more feathers get pulled out of a particular bird. In the quill of the larger feathers will be found a quantity of oil, and once a young bird tastes this oil, it will commence pulling feathers from other birds from that time on. The flight cages should be watched for birds of this kind, and as soon as detected they should be removed for a time into individual cages. In a large aviary, space is provided so that the birds can quickly fly when molested by another, but in a flight cage this is not the case, especially when more birds are in the cage than should be. There is no remedy other than to provide plenty of room for exercise. The quick removal of any bird pulling feathers, and possibly tieing on to the front of the aviary a piece of rope, with the end teased out, so that the birds will have something to take their attention away from one another.

(2) The tail feathers of adult birds will often get. broken by the use of small training cages, and in which the perches are placed a little too close to each end, or too close to the bottom of the cage. In passing from one perch to the other, as the birds will do possibly hundreds of times each day, the tail feathers touch the wires at the end of the cage or get soiled and broken by coming in contact with the tray of the cage. It is also possible for the primary feathers to become brittle and to break due to improper feeding, and a lack of those ingredients which would provide in a natural way the necessary amount of oil to keep the feathers soft and silky as they should be. Then again incorrect matings can be held responsible for this same trouble. In pairing the birds never mate two clears together unless they are opposite in clear color, i. e., Buffs and Yellows. No trouble will be experienced if a rule is made that in all pairs, one of the birds will be a green marked bird. Green being the fountain of color, two greens can be paired together without any detrimental effect to the length or texture of the feathers. Some fanciers keep a piece of unsalted bacon attached to the wire fronts of the cages during the moulting time, in order that a certain amount of animal fat can be assimilated by the birds. I think that better results can be obtained by the use of a fat which is locally known as "Call Fat." It is the thin layer of white fat taken from the carcass of a lamb, and the birds take to it quickly, and much benefit can be noted from its use, but it should not be used constantly, but only at the time when required, that being during the moulting season, and while the coat of new feathers are being produced. The diet that you mention is good, but I would suggest the elimination of Groats-Teazle and the Hemp Seed, and the adding of a larger portion of Flax Seed until the moult is finished. I might mention that a broken tail or wing feather can be pulled out, and this will be quickly replaced by a new feather. If left broken, the feather will of course stay that way until the next moult.

GOOD MOTHER GOES BAD
CLEAR EGGS

Question—(1) Reason why a hen which previously raised a nest of young birds well, should start plucking feathers from the young birds in the second nest, at six days old. (2) Reason why there should be one clear egg in each nest. (3) Why should a young bird die in the shell, and other eggs in the same nest hatch successfully?

Answer—The reason would be one of the following points: Red Mites in the nest, or the hen coming back into breeding condition too quickly. Some hens seem to inherit the habit of plucking, but as your bird raised her first nest, I would be inclined to think that Red Mites were the cause of the plucking. Occasionally hens will come into breeding condition quickly, and commence plucking in an endeavor to urge the young birds to leave the nest. In all cases when a hen commences to pluck her young, it is advisable to change the nest, and examine closely the soiled nest when removed. If no Red Mites are found, then adding as much Glauber Salts as will cover a dime to the drinking water, will help to regulate the hen, and reduce the desire to breed again too quickly. (2) In this question you have failed to state if the infertile eggs were found in the first, second, or later nests. If in the second nests, then I would suggest that the male bird was not paired to the hen soon enough. When a hen is in forward condition, the eggs will form and will be laid, no matter whether the male bird is in the cage or not, so it is quite necessary that the male bird should be paired back to the hen as soon after the raising of the first nest as is possible, and this is where the advantages of the double breeding cage will show itself. If in the cases you mention, the eggs were laid on the second or third day after pairing, then you can be quite sure that the infertile egg was formed before the birds were paired for the second nest. (3) Seeing that all young birds with one exception successfully hatched, it is not likely that unsuitable material for the making of the shell would be the trouble. Most likely the bird which was unable to break through the shell was a weak specimen, and unable to exert the necessary degree of pressure to break the shell. The condition of the parent birds has therefore a bearing on this question, but quite often as we find one weakling in other branches of animal and bird life so it is with our birds.

CONVULSIONS OR FITS

Question—What is the reason and cure for two young birds which are subject to convulsions or fits?

Answer—The first thing to do is to make quite sure of the relationship of the parent stock. It is almost sure that you have paired two birds which are closely related, and as a result you have got constitutionally weak progeny from them. Such birds should not be used for breeding stock, or the trouble will of course be magnified. If they were adult birds, then this trouble might be brought about by attacks of apoplexy or epilepsy. There is little that you can do in the way of treatment for the trouble in birds only two months old. However, I would cage the bird separately in as roomy a cage as possible. Feed on a stimulating diet, and keep the birds quiet for the time being. Add a few drops of Cod Liver Oil to the soft food, and every fourth day add six drops of tincture of iron to the drinking water. Unless the birds are of particular value, and if the fits occur quite

frequently, then I think your best plan would be to destroy them.

PUFFED—SLEEPS ALL THE TIME

Question—Give treatment for young birds which sleep continuously, and at other times sit with the feathers puffed out. Bodies very thin, and several birds have died. Ages from six to eight weeks.

Answer—One sentence in your letter gives the reason for your trouble. You say that "We use the best seed available and cannot understand why the birds do not thrive upon it." Young birds at the age mentioned above cannot possibly thrive or develop upon a diet of dry seed. At six to eight weeks they are hardly able to husk dry seed, but even if they were, they would not be able to get sufficient nourishment from the amount used to develop in the way that they should. In your desire to get the birds off soft food and on to dry seed, you are sacrificing the development of the young birds. It is simply a case of Mal-Nutrition, and as soon as you place young birds upon the diet suitable to their age, you will then note quite an improvement. Plan upon giving an allowance of soft food daily. Egg-food one day and bread and milk the next. Add a few drops of Cod Liver Oil to the bread and milk, and mix in well so that the birds will get full benefit. Keep a supply of seed before the birds, and as they are able to properly husk the seed, you will find that they will use more and more of it. Keep up the use of soft food until the birds are almost through the moult, when you can begin to gradually diminish the amount given, and also reduce the strength of the egg-food. Later you can give a teaspoonful of good Condition Mixture, which will help to tone up the birds and bring them into the best of song and condition.

EGG-BOUND

Question—What is the treatment of a hen sick as a result of egg-binding?

Answer—I am glad to know you were able to save the hen, and I think that you will find that she will in time get over the effects caused by the egg-binding. Instead of holding the bird over the "Kettle-Spout" you should have placed the hot water into a pitcher, and after covering the top of the pitcher with a piece of cheese cloth, you should have held the bird over the top of the cloth, with a small towel covering your hand and the body of the bird, so that the steam could penetrate into the feathers, but still not run the risk of scalding the bird as would be likely by the method that you used. You are right in saying that grit should be used at the time that the eggs are being formed. Finely powdered fowls' egg shells together with a piece of Cuttlefish Bone is the best material, and grit should not be given until all eggs have been laid. If the hen does not improve, write again and explain the symptoms fully. The heavy breathing might be the result of a cold contracted after the steaming you gave for the trouble.

WHEN TO REMOVE MALE BREEDER

Question—Two questions—First, concerning the removal of the male bird from the breeding cage during the incubation and raising period. No. 2—Cause and remedy for a hen bird which has gone bald.

Answer—From your letter I take it that in the third nest, you were able to find the cause of the failure in the earlier nests. I have found from much experience that 90 per cent. of healthy Roller hens can be depended upon to do their work of incubating and feeding the young without any assistance from the male bird. You will find in practice that most males will, when left in the breeding cage, remain gentle with the hen for several days after she has commenced to incubate the eggs. After this time, you will note that the male will be in constant song and that when the hen leaves the nest for food, the male will go to the nest and cover the eggs. When the hen wishes to return, the male will not always allow her to do so. In other cases you will find the male singing to the hen, and standing on the edge of the nest, he will pick at the feathers on the back of the hen, as though urging her to leave the nest. This often results in frequent quarrels. As nature has provided in the male bird the characteristic or ability to successfully breed with several hens in one season, I am sure that the male bird is far better employed in being mated to his second hen, rather than to allow him to disturb the first hen.

Of course there are the exceptions which prove the rule, and you will occasionally find the male birds which will not only feed and treat the hen well during incubation, but they will commence to feed the young birds from the first day. However, while I would not hesitate to return the male bird into the breeding cage, should his first or second hen prove a poor feeder, still I am sure you will get the best results, by allowing all of the hens to raise their broods, and mate the males to a second or third hen if necessary.

No. 2—You have not given me much information regarding the condition of the hen, and how long the trouble has been evident. I am not able therefore to give you the cause of the baldness. It is caused from two principal reasons: 1st, Close in-breeding; 2nd, An infection of the skin known as Fungoid Skin. Commencing with a fungus growth, this produces a scurvy encrustation on the surface,

and which spreads, making the affected part larger as time passes. If the trouble is caused by wrong breeding, then there is little that can be done, other than to bathe the head and after drying, apply a little sulphur ointment. The feathers will come in again at the time of moulting. For the second cause and if the bird is strong and healthy, then I would recommend a good hand-wash, using "Lifebuoy Carbolic Soap." After the bird is quite dry, then mix well together twenty drops of "Glacial Acetic Acid" into a teaspoonful of pure glycerine. Apply this every third day for two weeks. Keep the bird in an even temperature. Make sure there are no Red Mites in the cage. Use a good condition mixture, and add to the drinking water as much "Chlorade of Potash" as will cover a dime, every other day for two weeks.

QUIT SINGING

Question—Give reason and treatment for two male birds which have not sung since they were first mated in the beginning of the breeding season.

Answer—One important detail which you have failed to mention in your letter, is the results that you got from these male birds while in the breeding room. It is not at all uncommon for a male bird to go off song while in the breeding cage with the hens. In practice you will find that as the season progresses, so does the amount of song decrease. If you have obtained all fertile eggs from these male birds, then you have nothing to worry about, for as soon as they are over the moult, they will come back into condition and song. On the other hand, if you did not get fertile eggs from the hens mated to these males, it would indicate lack of condition. Without details on this point, it is rather hard for me to advise you. Keep the birds in a room with an even temperature. Allow them plenty of room for exercise. In addition to the staple seed (Canary and Rape mixed) give a little extra nourishing food each day. 1st, Bread and milk; 2nd, A small teaspoonful of a good condition mixture and in which should be Inga, Maw, Teazle, Hemp, Flax, Millet, Hulled Oats; 3rd, Give half a teaspoonful of egg-food made fresh. Examine the bodies of the birds, and if you find that they are thin, then add three drops of Cod Liver Oil to the bread and milk, and only give as much as can be cleaned up in half of the day. The condition that the birds are in, will be a good indication as to how much these stimulating foods should be used. Every third day for two weeks, put six drops of Tincture of Iron into the drinking cup. Good, clean, dry grit, and a piece of Cuttlefish bone should always be accessible at all times.

CONDITION FOR BREEDING

Question—Please publish the right principles to follow in order to bring both male and hen birds into proper breeding condition. 2nd, Give treatment for males in case a large number of infertile eggs are found in the nests.

Answer—This is a small question, but it requires a lengthy answer. There are many details that enter into the matter, and which could not be fully dealt with in this column. I am of the opinion that a large percentage of the losses each year can be directly traced to the mating of the pairs before the proper time. It is not possible to lay down a hard and fast rule, as to which is the proper time to pair up the birds, for that is controlled to a great extent by the location of the owner of the birds. Fanciers in the Eastern States are forced, owing to severe weather conditions during December, January, February and March, to apply a widely different system of management to their studs. They have to keep their birds in rooms in which artificial heat is necessary, while in milder climates this provision is not necessary or even advisable. Birds which are kept in warm rooms, will of course, come into breeding condition so much quicker. Heated rooms are not as conducive to health and condition as cold rooms, and this applies to the Roller more so than any other variety. Canaries can stand cold better than heat. Fluctuating temperatures must be avoided, for a room which is warm in the day, and cold at night will not only prevent proper conditioning, but if extremes are the case, then the birds are quite likely to go into a partial moult. This is almost sure to prevent successful breeding later in the Spring. The natural breeding season is, of course, in the spring of the year, when the days are longer and the nights not so cold. A temperature of 55 degrees during December and January, rising gradually to 65 during February and March. If these temperatures can be maintained, then the conditioning is as follows: Hen birds should be placed in a large aviary, or if the number of birds kept will warrant the use of a spare room, then so much the better. They should be given unlimited room for exercise. Hens which have been flying all winter will never give trouble from egg-binding, for this is only experienced when the hens have been kept in small cages during the winter. They should have a plain but stimulating diet. Canary and Rape seeds in equal parts. A little condition mixture. Bread and milk and weak egg-food, given each once during the week, always missing a day in between these foods. Once each week the hens should be given a liberal supply of Inga Seed. This seed contains a bland oil, which is very good for them. Males that are intended for stock only can be kept in another aviary or large flight cage.

Sufficient room must be allowed so that each bird can escape in case of quarreling. Male birds become very pugnacious towards one another as spring approaches, so they should be caged separately at this time. The same diet as given to the hens will be satisfactory in every way. With this treatment the birds will come forward and in a natural way. No attempt should be made to force by the use of stimulating food in greater or richer quantities than has been mentioned. The time for actual pairing must then be decided by the question of location as mentioned before.

Infertile eggs are the results of mating too early. While many birds will appear to be ready, still there are signs that can be watched for, and which are a sure indication of breeding condition.

SELECTING YOUNG ROLLERS

Question—How would you advise a fancier who is not familiar with the different parts of the Roller Song to separate the best birds from those not so good?

Answer—Your best plan would be to get in touch with some of the Fanciers in your locality, who are better acquainted with the song of the Roller than you are yourself. They no doubt will be glad to help you out of the difficulty. If you are not able to do this, then the only advice that I can give you is to make a study of the song of each of the young birds. You must work along the lines of what sounds HIGHLY-DISCORDANT and OBJECTIONABLE to you, will most assuredly sound the same to others. Listen attentively to not more than two of the young birds at a time. Mark down for each bird the number of changes that you can count in its song. Those which sing with the beak tightly closed, and which have the deepest and best tone, will be your best birds. Those which sing with the beak open, or which go high in certain parts of the complete song, and which high parts sound discordant when compared with the balance of the song, are the second best, and which are not necessarily faulty. By a process of elimination, you should try to grade the young males into three classes, and needless to say, these should be kept quite out of hearing of one another. If you do not take this precaution, then those which would be the best, will be spoiled by those which are now faulty.

You should join a club if you can attend the meetings. Get acquainted with other fanciers. Visit them and listen to their birds, and in this way you will gain a better knowledge of what is required in a good Roller singer.

DEFORMED CLAW

Question—Give treatment for a bird with the back claw on one foot growing up between two of the front claws, and thus crippling the bird.

Answer—The case is known as a "Slipped Claw" and it can be remedied if taken early. First of all wash the foot of the bird, and rub with a little sweet oil. Now take a small piece of adhesive court plaster, one inch long and one-eighth inch wide. Warm this so that it will stick well. Take the bird in your left hand, and gently bend back the bent claw, so that it will touch the leg of the bird. Now take the plaster, and give two or three turns around both the claw and the leg of the bird. If the bird is quite young, no pain will be given, but in an older bird the plaster should be put on loosely, and this can be renewed and tightened later. Leave the plaster on for at least one month, and when it is removed, the claw will stay in its natural position. This treatment should be given just as soon as the bent claw is noticed, as a permanent cure is far more probable, when taken in hand as soon as noticed.

FAULTY TUTOR

Question—Asks for advice regarding use of Tutor, which has good variety, depth and tone, but has one fault.

Answer—My advice to you is that you can with patience obtain the best results possible from training with this male bird. First of all the young tutor for a school of young birds is the father of the birds to be trained. This course is not always advisable however, due principally to the fact that the breeding season tends to spoil the song of the male parent. You have mentioned the fault as being a "Light Aufzug" and if you can give the necessary amount of time to your stock, you can complete the course of training, and at the same time prevent the young birds from hearing the fault that you mention. The first and principal rule to follow, will be never to allow the male to sing to the school, unless you are in the room. By a close study of the song of this bird, you will quickly detect the part of the song at which the Aufzug is introduced. Have the doors of the training rack closed, and place the Tutor upon a stand or table, so that his cage will be as close as possible to the center of the rack. I would use a standard type contest cage for the Tutor, and face his cage towards the rack. Take a seat behind the cage, so that the bird cannot see you. Partly open the doors of the cage, and place your hand upon the top of the cage. Allow the Tutor to sing freely, but immediately he reaches that portion of his song, when the fault is delivered, then by tapping the cage with your fingers, you will

stop his singing. If the fault is delivered at the end of the song, then this will be to your advantage. After a good lesson has been given in this way, remove the Tutor from the room. Try to give as many lessons as you can in this way, and you will find that later the young birds will follow very closely to the song of their father. Do not forget that the young birds have the inherited pre-disposition for the fault that you mention, and should they be allowed to hear it, then they will take up the fault very quickly. In listening and trying over the young birds from time to time, watch carefully for any that show an inclination towards the fault, and should any be found, then you should remove them to a separate rack, and out of hearing of the rest of the school. A slight Aufzug is not heavily penalized, and will be passed by many judges, if not given too loud, or discordant with the rest of the song. If you use an open training cage, then the Tutor might not sing as freely while you are sitting close to his cage, but if you can get the confidence of the bird to make this possible, then you can stop his song by simply raising your hand, for with the open cage the bird will be able to see the signal to stop singing as quickly as you make it. In time, by following this course, it is quite possible to get the Tutor to drop the fault. this is more likely than not.

SHEDDING—SORE FEET

Question—Asks for reason and treatment for a bird continuously losing feathers, and also suffering from sore and scaly feet.

Answer—From the details given in your letter I am afraid that you will lose this bird unless you take prompt steps. The continuous sleeping in the day time is not a good sign, especially in the case of an adult bird. The loss of feathers will result from the cage being kept in an unsuitable position. Close to a window which is frequently opened, or in a room in which the temperature is allowed to fluctuate, such as a kitchen. If gas is used for cooking, this presents another undesirable feature. I am inclined to think that Red Mites are the cause of the loss of feathers. My reason for thinking so, is because you have stated that the feathers under the wings are falling out, and when a bird is troubled with these pests it is under the wing butts that most of them will be found. You can quickly satisfy yourself on this point by covering the cage at night with a white cloth, and then examine the cloth closely when removed in the morning. Should Red Mites be in the cage you will find some of them on the cloth. Get another cage, and after thoroughly cleaning the same, transfer the bird from one cage to another every day. Red Mites are nocturnal, and as they leave the body of the bird in the early morning, you will find them in the ends of the perches, and in the dome at the top of the cage, and in any of the crevices in the fittings or ornamentation upon the body of the cage. Mix equal parts of coal oil, gasoline and turpentine in a bottle. Cut up a small block of camphor, and placing this into the bottle, shake the contents until the camphor is dissolved. With a small brush dipped in this solution, go carefully over the entire cage, and also dip the ends of the perches. Allow to stand for one hour, and then wash thoroughly with hot soapy water. Dry the cage and stand in the open to make sure that the fumes from the solution have left the cage. You can feel quite sure that no Red Mites can remain in a cage treated in this way. If the bird takes the bath freely, put a large tablespoonful of solution obtained by infusing one half ounce of "Quassia Bark" in a pint of boiling water. Later when the bird is stronger a good hand wash would be advisable.

It is quite natural as a bird gets older, for scales to form upon the lower leg and claws, but there is no necessity for soreness to result if the bird is properly taken care of. First examine the perches, and if they are small and round, have a new set of perches made. These should not be less than ¾-in. thick. They are better oval than round, as the flat or oval shape affords a more comfortable rest for the bird. You can remedy the soreness by following this treatment: Mix a teaspoonful of "Boric Acid Powder" in a cup of hot water. When cool take the bird in your hand, and with the claws drawn between the second and third fingers, hold the feet and lower legs in the solution. This will loosen the scales and heal any soreness. After drying, moisten the feet of the bird with a little "Olive Oil." This will keep the skin soft and prevent cracking and soreness.

Apparently the bird is in a rundown condition, and you will find that its body is quite thin. Feed on a liberal diet, giving a little fresh egg-food, bread and milk and condition seed mixture alternately. Supply clean dry grit and a piece of cuttlefish bone.

WHEN TOO OLD TO BREED

Question—Asks for the age at which a hen bird will have passed the stage of successful breeding.

Answer—A direct answer cannot be given to this question, for there are at least two details which determine the question. FIRST—The health, stamina and vigor of the hen in question. SECOND—The care and general management that the bird has been given from the first breeding season. Before the best average breeding results can be expected it is essentially necessary for the operator to select only the biggest and strongest hens for the

work. When these selections have been made in the fall, the best attention possible should be given to the birds. Plenty of room for exercise is important. A good wholesome but plain diet must be supplied, and care taken to see that the birds are not subjected to extreme temperatures. Commencing early in the year a period of conditioning should be followed, but no attempt should be made to force the birds by stimulating feeding into too early breeding condition. Hen birds which are neglected during the winter months, will seldom do well when the breeding season comes along. In speaking of the second detail, I have noted many cases in which the owners of good hens have completely spoiled their birds by working them too hard in the first season. A young hen in her first season should not be called upon to raise more than two good nests. With many the temptation to mate a good breeding and feeding hen for the third and sometimes the fourth nest is allowed to override the better judgment of the owner.

It is quite permissible to mate a hen for the third nest, but this should not be attempted until the bird is fully matured. Young hens which have done well with two nests in the first year, will often come back and produce twice the results in the second and subsequent seasons, but a young hen which has been worked out in the first season invariably proves a failure in the second year. Good healthy hens are at their best in the second season, and will continue to breed with slightly reduced results from that time onward. Four years can be considered a fair average for hens used in each of the years, but many cases are on record where hens have bred and raised their young in the fifth, sixth and even the seventh year.

SORE FEET—WON'T BATHE

Question—Asks for treatment for a bird with sore feet, and how a bird can be induced to take a bath.

Answer—Read the treatment advised in answer to question on "Shedding—Sore Feet." No doubt the scales on the lower leg and claws of your bird have cracked, due principally to the fact that the bird will not bathe. If you will see that the skin is kept soft by frequent applications of Olive Oil, I think it will remove the trouble.

Refusing the bath seems to be quite a common fault with many birds. I am inclined to think that this is brought about by a different type of bath being used, than the one to which the bird was accustomed when quite young. Young birds which are given a bath of the type which hang upon the front of the cage, will often refuse to use a bath which is placed inside of the cage. This also applies in the reverse direction. If you have had experience with hand washing, I would advise you to wash the bird in this way. Afterwards get a cheaper cage, and use this for giving the bath. Place a number of sheets of paper upon a table, and after removing the tray from the bottom of the cage, place the cage on the paper with a glass bath inside of the cage. You could spray the bird lightly, and then leave the room, and it is quite likely that the bird will finish its bath. Placing a spray of chickweed in the bath will sometimes entice the bird into the water. Once you are successful in getting the bird to start bathing, it will get over its nervousness, and will take a bath readily afterwards.

Question—Asks how to handle a bird with Avian Diphtheria—or Pox. What to do when the Pox appears.

Answer—You will find this serious disease quite prevalent during the summer months throughout many states, but cold weather seems to help eradicate it. Lumps of a cheesy like appearance may appear on the toes, face, and eyes, and although the bird seems hungry and tries to eat, often cankers form in the mouth and throat and bird will soon starve.

You will notice him wiping his beak as if trying to get food off the beak, which is caused by the lump distressing him. The eyes may finally be closed and he cannot see to find the food.

First of all, take the afflicted bird away from all others, use permanganate in the drinking water—putting in just a few drops which will make the water a pink color—be sure and not use too much for, you know it is poisonous. This will help to keep the disease from spreading to other birds which may have been in the same cage, also. Paint the lumps with mercurochrome, look in the mouth to see if cankers may have formed, and if so, paint them also. This will reduce the lumps—or scatter them. If the lumps appear on the toes only, your problem is not so great, but when near the eyes or in the throat—then danger of starvation is to be expected.

Feed "milk-sop", which is stale bread, soaked in sweet milk, and a sprinkling of poppy-seed over it, is a fine tonic and stimulant. Supply plenty of green foods, and a piece of orange. Be sure to burn all dead birds, for this disease is one to be avoided, if possible.

INDEX